THE THEATER AND THE DREAM

THE JOHNS HOPKINS UNIVERSITY PRESS
BALTIMORE AND LONDON

THE THEATER AND THE DREAM:
FROM METAPHOR TO FORM IN RENAISSANCE DRAMA

JACKSON I. COPE

The Johns Hopkins University Press, Baltimore, Maryland 21218
The Johns Hopkins University Press Ltd., London

Library of Congress Catalog Card Number 72-12782
ISBN 0-8018-1417-0

Library of Congress Cataloging in Publication data will be found on the last printed
page of this book.

Ornaments on title page and throughout text adapted from *Ursperger Chronik*, 1515.

FOR SUSAN

fairer than my dreams could frame

CONTENTS

ACKNOWLEDGMENTS

Most of the pages which follow have not been published elsewhere. But I thank the editors of *Comparative Drama* and *MLN*, respectively, for trying out earlier forms of the Prologue and Chapter VIII upon their audiences, as well as for permission to reprint them in the different context provided by this book. It is a context which I was able to formulate during precious months in Fiesole made free of teaching through the generosity of an American Council of Learned Societies fellowship in 1963–1964.

The notes are my partial recognition of debts to scholars who have taught me both details and perspective in Renaissance thought. Jonas Barish and Ira Clark cut their way through the jungle of the original manuscript, adventures for which acknowledgment here is an inadequate but most grateful thanks. C. L. Barber, Franco Fido, and Ray Waddington offered their best efforts toward making individual chapters coherent. Candida Allanbrook corrected much more than my Italian, and Jean Owen of The Johns Hopkins University Press suffered more that the reader might suffer less.

My last debt is less tangible. Robert Coover's talent and friendship brought the enterprise of criticism alive again after a long dry spell.

Michelangelo, "The Dream of Human Life."

PROLOGUE The Rediscovery of Anti-Form in Renaissance Drama

 Let us begin with a truism: we distrust form, in the theater as in the other arts. Theater has revived in Europe and in America in recent decades, but that revival has been carried forth upon a wave of anti-drama. What began as a movement toward freer communication between audience and players in the burgeoning arena houses of the fifties and early sixties became the ubiquitous "happening." Playwrights themselves have competed in making their medium its own strident message and frequently offer us the proposal that not only are life and drama near allied, but that life, like this particular theater, has as its final cause only theatricality. Whether one looks at Ionesco and Genêt, at Albee, at the West Coast mime troupes, or the *commedia dell'arte* revival in Stockholm, one meets the same insistence upon the epistemological primacy of the theatrical metaphor of and in the theater.

We are at a moment when taste, in our culture, is beginning to take on a coherent shape, most clearly reflected in this insistence upon the importance of theatricality. Such a moment might be interpreted as evidence of a breakthrough in sensibility, a new vision made possible when the scales of the past fall from the aesthetic eye. But our moment has not chosen to advertise its supposed uniqueness and originality. Perhaps because it follows a period of critical atomization symbolized by the New Criticism, its spokesmen seek to discern similarities, continuities—to be, in short, at root historic. Since its rich variety of methods both in making and rediscovering art are cohesively focused upon the exploration of anti-form, not only in the theater but in fiction and in graphics, and since the impulse is historic, we are in the process of coming to a new understanding of tradition. Where tradition was formerly defined (and therefore discerned) generically, thematically, iconographically, we are now redefining it in the broadest terms available to aesthetic discussion. We are slowly shaping the materials for a new history of literature which will recognize that art is its own best subject, that it has obsessively turned into a discussion of the possibility of form. Works repeatedly draw attention to the nucleus of the artistic transaction, the place where process and product turn inside out to offer a style of illusion opposed to that which we customarily understand when we speak of the illusion of reality created in mimetic art. Rather, continuously interchanging function, process and product fuse to create an effect stylistically analogous to the simple optical illusion, which demands as much from the process of the seeing eye as from the patterns of the object itself, with its spurious, ironic claim to a formal existence independent of that eye. Put another way, we have begun to question profoundly the efficacy of postulating a correspondence between the literary artifact and an extra-literary dimension which the letter translates into verbal form, a postulation which has led to theories of the work of art as a self-contained "structure" in the sense of an independent, architectural object. In place of this, we find critics frequently treating the work and the non-verbal world as a *diabasis*[1] in which both dimensions are preserved without prejudice as complementary phases of a single perception of reality. And nowhere have we enjoyed more success in recognizing and appreciating the values of this different illusionistic style than in studies of Renaissance drama.

For example, the playwright Lionel Abel examines what he labels the "metaplay,"[2] a form in which theatricality is essential to the characters' own self-projections, creating a struggle between author and protagonist. The attitude dictating such a drama is one skeptical of all "implacable values," to the extent that it believes fantasy to be "what one finds at the heart of reality." The study is motivated by a dramatist's wish to justify historically the post-Pirandellian theater at its most self-conscious by placing it within "the great tradition of Western dramaturgy." And this tradition is discovered to have the most aristocratic of dramatic pedigrees, emanating from the quintessential Renaissance of Shakespeare, Calderón, and Racine. "Now the Western playwright is unable to believe in the reality of a character who is lacking in self-consciousness," explains Abel: "We cannot have it both ways: a gain for consciousness means a loss for the reality of its objects, certainly for the reality of its main object, namely the world." It seems clear from such basic premises, he says, that "in the metaplay life *must* be a dream and the *world* must be a stage." It is not to the purpose to review the particular conclusions to which this thesis leads, but it *is* to the purpose to find a contemporary dramatist-critic rediscovering his traditional roots in the Renaissance by way of writing a history of dramatic form as a discussion of the very possibility of form.

However, we are left with a new question. If the anti-formal, or process-as-product, description of art is a reflection—even a reflex—of current cultural taste, can we trust the historic sense which locates similar phenomena in the Renaissance? Only if we can trust this sense are we justified in speaking of a redefinition of tradition, justified, indeed, in speaking of tradition at all. The test of true historicity begins to be met if we notice that the very qualities of Abel's "metaplay" are found at every turn in the work of a cultural historian whose explicit aim is to define another tradition. Jean Rousset's seminal study of French baroque, carrying over Wölfflinian categories, shifts the usual emphases by setting out an axiom which, stated almost at the close of the work, tacitly guides it from the beginning. It is simple: "With the debate concerning appearance and reality [*l'être*], one touches the heart of the seventeenth century. . . . the solutions may differ, but here is the problem to be resolved. It is also the problem of the baroque."[3]

Rousset follows two major manifestations through the labyrinths of seventeenth-century French literature, architecture, and casuistry with Argus-eyed rediscovery: the inevitability of metamorphosis, the omnipresence of Circean and Protean figures and myths, and the reasoned dominance of ornamentation and surface. Moral and aesthetic appearance supererogates an often merely hypothetical inner being, *le dedans* vanishes into *le dehors*, as in the peacock. This implies that man is a quick-change artist, a role-adapter, an actor, and therefore much of Rousset's survey is given over to the theater—that watershed upon which the great debate divides: "Passion or aversion for the theater, [this is] the sign of a greater opposition: here there is inscribed a veritable demarcation line; it divides those who offer themselves complacently to the experience of moving multiplicity and those who reject it or attempt to transcend it; two spiritual families, of fraternal enemies: the accomplices and the adversaries of a world in motion" (123). This fascination with drama is natural, because this age more than any other believed that "the world is a theater and life a comedy wherein one must assume a role," and it was destined "to make of the metaphor a reality; the theater invades the world, transforms it into an animated scene through its machines, and subjects it to its own laws of mobility and metamorphosis" (28). This fluidity takes a myriad of forms: in the theater and literature of cruelty, theatrical horrors and pain are transformed into pleasure; in the meditation of the Jesuit, but no less in the *Mausolée* of Mareschal, *The Revenger's Tragedy*, or Calderón's *El magico prodigioso,* death takes on movement and animation which merge with life itself; and in Shakespeare's *Comedy of Errors* or Brosse's *Les songes des hommes esveillez* life and dream illusions become so interwoven that Rousset can remark, "It seems that one sees the theater born in the form of a waking dream" (68; cf. 61–74). The theater itself was learning to exploit the theatricality of the world through endlessly repeated devices involving a theater within the theater, from the simply functioning internal masques of *The Spanish Tragedy* to the elaborate celestial amphitheaters which fuse court and stage both physically and mythically in sixteenth-century Florentine *intermedii* or in Bernini's baroque mirror play for a seventeenth-century *carnevale*.[4]

For Rousset the baroque manifests itself as a historic given: its theatricality is central, yet the stage looks into the mirror simply because it attained full professional maturity at this time. As to the counter-effect of a dream world which makes nebulous the boundaries of act and fantasy, this is only the game of "eternal vaudeville; there is no other end here than that of provoking shock, this is a vertigo expressed in the question repeated ceaselessly: 'Do I dream or am I awake?' " (66).[5]

This is a circular way of explaining the phenomena, and without seeing something of inner causes we are still on historic quicksand, vulnerable to the temptation to see only general outlines, to press plays into manufactured categories that distort their individual genius and thus are themselves in the end quite ahistoric. Yet the very fact that numerous studies, starting from whatever *point de départ,* return again and again to focus upon Renaissance drama, or the dramatism of the Renaissance, suggests that these archaeologists are excavating rather than inventing a tradition.

To shape the tools for digging beneath the surface manifestations to reach the vital sources of Renaissance dramaturgy, I should like to juxtapose the arguments of three twentieth-century observers, whose works span fifty years. They are as disparate from one another in time and in intent as they are from the earlier-mentioned historians, but they differ in that they, unlike Rousset, tend to see the aesthetic transaction as radically epistemological.

First we may examine an essay which does not deal with the drama at all, but whose emphases are central to our historic problem. José Ortega y Gasset in 1916 issued the first of a renowned series titled *El espectador.* This essay was allegedly written in response to a letter expressing concern at the passivity implied by the dedication of oneself to becoming a mere spectator,[6] and was titled "Verdad y perspectiva." Ortega calms the anxiety of his correspondent by explaining that he is reacting against a utilitarian age in which thought has become subordinated to the ends of politics, in which pure contemplation is rare, in which the search for truth itself is almost unknown. But, in his sense, to contemplate is precisely to be a "spectator": "The name enjoys a famous genealogy: Plato came upon it. In his *Republic* he concedes a special mission to what he calls φιλοθαμονες—friends of watchful observation. They are the speculatives, and the foremost of all these are the philosophers, the theorizers—that is to say, the contemplatives."[7] Ortega sets this conception against the Aristotelian deity whose abstraction is so great that he busies himself in thinking simply about thinking. His own spectator will participate in life (it will be recalled that Plato's viewers were to become governors), only reserving the ability and intention of withdrawing at intervals to sharpen his sight with pure theory (20). What he will see at such moments is, however, just the flow of life before him ("la vida según fluye ante él" [21]). It is at this point that the integral function of the visual imagery becomes apparent: Ortega's spectator adopts a premise antithetical to that underlying the two dominant traditions of Western epistemology: dogmatism and skepticism. Where proponents of these believe the point of view of the individual to be false, the author of *El espectador* affirms, "It seems to me that the individual point of view is the only point of view from which one is able to look at this world in its truth" (22). The man, says Ortega, who resists the seduction of exchanging his own retina for another, imaginary, one sees the world as it is. And this is each man's mission: "We are not to be substituted for; we are necessary. 'Only through all men does the Human rise into vivid being,' says Goethe. Within humanity each race, each individual, is a distinct organ of perception" (24). Here, then, is the challenge of the essay's title, "Verdad y perspectiva." "Reality is offered through individual perspectives. . . . The visual and the intellectual perspective are entwined with the perspective of values. Instead of disputing, let us integrate our visions in generous spiritual collaboration, and like the independent streams shaping the thick vein of the river, let us create the torrent of reality" (25).

It is clear that perspectivism, the seeing of that which is without but which can only be validated as real by the confluence of viewpoints, that grand union of "spectators" which the final quotation envisages, constitutes the fundamental notion which transmutes the visual images from metaphoric vehicle into epistemological tenor in Ortega's essay. I have chosen this as our first modern instance because to his almost exaggerated optimism Ortega adds a caution, a proviso stated in just the imagery so prevalent in Renaissance discussions of "vision"—which can be a thing seen, as by the spectators in a theater, but also something dreamed, something "visionary": "The spectator will look at the panorama of life from his heart, as from a promontory. He will wish to try to reproduce his particular perspective without deformation. That of which he has a clear notion will be set down as such; but also that will be set down as a dream which he holds to be merely a dream. Because one part, one form, of the real is the imaginary, and in a wholly complete perspective there is a plane where things desired make their life" (25).

Thirty years later Ortega gave a lecture in Lisbon titled "Idea del teatro" in which the hints contained in this proviso were developed into the principal rationale for drama.[8] The "idea" of the title is pseudo-Platonic; it does not embrace the presumably decadent modern theater which the aging Ortega found about him in 1946, but that ideal theater of the Athenian achievement and—inevitably—that of the later Renaissance, "the English and Spanish theater of Ben Jonson and Shakespeare, of Lope de Vega and Calderón" (26, 30).

The historical tie with our subject remains entirely implicit after this first statement; Ortega never turns back to examine individual plays. Rather, he examines theatrical space. A theater is an enclosed place which contains two interacting spaces: "the enclosed space, the 'inside' that is a theater, is, in its turn, divided into two spaces, the hall, where the public places itself, and the stage, where the actors place themselves" (35). But this dual space immediately introduces us to a dual function, which is its rationale: theater is a "spectacle," an art of seeing, and audience and actors can also be dichotomized as those who enter "to see" (para ver) and "to be seen" (para ser vistos [pp. 36–37; cf. 49]). Space has again become place, a point for viewing.

What we see in this theatrical space is a double vision: the actress, for instance, Marianinha Rey Colaço, and her characterization, Ophelia.[9] And yet, just this "known" double vision makes possible the triumph of unreality: "So, that which is not real, the unreal—Ophelia enclosed in the palace—has the power, the magical virtue of making that which is real disappear" (40). What does this make of theater? Metaphor: "The stage and the actor are the universal metaphor incarnate, and this is the theater: visible metaphor" (41). This, for Ortega, is the importance of drama. Theater being metaphoric, and metaphor being a form of the unreal, we attend for the metaphoric experience, the shiver of recognition that Marianinha is not Ophelia—with all that is implicit in that realization. We go to the theater because we feel drawn toward the unreal (49–50). And we feel this gravitation because man's life is a prison (such as Plato described, such as Calderón described), and the theater takes him out of this prison of "reality" by making him inexistent, taking him outside of life until he himself becomes a little "unreal" (54).

The companion essay included in *Idea del teatro*, "Máscaras," provides the complex argument by which this partial loss of identity and reality is justified as a desirable end for dramatic art. Man, soon discovering the existential self to be imperfect in light of its own aspirations, to be a limitation, desires henceforth to reach out and annex the other, that universe which is beyond the limits, and whose possession would thus enlarge the bounds of self: man passes through life wishing to "be other" (*ser otro* [92]). This otherness is first visited in and psychically annexed to that world which is most extraordinary, least habitual and predictable in man's experience, the world of dreams: "From the most primitive times man has considered that dreams and visionary states constituted, through their relative exceptionality and their extraordinary displacements, that which revealed to him this world that is *other* and, because it is other, is superior" (66). Indeed, we still know so little of the nature of dreams, warns Ortega, that modern man would do well not to underestimate more primitive cultures which judged explicitly that "in sleep a reality of a superior order presents itself intimately to him"—as Shakespeare and Calderón essayed to demonstrate, we might add.

Dreams, however little we may really know of their total bearing on the psychic economy, are subject to one crucial, incontrovertible observation. They are endowed with the same ambiguity, the same double being, as the actor, but the doubleness is a matter of space and vision, i.e., they have a simultaneous double existence inside and yet outside the mind of the dreamer: "Is the dream in us or are we in the dream?" (69).

Dreams, then, share a very objective spatial reality—an essential perspectivism, one might call it, recalling the interaction within the theater of those who come *para ver* and those who come *para ser vistos* —with the dramatic experience. But both theater and dream paradoxically incorporate the subjective movement of transcendence into the unreal: "Man the actor transfigures himself into Hamlet, man the spectator metamorphoses himself into a contemporary of Hamlet, participates in the life of the latter—he also, then, the public, is a player who *rises* above habitual being to an exceptional and imaginary state and participates in the world as it does not exist, in a world beyond [*Ultramundo*], and in this sense *not only the drama*, but also the auditorium and the entire theater in the end become a phantasmagoria—beyond life [*Ultravida*]" (57).

So this theater is the reflection of man's deepest, most persistent psychic being, a state which might be described, in a slight adaptation of Ortega's terminology, as ultraexistential. Man passes his life aspiring to be other than he is. But "the only possible way in which *one thing may be another is metaphor*—the being like or quasi-being. Which suddenly reveals to us that man has a metaphoric destiny, that man is the existential metaphor" (92).

Here Ortega has discovered a theatrical context to explain why his earlier essay on "Verdad y perspectiva" should have asserted so ambiguously, in the midst of its very physical, spatial treatment of men's vision of their universe, that "one form of the real is the imaginary, and in a wholly complete perspective there is a plane where things desired make their life." Life at its highest is a metaphor of aspiration, a dream whose double dimension impinges upon the daemonic, a theater in which our role of spectator, our attention to the scene, draws us inward to become an actor in an illusion which is more real than existence. Life is a dream, but dreams are more real than life. The world is a theater, but the theater is more real than this world.

It is instructive to move now from the Spanish philosopher-artist to an apocalyptic French actor of a slightly later generation, in the hope of establishing an important *concordia discors* which will further illuminate our point of departure. Antonin Artaud had been stage and movie actor, poet, director, critic, scenarist, and drug addict by 1927, when he began to write the manifestoes gathered as *Le théâtre et son double* in 1938.[10] These startling and influential essays call for a new drama which will press beyond the sterilities of formal and social concern to the "double," the shadow at the depths which is the precipitate, unpremeditated manifestation of the One behind multiplicity, the discovery of the mind which has "opened onto the belly, and accumulates from below a dark and untranslatable knowledge, full of subterranean tides, hollow structures, a congealed agitation" (152). "The theatre must also be considered as the double, not of this direct, everyday reality of which it is gradually being reduced to a mere inert replica—empty as it is sugar-coated—but of another archetypal and dangerous reality, a reality of which the Principles, like dolphins, once they have shown their heads, hurry to dive back into the obscurity of the deep" (48).

Such a theater, in contrast to the "storytelling psychology" of a modern aberration, involves the audience in anarchy, as poetry anarchizes language, breaking and destroying while it burrows to deeper layers of existence. This anarchy is what Artaud calls "cruelty," or the implacable force, rigor, and irreversibility of the life principles which teach us that evil is ever-present in the nature of being, that good is only an act willed and submerged: "We are not free. And the sky can still fall on our heads. And the theatre has been created to teach us that first of all" (79). And the theater "first of all," in every sense, for words of the past congeal, harden into form that in repetition defeats its own anarchic principle of being. However, the "true theatre," "because it moves and makes use of living instruments, continues to stir up shadows where life has never ceased to grope its way. The actor does not make the same gestures twice, but he makes gestures, he moves; and although he brutalizes forms, nevertheless behind them and through their destruction he rejoins that which outlives forms. . . . The theatre . . . is *no thing*, but makes use of everything—gestures, sounds, words, screams, light, darkness" (12). Theater employs these instruments because the best way to realize the "idea of danger" is by means of "the *objective* unforeseen, the unforeseen not in situations, but in things, the abrupt, untimely transition from an intellectual image to a true image" (43–44). Much of Artaud's collection of manifestoes is devoted to spelling out in detail this objective language, the poetry of *mise en scène*, of violent, surrealistic manikins and ten-foot symbols. And it becomes clear that his theater is a theater primarily concerned with perspectives: as when he announces a program of plays without script, modern *commedie improvvise*, such as "works from the Elizabethan theatre stripped of their text and retaining only the accoutrements of period, situations, characters, and action" (100), or when he reviews Jean-Louis Barrault's mime based on *As I Lay Dying*: "His spectacle . . . victoriously proves the importance of gestures and of movement in space. He restores to theatrical perspective the importance it should never have lost. It is in relation to the stage and *on* the stage that this spectacle is organized. . . . And there is not one point in the stage perspective that does not take on emotional meaning" (145).

Yet there is an insistent note of apparent contradiction which threads through the discussion, for—as with Ortega y Gasset—perspectivism, with all of its clearly objective implications, is absorbed into the spectator, or, as Artaud once put it in describing the "stage" of his "theater of cruelty," it may be a reversible equation, this relationship between seer and seen: "We abolish the stage and the auditorium and replace them by a single site, without partition or barrier of any kind, which will become the theatre of the action. A direct communication will be re-established between the spectator and the spectacle, between the actor and the spectator, from the fact that the spectator, placed in the middle of the action, is engulfed and physically affected by it" (96; cf. 81). It is just this strange involution by which audience and drama can be said less to "fuse" than to envelop one another in simultaneous union and separation which seemed to Artaud so mysteriously expressed by Balinese dancers. He describes "the gesture of the central dancer who always touches his head at the same place, as if wishing to indicate the position and existence of some unimaginable central eye" (63).

There is a further involution of Artaud's call for spectacles which would exploit the perspectivism of true theater, a call which appeared so simple initially. It may be seen in most succinct form in another of his attempts to describe the effect of the Balinese. He stresses their talent in objectifying spectacle: "There is an absolute in these constructed perspectives, a real physical absolute which only Orientals are capable of envisioning" (65). But in his next observation he describes the effect in another visual image: "the women's stratified, lunar eyes: Eyes of dreams which seem to absorb our own, eyes before which we ourselves appear to be *fantôme*" (66). The most objective theater is also the most subjective; and perspective, spectacle, ultimately emerge as the "double" of the dream:

> To consider the theatre as a second-hand psychological or moral function, and to believe that dreams themselves have only a substitute function, is to diminish the profound poetic bearing of dreams as well as of the theatre. If the theatre, like dreams, is bloody and inhuman, it is . . . in order to perpetuate in a concrete and immediate way the metaphysical ideas of certain Fables whose very atrocity and energy suffice to show their origin and continuity in essential principles.
>
> This being so . . . this naked language of the theatre . . . must permit the transgression of ordinary limits of art and speech, in order to realize actively . . . *in real terms*, a kind of total operation in which man must reassume his place between dreams and events. (92–93)

It is not surprising that a man who rejects the theater's "psychologism" because it does not reach to the roots of the psyche, whose theory of dramatic function is based upon the interaction between objective and subliminal reality, should give himself to an admiring critique of Ford's *'Tis Pity She's a Whore* (28–29), should have planned works from the Elizabethan theater "stripped of their text," and should even have planned an adaptation of *Arden of Feversham*, "a work entirely consistent with our present troubled state of mind" (99). Artaud's sense of the pertinence of Renaissance drama to his own theatrical aims and attitudes is natural; that is, of course, the point of my argument. But more than natural, it seems almost inevitable that the man who wrote the passage quoted above on theater and dream should have served as director to a production of that Renaissance play which it best describes of all the world's repertoire, Calderón's *La vida es sueño*.[11]

Artaud and Ortega y Gasset developed a dramaturgical theory which evidently, in large part, originated in their responses to Renaissance drama. It is not surprising, again, that the characteristic they seek to perpetuate in ideal drama is similar to the shape which our Renaissance historians, with various vocabularies, have been attributing to that same body of drama. This ideal is a theater of highly formalized physical spaces self-consciously aware of its own theatricality, and engulfing the spectator until he is aware that he stands both before and behind the mirror which the theater holds up to the *theatrum mundi*. Yet this theater which seems to master the spectator is ultimately the dramatist's objective correlative to a deeply subjective dream world in which the psyche overflows to inundate "form" with its own power, its chaotic anti-form. Rousset, we have seen, describes just such a theater in defining the baroque; Lionel Abel tells us that the Renaissance characteristic of self-consciousness dictated that in its "metaplay" we will find just such a double structure: "life *must* be a dream and the *world* must be a stage."[12]

Descriptive historians and prescriptive critics having drawn us by their several routes to focus in a new fashion upon Renaissance drama, it is a useful check to observe that we are brought to the same focal point by Northrop Frye's most extended examination of Shakespearean comedy, a book titled (happily, in the light of our discussion) *A Natural Perspective*.[13] Frye comes to literature as a mythically oriented cultural schematist, primed with preconceptions which are ahistoric in the sense that he is seeking universal structural patterns evolving from and into the differentiating accidents.[14] He begins by noting that Shakespeare moved more and more blatantly toward "mouldy tales" as his powers heightened, that he "deliberately chose incredible comic plots . . . with the specific function of drawing us away from the analogy with familiar experience into a strange but consistent and self-contained dramatic world" (19). The improbability of plotting is effected in such a way that "as in the *commedia dell'arte*, the spirit of which is so close to Shakespearean comedy, everything that goes on seems spontaneously improvised, precisely because its general convention is prescribed in advance" (30). The convention, as Frye's earlier readers will anticipate, is primitive convention, the festive form which comedy inherits from its ritual origins (53, 55).

The rite presupposes magic, Frye reminds us. When ritual acts become "narrated" into myth, the enactment of the myth pulls away from the magic toward sheer presentationalism: "the ritual acts are now performed for the sake of representing the myth rather than primarily for affecting the order of nature" (59). Drama is renouncing magic in the interest of its sheer existential being as story, and we find ourselves approaching a theory of drama (this time arrived at from origins rather than from final ends) similar to Ortega's theater which realizes man's destiny as an existential metaphor.

The narrative is, nonetheless, descended from myths, and even when the magic is renounced, and the actors have ceased asserting that "we are presenting the contest of summer and winter," "the bumps and hollows of the story being told follow the contours of the myth beneath" (61). Thus, of course, Frye accounts for the "festive" or "regenerative" essence of comedy. All myths have two poles, he argues, a natural (the sun) which is controlled by one personal and magical (Apollo), uniting two orders. What Shakespeare seeks, especially in the romances, is "the sense of nature as comprising not merely an order but a power, at once supernatural and connatural . . . controlled either by benevolent human magic or by divine will" (71). Since the narrative both follows and substitutes for the primal mythic shape, the audience becomes spectators and participants in this "connatural" stage order, and the same is true "*a fortiori*" of the author, who both creates and is bound into and observes his creation (100).

Frye then turns (as, by now, might be anticipated) to dreams—a private universe, incommunicable, yet its ultra-reality is hinted at as constantly by Shakespeare as by Freud or primitive man (in the preface, Frye observes that his own preferred title for the book was *The Bottomless Dream*). This dream wisdom, or vision, is re-enacted in festive comedy insofar as the balance of the outer, "natural" machine and the magical control are inverted: "The world of tyranny and irrational law is a world where what is real is given to us arbitrarily as a datum, something we must accept or somehow come to terms with. This is a spectator's reality, the reality we see to be 'out there.' The world of the final festival is a world where reality is what is created by human desire as the arts are created" (115). Invoking *The Winter's Tale*, however, Frye observes that "the action, therefore, moves from appearance to reality, from mirage to substance. . . . The real world, however, has none of the customary qualities of reality. It is the world symbolized by nature's power of renewal; it is the world we want . . . clearly not the world of ordinary experience, in which man is an isolated spectator" (116–17).

In Frye's view, then, art and nature become one, "connatural," as audience and author merge in and through a form which refuses limits, either those of what is normally labeled form or those of quotidian sensibility. "Normally we can forget . . . when we wake up from a dream"; the dream of drama, however, is Bottom's bottomless dream:

"In comedy there is a conclusion of awakening which incorporates the dream action, like Adam's awakening to find his dream true in *Paradise Lost*" (127–29).

What I have been sampling, and merely sampling, are the sorts of insights into the epistemological dramatic transaction that we have been given in recent years. And their focal point has been the shape of the Renaissance play. It is a little world which both boasts and mocks aesthetic objectivity as it incorporates the *theatrum mundi* into itself upon its own terms. As we begin to realize the paradoxical status of this dramatic Golden Age, it is revealing its riches to us at a level which underlies, and is no less breathtaking in its achievements than the glories we recognized under the critical tutelage of other generations.

In the following pages I hope that, however clumsily, some few new finds have been unearthed for the pleasure of modern judgments. They lay claim to being a literary history of sorts. One parent of this study, whose features will be discerned in most chapters, is a tracking of the several ways in which Florentine Platonism directly informed Renaissance criticism and practice of the drama. There is, clearly, no single fountainhead from which the inspired sophistication of the self-conscious drama of the Renaissance springs. However, the impact of Florentine philosophic thought has been wholly neglected; this is to neglect a major source—whether it is *the* major source each reader can determine privately in light of the argument. But this historic path casts its light only obliquely in some chapters. There the dramatic transactions discerned in plays directly in the Florentine tradition are compared with variations upon those transactions in important plays whose values have been missed by readers who start from a different place. Necessarily, then, this is a bastard child in the genealogy of literary criticism. Its other parent, who leads it from the path of literary history as strictly conceived, is *explication de texte*, in part because my own early nourishment was from that source, in part because it is my act of faith that even in trying to understand forms which assert the impossibility of form the most revealing discourse remains the formal one. Ultimately, then, despite the subtitle to this prologue, the book offers itself as a critical history of dramatic form in the Renaissance.

CHAPTER I Platonic Perspectives: Structural Metaphor from Cusa to Ficino

Ernst Curtius' topoilogical compendium shows how the old Platonic metaphor of "the tragedy and comedy of life" in the *Philebus* proliferated across Latin Europe and, with important impetus from John of Salisbury's *Policraticus*, leaped into the vernaculars.[1] Add to this Jean Jacquot's survey, wherein we learn how the *topos* traveled from its classical and medieval origins into the works of Renaissance humanists and thence into the theater itself,[2] and the story seems to be told. Or, looked at in another way, it scarcely seems to need a "history" when we recall that not long after Plato gave it impetus among philosophers, Menander wrote in the *Agroikos*:

> That man, o Parmenon, I count most fortunate
> Who quickly whence he came returns, when he, unvexed,
> Has looked on these majestic sights—the common sun,
> Water and clouds, the stars and fire. If thou shalt live
> An hundred years, or very few, thou'lt always see
> These same sights . . .
> So count this time I speak of some festival.[3]

But even here, at the origin of modern comedy in the work of Menander, the *topos* raises a paradox to tease the mind. If man is a player, that embodiment of life controlled because plotted, this theatrical sense already carries the seed of the opposing tendency to see life as evanescent, nothing more, perhaps, than a dream. Again the metaphor suggests Plato, and again Menander, whose fragmented *Koneiazomenai* reads like a snatch of dialogue from Shakespeare or Calderón: "[A] Is this then a dream? [B] If we are sleeping—no—but he offers us three talents as dowry. . . . [A] I am not awake. [B] Well, rouse up. He is making ready the wedding" (pp. 398–99).

But if the *topoi* are ancient, the Renaissance plays utilizing them are concerned with essential questions of epistemology which transcend the social ambience so often considered the limiting circle for dramatic action. Jacquot gives us little hope of accounting for this philosophic theater when he concludes that "all the aspects of the theme were already developed . . . from Plato to St. John Chrysostom, and . . . the role of humanism had principally resided in its transmission and diffusion."[4] Why, then, did this drama flourish so remarkably just in the wake of the humanists? And why did it appear as a mere catalogue, an apparent stimulus, but really an appendage, to Jacquot's survey, forming its climax only in a chronological sense?

The problem illustrates my conviction that when one begins with a *topos* and writes its history, aesthetic discussion becomes reductionistic, the individual play being the permanent catalyst that renews, by reorganizing, the essence of a *topos* it works upon. We will find this particularly true of Calderón's *La vida es sueño*, but that is only a remarkably thorough authentication of a process which each play discussed in the following pages will illustrate.

Furthermore, philosophers, theologians, ideational systembuilders are *artistes manquées*. Their materials are always too rich for their control. The radical ideas, those which are "new" in the sense that they rearrange prior structures, have a function analogous to that renewal of tradition encompassed by the artist when he individuates ideas into forms. Yet because he is not an artist, the philosopher sees the form through the blurred lens of that impossible oxymoron architectonic discourse; he is deaf to the music of his own poem and so misinterprets it. His truly radical ideas can be said less to take their shape from expression than to shape expression themselves. For all of his care, they seep through the interstices, complicating and embarrassing argument by their insistence upon sounding an independent harmony. This, at least, seems to be a useful premise from which to begin seeking the cause for a vitality in the Renaissance Platonists' revival of ancient *topoi* so strong that it gave drama a new dimension. In later chapters we will read some playwrights as though they were philosophers; here we will read philosophers as though they were poets.

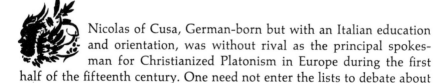 Nicolas of Cusa, German-born but with an Italian education and orientation, was without rival as the principal spokesman for Christianized Platonism in Europe during the first half of the fifteenth century. One need not enter the lists to debate about

his influence on two generations of Italian humanists in order to accept one uncontroverted conclusion: by whatever directions or indirections, his role of Platonic champion passed in the later decades of the *Quattrocento* to Marsilio Ficino.[5] It is in the work of these two great humanists that we will discover the structural power of the metaphors which make life into spectacle or dream, drama or vision.

In 1440 Cusa completed his first major philosophic work, the pious skeptical treatise *De docta ignorantia*. God, the creation, and Christ are examined in analyses which originate ultimately in the mystic theology of Dionysius the pseudo-Areopagite. The focal point is the Dionysian description of God as "the Maximum" who "is neither this nor that, neither in one place nor in another, for being all things, he is not any one of them."[6] And yet this more than Protean deity must be known by means of the feeble paraphernalia of human ignorance: "In every inquiry men judge of the uncertain by comparing it with an object supposed certain, and their judgment is always approximative; every inquiry is, therefore, comparative and uses the method of analogy."[7] This is a point which Cusa elaborates in specifically representational (and, therefore, implicitly aesthetic) as well as theological terms when he begins with the disarming reminder that all philosophers and theologians agree that the visible is a faithful reflection of the invisible, and that "the fundamental reason for the use of symbolism is the study of spiritual things." But the conclusion is far from reassuring: "We know for a fact that all things stand in some sort of relation to one another; that, in virtue of this inter-relation, all the individuals constitute one universe and that in the one Absolute the multiplicity of being is unity itself. Every image is an approximate reproduction of the exemplar; yet, apart from the Absolute image or the Exemplar itself in unity of nature, no image will so faithfully or precisely reproduce the exemplar, as to rule out the possibility of an infinity of more faithful and precise images" (25; *Opera*, p. 8).

As will be seen below, the ultimate poetic reconciliation of this statement with a knowledge of God will be achieved only years later in the treatise *De visione Dei*. But Cusa makes the point here in the hope of validating the imagistic exempla which carry the burden of demonstration throughout the treatise: those of mathematics.[8] If we are to arrive at the unknown, he argues, we must be certain at least concerning the properties of our images, or analogies. And where is that certainty most available? Clearly, says Cusa, in mathematics. But he does not mean "number" because "our knowledge of things is not acquired by completely disregarding their material conditions" (25; "appendicijs materialibus, sine quibus imaginari nequeunt," *Opera*, p. 8). He means, of course, geometry, that one abstract science which assigns itself as a working principle hypothetical place, position. After all, Cusa's God-Maximum from the beginning was defined not only as one who is "neither this nor that," but also "neither in one place nor in another." And not only is *De docta ignorantia* replete with diagrams and demonstrations of the coincidence of opposites by which "maximum" line, triangle, circle, and sphere are all contained in, phases of, one another, but the ultimate definition of God in the much-abused figure of the infinite circle here finally takes on its proper rationale and justifying milieu.[9]

Yet there is a disturbing undercurrent, as though Cusa knew that the moment that mathematics passes over into geometry, abstractness rather than materiality becomes the fiction, that even infinite space requires "place," "point"—or "point of view." "Only in God," he affirms, "are we able to find a centre which is with perfect precision equidistant from all points, for He alone is infinite equality. God . . . is, therefore, the centre of the earth, and of all spheres and of all things in the world."[10] "In the world"! With that phrase Cusa returns his argument to the explicit confines of the spatial, visible creation which his imagery of "mathematics" had attempted to make into a mere shadow and instrument of higher realms, of higher instruction. But it is what one might have anticipated all along, for when Cusa had come to demonstrate the "unity and infinity of the universe" (II, i), Man became the measure and demonstration of the earlier insistence upon the approximate, relative nature of all symbolism. Not simply Man, though, but Man as artist: "No two men are identical in anything; their sense perceptions differ, their intellects differ; and their activities, *whether they take the form of writing, painting or any other form of art*, are all different. Even if for a thousand years one man zealously tried to imitate another on some one point, he would never come to reproduce it exactly, though at times it may be that the difference is not perceived by the senses" (69 [italics mine]; *Opera*, p. 23). And, further, if this world is the world of artists, they are not writers, but painters, whose effects are perceived—or not perceived—by the senses. It is a point scarcely surprising in light of Cusa's personal background,[11] but one all-important to recognize when we read that one passage in *De docta ignorantia* in which he explicitly abandons the "abstract" imagery of geometry in favor of a directly material analogy for the relationship between God and the creation: "all in God is God, all things come from His unity and in all things He is what they are, like truth in an image. Yet it is as if a face were reproduced in its own image. With the multiplication of the image we get distant and close reproductions of the face. (I do not mean distance in space but a gradual distance from the true face, since without that multiplication would be impossible.) In the many different images of that face one face would appear in many, different ways."[12] Here is the bridge between *De docta ignorantia* and *De visione Dei*. Where the one has been a sustained, but marred, exercise in abstract analogism, the other will take up its imagistic cues and become a triumph which gives insight through the arts of sight. It transcends—and transgresses—the imposed limitations of the other in order to translate the vision of God through the aesthetic transaction between spectator and spectacle, the complexities of perspective. And, of course, the problem is complex, as is any vision, because (as Ortega warns) vision itself is ambiguous, being simultaneously internal and external.

De visione Dei, written in 1453 as a meditational guide at the request of the Benedictine monks of isolated Tegernsee, with whom Cusa had spent some days in the preceding summer, was partially translated into English in the seventeenth century by Giles Randall. The title of this redaction is instructive, in that the English Puritan clearly understood the ambiguity of the titular image of the Latin: he called it *The Single Eye, entituled The Vision of God*.[13]

As in *De docta ignorantia*, Cusa begins the later treatise by acknowledging that to bring divine things to human comprehension he must employ some comparison. The vehicle of analogy is established at the outset in a passage from which the entire work exfoliates: "Now among men's works I have found no image better suited to our purpose [here one observes Cusa's abandonment of the earlier proposition that no image is so faithful to its divine Exemplar "as to rule out the possibility of an infinity of more faithful and precise images"] than that of an image which is omnivoyant—its face, by the painter's cunning art, being made to appear as though looking on all around it. There are many excellent pictures of such faces . . . setting forth the figure of an omnivoyant, and this I call the icon of God."[14]

This icon, placed in a fixed position, will appear to be watching every viewer, yet when a viewer moves, the eyes seem to follow his motion; yet again, when two viewers move in contrary directions, the eyes seem to follow both simultaneously. If this capacity for omnivoyance can exist in the mere analogical simulacrum, and if it can therefore exist, as Cusa argues, in an even purer state in our abstract idea of "sight," then it certainly exists in the absolute vision of God, since "God is the true Unlimited Sight, and He is not inferior to sight in the abstract as it can be conceived by the intellect, but is beyond all comparison more perfect" (8; *Opera*, p. 182). We begin, then, with an image which immediately raises us to divine things and so goes beyond the material or even abstract imagination of this world. But it is an image formed by perspectives, and so it is inevitable that the divine world should be—if only gradually—reabsorbed into the physical, and that the double "vision" of God understood as a viewer viewed should by stages cease to be symbol and become description.[15]

Introducing the doctrine of *coincidentia oppositorum*, which was fully elaborated in *De docta ignorantia*, Cusa adapts it to an imagery entirely foreign to its application in the earlier work. "Thou hast inspired me, Lord," cries Cusa, "to do violence to myself, because impossibility coincideth with necessity, and I have learnt that the place wherein thou art found unveiled is girt round with the coincidence of contradictories, and this is the wall of Paradise where Thou dost abide. The door whereof is guarded by the most proud spirit of Reason, and, unless he be vanquished, the way will not lie open."[16] This is not a passing metaphor, but becomes a cornerstone for the entire treatise: "I begin, Lord, to behold Thee in the door of the coincidence of opposites, which the angel guardeth that is set over the entrance into Paradise" (46; *Opera*, p. 190); "Thou dwellest within the wall of Paradise, and this wall is that coincidence" (49; *Opera*, p. 191); "NOW and THEN . . . meet in the wall surrounding the place where Thou abidest in coincidence" (50; *Opera*, p. 191); "Therefore, it behooveth me to scale that wall of invisible vision beyond which Thou art to be found" (54–55; *Opera*, p. 192); "This Thy great Apostle Paul revealed unto us, who was rapt, beyond the wall of coincidence into Paradise" (87; *Opera*, p. 199); "While I imagine a Creator creating, I am still on this side the wall of Paradise" (57; *Opera*, p. 192); these and other passages conclude with the admission that the entire meditational method is capable of success only for those who will scale the wall, for Father and Son stand within Paradise, and "he that stayeth outside Paradise cannot have such a vision, since neither . . . are to be found outside Paradise" (104; *Opera*, p. 202).

This running image operates with just that simultaneous doubleness achieved by the initial imagistic conception of the omnivoyant viewer-viewed: it spatializes the suprarational aspects of mystical theology even while remaking the traditional space of Christian history into an interior landscape—the fortunate learner who comes to the vision of God through Cusa's book has already found a Paradise within him happier far. We begin to see how crucial the initial step was, where viewpoint, perspective, emphasized local motion as well. From this side of the wall of Paradise constituted by the absolute *coincidentia oppositorum*, God is precisely the sum total of each viewpoint, of every viewpoint. But it is his omnivoyant quality which permits him to reconcile all into a self-knowing Unity, which allows the icon's eyes to appear to travel across the room in contradictory directions. We are placed, and we move, that the movement may reveal the still point of God. But that stillness and unity itself can be known only through embracing its opposite, motion.

Sight is not the only sense, however, and Cusa introduces a new complicating factor when he makes himself, in his role of preacher, an analogue of God:

with Thee speech and sight are one, since . . . [Thou] art Very Absolute Simplicity. Thence I prove clearly that Thou seest at the same time all things and each thing.

While I preach, I speak alike and at the same time to the whole congregation . . . and to the individuals present. . . . And what the church is to me that, Lord, the whole world is to Thee. . . . Thou hast given me a face . . . and it is seen by all to whom I preach, individually and at the same time. Thus my one face is seen by individuals, and my one speech is wholly heard by individuals. . . . But if such a faculty were in me that to be heard were one with hearing, and to be seen with seeing, and in like manner to speak with hearing . . . then indeed I could hear and see all and each at the same time.

(45–46; *Opera*, p. 190)

With this transitional figure of the preacher in the pulpit, Cusa begins to merge the theater of the world in which God is both spectacle and spectator with the book of the world: "Thou speakest by Thy Word to all things that are, and callest into being those that are not: Thou callest them to hear Thee, and when they hear Thee then they are. . . . O infinite Power, Thy concept is Thy speech! . . . while Thou conceivest, Thou dost see and speak and work, and do all else that can be named" (47–48; *Opera*, p. 190).[17] This gradually evolving metaphor of the Word which grows out of the earlier metaphor of vision recalls us to the opening pages of the treatise, which were concerned with the primal need to express divine things precisely in metaphor. We begin seeking a proper metaphor, and find it in the visual image of the omnivoyant icon; now we have evolved the conception of creative metaphor, the fertile Word for that which is not until it is said. We find ourselves, I propose, at that juncture of interaction between speech and spectacle, word and perspective, which is exactly analogous to the dramatist's world, created by the verbal projection of idea into scene—a world which, like Cusa's, doubles back upon itself as the scene recreates those words for the spectators, who watch that they may listen.[18]

But, setting such analogies aside for the moment, let us examine this notion to see how in *De visione Dei* Cusa once more manipulates it to recreate even the Word as a physical entity, a thing to be looked upon: the Book.[19] We can begin with a passage which is the more developed echo of that we earlier met in *De docta ignorantia*,[20] a passage which makes more literal than usual the conception of man as the image of God: "Lord, I comprehend Thy face to precede every face that may be formed, and to be the pattern and true type of all faces, and all faces to be images of Thy face. . . . Each face, then, that can look upon Thy face beholdeth nought other or differing from itself, because it beholdeth its own true type."[21] Here is the ancient injunction *nosce teipsum* inverted from a looking within to a looking outward toward oneself in God. But at the other end of the treatise, Jesus becomes the one who looks out at man, since walking this world he "did use eyes of flesh like unto ours" in such special capacity that "from the aspect of the face and eyes of the men whom Thou sawest Thou didst truly judge of the passions of the soul." As the passage closes, Jesus by analogy becomes again the God who reads man as the book he has himself written: "From any one sign, albeit of the slightest, Thou didst perceive the man's whole thought, . . . even as the learned, from running their eye hastily over a book, can narrate the author's whole intent as though they had read it through" (106–7; *Opera*, p. 203).

The two passages are drawn together at the center of the treatise, where man looking upon God's icon and God reading man as a book unite to demonstrate that while the vision of God is the vision of an absolute reality conceived as form, yet that man is also a mere metaphor and shadow of that form:

when Thou, my God, appearest unto me as matter that may be formed, in that Thou receivest the form of whosoever looketh on Thee, Thou dost raise me up that I may perceive how he who looketh on Thee doth not give Thee form, but seeth himself in Thee. . . . Thou being as it were a living mirror of eternity, which is the Form of forms. While any looketh in this mirror, he seeth his own form in the Form of forms, to wit, in the mirror, and he judgeth the form which he seeth in that mirror to be a figure of his own form because it·is so with a polished material mirror. Yet it is the contrary which is true, for in that mirror of eternity what he seeth is not a figure, but the truth, whereof the beholder himself is a figure. Wherefore, in Thee, my God, the figure is the truth, and the exemplar of all things. . . . Thou appearest unto me like the shadow following the movement of one that walketh; but it is because I am a living shadow and Thou the truth that I judge from the change of the shadow that the truth changeth also.

(72–73; *Opera*, p. 196)

Man is a shadow, his motion—from which began the whole analogy of divine knowledge with perspectivism, viewpoint—a mere metaphor. Ultimately, though, it *has* been the just metaphor, the most appropriate.

We begin with a painting which resembles God, we finally learn, because God resembles a painter:

Thou, Lord, who maketh all things for Thine own sake, hast created this whole world for the sake of intellectual nature. Even so a painter mixeth diverse colours that at length he may possess his own likeness, wherein his art may rest and take pleasure, and so that, his single self being not to be multiplied, he may at least be multiplied in the one way possible, to wit, in a likeness most resembling himself. But the Spirit maketh many figures, because the likeness of his infinite power can only be perfectly set forth in many. . . . For were they not innumerable, Thou, infinite God, couldst not be known in the best fashion.[22]

Cusa begins *De visione Dei* with God as icon and closes with God as artist; he begins with man as viewer and closes with man as viewed. In the course of these transitions of viewpoint we are shown the logic by which the artist becomes God's metaphoric equivalent in the world. Himself a figure, a shadow, he is empowered with the god-like capacity to reveal and so to understand—to *view*—himself through the multiplicity of creative vicariousness. Metaphors turned icons: these are the media through which the artist-deity knows and is known in this book of the world,[23] or, better, in this script for the *theatrum mundi*, because when these media, shifting and merging, are wedded in a perspectivist matrix such as that embodied in this subliminal structure of *De visione Dei*, the artist God (as suggested briefly above) is prepared to emerge as playwright. Cusa does not say this directly; never, to my knowledge, did he use the theatrical metaphor. But he moves steadily toward the image of the shifting union of man and God as spectator and author in a theater, where their means of knowing one another can be described in those two words—sometimes overlapping, sometimes contradictory, in effect—with which we have become so familiar: perspective and vision. What Theseus said of actors, Cusa has already said of Man: the best in this kind are but shadows. The old theatrical *topos* has come to new life in Cusa's divine epistemology. Once reawakened, this impulse will not ebb throughout the course of the Renaissance, but will become more explicit, even if it never reaches a higher level of simultaneous sophistication and simplicity.

The inner tensions of Marsilio Ficino's web of cosmic powers binding man to supernal orders of being were summarized in an astonished question by his companion Pico della Mirandola on one memorable occasion. Ficino treats the moment half-humorously in writing to their friend Filippo Valori in 1488, but this experience, shared during a philosophic holiday in the hills of Fiesole, nonetheless epitomized the polarities of his folios of syncretic Platonizing:

We were imagining a villa placed at the edge of the hill in such a way as to escape the mists of Boreas, but without placing it in a hollow, in order to let it receive as much sun as possible in good weather. We wished, too, that it might be situated at an equal distance from the fields and woods, surrounded by springs, and turned toward the southeast, which Aristotle proposes concerning construction in his treatise on family government.

While we were giving ourselves up to this imaginary architecture, suddenly it stood before our eyes. Pico exclaimed: "Dear Ficino, haven't we there suddenly before us, simultaneously thought and seen, the very thing we so vividly imagined and wished for? This is what happens every day to dreamers [*quod quotidie somniantibus accidit*]. Or have we perhaps raised up the form we contrived in our spirits by the force of imagination alone? Unless a philosopher has had it built according to the just rules of architecture.[24]

The ambivalence of places which seem both interior and architectural, imaginary yet externally real, engulfs the visionary himself with a wonder so incandescent that Pico's question echoes again and again down through the years of Platonic dominance in the Renaissance. Life, like the perfect villa, suddenly appears before us in the light of that strange yet quotidian mystery which "happens every day to dreamers." But is it man's dream, or is he himself, with this world, but the shadow of a deific dream?[25]

The answer for Ficino is that both are true. Writing to Lottieri Neroni in a letter titled "Anima in corpore dormit, somniat, delirat, aegrotat," he explains that all worldly actions are but dreams of the sleeping (*dormientium somnia*), dreams which only philosophers following in the footsteps of Plato know to be illusory, from which only Platonic truths can awaken us.[26] The *Republic* is the great source for the metaphor, in all of its complexity, of course, and Ficino not infrequently returns to it,[27] but perhaps the most interesting and characteristic expression of this aspect of Ficino's thought is a passage in the *Platonica theologia* where, after speaking of the ways intemperance imprisons man in his body, he says: "The ruined souls of these are fallen into a like great madness here in this life through corporal passions with those persons who would rashly set shadows above the chiefest of goods, who would love shadows and would fear shadows" (*Opera*, p. 420). Following this account of terrestrial life, he proceeds at length to describe hell itself as evanescent, like a dream, but still a nightmare from which none awaken: "The gates of Pluto cannot be unlocked; within are the people of dreams [*populus somniorum*]. Plato says in the seventh book of the *Republic* that he finds the rational soul sleeps profoundly in this life, and before it can be awakened, it dies; and after death it is weighed down even more deeply by sleep, and confused by yet more violent nightmares [*somnijsque acrioribus perturbari*], which, properly speaking, is the state designated as Tartarus" (*Opera*, p. 422).[28]

For all of this negative development, however, there is within Ficino's system room for another world of dreams, the world of those divine dream visions which are the highest knowledge—indeed, are "magical," in his usage. Paradoxically, these dreams are available to that same Platonic philosopher whom we have found him insisting to be the only waking man among the somnambulant masses; they seem to wake only to dream again at a higher pitch.[29]

The dream as metaphor for life or as a vision of knowledge is ubiquitous. Setting aside its Platonic associations in antiquity, the equation fostered one of the most fertile genres of medieval literature: the dream allegory. But, of course, it was Dante who climaxed that genre, and in so doing deeply impressed the metaphor upon the Florentine imagination. Admirers of Plato and Dante, Florentines seem to feel obligated to rework the metaphor endlessly as the frame for almost any genre. One may briefly recall that Boccaccio used the form in the *Corbaccio* and *Amorosa visione*, that the tradition of direct imitation of Dante continued in the ambitious versifications of Palmieri and Ugolino Verino,[30] that Leonardo Bruni was enthusiastic about the visionary hermetic book described as the *Liber altividi de immortalitate animorum*,[31] and that the heritage was embraced by those associated with Ficino at Careggi. Poliziano narrated Giuliano di Piero de' Medici's dream vision of the celestial Venus in *Stanze per la giostra* (II, 29–38), and Alberti explored the dream of a philosopher observing the river of life in *Fatum et fortuna*.[32] Yet later generations of Medici associates were still continuing the tradition in the elaborate symbolic pageantry of *Il trionfo de' sogni*, which paraded Florence for the nuptials of

Francesco de' Medici and Joanna of Austria in 1556, and in the dream ballet performed in 1608 for the wedding of Prince Cosimo and Archduchess Maria Magdalena.[33]

Perhaps the most interesting instance, from our point of view, is Michelangelo's little drawing of the dream of life, "Il sogno." Panofsky describes it as follows: "a youth reclining on a box filled with masks of all descriptions, the upper part of his body supported by the terrestrial globe. . . . He is surrounded by a semi-circular halo of smaller groups sketched in an unreal, vaporous manner and thus easily recognizable as dream-visions; they represent unquestionably the seven Capital Sins. . . . But a winged genius or angel descending from heaven, awakes the youth by sounding of a trumpet."[34] The striking aspect of the piece, of course, is the explicit parallel it draws between life as a dream and as theater, a parallel which in this instance leaves unanswered the further question it engenders: is life a dream-like play conceived by man, or a dream likened to a play by the sleeper's imagination? This ambiguity clouding the relationships among life, drama, and sleep is, according to Panofsky, Michelangelo's most abstract and yet direct tribute to Ficino's influence because, if the ambiguity persists from one point of view, from another it is resolved. The youth has slept in this world of illusion, but now he awakens, and the movement is toward the divine realm which alone is real, as Ficino never tired of insisting.

There is another observation to be made concerning this symbolic drawing which is, I believe, of utmost importance. The heavily articulated musculature of the figure, wrenched into a strained right-angle position at the legs, is markedly, even unrealistically, plastic. The additional torque of the torso and the obvious pressure transmitted through the fingers of the left hand not only enhance this figural volume but involve the supporting terrestrial ball itself in the receipt and extension of the implied weight and depth. This thrust is partly countered by the indistinct volume curve of the lower portion of the globe and seems to be dissipated before it arrives at the box, upon which both globe and figure seem scarcely to weigh. But this impression of fading force is, in turn, countered again at the lower edge by the emphatic depth of the box and—unexpectedly—by the masks themselves. These drive a cone of space directly toward the spectator with their staring postures, even as the central figure's fixed gaze creates a perspective beyond the trumpeter, who recedes slightly into the background just out of the youth's line of vision. The point of this amateur digression into graphic analysis is to emphasize the emphatically solid spatial volumes, surprising in the depiction of life as a dream. But this indisputably physical quality of the shadow world is also just what we find when we look further into the imagery of Ficino. As in the drawing, the physical aspect of Ficino's descriptions of man's state opens out through imagery of sight and the eye to give spatial depth, perspective, to a world which ends by being as visual as it is visionary.

The youthful Ficino had been beguiled from his earliest years by optics and the study of perspective, as his biographers all assure us: "At that time he applied himself more vigorously to mathematics and astronomy, in which anyone can readily judge how much progress he made in a short time by his many compositions. He gave himself also to the study of perspective, and I have seen in manuscript some of his considerations on vision with some others on mirrors, both plain and concave.[35] . . . and when he was twenty-one years old he knew so much of [philosophy] that he was able to solve for Antonio Serafico certain doubts concerning vision and the rays of the sun."[36] Thus it is not entirely surprising that he should once describe God indirectly (in *Liber de sole*) by defining the analogous powers of the sun, nor that his matured system should be permeated by physical dimensions in space when he is describing states of the soul. But perhaps the truth is that perspectivism and its corollary need for a spatially oriented imagination is not only personal but, like the emphasis upon the dream metaphor for life, a mode of conception which was nurtured in Ficino by his milieu. Hans Baron has singled out Leonardo Bruni's *Laudatio urbis florentinae* (1403–4) as a new departure in the genre of civil panegyric because it coalesces attempts to explain the political and the physical atmosphere of Florence on a single principle: "In the *Laudatio* . . . the first attempt is made to discover the secret laws of optics and perspective that make the Florentine landscape appear as one great scenic structure. The site of the city, so Bruni points out, is almost the geometric center of four concentric circles. . . . so, the picture of the *urbs florentina* as the geometric center of the surrounding countryside is a striking anticipation of the ideal of the 'perfect city,' and of what has been called the 'geometric spirit' of the Renaissance."[37] This description of Bruni's treatise is echoed in the little scene between Ficino and Pico in the Fiesole hills, with its similar insistence upon the union of landscape and phlosophic perfection. Between the two historic moments Alberti's genius for perspective had emerged in Florence.[38]

In any case, Ficino displays a highly developed sense of space as a balance to his equally acute sense of evanescence. As an instance, one notices he adapts the description of God as an infinite circle, a description found earlier in Cusa, a circle where the center is everywhere and the circumference nowhere; and yet, asserts Ficino in a passage which moves agilely from hypothetical to positive constructions, if this unimaginable image were to possess a place in the cosmos it would certainly be—indeed, it is—that of the sun.[39] Nothing could give a clearer indication of Ficino's psychic perspectives: so wedded is his vision to material space that he compromises a traditional metaphysical paradox in order to project for it a local habitation and a name. It is an unwitting compromise which we have seen anticipated by Cusa, but now is made even more specific, more closely involved in that cosmos which one discerns from both telescope and textbook as defined place.[40]

The key to this apparent anomaly lies in Ficino's central axiom concerning the importance and nature of contemplation.[41] Contemplation becomes almost exclusively physical in Ficino's vocabulary, in his conception of the soul's gravity ("natural concinnity," a later English Platonist would call it) which draws those so given downward toward their corporeal bearings even as it assures more refined beings of an ascent toward deity: "Similarly [to the buoyancies of the nine orders of the angelic hierarchy] Christians reckon reprobate souls who living make themselves into nine degrees of reprobate demons, by the same similitude, to be hurled down almost by natural weight [*quasi pondere naturali putant praecipitari*]."[42]

In another mode of statement, however, more traditional, contemplation becomes the "vision" of God, the seeing of all things in God (recalling the bond between Cusa and Ficino). This vision is seldom pure: we are all Januses, looking back as well as upward;[43] or we are like a man whose life is passed standing on his head, one eye cast to the heavens, the other to the earth, who scrambles with lips, nostrils, fingers to catch what he sees below, but is reduced to his non-prehensile toes in trying to reach what he might see above.[44] But that which we do see when we gaze upward in true contemplation we see in the highest context of beauty and knowledge; we see it in God as a reflex of our seeing it at all, since visual beauty is the highest aesthetic category.[45] There is a thorough rationale. Light makes beauty in the world as well as providing the modality for contemplation. Therefore, the sun is the proper place of God's residence as he is understood to participate in this world. It is a natural union, since God's own image is that of the eye. God is the eye by means of which all eyes see and, according to the word of Orpheus, is that eye which sees all in each object and perceives all things in himself.[46] Light, then, is the divine medium, and vision the divine act of knowing. Ficino goes further yet, though, and reaches Cusa's conclusions by a different route. Man as spectator sees, and thus imitates the *oculus infinitus* which is God. But God's seeing is an act of creation by which he perceives himself in the diversity of others; by analogy, man's vision is a form of creativity, the physical eye giving the soul insight through sight into the true nature of forms. And the evidence for the creativeness of the act lies in man's ability to master the world which he views, the plants, the beasts, the elements themselves. This man who reigns over what he surveys is very near to being a deity himself.[47]

Ultimately, man's vision is even more than this quasi-creative reflection of God's greater power as the *oculus infinitus*.[48] Standing at the center of the universe, not looking backward as a body-ridden Janus nor with that upside-down vision which makes of man's life a circus act of acrobatic misery and mistakes, but rather upward toward the clear creative center, the divinely symbolic sun, man becomes again what he had been in the Platonic vision of Cusa. He becomes the indispensable spectator in this prodigious theater of the world whose looking upon it enables God himself reflexively to complete the creative act by seeing "all in every object," and so "all things in himself," even as—to complete that visual-spatial analogue Ficino is so fond of—"the light of the sun, font of all colors, which is (so one may call it) monochrome, perceives itself as if it were omnicolored."[49]

From Ficino's walk with Pico we have arrived at something very like the relationship between Cusa's omnivoyant and his viewers. Man sees because he has a perspective point (this time at the center of the creation) and is himself created by the seeing, the "vision," of God. One could offer some later historic observations on this point. Pico in his *Oratio*, for example, adapted the conception of man having his place at the center of the universal stage to the myth that all other posts in the creation had been exhausted before his creation. Thus man is by origin an actor, able to assume all places and guises without being limited by any one of them. To pass to the early sixteenth-century, Ludovicus Vives' famous little fable of man was derived from Pico, and he developed its theatrical suggestions. Now the creation itself is narrated as a play for the entertainment of the gods in which man's mimic talents appear so divine that by general consent the illusion is broken, while man climbs into the galleries of heaven to become spectator of that play in which he had been actor but a moment before.[50]

But our concern is not to write the history of a popular *topos*, but only to set the scene for reading certain plays which enriched the Renaissance theater at the highest point of dramatic achievement in European history. Let us begin that reading, then, by turning to an English playwright who revealed on the stage how the theater of this world is watched over and directed by another, and how that other world is accessible by means of contemplation—by, precisely, the dream visions of Ficino's saturnine philosopher. For Ficino himself knew that "humanum genus in terris est Dei ludus. Ludi quidem huius et fabulae author est ipse Deus" (*Opera*, p. 884).

CHAPTER II George Chapman: Myth as Mask and Magic

Among Elizabethan and Jacobean poets none was more committed to mythic vehicles for "dark" philosophy than George Chapman. The epistle introductory to *Ovids Banquet of Sense* is a manifesto of philosophic poetics:

The prophane multitude I hate, & onelie consecrate my strange Poems to these serching spirits, whom learning hath made noble, and nobilitie sacred. . . . that Poesie should be as peruiall as Oratorie, and plainnes her speciall ornament, were the plaine way to barbarisme. . . . Obscuritie in affection of words, & indigested concets, is pedanticall and childish; but where it shroudeth it selfe in the hart of his subiect, vtterd with fitnes of figure, and expressiue Epithetes; with that darknes will J still labour to be shadowed.[1]

It has long been acknowledged that Chapman's Platonic views were even more often derived from his reading in the works of Ficino and the Florentine circle than his marginal glosses suggest,[2] and this very darkness of poetry comes equally from that source. It is to the Florentines that we must turn if we are to recognize in Chapman's comic corpus two plays which seriously probe the bearing of dreams and theatrical illusion upon the course of events in the active life of society. These are Platonic plays in that they examine, respectively, the two poles of vision which Ficino argues may attract man. In *The Gentleman Usher* the divine dream vision of the contemplative philosopher directs life into the pattern of an unexpected *commedia divina*. In *The Widow's Tears* the diabolic nightmare turns man himself into a shadow, a mocking, illusory inversion of his own best hopes. In both plays the mode of development is mythological; it is upon this account that we must remind ourselves of the Renaissance Platonists' impact upon Chapman's understanding and use of mythology.

Ficino himself, even while equating the themes of the three great epics of Homer, Virgil, and Dante by interpreting them as allegorical histories of the soul, insisted that divine things, the transcendent, are beyond mere conceptualization. Man's need to bridge this spiritual abyss, to know the inconceivable, is the explanation of his need for myth.[3] We have seen Ficino at times to be a thoroughly conceptual allegorist as he removes all traces of narrative in spiritualizing Plato's Tartarus or in converting Tantalus into a rather banal symbol of man's general spiritual yearning.[4] Yet certain mythological figures, most notably Saturn and Orpheus, became pivotal to his complicated description of cosmic and microcosmic interaction. That they were more than a convenient symbolic shorthand for intellectual melancholy and poetic-religious inspiration is clear from what we know of Ficino's personal re-enactment of Orphic chanting, for instance.[5] Here there can be no question of conceptual sterilization, since Ficino went to the effort to build an "Orphic" lyre, to decorate it with phrases from the hymns, and to create personal ecstasies by chanting the hymns to the accompaniment of this lyre while drinking the prescribed wine, which invited a darker god to enhance the reawakened scene rooted in the Ur-history of magic.[6] There could be no more vivid evidence that young Ficino earnestly meant his assertion that mythic fictions and figures speak to the soul at a level different from conceptual forms of discourse. Here the mythic act is, if we may so call it, both universal and cultic. If it re-establishes communication across fundamental and lasting channels of "magic" cosmic energy, it does so in a private, secret ritual hidden from the gaze and the capacities of the vulgar. Pico records that Plato wrote to Dionysius "per aenigmata" in his letters on the supreme substance in order that, should these letters fall into unknown hands, they would remain unintelligible; he also records that Aristotle's notes on divine things in the *Metaphysics* might be said "editos esse et non editos."[7] John Colet remarked in his marginalia upon a copy of Ficino's *Epistolae* that "Plato . . . believed that since its [wisdom's] true value could not be properly displayed, it should be fittingly hidden. And so he clothed his ideas in obscure . . . dress in order to hide them and make the stupid reader miss them. . . . those who bring their light with them may penetrate his mysteries."[8] *The Gentleman Usher* is such a Platonic "mystery," and the word is one favored by Chapman in discussing his own poetry. In *The Shadow of Night* he had framed the "Hymnus in Cynthiam" as "an argument to rauish and refine / An earthly soule, and make it meere diuine" (ll. 154–55) when "iudgement shall displaie, to purest eyes / With ease, the bowells of these misteries" (ll. 168–69). This was a conception of the relation between deep truths and the true philosopher which Chapman never tired of rephrasing. Contrasting the "sleight man" and the philosopher in *Petrarch's Seven Penitential Psalms* (1612), he warns:

> Their imperfections yet are hid in sleight,
> Of the felt darknesse, breath'd out by deceipt,
> The truly learn'd, is likewise hid, and failes
> To pierce eyes vulgar, but with other vailes.
> And they are the diuine beames, truth casts round
> About his beauties, that do quite confound
> Sensuall beholders. . . .[9]

Late in life, Chapman would discover the allegory of the *Odyssey* to be more moral than mysterious,[10] but in 1614 (the year of Jonson's daring hidden allegory in *Bartholomew Fair*[11]) he was still championing the "mysterious" rites of poetry in "A Free and Offenceles Ivstification: Of a lately publisht and most maliciously misinterpreted Poeme; Entituled. Andromeda liberata": "As *Learning*, hath delighted from her Cradle, to hide her selfe from the base and prophane *Vulgars*, her ancient Enemy; vnder diuers vailes of *Hieroglyphickes*, Fables, and the like; so hath she pleased her selfe with no disguise more; then in misteries and allegoricall fictions of *Poesie*."[12] And certainly *Andromeda Liberata* was no mere "moral" fiction.

One might object that the comic stage constitutes a much clumsier and more improbable instrument for philosophic investigation than does allegorical narrative, but Chapman himself apparently did not feel the weight of the objection. In the final sonnet of "A Coronet for his Mistress Philosophy" he called his philosophic muse to witness against "such as scorne to tread the Theater" because "noblest wits, and men of highest doome" have graced the stage under her aegis: "The Theaters of *Athens* and of *Rome* / Haue been the Crownes, and not the base empayre."[13] Twelve or fifteen years later he carried the point onto the stage itself in *The Revenge of Bussy D'Ambois*, when Clermont and the Guise, in hearing of the treacherous Baligny, compare ancient and modern stages. Here the philosophic potential of drama is argued not only by the invocation of authority from Democritus and Epictetus, but by that of the world theater *topos*:

> *Guise.* I would have these things
> Brought upon stages, to let mighty misers
> See all their grave and serious miseries play'd,
> As once they were in Athens and old Rome.
> *Clermont.* Nay, we must now have nothing brought on stages
> But puppetry, and pied ridiculous antics:
> Men thither come to laugh, and feed fool-fat,

Check at all goodness there, as being profan'd:
When, wheresoever goodness comes, she makes
The place still sacred. . . .
. . . .
Baligny. Why, is not all the world esteem'd a stage?
Clermont. Yes, and right worthily; and stages too
Have a respect due to them. . . .
. . . .
. . . If but for this, then,
To make the proudest outside, that most swells
With things without him and above his worth,
See how small cause he has to be so blown up,
And the most poor man to be griev'd with poorness,
Both being so easily born by expert actors,
The stage and actors are not so contemptful
As every innovating Puritan,
And ignorant sweater-out of zealous envy,
Would have the world imagine.[14]

I will argue that Chapman's muse of philosophic drama was identical with that dark lady who shadowed the narrative poems "in misteries and allegoricall fictions." It remains only to ask what mythology has to do with dreams. And the answer, by this point in our survey of Florentine foci, is almost reflexive: if myths are signs, figures which make available what we might term "supradiscursive" realizations concerning the soul's relationship to its divine origin and aspiration,[15] certainly dreams have a common genesis, with their psychic deployment into imagistic symbols that eventuate in insights, visions unguessed in the waking state.[16] Where reason ends, images begin. And with the images, with myth and dream, begin responsibility, for it is only through these media that man wakens from the sleep of life.

These attitudes are what George Chapman learned and breathed more deeply into the body of his work than most artists even in the late Renaissance, when allegorical impulses had become a conditioned response to mythology.

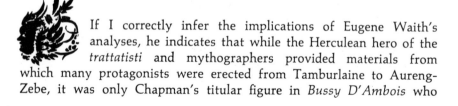

If I correctly infer the implications of Eugene Waith's analyses, he indicates that while the Herculean hero of the *trattatisti* and mythographers provided materials from which many protagonists were erected from Tamburlaine to Aureng-Zebe, it was only Chapman's titular figure in *Bussy D'Ambois* who was conceived as symbol, as a paradoxical *Hercules redivivus* for "the more sophisticated spectators" who might realize with the author that the play "seems to be moving on two parallel lines, one of which is the adventures of the historical Bussy, the other a progressive revelation of a mythic figure, a Hercules disguised as Bussy."[17] It is a likely conclusion, following from what we have just noted about his Platonic heritage, that Chapman so veiled another "mystery" in myth. But even so, the Herculean aspect of Bussy hidden beneath the "pervial" surface of his court scandal serves ultimately, in Waith's reading, only to emphasize "the moving dilemma of a great-spirited man who attempts to live by a heroic code in a world dominated by Machiavellian policy."[18] In *The Gentleman Usher* Chapman adapted the Herculean protagonist to even better effect, creating a truly Platonic Hercules whose success is imaged through the transcendent magic of a vision which sees the world as a masque of policy. And that which puts down policy is the harmonious source of vision itself: patience.[19]

The first scenes of the play are dedicated to theatrical spectacle, to masque and grotesque anti-masque which serve as symbolic plays-within-the-play. And yet there is a cross-current even here, as a prelude of prophetic dream throws these carefully prepared shows strangely out of the focus of manipulated control which is implied in symbolic spectacles.

The plot of *The Gentleman Usher* centers upon old Duke Alphonso's rivalry with his son Vincentio for the love of youthful Margaret, daughter of Earl Lasso. Into this perverse romantic situation are threaded the vicious, jealous pretensions of Margaret's aunt, Cortezza, and of three male witwoulds: Medice, evil counselor to the Duke; Poggio, hapless and witless nephew to Vincentio's friend Lord Strozza; and Bassiolo, "gentleman usher" to Margaret's father. But gradually it is Strozza, a manipulator who out-manipulates the schemers surrounding Vincentio and himself, who emerges as the protagonist. From the beginning through act IV the action centers upon plans for a boar hunt led by the Duke, a hunt which ends in a treacherous, nearly fatal attack upon Strozza by a minion of Medice. But in the earliest scenes the hunt is transmuted into the symbolic love hunt of a court masque through which the Duke woos Margaret, and it is still further delayed by an answering masque performed for the Duke's entertainment at the behest of Lasso.

In the opening scene the impending hunt is introduced in a nervous interview among Poggio, Strozza, and Strozza's wife Cynanche. Poggio has awakened late because of a dream of grotesque violence involving his horse, followed by another, equally grotesque, of love-servitude to Margaret. The tangential bearings of dream on reality are suggested when Poggio closes his account of equine disaster with the plaint, "Slud Aunt, what if my dreame had beene true (as it might haue beene for any thing I knew)."[20] Strozza immediately associates the dream violence with the hunt through his ironic yet ambiguous epithet "furious" for the nephew (who closely approximates a type of child-like but prophetic fool popular on the stage at the time in all his individuations, from Lear's jester to Jonson's Bartholomew Cokes):

> Well said, my furious nephew: but I see
> You quite forget that we must rowse to day
> The sharp-tuskt Bore: and blaze our huntsmanship
> Before the duke. (I, i, 18–21)

As Poggio disappears to prepare, Cynanche moves his dream of violence a plane closer to the actual hunt with her own misgivings: "My Lord I fancie not these hunting sports"; "Take heede for Gods loue if you rowse the Bore, / You come not neere him" (I, i, 49–62).[21]

Reassured by Strozza, Cynanche leaves, to be replaced by Vincentio and the return of Poggio, in a highly excited state. He brings reports which again seem grotesque, yet are more discomforting as unnatural omens than the dreams which they translate into reality, completing the transition initiated by Cynanche. Strozza's hounds and horses have turned, "and *Kilbucke* being runne mad, bit *Ringwood* so by the left buttocks, you might haue turnd your nose in it" while simultaneously "your horse, Gray Strozza too haz the staggers, and haz strooke bay-Bettrice, your Barbary mare so, that shee goes halting" (I, i, 136–51).[22] Before he was only amused by Poggio; now Strozza is inclined to think him ominous: "What poison blisters thy vnhappy tongue / Euermore braying forth vnhappy newes?" (I, i, 153–54)[23]

The sense of nature gone wild is quieted immediately, however, by the entrance of Duke Alphonso to announce that

> Tis no true hunting we intend to day,
> But an inducement to a certair, shew,
> Wherewith we will present our beauteous loue. (I, i, 164–66)

The hunt is to be safely manipulated into a masque for Margaret, and this dramatized conceit becomes symbol when Strozza *ex tempore* narrates the show in which the Duke himself is brought before his mistress "bound" by Sylvanus the enchanter and attendant spirits. As in the portentous dreams, Chapman again tantalizingly maneuvers the masque-within-the-play in such a manner that Strozza is able to fashion a gloss which is both truth and fiction, in that it recounts the love hunt being enacted in the masque in terms of the boar hunt which has been the fictive mask for the masque:

> His Grace this morning visiting the woods,
> And straying farre, to finde game for the Chase,
> At last, out of a mirtle groue he rowsde
> A vast and dreadfull Boare, so sterne and fierce,
> As if the Feend fell Crueltie her selfe
> Had come to fright the woods in that strange shape.
> . . . .
> Horror held all vs Huntsmen from pursuit,
> Onely the Duke incenst with our cold feare,
> Incouragde like a second *Hercules.*
> . . . .
> Hunted the monster close, and chargde so fierce,
> That he inforc'd him (as our sence conceiu'd)
> To leape for soile into a cristall spring,
> Where on the suddaine strangely vanishing,
> Nimph-like for him, out of the waues arose
> Your sacred figure like *Diana* armde,
> And (as in purpose of the beasts reuenge)
> Dischargde an arrow through his Highnesse breast,
> Whence yet no wound or any blood appearde:
> And this Enchanter with his power of spirits,
> . . . .
> . . . strooke vs sencelesse, while in these strange bands,
> These cruell spirits thus inchainde his armes,
> . . . .
> [*Enchanter.*] Bright Nimph, that Boare figur'd your crueltie,
> Charged by loue, defended by your beautie.[24]   (I, ii, 78–113)

Vincentio later protests to Strozza that his speech of interpretation has been too persuasive, benefiting Alphonso's cause before Margaret, and the Duke himself is clearly pleased. Neither, apparently, has listened attentively to the allegory. If Alphonso has been like a second Hercules, it has scarcely been in the classical pattern, for the boar has triumphed in metamorphosis. Alphonso's ultimate "release" by Margaret, which closes the masque, is a forced game urged by the Duke's supporters; it derives no more logically from Strozza's myth than does the Enchanter's conclusion.[25] Indeed, the entire masque seems so distant from the Hercules legends that on the surface it suggests more strongly the Platonic *concordia discors* in which Venus arms herself with the weapons of Diana, and "the union of Chastity and Love through the mediation of

Beauty is . . . expressed by one hybrid figure in which the two opposing goddesses . . . are merged into one."[26]

The puzzlement is increased by the pageant which Lasso subsequently presents for his noble guest. Performed by rustic broom-men, rushmen, and bugs, with the simpleton Poggio as narrator, this actually functions as a comic anti-masque to the masque proper. But the moral of both is the same: if Margaret is invited to embrace the Duke at the end, it is (like Alphonso's release in the first masque) in spite of the lesson of the dance:

> as our country girls held off,
> And rudely did their lovers scoff;
> Our Nymph likewise shall onely glaunce
> By your faire eies, and looke askaunce
> Vpon her feral friend that wooes her,
>
> . . . .
> . . . though the rurall wilde and antike,
> Abusde their loues as they were frantike;
> Yet take you in your Iuory clutches,
> This noble Duke, and be his Dutches.   (II, ii, 102–17)

Poggio's climactic broom speech not only supports the rejection of passion but asserts a bond with the first masque through an answering Herculean reference:

> Grim *Hercules* swept a stable with a riuer,
>
> . . . .
> Philosophy, that passion sweepes from thought,
> Is the soules Broome, and by all braue wits sought,
> Now if Philosophers but Broomemen are,
> Each Broomeman then is a Philosopher.   (II, ii, 57–67)

I have called the presentation an anti-masque and this an "answering" allusion because it assigns to Hercules a role different from that he played in the masque of the love hunt. There he stood as the apparent victim, here as the symbol of victory over passion.[27] If we turn to the mythographers whose compendia Chapman utilized, this apparent discrepancy in his Herculean symbolism disappears, to reappear as a familiar, traditional synthesis.[28]

Invariably the mythographers devote several pages to the deeds and iconography of Hercules, that most exciting of the pagan gods. And if they differ in many particulars, none fails to focus a part of his exegesis upon Hercules as the great representative of man's spiritual triumph over the passions, often making him the exemplar of apotheosis through his deliberate rejection of the body.[29] Vincenzo Cartari achieves a tour de force in explicating the labors and the traditional static iconography in a single brief and cohesive account which can stand for many other less economical versions:

[Hercules] was called a tamer of monsters; but because there are no uglier or more horrible monsters, nor tyrants more cruel among mortals than the vices of the spirit, some have wished to say that the strength of Hercules was not of the body but of the spirit, with which he overcame all those disordered appetites which, rebels against reason, disturb and harrass man continuously like ferocious monsters. And *apropos* of this Suidas writes that the ancients, in order to show that Hercules was a great lover of prudence and virtue, painted him dressed in a lion's skin, signifying greatness and generosity of spirit, and placed a club in his right hand, which signifies a desire for prudence and knowledge. With this they feigned the fable that he had smitten the fierce dragon and carried away three golden apples which it guarded. These he held in his left hand, signifying that he had overcome sensual appetite and thus had freed the three powers of the soul, ornamenting it with virtue and with just and honest deeds.[30]

Cesare Ripa describes a number of Herculean icons under the rubric of *virtù* in his *Iconologia,* and one repeatedly meets the lion of spiritual fortitude and the boar of corporeal passion, each necessary and necessarily harnessed together by Hercules. There is one definition of heroic virtue in his exegeses which passes beyond the merely moralizing comments on the iconographic plates, however: "heroic virtue in man is that state in which reason has so overcome the sensitive affections that it arrives at a point whence it cannot be separated from virtuous means; one made so pure and illustrious transcends human excellence and draws near the ranks of the angels."[31]

With the last phrase Hercules moves from the classical pantheon into the celestial choir of the Christian saints. It was not, of course, a recent journey, although one seldom reflected in the mythographic compendia. There had been those Fathers like Lactantius who dismissed Hercules as a barbarian who clearly had followed the opposite way from that of virtue. However, as the patristic tradition of attack succumbed in large part to neoplatonic syncretism in the Renaissance, even those commentators who took note of Hercules' lapses did so with an eye upon his eventual apotheosis.

That apotheosis is more prominent in the exegetes upon Ovid than in the compilers of mythic handbooks, since the former had the encouragement of the *Ovide moralisé* tradition and were also compelled to emphasize and explain the Nessus and Oeta episodes. We discover, for instance, in Giuseppe Horologgi's annotations to Giovanni Andrea dell' Anguillara's popular translation of the *Metamorphoses* a reconciliation of the two Herculeses—the passionate pagan sinner and Ripa's triumphant saint.[32] Hercules, explains Horologgi, is the lover of glory who sees himself being robbed of his hard-earned fame (Deianira) through lasciviousness (the centaur). He kills this passion with an arrow dipped in his own virtue, but the poisonous shirt is the revenge which passion takes upon the man intent on glory. This allegory is but prelude to the climax of Horologgi's reading: "he burns himself and is rejuvenated, because as at first we pass from a lascivious, dishonest, and vicious life to one temperate, honorable, and praiseworthy by burning out the evil affections, so we return young again to virtue and to glory; and thenceforward we are lifted to Heaven again on wings of contemplation, and numbered among the Gods, who are those that have turned all their thoughts upon God, becoming Gods by participation, in the way the Psalm says: "I have said that you are Gods" [*Ho detto che voi sete Dei*]."[33] Hercules Oetaeus has become the very prototype of Christian promise: paradise well lost that it may be regained upon a transcendent plane happier far. With these reminders of an often-told history, we are equipped to examine those resonances of the Herculean myth which couple masque and anti-masque, and which finally structure the principal action of *The Gentleman Usher*.

The first masque deliberately confuses myth and, therefore, motive. It seems to fall neatly into the tradition which associates Venus and venery, love and the hunt, a pattern woven by Chapman's contemporary into *Venus and Adonis* and *Twelfth Night*. But with the introduction of Hercules, the hunt becomes, willy-nilly, symbolic of the control of passions, capture of the rampant boar. And, willy-nilly, the boar turned upon the hunter becomes Diana, to reaffirm the symbolic Herculean feat by which the monster was brought to leash.[34] It must be so, because Alphonso is the unnatural lover, *Hercules furens* raging in passion's slavery, while the masque prophesies Hercules' transcendence of passion. The old Duke raging in the shirt of Nessus is here promised that chastity he does not yet seek which will come, when it comes, from one who is truly "a second Hercules," one who has learned and teaches that "philosophy" which sweeps passion from the thoughts.

The contradictory confusions of the masques, the overtones of something above controlled theatricality when dream disturbs the world of contrived symbol—these aspects of the supranatural impinging upon the action are supported by the strange markings upon the three witwoulds. We have noticed Poggio's dreams, his prophecies in nonsense, the repeated emphasis upon his role as the innocent but inevitable carrier of bad news. If he speaks folly, it is truth. "I am the veriest foole on you all," he cries, and "therein thou art worth vs all, for thou knowst thy selfe," responds Vincentio (III, ii, 219–21). Bassiolo, the "gentleman usher," is gulled through his own vanity into uniting Vincentio and Margaret, and the scenes of his presumptuous intimacy with Vincentio strike notes strongly recalling Malvolio's cross-garters. Yet the fact remains that he alone has joined with Strozza in forwarding this natural union. And when, again like Malvolio, he stands most mercilessly exposed before the court in his simpering claims upon Vincentio, a reformed Alphonso refuses to be drawn to laughter or scorn, but is bemused at a fool whose innocence improbably "saw the fitnes of the match, / With freer and more noble eies then we" (V, iv, 175–76; cf. V, iv, 162–64). These eerie marks are counterweighted by the unnatural pretensions of both Poggio and Bassiolo to a courtly status for which neither is equipped; and the two strange extremes meet in the figure of Medice. For if the pretensions are a focus of satire in Bassiolo and of farce in Poggio, they flicker in a diabolic, pseudo-tragic light around Medice. Revealed in the denouement as the would-be murderer of Strozza, Medice is discovered to be Mendice, king of the gypsies, who was motivated in his intrigues by dark influences from "an old Sorceresse" (V, iv, 258 ff.). By this point we have already seen him grievously wound Strozza and Vincentio, the attack upon the latter being characterized as "blacke witchcraft . . . . diuelish wrath of hell" (V, ii, 61–62). Unmasked publicly through Strozza's "diuine relation," Mendice finally flees the stage to "hide me from the sight of heauen" (V, iv, 277).

These strange butts, Poggio's strange dream, Cynanche's premonitions, the metamorphic vision of the first masque with its Enchanter, Mendice's sorcery—all these hover like indecisive shadows over the action of the drama until they are illuminated by the brilliant flash of Strozza's vision, a vision which makes him, indeed, as Schoell said, "a mixture of Christian mysticism and pagan stoicism."[35] But Chapman urges us throughout to see him more specifically than this, as the mythic center in which these traditions merged, the Christian Hercules.

The turning point for Strozza, as for the play, is an incident which moves toward tragedy in a way unprecedented in Chapman's earlier comedies (if we discount the farcical murder of Prince Doricles in *The Blind Beggar of Alexandria*) and approached again only in *The Widow's Tears*. On the day following the masques Alphonso orders an actual hunt, in which Strozza is painfully wounded. As at the opening of the play, there is a sense of fatality when the hapless messenger of doom Poggio rushes on stage to announce this "accident" to his aunt, Cynanche.

Almost immediately Strozza is carried in, overwhelmed by a desperate agony:

> Must we attend at deaths abhorred doore,
> The torturing delaies of slauish Nature?
> My life is in mine owne powers to dissolue:
> And why not then the paines that plague my life?
> Rise furies, and this furie of my bane,
> Assaile and conquer. . . .
> . . . .
> Resolue and rid me of this brutish life,
> Hasten the cowardly protracted cure
> Of all diseases: King of Phisitians, death,
> Ile dig thee from this Mine of miserie.   (IV, i, 34–46)

His wife, more terrified by this desperation than by the physical wound, in order (as she soliloquizes) to "salue with Christian patience, Pagan sinne," attempts through "fained patience to recomfort him" when she offers Strozza the reminder that

> afflictions bring to God,
> Because they make vs like him, drinking vp
> Ioyes that deforme vs with the lusts of sense,
> And turne our generall being into soule. . . .   (IV, i, 62–65)

Her exhortations reach a climax with the proud assertion that "Patience in torment, is a valure more / Then euer crownd Th'Alcmenean Conqueror" (IV, i, 55–56). The allusion indicates the prototype of Strozza's anguished outcry against the torture of a treacherous and incurable wound, as well as its significance: it is "Hercules Oetaeus" burning in the shirt of Nessus.[36]

Soon after Cynanche's expostulations with her husband we see them together again; and the brief time that has elapsed has worked a miracle: the wounded Strozza now volunteers a long panegyric upon the value of a true wife, explaining that Cynanche's "diuine advice," her "heauenly words," have healed him:

> My free submission to the hand of heauen
> Makes it redeeme me from the rage of paine.
> For though I know the malice of my wound
> Shootes still the same distemper through my vaines,
> Yet the Iudiciall patience I embrace,
> (In which my minde spreads her impassiue powres
> Through all my suffring parts;) expels their frailetie;
> And rendering vp their whole life to my soule,
> Leaues me nought else but soule. . . .   (IV, iii, 43–51)

As Cynanche had proposed, affliction has turned his "general being into soule" (IV, i, 65). Re-created in the fire of suffering sustained, Strozza experiences in his person a paradox suggestive of the Herculean apotheosis—and of the Christian:

> Humilitie hath raisde me to the starres;
> In which (as in a sort of Cristall Globes)
> I sit and see things hidde from humane sight. (IV, iii, 61–63)

This holy vision becomes prophetic (through "that good Angell, / That by diuine relation spake in me" [V, iv, 199–200]) in assuring him that on "the seuenth day" the arrow will fall from his healed wound, a prophecy underlined by Strozza's almost incantatory repetition of the magic number "seven." He further amazes his skeptical audience when, rapt beyond their comprehension, he also sees a vision of mortal danger to Vincentio, who has left his father's hunt in the hope of enjoying some stolen hours with Margaret. The dream of danger is soon verified as Cortezza, the drunken sister of Lasso, leads a suspicious Alphonso to the lover's tryst, reviving with perverted emphasis the analogy between love and the hunt:

> Their confidence, that you are still a hunting,
> Will make your amorous sonne that stole from thence,
> Bold in his loue-sports; Come, come, a fresh chace,
> I hold this pickelocke, you shall hunt at view.
> What, do they thinke to scape? An old wiues eye
> Is a blew Cristall full of sorcerie. (IV, iv, 50–55)

Malevolent and lecherous, Cortezza joins the venomous Medice-Mendice in setting up an imagistic counterpoint of diabolic sorcery, black magic, against the divine benevolence of Strozza's healing powers and mystic visions. And in the final act, set a week after the day of the near-tragic hunt, this transcendent war between spiritual and demonic magic (up to this point a muted battle which has gradually emerged from the early dreams of Poggio) explicitly comes to dominate and to enlarge the action. Strozza, now miraculously healed, assures his physician that

> t'was no frantike fancie,
> That made my tongue presage this head should fall
> Out of my wounded side the seuenth day;
> But an inspired rapture of my minde,
> Submitted and conioyned in patience,
> To my Creator, in whom I fore-saw
> (Like to an Angell) this diuine event. (V, ii, 1–7)

The good Doctor Benevenius glosses the lesson of this "right christian president":

> What a most sacred medcine Patience is,
> That with the high thirst of our soules cleare fire
> Exhausts corporeall humour; and all paine,
> Casting our flesh off, while we it retaine.[37]   (V, ii, 10–13)

We have already met the transcendence of passion through suffering, the apotheosis of one "Submitted and conioynde in patience / To my Creator," in the Christianized Hercules Oetaeus of the commentators; let us further remind ourselves that patience is the lesson they, too, sometimes teach. As Sandys suggested, Nessus' shirt *put on by Hercules, he broyls with heate, which subdues his fortitude with intollerable torments: who in his anguish disputes: with the Gods . . . (an impatience unto which the best of mortall men haue beene subiect . . .).*[38] By and large, Renaissance dramatists, following Seneca, emphasized this "impatience,"[39] but Chapman was no ordinary dramatist. He was, rather, as we have noted, an eclectic yet serious Platonist who drew his imagery as well as his vision from the legacy of Ficino's Florence. When we turn again to Ficino, this time as an interpreter of mythology, we discover an exclusive emphasis upon that *Hercules patiens* who succeeded and transcended *Hercules furens*. And we recover, too, the orientation of Strozza's magic dream vision.

For Ficino, Hercules was an exemplar of those victims of epilepsy who shared with other prophets the experience of self-transcendence, of leaving the body in life: "Quo excelluisse Hercules dicitur, Arabesque permulti, qui comitiali morbo corripiebantur."[40] Suffering leads to God rather directly. And if we place this view of Hercules' significance within the total complex of Ficino's thought, it gives a light which clarifies Chapman's play, arguing from a reasoned system the supernal validity of dream. We know how Ficino reverses the perspective of society, teaching that only philosophers are awake to divine things while others dream in waking. The body, "things," constitute a shadow world which must be transcended by the divine rapture of knowing.[41] Thus in dreams lie a responsibility and reality such as Strozza experiences after transcending the corporeal; or, to invert the equation in yet another dimension, man is "a dream / But of a shadow, summ'd with all his substance," as Chapman's Bussy reckons him.[42] Those who, escaping the corporeal shadows, are able to see reality as dream and dream as reality are those who, like Hercules, are "rapt" beyond the Platonic cave of this world to a more direct communion with their "Creator" (it should not be forgotten that Ficino considered his *De raptu Pauli* important enough to translate it into Italian himself[43]). But Ficino associated transcendent rapture with suffering: one emerged from time to time into the reality of the eternal dream through the interior ascent which begins in corporeal misery.[44] So it was with Strozza and with Hercules.

The interior ascent toward an unmediated vision is articulable process as well as promise in Ficino's system, and the process is dependent upon that concept which has been echoing like a refrain through the speeches of Strozza and Cynanche: "patience." It is this trait which focuses Ficino's discussion of the wise man's spiritual transcendence.[45] "All other virtues consist in doing well; patience alone in suffering well," wrote Ficino.[46] And to Antonio Cocchi he explained: "I think that patience prescribes mainly three things. First that you may be willing to suffer gladly evils which nature itself commands you to be unwilling to suffer. Secondly, that those things which fate has decided to be necessary you transform into voluntary ones. Thirdly, that you turn all evils into goods, which is God's task alone. [Patience, therefore] commands us . . . to make ourselves equal to God. . . . For only impatience causes misfortunes, which might be confined to external things and to the body alone, to pass into the soul as well."[47] One can listen for the echoes of such a passage in Strozza's triumph over the physical agony of his wound, as when the doctor affirms the power of the "most sacred medicine Patience . . . Casting our flesh off, while we it retaine." But Ficino goes further in explaining just how man effects that visionary rapture which Strozza experiences as the reward of patience, understood in its root sense:

Since it is impossible to approach the celestial seats with a corporeal bulk, the soul, taking thought as its guide, by the gift of philosophy, transcends through contemplation the nature of all things. . . . to speak comprehensively, since philosophy is a celestial gift, it drives earthly vices far away, bravely subdues fortune, admirably softens fate, safely uses mortal gifts, abundantly offers immortal gifts. . . . O sure guide of human life, who first defeats the monsters of vice entirely with the club of *Hercules*, then with the shield of Pallas avoids and overcomes the dangers of fortune, and finally takes human souls upon the shoulders of Atlas, frees them from this earthly exile, and returns them truly and happily to the celestial fatherland.[48]

In Ficino's view, this is the path of divine patience by which *Hercules Oetaeus* arrives at the role of prophet in rapture, raised to the stars on the *scala* of suffering. And it is the path along which Strozza follows the Alcmenean conqueror of self.[49]

In yet another comment on patience in suffering, Ficino said:

Our body is attracted in a powerful attack by the body of the world through the forces of fate . . . and the power of fate does not penetrate our mind if our mind has not previously immersed itself in the body subject to fate. So no one should trust his own intelligence and strength enough to hope he can wholly avoid the sicknesses of the body [*morbos corporis*] or the loss of things. Every soul should retire from the pestilence of the body [*corporis peste*] and withdraw into the mind, for then fortune will spend its force on the body and not pass into the soul. A wise man will not fight in vain against fate, but rather resist by fleeing. Misfortunes cannot be hunted down, but can only be fled.[50]

The masque of Hercules and the chaste boar had been Alphonso's spectacle of the frontal assault upon fate; *Hercules furens,* he had caught the arrow of passion as the beast of the body turned upon him. And yet that beast had been, in spite of his own will, a benevolent prey—as Strozza explains, passion pursued becomes passion providentially spent. And when the same arrow of misfortune pierces Strozza's side, he, wiser than the Duke, acted the role of the divine philosopher, *Hercules patiens:* through his interior ascent from the pestilent body he did, in fact, turn his "generall being into soule." In the love hunt, symbolized by Strozza at its divine level, the victor is not the hunter, but the prey.

If Chapman emphasizes illness, we can annotate his intentions here, too, from Ficino's thought. Like the author of *The Gentleman Usher,* the Florentine was obsessed with the medical, psychosomatic aspects of self-transcendence. Soellner has traced the tradition of his interest, insofar as it relates specifically to Herculean mythology, from the pseudo-Aristotelian *Problemata,* a handbook immensely popular in the Renaissance. There Hercules' madness was attributed to epileptic melancholy, with the note that "epileptic afflictions were called by the ancients 'the sacred disease, after him" (953ª)—Galen's νοσος 'Ηρακλειη, *Herculeus morbus.* But Soellner points out that "the Neoplatonists of the Renaissance gave a new twist to the idea of the epilepsy of Hercules by explaining it as something of a spiritual achievement. They fused a popular medieval superstition about the prophetic gift of epileptics with the pseudo-Aristotelian theory of the excellence of epileptic melancholiacs as exemplified by Hercules."[51] This new version of a medieval tradition owed a great deal to Ficino's image of himself as a melancholiac seer whose power came from morbidity. It is a self-portrait which is reflected in his extensive writings on natural magic, and which permits us to refine more precisely the function of Strozza in bringing into focus the theme of Chapman's play about the absorption of artifice into vision and dream. Indeed, intentionally or not, Strozza (in the milieu which Jacquot so felicitously tags "une Italie de rêve") becomes not merely a modern Hercules, but imitator of that imitator of the great epileptic of myth, an icon for Ficino himself.

Ficino insisted that he was a "Saturnine" victim of that ambiguous gift of intellection which is marked by the stars as contemplative melancholy. It was a gift which—as the "epileptic" diagnosis for Hercules supposes—Ficino developed into a complex of physiologico-astrological magic that could be rationalized as medicine.[52] But he was undoubtedly influenced more by familial tradition than by the horoscope he cast for himself because he carefully reported in later life how both his father, a young physician, and his mother gave him a personal legacy of prophetic visions and dreams. The father, called to inspect an injured farmer, gave the man up as fatally wounded. Returning home, he paused under an oak tree to rest, and there experienced a vision in which a beautiful young woman accused him of ingratitude to God for not employing his gift of healing more generously. Three days later the farmer's father arrived to plead for the doctor's return. When he did return, to his amazement he found the man still alive and was able to cure him. Later he learned that the family had been praying to the Virgin at the very moment when she appeared to him on the road (*Opera*, p. 644). Ficino's mother, Monna Sandra, had had dreams correctly presaging deaths in the family (*Opera*, p. 615). Ficino himself inherited this prophetic gift; he often cast successful horoscopes, successfully predicted both war and plague in 1477, and once (a direct analogue to Strozza's experience) was promised recovery from his own serious illness in a dream.[53]

As Strozza cried in petition at the outset of his suffering, "Rise furies, and this furie of my bane, / Assaile and conquer" (IV, i, 38–39), so Ficino elaborated a system in which fury played a principal part. He described four *furores*, those induced by poetry, mystery, prophecy, and love, concluding that "no man possessed by *furor* is content with ordinary speech but breaks forth into shouting and singing and chants. Wherefore any *furor*, either that of prophecy, or of mysteries, or of love, since it leads to singing and poetry, can rightly be said to find its completion in the poetic *furor*."[54] Strozza's invocation of the aid of the Furies seems pointed when we recall that at the beginning of the play he had addressed the other prophetic character, Poggio, as "my furious nephew." In Poggio, as in Strozza, the fury of prophetic vision—as Ficino explains—makes him a true poet, possessor of the divine afflatus. In the light of this insistence that true poets are furious seers, inspired dreamers, we come to appreciate how fully Chapman has prepared the antithesis between the theatrical art futilely employed by the authors of the masques and the grotesque dreams of furious Poggio. We now know, too, why Strozza's reading of the poetic masque was not only more "poetic" but more true than the masque itself.[55] The carnal boar metamorphosed into Diana, the broom-man philosopher who "passion sweeps from thought," were obscured promises (made only partially "peruiall" through the veiled prophecy of their Herculean allusions), types of Strozza, the rapt physician who verifies a dream of health snatched in angelic vision.

Medicine, however, permeates the play's last scenes in many other respects, reminding us of how the Renaissance critical debate on Aristotelian *katharsis* in art sought a grounding between the extremes of passion psychology and religious lustration.[56] That Mendice should masquerade as Medice is more than a pun, as we see when the result of his machinations is the soul-healing paradox of the wounds suffered by both Strozza and Vincentio, and this medical focus is carried into yet another channel of action by the venomous disfigurement and miraculous restoration of Margaret's beauty.

In act IV it becomes apparent that the fundamental structure of *The Gentleman Usher* is the interaction between the mutually illuminating events involving Strozza and those involving Vincentio and Margaret. We have been reviewing Strozza's wounding and consequent translation through patience to a state of divine vision and prophecy. We have not noted, though, that in attributing his new-found patience to Cynanche, Strozza describes a "true wife" as one whose

> true woorth
> Makes a true husband thinke, his armes enfold
> (With her alone) a compleate worlde of gold. (IV, iii, 35–37)

In the immediately preceding scene, Margaret and Vincentio meet secretly while the others hunt. Fearing that Alphonso and Lasso intend to betroth Margaret to Alphonso and so frustrate the young lovers, they enact a rite of "natural marriage" before God. In this self-authorized ceremony under the eye of deity alone Margaret proposes an image of marriage to which Strozza's eulogy is an echo. She pledges that

> If you be sicke, I will be sicke, though well:
> If you be well, I will be well, though sicke:
> Your selfe alone my compleat world shall be,
> Euen from this houre, to all eternity. (IV, ii, 175–79)

A further analogy between the two actions is seen in the lovers' insistence that their marriage is valid because it accords with divine and natural law; they defy the laws of a society which is itself unnatural—as demonstrated by Alphonso's rivalry with his son or Mendice's success at court almost as clearly as by Poggio's report on the unnatural combat of dogs and horses. At the critical point in their tryst, Margaret queries rhetorically:

> may not we now
> Our contract make, and marie before heauen?
> Are not the lawes of God and Nature, more
> Than formall lawes of men?   (IV, ii, 129–32)

This anti-Hobbesian view of man in a primitive state of nature recurs later in more titanic tones when Strozza defends his defense of the young couple against the Duke's mandate:

> A vertuous man is subiect to no Prince,
> But to his soule and honour; which are lawes,
> That carrie Fire and Sword within themselues
> Neuer corrupted, never out of rule.[57]   (V, iv, 59–62)

For a moment early in the final act of the play Alphonso realizes that his command (disobeyed by Mendice in the event) for Vincentio not to be harmed is motivated by "Nature's" power in man (V, i, 162–65). When he is ultimately confronted by a wounded Vincentio, a disfigured Margaret, and Strozza as spokesman for natural man, the Duke recognizes his own lapse from natural sentiments and laments:

> O would to God, I could with present cure
> Of these vnnaturall wounds; and moning right
> Of this abused beautie, ioyne you both,
> (As last I left you) in eternall nuptials.[58]   (V, iv, 84–87)

Thus calmed through the hard pedagogy of Strozza, Alphonso resigns the role of unnatural tyrant, and in the denouement drives Mendice from court and blesses the marriage of Vincentio and Margaret. We are perhaps justified in recalling Sandys' eulogy upon another virtuous winner: "*Yet* Hercules *better deserued a Deity then all the rest of the* Heroes: *who conquered nothing for himselfe: who ranged all ouer the world, not to oppresse it, but to free it from oppressors and by killing of Tyrants and Monsters preserued it in tranquillity.*"[59] And "tranquillity" is just the word, because Strozza's analogy with Margaret and Vincentio must be completed, the moral bond with natural magic welded tight, by the establishment of "patience" within the patients as well as the physician.

It is clear that Vincentio and Margaret exhibited an initial impatience in attempting to abrogate the fullness of providential time with a union "now"—a term of temporal pressure repeated throughout their marriage ritual.[60] The impatience exhibited in this scene of star-crossed lovers is juxtaposed to the fury of *Strozza agonistes* in the preceding scene as an analogue, but set in profounder perspective by the following scene, in which Strozza has been translated to the certitude of patience through his own wife's efforts. In short, act IV establishes the primacy of "natural" man over the contrived tyrannies of society, only to bring this Rousseauistic attitude immediately into question by underlining patience under providence; ripeness is all.

In act V we see the result of this crucial discrepancy between Strozza and the lovers. In the opening scene, as we have noticed, Alphonso begins to feel the tug of nature. But the machinery for filicide is already in motion, and in the second scene we hear both Strozza's crescendo of poetry upon patience and his visionary knowledge that Vincentio has been wounded in body or soul—alternatives which can be coped with by the divinely contemplative healer. Strozza orders the Doctor to

> beare with you
> *Medcines* t'allay his danger: if by wounds,
> Beare pretious Balsome, or some soueraigne iuyce;
> If by fell poison, some choice *Antidote*,
> If by blacke witchcraft, our good spirits and prayers
> Shall exorcise the diuelish wrath of hell,
> Out of his princely bosome.   (V, ii, 57–63)

The following scene reveals Margaret, believing Vincentio to be dead, inviting the willing connivance of Cortezza in her self-disfigurement. Encouraged by the hypocritically reticent aunt, the girl smears over her face a violent acid.[61] In destroying her own beauty Margaret is—albeit tempted by a wicked agency—attempting that escape from the body and its passions which Strozza has effected in becoming "nought else but soule." However, she has done so in the wrong phase. She is God's subject *furens*, not *patiens*, and therefore echoes the pre-visionary courtier Strozza, rather than Strozza the seer made patient with providential promises. As the scene closes, Margaret's apostrophe uses a medical image to draw her furious grief, and Alphonso's unnatural passion, into the aura of demonic magic which counterpoints the spiritual magic of Strozza and his cures:

> Smart pretious ointment, smart, and to my braine
> Sweate thy enuenom'd furie, make my eyes
> Burne with thy sulphre, like the lakes of hell,
> That feare of me may shiuer him to dust,
> That eate his owne childe with the jawes of lust.   (V, iii, 78–82)

The play's last scene is constructed around a sharp concentration of the movement by which Margaret, Vincentio, and Alphonso all run that course of conversion from *homo furens* to *homo patiens* for which Strozza has already been pattern and spokesman.

As Alphonso and Lasso exchange their first premonitions of the danger to Vincentio, the demonic Cortezza—who embodies fully the perverted lust of the aging which is only a passing, unnatural passion in Alphonso—rushes in to report Margaret's self-abuse; she is immediately followed upon stage by the disfigured and disheveled Margaret, who frantically accuses Alphonso of destroying her beauty, Vincentio's life, and the natural expectations of love, sealing her attack with a curse. Alphonso, staggering under this assault, then receives a messenger who reports Vincentio's dangerous wound. Before he has an opportunity to react to either discovery, Strozza, Cynanche, Poggio, and Doctor Benevenius appear on the one side and Mendice with his wounded son on the other. The stage is now a tableau of passion's slavery: Alphonso stands at bay, faced by the diabolic Cortezza and medicine-man Mendice and by the spiritual visionaries and physicians, and looks upon the dreadful results of his passion.

It is now that Strozza attacks the unnatural tyranny which could foster a filicide; Alphonso replies in imagery which recapitulates Strozza's own Herculean experience of physical suffering and spiritual transcendence:

> How thicke and heavily my plagues descend!
> . . . .
> Poure more rebuke vpon me worthie Lord,
> For I have guilt and patience for them all.   (V, iv, 67–70)

His first generous thought in the state of patience is for the young lovers. Vincentio responds in a fashion that reveals how he, too, has passed into a spiritual transcendence of physical accidents, has learned Ficino's dictum that "every soul should retire from the pestilence of the body and withdraw into the mind, for then fortune will spend its force on the body and not pass into the soul":

> since I make no doubt I shall suruiue
> These fatall dangers; and your grace is pleasde,
> To giue free course to my vnwounded loue;
> T'is not this outward beauties ruthfull losse,
> Can any thought discourage my desires:
> And therefore, deare life, doe not wrong me so,
> To thinke my loue the shadow of your beautie,
> I wooe your vertues, which as I am sure
> No accident can alter or empaire;
> So, be you certaine nought can change my love.   (V, iv, 90–99)

Vincentio, too, can now say with Strozza, "the Iudiciall patience I embrace / . . . Leaues me nought else but soule" (IV, iii, 48–51). And, in Margaret's response, the circle of self-conquest is completed. She tenderly rejects his offer, but rejects it because she has learned to await the fullness of time:

> when the most needfull rights
> Of Fate, and Nature, haue dissolu'd your life,
> And that your loue must needs be all in soule,
> Then will we meet againe: and then (dear Loue)
> Loue me againe; for then will beautie be
> Of no respect with loues eternitie.   (V, iv, 110–15)

All are now become *homines patientes*, and it remains only for a final act of spiritual healing to complete the harmony. Doctor Benevenius, who, with his pious chorus, has almost become Strozza's alter ego,[62] steps forth upon the moment of Margaret's patient acceptance of suffering. Petitioning "Heauen, and Art," he applies to her face "an Elixar drawne through seuen yeares fire" (V, iv, 124) which will restore her outward beauty in neoplatonic harmony with her inward state. Then, "if heauen consent," he prophesies a cure for Vincentio on the seventh day thereafter. Thus the spiritual healing of the visionary Strozza has been re-enacted upon his friends down to the smallest detail. Patience has re-created the bodies of all the protagonists under the transcendent mark of spirit.

One may well question, though, why concinnity was not kept by making Strozza the direct instrument of the later cures, as he was of his own. The answer lies in the final hundred lines of the play, which seem at first to confuse, if not abrogate, the thematic development toward harmony in patience. Benevenius having restored the lovers' hopes, Mendice is brought in for questioning, and Strozza attacks him so passionately that he must be restrained by the Duke and Vincentio so that Mendice may confess and be exiled rather than be killed on the spot. Strozza at this point repeatedly recalls the vision which has effected restoration through

> that good Angell,
> That by diuine relation spake in me,
> Fore-telling these foule dangers to your sonne,
> And without notice brought this reuerend man
> To rescue him from death. (V, iv, 199–203)

This same angel has assured Strozza that Mendice is a vile impostor, meriting death. "Which," says Strozza "will instantly appear, / And that I feele with some rare miracle" (213–14). Strozza's

> spirit propheticke
> Hath inward feeling of such sinnes in him,
> As aske the forfait of his life and soule (220–22)

and he knows "it is heauens iustice / To plague his life and soule." Acting as justice's minister, Strozza now draws his sword, crying at Mendice, "and heer's heauens iustice" (232–33), at which point he is restrained by the Duke. Under these pressures, Mendice confesses that he has been supported by gypsy sorcery and is driven into exile in limbo, crying, appropriately enough for the demonic agent he has been, "Ile runne and hide me from the sight of heauen" (277). Thus, at the close, the larger implications of the tragicomedy of *The Gentleman Usher* are made explicit in almost paradigmatic fashion: comedy emerges from the threat of tragedy, in the medieval sense of the two terms, as it always must in the divine creation because spiritual magic has exorcised the demonic.

This anger of Strozza's, then, has been an inspired anger. "My hand / Forbidden is from heauen to let him liue," Strozza cries (227–28). But both Strozza and heaven do permit Mendice to live, and the rationale for the patient man's anger must be sought in the announcement which precedes his wild entrance. Strozza, remarks a courtier, is "burning in zeale of friendship" (V, iv, 39). Zealous anger constitutes the final bond between Strozza and the tradition of exegetical commentary upon Hercules. Waith has shown the path by which Hercules' irascible nature is transmuted into a manifestation of the Christian concept of righteous indignation: "Thomas Aquinas uses this term, *ira per zelum*, for a praiseworthy anger which is in accordance with right reason. He quotes

Gregory the Great as saying that *ira per zelum* troubles the eye of reason whereas sinful anger blinds it. It is important to remember that the terrible rage of Hercules, vanquishing monsters and chastising tyrants, or suffering in his poisoned robe, could have the meaning of that justifiable anger which is not opposed to reason and which the great man requires in his struggle with a corrupt world."[63] So *The Gentleman Usher* closes in comedy: Strozza's paradoxically angry patience drives the demonic physician from the court, and spiritual harmony is restored through the healing vision of a more truly Herculean hero than the posing and defeated Bussy.[64]

In a fashion he probably never dreamed, *The Gentleman Usher* verifies Guarini's contemporary assertion that tragicomedy alone provides *katharsis*. Here Chapman has shown that tragedy is a true lustration which purges man of passion; but also that man so purged transcends tragedy to take his role in the divine comedy of the creation.[65] Strozza's prophetic dreams raise him to the world of the imagination (Ficino had seen that prophetic *furor* always ends in making a man a poet), and so he becomes the only true playwright and manipulator in a world of art, artifice, and deception. Mendice, the demonic, could not explicate the masque of lies which was the feeble theatrical invention of the passion-ridden Duke at the opening of the play. Strozza, dreaming prophet, opens by interpreting the masque in a sense which the others cannot seize upon, and closes the play as the instrumental voice of the greatest playwright, who raises the action from the theatrical spectacle of courtly intrigues to the spiritual theater of the soul in which God is both seer and seen.

 Strozza and the satellite characters who follow him along the path to patience have been tested by providence. But man, too, tests man. In a contingent world he would have certainty, and with this appetite he gnaws at the vitals of reality, attempts to extirpate from it a heart of the matter which will somehow stay palpitating and palpable in his hand. This is the Renaissance rationalist, the anti-dreamer who asks and asks, "Who are you?" Neither Faustus nor Mephistopheles, he is both, trying everything by his touchstone of doubting hunger until he finds himself standing over the corpse of his own desires in a world which he has made over in the image of the operating room, a grand theater of experiments. This is the highest impatience of pride, the obverse of that inspired certainty which Strozza received through a dream interpreted in the tongues of angels.

Chapman was as fascinated by error as by virtue, for either suggested to his Platonic sense of earthly evanescence epistemological as well as psychic explorations. His early comedy *All Fools*[66] has much in common with the surviving plays he is known to have written in the 1590s. In the young demon plotter Rinaldo one finds a more sophisticated inheritor of the manipulator's mantle worn by Irus in *The Blind Beggar of Alexandria* and Lemot in *An Humourous Day's Mirth*. But for the first time the plot has become truly comic and the tone, if one may be intentionally vague, "Elizabethan" or "Jonsonian" as such tags are applied to comical satire in the nineties. The young wits who hide secret amours under those paternal eyes which are so keen upon discovery, the streak of sensuality under the gray beards of bourgeois propriety—in short, the familiar situations of the *commedia erudita*—are set in Florence, but it is that Florence of the earlier version of *Every Man in His Humour*, more easily recognizable as the London of gallants and gulls of Dekker's pamphlets. The ballet of scheming in which Rinaldo induces now one, now the other, of the gallants' fathers to house the young lovers and ironically, to abuse each other for credulity is linked in a double-plot relation to the May-December marriage of Cornelio and Gazetta by the themes of jealousy and vigilance. The near-divorce of this last couple, Cornelio's brief duel with a supposed rival, and the peripety by which Gostanzo surprises his seemingly modest son Valerio in flagrant leadership of a tavern orgy bring the play close to tragic consequences. The grotesque, primitive laughter of Irus in *The Blind Beggar*, where desertion, theft, and murder are gaily accepted in a comic denouement, has been left behind, nor has Chapman progressed into the tragicomic pattern which turns the similar age-youth conflict into the philosophic modulations of the Alphonso-Vincentio-Margaret triangle. Rather, *All Fools* closes with Valerio calmly facing down his father with a fine mock encomium on "Horn," that universal attribute of man which yet "is incorporall, not falling vnder sence, nor mixt of the grosse concretion of Elementes, but a quintessence beyond them; a spiritual essence inuisible, and euerlasting" (V, ii, 247–49). To this, the father cries "notable wag," the elders join hands with the youngsters, and send them off with a blessing spoken by Gostanzo:

> Very well done, now take your seuerall wiues,
> And spred like wilde-geese, though you now grow tame:
> Liue merily and agree,
> *Hornes cannot be kept off with iealousie.* (V, ii, 307–10)

All Fools is, on the whole, more generically typical than Chapman's eccentric plays usually are. Still, throughout there runs a marked strain of discussion which gives the hackneyed action a significance lacking in its *Cinquecento* Italian and ancient Roman forebears and draws it closer to the comedy of Wycherley or Farquhar.

"*Hornes cannot be kept off with iealousie*": this is the closing note, wisdom Gostanzo has learned from Cornelio's own father, who had been a "wise Gentleman" with a wife who "was wise, a most flippant tongue she had, and could set out her Taile with as good grace as any shee in *Florence*, come cut and long-tayle; and she was honest enough too" (V, ii, 181–84). Honest enough, but with a humor sometimes! Cornelio's father in his wisdom "made a Backe-doore to his house for conuenience, gott a Bell to his fore doore, and had an odd fashion in ringing, by which shee and her Mayde knew him; and would stand talking to his next neighbour to prolong time, that all thinges might be ridde clenly out a the way before he came. . . . This was wisedome now, for a mans owne quiet" (V, ii, 189–94).

But this is only one fact of the matter. If horns cannot be kept off by jealousy, they can be put on; as Valerio opines, "some foolishly fearefull, would imagine the shadow of his Eares to be Hornes" (V, ii, 285–86). In the closing mock-encomium, Valerio is counterpointing the satiric setpiece in praise of women earlier spoken by a young page, and there too "horn" is half-created by the male imagination:

> Now (sir) for these Cuckooish songs of yours, of Cuckolds, hornes, grafting, and such like; what are they, but meere imaginary toyes, bred out of your owne heads, as your owne, and so by tradition deliuered from man to man, like Scarcrowes, to terrify fooles from this earthly paradice of wedlock, coyn'd at first by some spent Poets, . . . who, like the Foxe, hauing lost his taile, would perswade others to lose theirs for company? Agayne, for your Cuckold, what is it but a meere fiction? shew me any such creature in nature; if there be, I could neuer see it, neyther could I euer find any sensible difference betwixt a Cuckold and a Christen creature. . . . your Cuckold is a meere *Chymaera*, and . . . there are no Cuckoldes in the world, but those that haue wiues.[67] (III, i, 227–40)

Horn *is* half-created—surprising in this comedy which is explicitly and unexpectedly free of adultery. At the close, Cornelio asserts he has made all fools, gulled the gullers in the last turn, by inheriting his father's wise blinking at appearances, and that he has only pretended to wish a divorce from Gazetta, only pretended to be jealous "to bridle her stout stomack." In full assembly he makes a confession of contented cuckoldry which his supposed rival already has repeatedly assured us is untrue: "I did traine the Woodcocke *Dariotto* into the net, drew him to my house, gaue him opportunities with my wife . . . let him alone with my wife in her bed-chamber; and sometimes founde him a bedd with her, and went my way backe againe softly, onelie to draw him into the Pitte" (V, ii, 204–10). The cuckold has grown his own horns, but there is a still deeper incision into the pattern of pretence and reality. Here Cornelio has created only a public mask of folly to cover that other mask of jealousy he had once proudly worn ("let me still be poynted at, and thought / A ielouse Asse, and not a wittally Knaue" [II, i, 287–88]). But if Gazetta has no part in creating Cornelio's horns, those horns have re-created her; the shadow of his ears has fallen across her heart:

> did euer Husband
> Follow his Wife with Ielousie so vnjust?
> That once I lou'd you, you your selfe will sweare.
> And if I did, where did you lose my Loue?
> In deed this strange and vndeserued vsage,
> Hath powre to shake a heart were nere so setled:
> But I protest all your vnkindnes, neuer
> Had strength to make me wrong you, but in thought.   (II, i, 261–68)

Here is a tragic moment of metamorphosis, a touch of Middleton's Bianca, in the center of a traditional comedy of intrigue. If it is suggested that we not look too closely at the invisible substance which is the psyche, that the only peace is the way of Cornelio's father hemming at the door, it is also suggested that our corrupt and squinnied vision may itself devour the virtue of which we seek ocular proof. When he came to treat the Petronian legend of *The Widow's Tears*, Chapman pushed beyond the comedy of social masks and created a sustained extension of the terrible potential for metamorphosis into which Gazetta's admission gives one a brief glimpse.

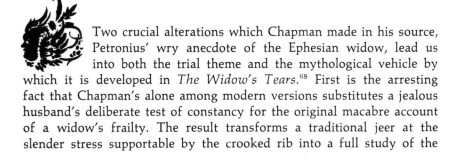 Two crucial alterations which Chapman made in his source, Petronius' wry anecdote of the Ephesian widow, lead us into both the trial theme and the mythological vehicle by which it is developed in *The Widow's Tears*.[68] First is the arresting fact that Chapman's alone among modern versions substitutes a jealous husband's deliberate test of constancy for the original macabre account of a widow's frailty. The result transforms a traditional jeer at the slender stress supportable by the crooked rib into a full study of the

destructive search for certainty touched upon in *All Fools.*[69] We are, in brief, invited by the adaptation to assume that Chapman is more interested in the folly of tempter than of tempted. Second, while the sacredness of Ephesus to Diana undoubtedly led him to name his heroine Cynthia, Chapman's removal of the scene to Cyprus places his own Diana in the milieu sacred to Venus so defiantly that a mythically alert auditor is forced to search out an explanation.

Pursuing the implications of these initial aesthetic maneuvers, one notices that, with the exception of *The Blind Beggar of Alexandria*, *The Widow's Tears* stands alone among Chapman's comedies in carefully maintaining a pre-Christian setting. It is a Hellenic world into which creep no Christian anachronisms, in which speaker after speaker affirms his piety—or lack of it—by swearing on the gods of the gentiles. This insistent Hellenic historicism, along with the mythological overtones of a Cynthia lodged in Cyprus, serves to help us immediately allegorize the demon-plotter revealed in the opening scene of the play. No mere stage wit, no Rinaldo or Lemot or Valerio, Tharsalio invokes the goddess Confidence before the action begins, thus translating and worshipping his own name and nature ($\theta\alpha\rho\sigma\alpha\lambda\varepsilon\sigma\varsigma$). This immediate identification may universalize, but does not unriddle, the dramatic, psychic, and epistemological questions which it will arouse; indeed, it rather sets the questions in the open *as* questions. For if Tharsalio clearly prefers to translate his name and his function as that of dashing and courageous confidence, other lexicographers might read it as presumption and foolish overweening.[70] Within a dozen lines, when Tharsalio rejects the blind goddess Fortune, only to address her sister deity,

> *Confidence.*
> Shee be my Guide, and hers the praise of these
> My worthie vndertakings   (I, i, 12–14)

the dialectic of ambiguity which is *The Widow's Tears* has begun. No problem play has ever been more swift in laying bare the "problem": who is Tharsalio, boldness or blindness?[71]

The opening scene[72] as a whole continues this brilliant economy: in fewer than two hundred lines plot, personalities, and problem have been presented in an interplay of dialogue and staging which dictates the focus of all that follows. Briefly, Tharsalio enters, preparing his luxurious court dress before a hand mirror while invoking his new deity. Immediately he is joined by his brother Lysander (also carrying a mirror), Lysander's wife Cynthia, and others. An occasion is in preparation, and Tharsalio turns to Cynthia to ask a compliment upon his new suit: "How like you my aspect?" She, in turn, chooses to mistake his obvious meaning: "Faith no worse than I did last weeke, the weather has nothing chang'd the graine of your complexion." With Tharsalio's rejoinder the challenge to read psyches in physiognomies is set: "A firme proofe, 'tis in graine, and so are not all complexions" (I, i, 18–21). The lady is discreet, sensible, and believes in the validity of appearances; Tharsalio is cynical in the abstract and adopts partisanship in the debate upon "painting" which stretches across the Renaissance.

After this prelude on appearances and what underlies them, the brunt of which argument is turned at once upon women by Tharsalio, attention is returned to his new suit, which Lysander blesses by wishing for his brother that "Fortune send you well to weare it: for shee best knowes how you got it." Tharsalio smugly acknowledges the source: " 'Tis the portion shee bestowes vpon younger Brothers, valour, and good clothes" (27–30). This is surprising—and a signal of his confusion —because he has rejected "weake Fortune," the "blinde imperfect Goddesse," only moments before. If his clothes are the heritage of such a debilitated deity, if his valor (another word for "confidence"?) is plucked from the same stem, are we not to suspect that her blindness, too, is shared by a minion who rejects outsides while taking confidence in them, rejects his deity while comfortably assimilating her presumably worthless gifts? Something of this doubt is struggling in Lysander's mind when he explicitly translates the philological question of Tharsalio's identity. Confidence is well enough, but, he warns, "be not too forward" (39).

Now we learn of Tharsalio's project, the real cause for his suit: Eudora, the widow of the Governor whom Tharsalio had once served and now aspires to bed. Everyone is aghast at this audacity: he is a servant, she a lady and what is more, is sworn to chastity in respect for her dead husband. But Tharsalio casts objections aside with a shrug: Confidence is the goddess who will lead him between those silken sheets because, in the end, "Fortune waits vpon her; *Cupid* is at her becke" (59–60). It is a trinity in which one more sensitive to his own implications might hesitate to confide—the blind leading the blind. But "confidence," "confidence," "confidence" has threaded the trialogue amongst Tharsalio, Lysander, and Cynthia like a necklace which will become a noose, and when Cynthia, shocked, interposes the objection posed by the Countess' oaths, Tharsalio looses the trap beneath the gibbet. You, too, he says to his sister-in-law, might have sworn that should you outlive Lysander you would (the words have been hers) "preserue till death, the vnstain'd honour of a Widdowes bed" as well as the Countess. Then, with a sudden turn upon Lysander he confronts the question which will

culminate in the trial of Cynthia: "Would you beleeue it Brother?"
Lysander seals the course of the plot like a poor Othello: "I am therein
most confident" (87).

The challenge to a testing is not yet; Tharsalio is cynical, painting
a picture prophetic of the widow embracing her own husband's murderer, some "confident" ruffian. Then, when Lysander becomes restive
under this goading, Tharsalio holds up his own mirror (Lysander's, limp
in his hand, becomes both symbol and forecast of his own self-cuckolding and its significance, although we cannot yet know it) and removes
the conversation through metaphor into generalization: "Looke you
Brother, this glasse is mine." And goes on: "While I am with it, it takes
impression from my face; but can I make it so mine, that it shall be of
no vse to any other? will it not doe his office to you or you: and as well
to my Groome as to my selfe? Brother, Monopolies are cryed downe.
Is it not madnes for me to beleeue, when I haue conquer'd that Fort of
chastitie the great Countesse; that if another man of my making, and
metall, shall assault her: her eies and eares should lose their function"
(I, i, 106–12).[73] Cynthia accuses Tharsalio of infection from that Italian
air in which he has recently been traveling, which "poisond the very
Essence of your soule, and so polluted your senses, that whatsoever enters there, takes from them contagion, and is to your fancie represented
as foule and tainted" (118–20). "No sister," replies Tharsalio, "it hath
refin'd my senses, and made me see with cleare eies, and to iudge of
obiects, as they truly are, not as they seeme, and through their maske to
discerne the true face of thinges" (122–24). The couple laugh good-
naturedly at Tharsalio's confidence, leaving the stage to allow him a final
brief soliloquy which, like that opening the scene, is an invocation of
the "third blind Deitie," Confidence.

A pattern which will control the play is now clear. Confidence is set
against caution, good faith, and a Spenser-like faith in wedded chastity.
And that confidence which is so certain that its clear eyes discern the
true face of things is pawned repeatedly to blindness. To make the situation even clearer, its spokesman Tharsalio adopts the mirror as his iden-
tifying property and argument: what he sees is a projected image of his
own complexion, constant in grain only to its own assurance that inconstancy is an absolute quality of nature (why, then, one might ask,
abandon that fickle lady Fortuna?). But there is a monitory countercurrent, for Lysander, too, holds a mirror; he too invokes "confidence,"
if in an opposite principle of constancy. And what, finally, of the mirror
itself as a conspicuous design? If it takes the shape of all things *in
propria natura* it is the symbol of metamorphosis, change, appropriate
to Cynthia as the lunar deity of cycles. Still, can one ever discern "the

true face" of anything but ourselves in the mirror? If it is to be symbol of the world's way, does it not tacitly invert Tharsalio's argument for fickleness and demonstrate rather Cynthia's point that whatever we see out there in the otherness is polluted by our senses and "takes from them contagion"? If he sees with clear eyes upon looking into the *speculum mundi*, has Tharsalio not forgotten the lesson of Cusa's or Ficino's epistemological and moral perspectivism, i.e., that every eye sees a single true but fragmented vision of the real?

The action of *The Widow's Tears* appears to validate this line of inquiry, since the scene immediately changes from Tharsalio's invocation to bring Lysander back before Countess Eudora's villa in order that a serving man may hide him where he can watch Tharsalio's outrageous attempt upon the lady, or—to use Lysander's own language of the theater when he turns to the servant—"you shall fauour me so much to make me a spectator of the Scene" (I, ii, 4–5).

What Lysander sees is Tharsalio bursting upon the Countess and the train of a silly suitor, unmasking the shallow pretensions of the cowardly courtier, and being driven out the door for his efforts by the incensed tongue of the lady whose privacy has been invaded by her quondam servant. Tharsalio himself interprets the scene as a defeat, in spite of his satiric stripping of the gull, evidencing his vexation with the "Saturnian Peacock" Eudora[74] before Lysander reveals himself in order to read a lecture against overconfidence. The vexation and the epithet alike indicate that Tharsalio, like all the others who mention her, fully accepts the loyalty of Eudora to her late husband, since the Saturnian peacock is the iconographic property of *Juno jugalis*, deity of marriage.[75] She *is* a virtuous and chaste widow. Her disgust with the suitor as well as the upstart Tharsalio, the respect she universally attracts, the good sense of her lady attendants (one of whom is Sthenia [σθενεια], an epithet of Athena[76]), her mythic associations—all these signs indicate that she is what she appears to be. If she swears by Venus twice in the course of the scene played out before Lysander (I, i, 39, 149) it is because she is a Cyprian lady, and yet that seed is sown, infinitesimal as it is in the face of the other evidence, and Tharsalio has far from given up.

That the oaths sworn upon the love goddess are to be noted is underlined by the conversation between Tharsalio and Lysander which follows. Tired of being called to heel for his own "confidence," the fortune-hunter applies to his brother the general principle of woman's frailty which he had earlier brought to bear upon a hypothetically widowed Cynthia: "Well Sir, you lesson my Confidence still; I pray heauens your confidence haue not more shallow ground" (I, iii, 34–35).

The technique is that same insinuating retreat with which Iago ambushed Othello at just about the same time. Tharsalio spoke, Lysander insists, "as to your selfe, but yet I ouer-heard" (55–56). Then the demand direct: "Know you ought that may impeach my confidence. . . . hath your obseruation discouered any such frailtie in my wife?" And Tharsalio sets the challenge as directly: "Nay, Brother, I write no bookes of Obseruations, let your confidence beare out it selfe, as mine shall me" (45–49). The hook has been baited, and when Lysander insists, the undertone of Venusian Cyprus suddenly leaps into focus by the rule of contraries, and Cynthia's name, like Tharsalio's, becomes symbolic as well as individual:

> *Tharsalio.* Brother? are you wise?
> *Lysander.* Why?
> *Tharsalio.* Be ignorant. Did you neuer heare of *Actaeon?*
> *Lysander.* What then?
> *Tharsalio.* Curiositie was his death. He could not be content to adore *Diana* in her Temple, but he must needes dogge her to her retir'd pleasures, and see her in her nakednesse. Doe you enioy the sole priuiledge of your wives bed? (59–66)

Like the mythological masques in *The Gentleman Usher*, this is a strangely allusive warning which the speaker himself cannot fully explicate. Drawing Lysander on with admonishment against "vain curiosity," that disease of scholars and husbands in the Renaissance, Tharsalio has chosen the mythic vehicle which demonstrates that Cynthia is, indeed, chaste, and that Lysander can only destroy himself, not that chastity. The myth plays off against the *non sequitur* of the final question. Ironically, Tharsalio states the whole lesson of the myth and of the plays in a generalization which he never takes to his own heart: "Your Sages in generall, by seeing too much ouersee . . . happinesse" (73–74). In Tharsalio's view, happiness is ignorance; in the myth it is wisdom. In act II Tharsalio picks up the myth for a now thoroughly unsettled Lysander and gives it a perversely suggestive coloring, while simultaneously urging the terms of the test—Lysander must feign death and watch his "widow's" reactions:

> *Tharsalio.* . . . Beware of curiositie, for who can resolue you? youle say perhaps her vow.
> *Lysander.* Perhaps I shall.
> *Tharsalio.* Tush, her selfe knowes not what shee shall doe, when shee is transform'd into a Widdow. You are now a sober and staid Gentleman. But if *Diana* for your curiositie should translate you into a monckey; doe you know what gambolds you should play? your only way to bee resolu'd is to die and make triall of her. (II, i, 22–29)

Lysander has become an Actaeon *before* the fact of seeing too much in the mirror of his own sensual pollution.

Let us take stock for a moment. The female protagonists on both levels of the double plot have been identified by myth and milieu as types of virtue and chastity put to arbitrary test. The real test lies beyond their individual destinies, though. The principle being tested through these women is "confidence." Tharsalio thinks the confident man is one who sees cynically "with clear eyes" into the real essence of things, while he pretends to exhort his brother to restraint which places "confidence" in others. Lysander teaches Tharsalio to be an over-reacher, even as he is falling into the web Tharsalio has woven from his brother's jealous lust to "know." It is difficult to choose the larger loser: if Tharsalio follows the blind goddess in his search for clear sight, Lysander follows in the track of Actaeon, who looked too precisely upon the goddess.

 Eudora has been a *Juno jugalis*; Cynthia is a Diana. Yet Eudora has sworn by Venus, and it becomes a habit in her ambience: "Ovr *Cypriane* Goddesse saue you good Honor," cries her servant Argus (II, ii, 51); "*Venus* pardon me," he begs of Eudora, while describing Tharsalio as "the most incontinent, and insatiate Man of Women that euer *Venus* blest with abilitie to please them" (II, ii, 81, 72–73); her waiting lady cries (somewhat confusedly) "*Venus* keepe her vpright, that shee fall not from the state of her honour" (II, iv, 15–16); and even Sthenia swears "by *Venus*" (II, iv, 71). Ultimately, ambience triumphs, to everyone's amazement. The panderess Arsace and the blind gentleman usher Argus having been bribed to press his case, Argus can at last assure Tharsalio that Eudora's eyes are opened (or closed?) by the blind archer: "I saw *Cupid* shoot in my words, and open his wounds in her lookes" (II, iii, 7–8). She may yet protest, but Tharsalio has learned about *concordia discors*, and almost anticipates the law of self-contrariety within the pagan gods—and goddesses.[77]

Defending Argus' failure to expel him from Eudora's palace, Tharsalio explains: "Madam, this fellow only is intelligent; for he truly vnderstood your command according to the stile of the Court of *Venus*; that is, by contraries: when you forbid you bid" (II, iv, 124–26). He is right. Tharsalio, aided by the blind goddess Confidence, has metamorphosed Juno into Venus, the chaste widow into the itching bride. As he goes gaily to announce his impending nuptials to Lysander and Cynthia, he disguises himself in a worn cloak so that Lysander may attempt to "school" him once more. Then with a gesture he throws open the cloak to reveal the brilliant suit which he now belittles as "these simple fragments of my treasurie" (III, i, 64), and cries in ironic triumph, "Now I confesse my ouersight, this haue I purchas'd by my confidence" (58–59).

But wherein lies the irony? "Oversight" may mean, as Tharsalio believes, "foresight,"[78] but does it signify this when one marries a Juno metamorphosed into an itching Venus through the agency of sleeping Argus and a panderess, when one turns the world topsy-turvy, as, in taking her servant for her new husband, Eudora must "stoop to make my foot my head" (II, iv, 152), when, to put it in Chapman's crudest terms, Tharsalio has exerted enough force to prove the potential validity of his belief that "these angrie heates that breake out at the lips of these streight lac't Ladies, are but as symptoms of a lustfull feuer that boiles within them" (II, iii, 21–22)?[79] Having completed his Pyrrhic victory, Tharsalio turns upon the astonished Cynthia to remind and threaten her: "Here are your widdow-vowes sister; thus are yee all in your pure naturalls; certaine morall disguises of coinesse, which the ignorant cal modestie, ye borrow of art to couer your buske points" (III, i, 88–91). She rejects the thesis and the Countess with an ominous oath. The latter's action has not only been too premature but is in itself reprehensible; Cynthia claims she would never take a second lover to her bed. Lysander, burning under Tharsalio's innuendoes and success, asks the fatal question: "No, wife?" The reply is pathetic, almost tragic after one has observed the mythic counter-point of Eudora's metamorphosis: "By *Iuno*, no" (115–16). Juno has already been transformed as the subplot runs its course; it is now Cynthia's turn to prove that she carries the seeds of contradiction within herself.

That she is a Diana has been acknowledged by Tharsalio early—in conjunction with the assurance that she is also Venus in waiting: "Truth is I loue my sister well and must acknowledge her more than ordinarie vertues. But shee hath so possest my brothers heart with vowes, and disauowings, sel'd with oathes of second nuptialls; as in that confidence, he hath inuested her in all his state, the ancient inheritance of our Familie. . . . so as he dead, and shee matching (as I am resolu'd shee will) with some yong Prodigall; what must ensue" (II, iii, 65–71). It is the function of the last acts to demonstrate this second metamorphosis, to which Eudora's has been but the prelude.

The trial proper has begun. The nuptials of Tharsalio and Eudora take place under a battery of sexual jokes, culminating in a masque which brings together the Countess' daughter and Tharsalio's nephew (the latter a Cupid who pricks the girl while masking as Hymen). Meanwhile, Lysander pretends to journey and sends news back of his own murder to test Cynthia's vows. His accomplices are Tharsalio and the unwilling servant Lycus. Cynthia, to the astonishment of all Cyprus, descends with the supposed casket into Lysander's tomb to fast and grieve, taking with her only a maid-servant, Ero. Lysander disguises himself as a soldier who must guard the crucified bodies of some thieves and by rhetoric insinuates his way into the tomb and then into Cynthia's arms and desires. The cruelty and insensate nature of the test is emphasized when the humane Lycus cries out against the "vngrounded humour" of racking "a poore Ladies inno-cencie" and feelings, only to draw Lysander's reply: "I am resolu'd, if shee be gold shee may abide the tast [sic]" (III, i, 1–6). If she be gold— or if she be a goddess; but if she be a woman? And even as Eudora's Cyprian oaths warned that she had reached the limits of fleshly endur-ance, so we have a mythic as well as psychic premonition concerning Cynthia. For has not her waiting lady and confidante, her companion in the tomb, been from the first that infiltrator from Venus' camp, "Ero"?

One must watch the developing metamorphosis from the perspec-tives offered by three viewpoints, since *The Widow's Tears* is concerned with "testing" in the impatient hope of forcing certitude. As though he himself were impatient with the sheer vehicular details of the interstices, Chapman makes a leap over the action between acts III and IV, rare in Elizabethan and Jacobean drama, and relegates the report of Lysander's murder, his burial, and the five days of Cynthia's self-immolation within the tomb to a few explanatory remarks after the fact. Not action, but interpretation, is all, in this funereal comedy authored by Tharsalio and Lysander. And the interpretations we must hear are those of the dia-metrically opposed brothers and of Lycus, the sober choral voice. Both brothers treat him as a respected peer, confide in him, accept admonition from him: he plays Horatio to Hamlet and Claudius simultaneously.

From the beginning Lycus is privy to the details of Cynthia's "trial," and from the beginning he warns against the danger and folly of con-fidence in its negative sense. Learning that Tharsalio insists upon

Lysander's feigning death, Lycus has a clear eye for all participants in this perverted triangle. Tharsalio, he realizes, is interested only in setting Lysander's "braines a-worke" to divert attention from his own initial rebuff by Eudora. Lysander would be more than foolish to accept the bait: "That were a strange Physicke for a iealous patient; to cure his thirst with a draught of poison" (II, i, 54–55). Finally, concerning Cynthia herself, she is, as far as flesh can go, proved, says Lycus; Lysander himself *could* alter her with his "confidence" which asks that she be that humanly impossible thing, the deity who shadows her as namesake —and yet here that possibility is merely hinted at:

> The world hath written your wife in highest lines of honour'd Fame:
> . . . .
> Nor thinke he [Tharsalio] can turne so farre rebell to his bloud,
> Or to the Truth it selfe to misconceiue
> Her spotlesse love and loialtie; perhaps
> Oft hauing heard you hold her faith so sacred
> As you being dead, no man might stirre a sparke
> Of vertuous love, in way of second bonds;
> . . . .
> T'may be, in that point hee's an Infidell,
> And thinkes your confidence may ouer-weene. (II, i, 57–71)

The warning is lost upon Lysander; the trial runs its course. And with the consequent demonstration of Cynthia's real grief, Lycus reads a lesson on overweening to Tharsalio also: "The edge of your confidence is well taken off" (IV, i, 3). Tharsalio is still Tharsalio, and sneers that he will bide his time. If Lysander has written the morality play of the tomb, Tharsalio believes that Cynthia is also quite conscious that she is playing in a "spectacle," and if she takes her "Cue" from Lycus' own "plaine acting of an enterlude," she is not skilled enough: "This straine of mourning wi'th' Sepulcher, like an ouer-doing Actor, affects grosly, and is indeede so far forc't from the life, that it bewraies it selfe to be altogether artificiall" (96–98). Lycus is astonished and outraged at Tharsalio's callousness: "Performe it, call you it? . . . you wager of her passions for your pleasure, but shee takes little pleasure in those earnest passions. I never saw such an extasie of sorrow. . . . I assure you Sir, I was so transported with the spectacle, that in despight of my discretion, I was forc't to turne woman, and beare a part with her" (31–40). Lycus knows that Cynthia is a daughter of Diana. He knows, too, however, that there is no impossible absolute beneath the sphere of the moon and, in closing, comments upon both Tharsalio's cruel cynicism and the inevitable potential for metamorphosis which is nature's livery:

I meruaile what man? what woman? what name? what action doth his tongue glide ouer, but it leaues a slime vpon't? Well, Ile . . . not say but shee may proue fraile:

> But this Ile say, if she should chance to breake,
> Her teares are true, though womens truths are weake. (128–33)

This gnomic couplet on the simultaneous possibility of faithfulness and faltering, of contrary principles in a single human being, has major dramatic importance because it is placed between two extreme views of Cynthia's behavior which explicitly return the test to the ambience of the Venus-Diana mythic scheme. Before leaving the stage free for Lycus' comments, Tharsalio reaches a new height of cynicism in interpreting Cynthia's fasting and weeping: "For this does shee looke to bee Deified, to haue Hymnes made of her, nay to her: The Tomb where she is to be no more reputed the ancient monument of our Familie . . . but the new erected Altar of *Cynthia*" (109–12). In acting the goddess, Cynthia would become Diana proper.

Lycus closes this conversation with his moderator's judgment, but the following scene opens with the opposite excess of Lysander, who discovers in the mourning Cynthia the "enuie of the Deities" (IV, ii, 2). If all is less than it appears for the cynical Tharsalio, all is more than is possible with Lysander:

> Yet must these matchlesse creatures be suspected;
> Accus'd; condemn'd! Now by th'immortall Gods,
> They rather merit Altars, Sacrifice,
> Then loue and courtship.
> Yet see the Queene of these lies here interred;
> Tearing her haire, and drownd in her teares.
> Which *Ioue* should turne to Christall; and a Mirrour
> Make of them; wherein men may see and wonder at womens vertues.
> (IV, ii, 3–11)

But we have learned from the opening scene of the play the ambiguous nature of mirrors: they are images of metamorphosis because everyone sees in them just what he brings to them, what he seeks: himself.

Lysander has begun his search for certainty with an absolutist's simple maxim: "I will beleeue nothing but what triall enforces" (III, i, 170). What he sees is Diana at her altar. In the first encounter within the tomb, disguised as the Petronian soldier, he tests her with the more than willing assistance of Ero, whose bawdy behavior fulfills the promise of her suggestive name and aligns her with Venus' minions. Ero equivocates the mythic structure (with dangerous overtones for those who remember the history of Eudora) by insisting that Lysander is a messenger from Juno (IV, ii, 93–94). But no gates give way to his first probings, and when the test concludes, Lysander prefers to return to the language of the more absolute myth, to the prejudice for whose sake he had entered the tomb:

> O *Cynthia*, heire of her bright puritie,
> Whose name thou dost inherit; Thow disdainst
> (Seuer'd from all concretion) to feede
> Vpon the base foode of grosse Elements.
> Thou all art soule; All immortalitie.
> Thou fasts for *Nectar* and *Ambrosia*.   (IV, ii, 179–84)

It is a truth turned absurdly false by the rhetoric of idolatry. Lysander's exaggeration of θαρσαλεοσ to the point of parody comes at the very moment in which he has nurtured the seed of Venus within Cynthia's bosom. It may be called Ero, but its strength comes from the vain curiosity of Lysander.

Immediately after hearing these fatuous self-assurances by the tempter, we watch the transition scene proper, in which the threatened metamorphosis occurs before our eyes—and Lysander's. Cynthia is at last induced to emerge and breathe the fresh night air, led forth by an Ero now made totally drunk by the bottle Lysander has left in her keeping. The emergence from the tomb is a symbolic life gesture, of course, in itself a silent commentary upon the inhuman terms which alone can satisfy Lysander's demand for more than human certainty. Ero senses the renewed human dimensions in which the action will henceforth be framed, and chides her mistress for her faith in that distant deity we have come to recognize as a mediation point between Diana and Venus: "Did you looke forsooth that *Iuno* should haue sent you meate from her owne Trencher, in reward of your widdowes teares?" (IV, iii, 10–12). No, the nourishment has been brought by the living man, the soldier. So it is that, after the long struggle, Ero induces Cynthia to assert symbolically her woman's need for life by sipping from the bottle. No sooner has she done so than Ero vents a casual but pertinent oath in pouting, "I would to *Venus* we had some honest shift or other to get off withal. . . . Ile not turne Salt-peeter in this vault" (27–29). It is the first mention of Venus which has ever entered Cynthia's ambient,[80] and its significance is underlined in a few minutes by the kiss Lysander places upon her silent lips. Diana has become Venus.

For once Tharsalio follows Lysander at a slight distance, just far enough behind to provide a backdrop of farcical, frenzied reaction for his inevitable fallibility. At this moment he becomes a reincarnation of the blind beggar Irus ranting as Count Hermes, or of Haphazard and Ambidexter and all the long tradition of irresponsible, irrepressible Vices. Lycus' expostulations finally break down Tharsalio's cynicism. It is too much, admonishes this would-be reformer,

> to runne on
> With an opinion against all the world,
> And what your eies may witnes (V, i, 2–4)

Cynthia is chaste. Confidence crushed, Tharsalio capitulates uncondi- tionally: "I must confesse it *Lycus*" (7). He hurries to enter the tomb now, not to get the ocular proof, which he ironically waives, but to gently induce Cynthia to return to life and the knowledge that Lysander is alive. But eyes he has, and when he looks (inverting Lysander's earlier role as spectator to Tharsalio's own seduction of the widow Eudora), it is at the very juncture at which Cynthia has abandoned Diana to become Venus' lady. "A Souldier with my sister? wipe, wipe, see!" (V, i, 24). Dancing, he sings out gaily in triumph: "She, she, she, and none but she. / Shee only Queene of loue, and chastitie" (31–32). Venus and Diana—both. He says it, and still does not heed or understand the *concordia discors* of his own epithet. A moment before he had accepted Cynthia as all Diana, just as Lysander had done; a moment later all is Venus. His renewed confidence in confidence is wild, and its hyperbolic rhetoric obscures some important ironies:

> O had I held out (villaine that I was,)
> My blessed confidence but one minute longer,
> I should have beene eternis'd. Gods my fortune,
> What an vnspeakable sweet sight it is?
> O eies Ile sacrifice to your deare sense,
> And consecrate a Phane to Confidence. (V, i, 52–57)

It is *he* who sought to be "eternis'd" for his constancy, a desire he projects upon Cynthia, who appears to be acting a role only when seen in the mirror of his own absolute ambitions. And it is the eyes, those weak organs he would not credit when appearances were against him, that he will worship. It is a worship little consonant with a "Phane to Confidence," the blind deity who sees only what she wishes to see. No character is so thoroughly without compass in the darkness of distrust, mistake, and change which blankets the action of *The Widow's Tears* as the great manipulator whose first claim and last is to be able to "see with cleare eies."

Lysander and Tharsalio, psychic antipodes when the play opens, by the end have achieved unity through a shared error. Once absolute for confidence in Cynthia, Lysander after the metamorphosis is as absolute in his gynephobia: "Put women to the test; discouer them; paint them, paint them ten parts more then they doe themselues, rather then looke on them as they are" (V, iii, 66–67). He has seen Medusa in the mirror.

To realize how deeply Lysander is lost in the maze of errors growing from the simple premise that identity, reality, stands in any constant relation to appearances, one must recall the last stages of the monstrous farce of the tomb. While Lysander is busily destroying his own happiness by wooing Cynthia, Tharsalio "sees" them. But his clear eyes do not penetrate Lysander's military disguise, and he sets out to avenge the stain upon his brother's honor by stealing one of the crucified corpses which the soldier is guarding, knowing the law by which a negligent sentry must himself replace a lost victim upon the cross. Lysander thus emerges from the tomb to find himself a hunted man and rejoins Cynthia to escape the patrols. Having returned to life, she is unwilling to support yet another death, and compounds his horror with the grisly but comprehensible suggestion that they place her "dead" husband's body on the cross as a substitute. Dazed with the tempest of disillusionment he has loosed upon himself, Lysander determines on yet another trial. He goes off to get the tools to open the casket and hoist the body, vowing that if Cynthia actually attempts to act upon this macabre plan he will kill her. When we next see him, he is pausing before the tomb with the crowbar and halter with which he will pretend to desecrate a corpse that is no more than the shadowy symbol of his own dead happiness. Laying these suggestively suicidal properties aside, he again puts on his military disguise, accompanying the action with a soliloquy:

> Come my borrow'd disguise, let me once more
> Be reconciled to thee, my trustiest friend;
> Thou that in truest shape hast let me see
> That which my truer selfe hath hid from me,
> Helpe me to take reuenge on a disguise,
> Ten times more false and counterfait then thou.
> Thou, false in show, hast been most true to me;
> The seeming true hath prou'd most false in her.   (V, v, 1–8)

Lycus had warned that Diana could become Venus; Tharsalio instinctively knew that Diana and Venus were one, even if he did not understand the implications; and Lysander will simplify even this by saying, in effect, "Venus is, Diana never was," as he had earlier stated, with equal aplomb, "Diana is, Venus can never be." But he must compound even this fool's equation by reversing it for his own case: "I *was* real, I *am*, therefore, disguised." But what disguise could be more true to Lysander's jealous nature and actions than that of the Argus-eyed guard who sleeps and so dies under self-hypnosis, and now carries the tools which tacitly speak of his murder of his own happiness—indeed, himself?

In tragicomedy death is averted, and all revive to savor a new life. But *The Widow's Tears* is not tragicomedy; it is a metaphysical joke—metaphysical because it is conceived as an analysis of reality, joke because the Death Brothers, Tharsalio and Lysander, never understand the crucial lines of their own script. For instance, to reinterpret these observations, Lysander has buried a true Cynthia under the mere shadow of Venus. His happiness has been killed by an adultery which does not exist any more than the corpse exists in the coffin. He wears only the horns of a would-be self-cuckold who has not even succeeded in this except in spirit.[81] We may remember the jealous old Cornelio of *All Fools* and Valerio's epigraph to the action of that play: "your Cuckold is a meere *Chymaera*." The words were appropriate to *All Fools* but are profound when applied to *The Widow's Tears*, wherein we see that Lysander has dissolved not only Cynthia-Diana but himself; that not just the adultery but the man himself has become a "meere *Chymaera*," one who denies his own substantial past. Cynthia has won full right to Gazetta's words:

> this strange and undeserued vsage,
> Hath powre to shake a heart were nere so setled:
> But I protest all your vnkindness, neuer
> Had strength to make me wrong you, but in thought.

There are two apparently casual generalizations early in the play which apply the metamorphosis theme directly to Lysander himself as well, and make his self-murder more than a plot mechanism. The first is the belief of Eudora's servant Argus, true as far as it goes, that "you Wenches haue the pregnant wits, to turne Monsters into husbands, as you turne husbands into monsters" (II, iv, 38–40). The other is Eudora's warning that "Misgiuing mindes euer prouoke mischances" (III, ii, 56). It is by now completely clear that in *The Widow's Tears* jealousy is only a particular expression of the search for that false grail, absolute certainty, and that search eventuates in destruction when Actaeon follows Diana, if we remember Tharsalio's mythic reminders.

When Tharsalio realizes that Lysander is the soldier, he descends into the tomb and gives Cynthia warning. Thus forearmed, when Lysander returns as the soldier, with halter and crow, she teases him with gruesome proposals, and then suddenly turns upon him. If Diana has been turned to Venus by her own husband, she now turns the hounds upon an over-curious Actaeon. Lysander opens his lips to accuse her and reveal his "true" self: "are not thou the most—". But Cynthia cuts him short by holding up a mirror which is at last openly labeled "nosce teipsum":

> Ill-destin'd wife of a transform'd monster;
> Who to assure him selfe of what he knew,
> Hath lost the shape of man.   (V, v, 77–80)

And, as though recalling Valerio's mock encomium on "horn," she adds a brutal coup de grace:

> Goe Satyre, runne affrighted with the noise
> Of that harsh sounding horne thy selfe hast blowne,
> Farewell; I leave thee there my Husbands Corps,
> Make much of that.   (83–86)

That Diana should become Venus is an ever-present human potentiality. That man should become monster and grow his own horns is a reflection of perverted ambitions unnatural in that they aim beyond nature's limits. There is no recovery here; even as he is being released from a death penalty which is no longer meaningful because with Cynthia's accusation he has effectively ceased to exist, Lysander's last words upon stage are a cry de profundis: "O brother, this iealous phrensie has borne mee headlong to ruine" (V, v, 269).

The final scene compounds the aura of decay and impending death. Lycus is arrested for the murder of Lysander, Lysander stands in danger of crucifixion for his negligence, and the background is a cross and a tomb, but placed in a pagan world, without any hint of resurrection. Yet this last scene, played in a graveyard, is the most farcical of all, with its grotesque puppets posturing in a parody of hell. It is an effect we must explain with reference both to its medium and its aim.

As to the medium, after all the claims of clear sight, insight, and farsightedness by the players, the threat of death is waved away when a soldier points to the coffin and explains: "there's no bodie, nothing. A meere blandation; a *deceptio visus*. Unlesse this souldier for hunger haue eate vp *Lysanders* bodie" (V, v, 138–39). Who speaks more metaphoric truth in the play than this poor supernumerary? And Lycus himself steps in to effect his own release with a development upon the soldier's words which is the last echo of the Venus-Diana myth. "The body," he explains, "was borne away peece-meale by deuout Ladies of *Venus* order, for the man died one of *Venus* Martyrs. And yet I heard since 'twas seene whole ath' other side the downes vppon a Colestaf betwixt two huntsmen, to feede their dogges withall" (141–45: "two huntsmen"—Tharsalio and Lysander?).[82]

Judgments and justice eventuate in pardons, and the play closes with a foolish governor, a deficient Duke of Vienna, turning over his brief ascendency to allow Tharsalio to exit as the peacemaker. Agony and folly, death and marriage merge in a cacophony in which the last gesture of disharmony is Tharsalio's reuniting a silent and despairing Lysander and a silent Cynthia, his "only constant Wife" (V, v, 292). The whole is a bad joke, an outrageous joke, to the end: the only safe cuckold is the only certain cuckold, a self-portraitist.

The grotesquerie in the final scene is developed within a framework which distances the action to clarify how far the characters stand from their own realities, from involvement in the contingency of personal being. When Lysander is hidden by Lycus so that he may be "spectator of the Scene" in which Tharsalio woos Eudora, he is more than metaphorically watching a performance. His detachment from his brother's discomfiture is that of a spectator at a comedy. And when Tharsalio seems rebuffed, Lysander emerges chuckling at the denouement and his own anticipation of it: "This brauing wooer, hath the successe expected; The fauour I obtain'd, made me witnesse to the sport; And let his Confidence bee sure, Ile giue it him home" (I, iii, 1–3). Giving it home, Lysander provokes Tharsalio's determination to bring him down with jealousy: one play brings on the other, that elaborate drama of death in which Lysander, Lycus, and Tharsalio all play their roles to place Cynthia in the tomb, where Tharsalio sees her only as an exaggerated actress taking her cues in the spectacle they have arranged. To treat life with the deliberate manipulation proper to a play, in the confident belief that roles can be shed after the "real" being of others has been tested, has begotten spectacle upon spectacle for blind spectators. Or, to coordinate the theatrical aspects of *The Widow's Tears* with its exploration of "confidence," one could say that in their pride these characters forgot that the great theater of the world is a site for *Dei ludus* and aspired to be not only spectators but authors. With such mistaken ambitions it is appropriate that their histories draw to a close in a theater of unmeaning, a play without a plot.

The conclusion rapidly, almost cursorily, sketched in the last three hundred lines of the play is superfluous to the action, the psychic consequences of which have run their course. If Lysander and Cynthia are rejoined in a resurrection from the tomb, they are a Leontes and Hermione who cannot awaken again. The significance of the close is not in any change of development but in the symbolic maturation of the theatrical imagery as the final comment of Chapman upon his characters and play.

The Governor of Cyprus is announced as no other symbol of tragicomic balance and restored harmony has been, giving to the whole an aura of absolute absurdity in all senses of that word. "Stand aside," shouts a guard, and his captain introduces the ruler with a wry aside: "Roome for a strange Gouernour. The perfect draught of a most braineless, imperious vpstart. O desert! where wert thou, when this woodden dagger was guilded over with the Title of Gouernour?" (V, v, 151–55). Tharsalio elaborates the implied image: "the Vice must snap his Authoritie at all he meetes, how shalt else be knowne what part he plaies" (201–2). The spectacles proposed by man have been subsumed into the Interlude of Cyprus wherein the Vice becomes King.[83]

But he is not an Ambidexter or even an Haphazard; he is Confidence, and Confidence is blind. Like Tharsalio and Lysander, he sees before he looks: "A villaine," cries the Governor concerning Lycus, "whose very sight I abhorre; where is he? Let mee see him" (160–61). "Hee's able yee see to iudge of a cause at first sight," says Tharsalio (182–83) because, as the Governor himself confirms, "in matters of iustice I am blinde" (191). This is a special blindness, though, annunciated by the earlier metamorphoses. The Governor is not randomly mistaken but represents a world inverted. "Ile turne all topsie turuie," he says, "and set vp a new discipline amongst you" (209–10). Topsy-turvy the world of *The Widow's Tears* has been, but to set it right again the blindly confident Governor threatens to expel all that it contains. Strange wisdom issues from this fool: "I will whip lecherie out ath' Citie, there shall be no more Cuckolds. They that heretofore were errand Cornutos, shall now bee honest shop-keepers, and iustice shall take place. I will hunt ielousie out of my Dominion. . . . Ile haue all yong widdowes spaded for marrying again. . . . To conclude, I will Cart pride out ath'

Towne" (V, v, 224–41). But we know, of course, that it is a mock wisdom. Blind confidence speaks of expelling pride and promises to prevent the actions which have just run their destructive course. It is proper that the Governor should select the sleepy Argus as new favorite in his cortege and that Tharsalio should gently put this puppet ruler back in his box and himself close the play he has directed as a mockery of romantic harmony. As *The Widow's Tears* began, so it closes under the auspices of the blind: Argus, the Governor, and Tharsalio, husband (through Argus' aid) to the former Governor's widow.

So much for the theatrics with which the final scene enhances the play's effect; it remains to determine its end. If his vision of the world is topsy-turvy, no one is more devoted to appearances than Tharsalio himself. From his suit and hand-mirror at the opening to his establishment of a manifestly discordant "harmony" at the close, he reveals himself as master and chief victim of a hell of his own invention. He no sooner has entered Eudora's household to bully her suitor than she turns in amazement to demand of the latter:

> what Deuill sees
> Your childish, and effeminate spirits in him,
> That thus yee shun him? (I, ii, 126–28)

Soon Lysander, his jealousy aroused by this fraternal Iago, curses "All the Furies in hell attend thee" (II, i, 34) and conjectures that he has

> Turn'd Deuill . . . and stuft his soule
> With damn'd opinions, and unhallowed thoughts
> Of womanhood, of all humanitie,
> Nay Deitie it selfe. (46–49)

"Let him be the Deuill," challenges Eudora (II, ii, 74), and Argus implies that he has the witchcraft to be one (77–82). As in *Othello*,[84] the diabolism is transferred from Tharsalio to his victim when Lysander begins to tempt and then to damn Cynthia with the cry, "Hell be thy home" (V, ii, 33)[85] or with the curse "All the infernall plagues dwell in thy soule" (V, iii, 62). But, as Tharsalio affirms, the instrument of transferal has been his own creation, "that furious, frantique capricious Deuill iealousie" (120–21).

The horror is that Tharsalio is not Iago. If he is a devil, he is only a devil of lath, like the Governor, the Vice of a stupid interlude. At first he wants only to turn the tables upon Lysander because the latter has been callous enough to make an ironic and superior comment upon the "scene" he has played out with Eudora, much to his discomfiture. When he has ocular proof of Cynthia's metamorphosis in the tomb, he argues with Lycus that the revelation will cure Lysander's jealousy rather than madden him (V, i, 59–65), and his first thought is to avenge his brother. When, in time, he recognizes Lysander himself as the soldier, his good will turns toward Cynthia, whom he alerts: "This was a proiect of his owne contriving to put your loialtie and constant vowes to the test; y'are warned, be arm'd" (V, iii, 156–57). He is a very human, sometimes even humane, devil, one whose heart has softened in the midst of his scheming, who loses confidence in inconstancy itself at times, and who tries to seal the action with an impossible reunion of Cynthia and Lysander, and this in the context of a wedding masque to celebrate the nuptials he has arranged for his nephew—a union of love.[86]

To understand the point of the topsy-turvy world of *The Widow's Tears*, we should return to Chapman's interest in Ficino and the Platonism of Florence. It was in Ficino's letters that we earlier found the symbol which comes to dominate and explain the play. It is, of course, man on his head, touching divine things only by the inept waggling of his toes while his eyes and brain try to catch the shadows here below (Eudora, we may recall, in taking Tharsalio, made "my foot my head"), trying to possess some absolute substantiality where nothing truly exists. This topsy-turvy figure is antipodes to the patient Strozza, whose inspired dreams and prophetic reading of myth rewarded his Platonic faith and Herculean *furor* in *The Gentleman Usher*. His faith and patience made of him a demi-divinity, led him halfway to the heavens before he had left this world. It is inevitable, then, that Tharsalio should himself be a mere demi-devil. In *The Widow's Tears* man willfully misinterprets his own myths and acts out an ironic role in the pseudo-philosophic puppet plays through which he tries to locate absolutes in a shadow world. As we earlier heard Ficino say in half a dozen ways, "The gates of Pluto cannot be unlocked; within are the people of dreams." The soul slumbers in this life, "and before it may be awakened, dies; after death . . . to be confused by yet more violent dreams; which, properly speaking, is designated by the name Tartarus."

If the metamorphoses of *The Widow's Tears* have taught us anything, it is how we evolve out of our own potentialities. Strozza has passed from courtier to visionary and, perhaps, to saint. Tharsalio has gone the other way. If he lives in hell, it is only projected from his own psyche, mirror image of himself, as evanescent yet as permanent as Lysander's horns. Looking into the tomb and seeing Cynthia kissing the soldier, he whispers in awe: "By heauen I wonder now I see't in act, / My braine could euer dreame of such a thought" (V, i, 48–49). As Ficino could have told him and as Chapman knew, it is a dream from which he never can awaken.

 Let us turn briefly, by way of epilogue, to a play which must certainly have been one of Chapman's last, perhaps his very last, effort for the stage, *The Tragedy of Chabot.* Here again he presents that temptation by trial which in his world brings on only universal loss and remorse.[87] The milieu is different in this historical play. Jealousy and incredulity is aroused not by a wife but by a court favorite whose sense of justice is so lofty that his rivals are able to sow a seed of doubt as to its genuineness in the mind of Chabot's mentor, Francis I. The critical act is Chabot's: he stands out against his rival for favor, Montmorency, by tearing up and refusing to honor or sign a bill upon which the opposition party has gained the thoughtless King's signature. His defiance in the name of principle is pressed until he is brought to trial for treason. The King conceives of this as a lesson to humble overweening pride and intends to pardon Chabot all along, while even Montmorency who recognizes Chabot's incorruptibility, has pangs of conscience over the affair.[88] But to Francis' amazement and discomfiture, Chabot refuses to accept pardon for what he knows demands none, and so his trial becomes the King's own (IV, i, 213–92). All seems to be going well enough when Chabot's insistence brings about a public revelation of justice and its abuses, and act IV concludes with the King's contented benediction upon his favorite:

> Come, Philip [Chabot], shine thy honour now for ever,
> For this short temporal eclipse it suffer'd
> By the interpos'd desire I had to try thee,
> Nor let the thought of what is past afflict thee
> For my unkindness; live still circled here,
> The bright intelligence of our royal sphere. (IV, i, 455–60)

As Lysander learned in the tomb, when he so smugly decreed of Cynthia, "if shee be gold shee may abide the test," the King declares of Chabot, "If he prove / No adulterate gold, trial confirms his value" (IV, i, 29–30). To this simplistic pontificating the Queen replies:

> Although it hold in metal, gracious sir,
> Such fiery examination and the furnace
> May waste a heart that's faithful, and together

With that you call the *faeces,* something of
The precious substance may be hazarded.   (31–35)

She is right, of course. Between acts IV and V Chabot, exonerated of
wrong and even exalted for righteousness, has fallen ill. The last act is
filled with medical imagery, with the attempts of Chabot's father and
friends to keep Francis from seeing the shadow of death he has cast
upon his favorite by the gratuitous trial, and with the King's last-minute
attempt to restore the loyal but dying Chabot.

Chabot at his mock-trial had come to see this world for what it is
to Chapman's Platonic protagonists: "He stands as all his trial were a
dream." The cynical court secretary comments, without knowing how
deeply it cuts, "He'll find the horror waking" (IV, i, 209–10). Chabot
dies of a broken heart, and the erring and human physician Francis cannot cure him of it. The trial cannot be recalled; it has destroyed the
substance of justice[89] as thoroughly as Lysander's testing destroyed his
Cynthia, as Cornelio's jealousy destroyed Gazetta's love. Still, as Chabot
dies there is a combined eulogy and elegy which sends him "a victory
in's death"; the words are the King's, who concludes,

> this world
> Deserv'd him not. How soon he was translated
> To glorious eternity.   (V, iii, 206–8)

It is a pattern of destruction and apotheosis which is familiar in
Chapman's work. Chabot is a Cynthia whose trial fuses into that not
of a Bussy but of a Strozza; jealous love has killed him only to transport him. It seems an almost inevitable stroke of poetic and Platonic
consistency that the mythic arrow which transformed Strozza should
many years later reverberate in the mind of Chabot and that of his
creator, whose poems have seemed so dark to every generation from his
own because they lie in the shadow of their own myths:

> *King.* Doth that [my unkindness] afflict him?
> *Father* [*of Chabot*]. So much, though he strive with most resolv'd and
> adamantine nerves,
> As ever human fire in flesh and blood
> Forg'd for example to bear all, so killing
> The arrows that you shot were (still your pardon),
> No centaur's blood could rankle so.   (V, i, 81–86)

CHAPTER III Critics and *Commediografi* in Sixteenth-Century Florence

Having seen the English disciple re-create the Italian philosopher's interacting metaphors for reality as dramatic action, we should now recall that Chapman stood alone among contemporary dramatic poets in his enthusiasm for the folios of Florentine philosophy. Indeed, this enthusiasm for what we may tag the *Platonica theologica* was probably unmatched among those Englishmen who have left written records of their intellectual activities from the time of St. Thomas More to that of Henry More. In Chapter VIII we will encounter a later seventeenth-century Spanish playwright whose masterpiece turned Ficino's texts to account by dramatizing Plato himself. Between Chapman and Calderón, though, the Platonic debt of our dramatists is indirect—one might fairly say non-existent were it not for the impact of the Ficinian epistemological metaphors upon later Florentine criticism. But this influence in the sixteenth century represents a new emphasis upon the complex union of the formative imagination of the artist and the dissolution of form which deeper considerations of the imagination brought about.

If Ficino was the Renaissance proprietor of Plato, the heretical and caustic Modenese Ludovico Castelvetro was the proprietor of Aristotle. It was he who finally disentangled the *Poetics* from Averroes,[1] but his own immense *Poetica d'Aristotele vulgarizzata, et Sposta* (1570) demonstrates, as one critic remarks, "a basic scorn for the text of the *Poetics.*"[2] His attitudes are difficult to disentangle, partly because, like many Renaissance commentators, he ran as he wrote,[3] and partly because he was groping toward a sense of the transactional nature of the poetic act. Himself an academician and playwright,[4] he sought to delineate the especially complicated form that transaction takes when an author's projection and an audience's perception must be mediated by an actor. The Prologo to his youthful play *Gl'ingannati* enters with a physical and verbal gesture toward the perspective stage, reminding the audience that, for all its careful "realism," it consists only of "questo apparecchio." The play is a projection around a Plautine plot of the poet's imagination of Modena constructed from a web of local allusions. Yet, like the Prologue to *Henry V*, this one comes to remind the audience that the actors' and author's "facende, senza voi, son fredde e presso che perdute e, se non ci si ripara, se ne vanno in un zero" ("efforts, without you, are unconvincing and almost lost and, if you don't do something about it, end up nothing but a zero").[5] It was inevitable that this early play should have been provided with a Prologue: the Prologue was an important heritage of Latin comedy and its proper function one of the most-debated questions of sixteenth-century Italian criticism.[6] But what is immediately interesting is the older Castelvetro's rejection in the *Poetica* of just the bridging function, the appeal to the audience's imaginative participation with the actors in making the play, which the young Castelvetro embodied in his *Prologo*: l'istrioni "m'hanno spinto qui per imbasciadore, oratore, legato, procuratore o poeta" ("the actors have thrust me out here as an ambassador, orator, legate, attorney, or poet").[7] It is interesting because the later Terentian position throws into relief his continued concern with, but revised conception of, the auditor's imagination, a conception which both stimulated and made possible the direct rebuttal of Francesco Buonamici in Florence and the indirect rebuttal of Jacopo Mazzoni in his defenses of Dante's comedy.[8]

It should be remembered that *Gl'ingannati* was performed before a highly select private audience by the sophisticated members of the Accademia degli Intronati: the audience being treated of in the *Poetica* is much different, "genti grosse," "la moltitudine rozza." They are people incapable of "understanding disputes on the sciences and arts,"[9] just those disputes so popular in dozens of Renaissance prologues. And it is this limitation of the audience which, for Castelvetro, makes poetry of all sorts an improper vehicle for teaching; able only to follow the changing fortunes of the world, they cannot be tutored, only entertained. The end of poetry is to delight (16–17). And one delights by verisimilitude, by convincing the audience that it is, indeed, watching men in the world. There is no need here to enumerate Castelvetro's familiar guides for tightening the rules of unity, except in those respects in which his insistence upon formal properties springs directly from his conception of the audience. Part of the paradox discernible in his thinking about drama is precisely that his exhaustive and haughty prescriptions and proscriptions for its form are largely dictated by his estimate of the viewers' imaginative needs and powers.

The most notorious of these estimates, perhaps, is that in which

Castelvetro takes issue with Aristotle's remark (1451a) that the relation between the length of tragic plots and the time necessary for their presentation is only accidental. Performances, Castelvetro insists, must exceed two hours in length because no audience would go to the trouble of attending only "o per vna hora, o per due anchora" (95ᵛ). But performances cannot exceed twelve hours, "non potendo il popolo stare in theatro senza disagio insupportabile più di dodici hore" ("the people not being able to remain in the theater more than twelve hours without insupportable discomfort") (97ʳ).¹⁰ This sense of the limits of human physical endurance delimiting the tragic plot is coupled later in the *Poetica* with the limitations of human vision delimiting the place of tragedy: "nella tragedia è ristretto non solamente ad vna citta, o villa, o campagna, o simile sito, ma anchora a quella vista che sola puo apparere agliocchi d'vna persona" ("in tragedy [the scene] is restricted not only to one city, or villa, or countryside, or similar place, but also to that view which alone could appear to the eyes of one person") (296ᵛ). These comments clearly reflect an audience which is mesmerized by a real world substituted for their own, completely empathic with the mirror world upon the perspective stage (could the young author of *Gl'ingannati* who translated Modena to Siena, as Plautus so often boasted of translating Athens to Rome, have conceived of such a malleable audience?). Yet other remarks in the course of the *Poetica* reveal that Castelvetro also knew that one sometimes had to depend only upon the imagination of the audience to sustain the illusion, that sometimes the actor had to renounce his domination of the translation of word into world.

For instance, he argues that logically we ought to be more impressed by seeing horrible events staged than by hearing them merely reported, but the fact is quite the reverse. He gives as evidence the diminished dramatic effect when the *sacre rappresentazioni* become too literal: "se alcuno ne dubitasse ritruouisi alla rappresentatione della passione di nostro signore doue cio s'vsa & spetialmente a Roma & contenga le risa se puo" ("if anyone should doubt it, let him visit the representation[s] of the passion of our lord where it is a custom, especially at Rome, and let him who can contain his laughter") (161ʳ). Returning to the same point later, Castelvetro bans from staging all actions of "vccidere, crucifiggere, impiccare, collare, martoriare, trasformare & simili." He does so because "queste sono attioni, lequali . . . danno a veditori il piu delle volte da ridere, la doue sono introdotte per far piangere" ("these are actions which . . . most of the time make the viewers laugh where they are introduced to make him weep") (304ᵛ).¹¹ But an even worse dramatic sin than this one of inadvertent illusion-breaking is the deliberate confusion

of imaginative levels by means of a prologue: "Percio che se la rappresentatiua dee hauer luogo, & porger diletto, non si dee fare vna attione
contraria, che è la narratiua, la quale distrugge, et annulla ogni verisimilitudine della rappresentatiua. . . . Et in questo . . . pecca . . . Plauto, &
. . . Terentio . . . con le persone de loro prolaghi, per gli quali si palesa
l'argomento della fauola che si dee rappresentare, & si manifesta come
non vera contra a quello che sarebbe douero a fare" ("Since if the representative [action] must have a place and give delight, one must not make
a contrary action, that is, the narrative, which destroys and annuls every
verisimilitude of the representative. . . . And in this . . . Plautus and
Terence sin . . . with the persons of their prologues, through whom the
argument of the plot is revealed which one should represent, and it is
manifest that it is not true contrary to what should be done") (13ᵛ; cf.
57ᵛ). Again and again Castelvetro returns adamantly to this prohibition
in his several annotations upon the corpus of Latin comedy. On the
Mercator he comments (in sharp contrast to Mazzoni's later argument
for the author as character) that "pecca il prologo, che essendo persona
comica, non può essere insieme prologo, rivolgendo il parlare a veditori,
i quali non sono persona comica" ("the Prologue errs, in that being a
comic persona he cannot at the same time be a Prologue, turning his
speech to the audience, who are not comic *persone*").[12] And on the
Amphitryo he remarks: "Io non so qual tragedia, o, comedia mi leggessi
mai che meno mi piacesse. Prima il prologo non si conviene a Mercurio,
si come a colui che è persona della comedia. . . . rivolgesi piú volte il
parlare a veditori, il che io reputo grandissimo vizio" ("I do not know
what tragedy or comedy I ever read which pleased me less. First the
prologue is [a role] not suitable to Mercury, inasmuch as it is not suitable
to any who is a persona of the comedy. . . . he turns his speech several
times to the audience, which I hold for a most grave vice").[13]

The entire force of Castelvetro's dramatic criticism is coercive: the
spectator's attention is focused upon the world of the play as thoroughly
as his eyes, led to that vanishing point beyond the last *palazzi* of the
perspective stage. No physical or psychic discomfort, no improbability
of plot, no creaking of winches in the wings must be permitted to allow
the psyche to escape back into acknowledgment of that other world
from which it watches. The double awareness of Ortega y Gasset's spectator has been recognized, only to be sundered. And the most important
and dangerous element in the shaky compound of illusion is the actor,
whose doubleness must also be divided and denied. He must cease to
be actor and assume only the dimension of character, of *persona comica*.
It is for this reason that such apparently undue emphasis is given to
attacks upon the Prologue who doubles as a character or who, in speak-

ing directly to the audience, disillusions them—for this reason, but also because the scorned popular dramatic forms with which the *commedia erudita* was in competition were making a mockery of the entire aesthetic of illusion, washing away the rules with a pragmatic success which was still defying theory years after Castelvetro's struggle with the problem.

Let us look briefly at two Florentine examples, both earlier than Castelvetro's *Poetica*. The earliest is the very sophisticated *sacra rappresentazione* titled *Quando Abraam cacciò Agar sua ancilla con Ismael suo figliuolo*.[14] It was presented by the boy company Del Vangelista (also known as L'Aquilini) in the hills of Fiesole, where Ficino and Pico had dreamed their ideal villa into existence. Written while Savonarola's memory was still fresh, it may have been enjoyed by Ficino himself, since L'Aquilini were sponsored by Lorenzo il Magnifico, who enrolled his own children among its players,[15] or it may have been played in the last weeks when Ficino lay dying in Florence. In any case, *Abraam cacciò Agar* was so popular that it long survived its original production, passing through six and possibly seven editions by 1610.[16] It is, in short, perhaps the best representative of the genre which suddenly emerged from the *laudi* as full-blown drama in Florence in the age of Lorenzo and the Platonic academy. Like a number of other *sacre*, *Abraam cacciò Agar* is a biblical prodigal son narrative enveloped by a *frottola*, a framing verse induction and conclusion around the scriptural narrative itself.[17] So attractive was this frame tale that it was independently published under the title of *Frottola d'un padre che avea due figliuoli*.[18]

In this *frottola* a Florentine father decides to take his sons Antonio and Benedetto to the convent of Santa Maria delle Murate for vespers,[19] in order that they may

> enjoy their sweet songs,
> In which you will seem to hear holy angels
> Singing in the Heavens. (4)

It is already a complicated bridging joke, a version of Hamlet's "little eyases," in which the author makes the father appear ludicrously simple, even old-fashioned, before a more knowing audience, draws attention blatantly to the strains he puts upon that audience's imagination with mimetic impossibilities, and perhaps even offers dubious, backhanded compliments to a rival company.

Not only was *Abraam cacciò Agar* played in the Fiesolan hills, but the action of the *frottola* begins in Florence, only to move to Fiesole, where father and sons will watch a *sacra* presented by the Vangelista boys. The Murate was not chosen at random. It was a convent which

had been patronized by Caterina Sforza and to which she had recently
sent or was about to send her minor children and her portable wealth
as she prepared to face Cesare Borgia's siege of Forlì.[20] Thus the *frottola*
sets two well-known companies of young performers in competition by
means of the father's decisions and revisions about what seems the most
profitable entertainment for his sons. The attraction offered at Santa
Maria delle Murate may have been nothing more dramatic than the
angelic singing of novices and nuns in one of the more exclusive convents. If so, the allusion draws attention to the daring of the spoken
frottola in which that allusion is made. *Bel canto* was the norm for de-
livery of the *sacre rappresentazioni* and constitutes the mode of performance for the biblical narrative of *Abraam cacciò Agar*. While
D'Ancona[21] has argued from textual hints that a few precedents may
have been available, the recitative rather than musical character of the
frottola was unexpected enough to convince the mid-sixteenth-century
Florentine annalist Vincenzo Borghini that it was an innovation: "The
first, I wish to record, that stripped away song was the Herald, in that
frottola which all the boys of my time knew by heart, 'Anton! Chi
chiama?' [the opening lines of *Abraam cacciò Agar*], although the *festa*,
as they called it, was recited in *bel canto*, but that opening was recited
in prose, which appeared a strange thing at first, but was gradually enjoyed and put into practice."[22]

The convents, however, sometimes also presented *sacre* in competition with the male companies such as the Aquilini, and even some
frottole (as well as allusions by later sixteenth-century Florentine
commediografi such as Cecchi and Grazzini) toy coyly with the trans-
vestite titillations offered by the little nuns playing at soldier long before
Viola landed in Illyria.[23] We have little information on such conventual
activities before the latter half of the sixteenth century, but that they
must have been sufficiently notorious to raise eyebrows much earlier is
suggested by a warning from the Council of Cologne as early as 1549.[24]
Whether it was to a vesper choir or a rival *sacra*, the author of *Abraam
cacciò Agar* decided upon an allusion which would defy illusion, while
challenging the demi-operatic nature of the *sacre* by flaunting his own
"realism" in pitting drama in prose ("*a parole*") against the rival and
generic tradition of song.

The audience for such *sacre* as this was, like the actors, in large
part boys, who were expected by their accompanying parents to carry
away lessons in decorum treacherously disguised under the delights of
an evening's colorful outing in the hills or the churches where these
musical playlets were performed[25]—indeed, just such an audience as that
of father and sons in the *frottola*. This is the first mirror which the play

holds up to its audience, shattered by the allusion to the Murate but reinforced by the father's references to the present times in Florence. Before setting off for the entertainment, the father questions the prodigal Antonio about his desires, which are all focused on freedom, spending money, and clothes—clothes of every variety: French berets, French trousers so tight they look painted on, silk jackets, etc. It is this which offers the father an opening to denounce the unrestrained riot of youthful luxury and fads in these bad post-Savonarolan days:

Cresciute le berrette
E scemati e' cervelli,
E' panni son più belli
E gli uomini più stolti.
[The caps have grown
And the brains are shrunken,
The cloth is more beautiful
And the men more foolish.]   (7)

Yet only a short time before, he tells the Florentines, theirs was a city almost returned to Christian living; now it is insane and miserable in its whirligig of fashion.[26] But all hope is not yet to be abandoned because there are those young men like Benedetto who, upon questioning, reveals that, in contrast with his brother, he has a single modest vice, lust for books—and this only because he is uncomfortable about borrowing them: "O buon mio Benedetto, / Tu hai il nome e' fatti" ("O my good Benedetto, / You have the nature as well as the name"), boasts the father (8), and the name will be used to consolidate the several levels of conversion to virtue as Isac ("che Dio ti benedica" [17]) and, finally, Antonio ("E vôti perdonare / Antonio, e benedire" [37]) become "benedetti."

But Antonio must be converted through seeing himself in the mirror of another prodigal, even as the conversion of any little Florentine *birbone* in the audience must come about through the mirror provided by the careless Antonio. So at this point the father changes his plans and decides to take the boys to Fiesole and the *festa*[27] of the Vangelista group, who, he pointedly tells Antonio, "play it all for your benefit" (9).

The mirror of illusion is cracked again by parody, as the trio pretend to struggle up the hills breathlessly to the very spot at which they stand initially, yet it is immediately restored as they approach a harried *festaiuolo*[28] to ask about the play, thus becoming less the focus than mediators between the audience and that third area at which its imagination has to make peace between realistic mimesis and palpable pretense.

This level, which participates in both the *frottola* and the *sacra* or *festa* proper, is that in which the actors mimic their profession. The *festaiuolo* is upset because one of his players has not yet arrived, but he is finally induced by Benedetto to summarize the plot of the *festa*, the history of the prodigal Ishmael and the pious, filial Isac and the conversion of Ishmael in the wooded hills. Thus the *frottola* frame has been used to rationalize the usual *annunziazione*, to incorporate into the drama itself the summary Prologue of the Plautine type which Castelvetro so lamented because of its sin against illusion, against verisimilitude. This reformed "Prologue," then, is the first sinner converted by the play.

Now the missing actor arrives on horseback, and there is a shock of the absurd when he turns out to be a quarrelsome hunchback (12). He is assigned his place, and it is that of one of the worst of the bad companions of Ishmael, one whose only part in the action is to draw a weapon at one point and, for no reason, threaten the others. Again, within the framework of "realism," the author is calling for attention (from the fathers if not the sons, from the sophisticated if not the modest) to the nature of the little play, this time symbolically. The *gobbo* is, of course, a resurrection figure, the pulcinella who, with his hump and club, was a revived daemon, a soul returned from the dead in fertility celebrations long before he became a major *maschera* of the *commedia dell'arte*.[29] And the *sacra* of *Abraam cacciò Agar* is itself a history not only of spiritual but of literal resurrection: Agar leaves Ishmael to die of starvation in the wilderness; Agar's prayers are then answered by the sudden appearance of a miraculous, life-giving fountain. Revived, Ishmael joins his mother in penitent prayers for forgiveness of his jealousy and his temptation of his good brother Isac into the ways of sin whose wages he has found to be death. The *gobbo* figure places the Old Testament story of salvation, in which the participants self-consciously look forward to a better future under the savior Christ (15–16), within a larger, more primitive context of renewal. The *gobbo*, like the *frottola* frame, breaks the mimetic illusion of the little players' biblical history in order to give it a reality greater far within the imagination of that ideal spectator who does not wear the perversely ideal, but impossible, blinders prescribed by Castelvetro's realism.

In the end, neither Antonio nor his father was quite so literal as Castelvetro feared. The prodigal recognizes himself in the parable and returns to reality by kneeling in imitation of Ishmael to beg his father's forgiveness for his folly. This folly has been denounced by Isac, who acts out in his world, before Ishmael and his companions, the lament about youth of the father in the *frottola* (23). A ripple of doubtful identity courses throughout Ishmael's relationship with his brother ("Ipocrito . . . Tu credi ch'io non sappia chi tu se'?" ["Hypocrite . . . do you think that I don't know who you are?"] [27]). But now Antonio, in this mirror, both discovers and liberates himself by recognizing that the truth of drama is archetypal: "Io sono uno Ismael" (37). The boys have had a double opportunity to learn their lesson of repentance and better behavior, but now, before the fathers lead them on the long walk back down to the great city in the valley, the author offers the elders their own opportunity to step back through the looking-glass of the play. If Puck will tell Shakespeare's audience to mend the play's faults, the father in this *frottola* will tell the *festaiuolo* to mend his play's faults: "There have been some unimportant errors, especially in the unpolished, loose verse, [and] in some off-key singing." But, in the end, it has been a good play; and none are without errors (38). It has been a good play because in teasing the imagination of the spectator with its shifting distances from his reality it has remade that reality. It is because he was not trapped by mimesis that Antonio could cry out in renewal and recognition: "Io sono uno Ismael." The *sacre rappresentazioni*, like all religious dramatic forms, evolved from ritual. If ritual is efficacious imitation, we might say fairly that this sophisticated little play-within-a-play has fulfilled its function.

Giovanbatista dell'Ottonaio, probable author of *Abraam cacciò Agar*, was also the author of numerous popular *canti carnescialeschi*, street songs for the carnival parades and pageants which were brought to their peak of luxury and art by the enthusiastic support of Lorenzo de' Medici. Antonfrancesco Grazzini, a popular author better known under the ichthyophilic title of *Il Lasca*, which he assumed as a member of the Accademia degli Umidi, intent upon preserving this aspect of Florentine culture, collected Ottonaio's texts and others for publication. But Paolo dell'Ottonaio, Giovanbatista's brother and literary executor, publicly protested about the impurity of the texts and blocked their publication in Grazzini's anthology.[30] This quarrel, along with an earlier one within the Accademia degli Umidi, was doubtless instrumental in preventing Florentine staging for most of the comedies written by Grazzini, whom the antiquarian Filippo Valeri at the end of the century posthumously named the modern Terence.[31]

One of these unstaged comedies was *La strega*, a self-consciously "modern" play written between 1550 and 1566, which will serve as a second Florentine challenge to the Castelvetran critical notion that a stable reality level should be sustained throughout a dramatic presentation.[32] An Induction precedes the play, a debate between the conservative Prologo and the dramatic iconoclast Argomento. The latter objects to mere imitation of ancient New Comedy, as had the prologues to two of Grazzini's earlier comedies: "Aristotile e Orazio videro i tempi loro, ma i nostri sono d'un altra maniera. . . . in Firenze non si vive come si viveva già in Atene e in Roma" ("Aristotle and Horace saw their own times, but ours are different. . . . in Florence one does not live as they used to do in Athens and in Rome").[33] Prologues are rejected by Argomento as inorganic; arguments are rejected by Prologo as old-fashioned —and La strega is slyly misidentified by Prologo as a play without an argument. But Argomento also plays sleight-of-hand in taking over the Prologue's usual function to sweep our attention toward the perspective scenery in setting forth the place: "la scena si conosce benissimo esser Firenze; non vedi tu la Cupola, bue" ("you know very well that the setting is Florence; don't you see the Cathedral, you ox") (184). These interlocutors can agree upon only one thing: the elaborate machines and pomp of the intermedii have engulfed the plays they once served: "it used to be that the intermedii should serve comedies, but now the comedy only serves the intermedii" (186). The present comedy, asserts Argomento, will be more modest—or more assertive—in renouncing these elaborate interludes. But Prologo wants an adherence to decorum, to comic precepts, citing the pseudo-Ciceronian definition of comedy. In response, Argomento calls this old-fashioned ("all'antica"), adding a synonym for the conservative stance: "tieni del fiesolano" (186). While it is proverbial,[34] the phrase is of dubious appropriateness when thrown back at a Ciceronian citation, with its implications of the rougher barbarisms of the hill peasant's mentality. And this is just its point: it reminds the audience of the popular comedy in which such peasants played so large a role, in contrast to the commedia erudita. The puzzled Prologo suggests that if the classical precepts are to be discarded one might as well call in the rough-and-tumble players of the commedia dell'arte ("Si potrebbe anche mandare a chiamare i Zanni"), that dominant and immensely popular theater which the dramatic critics of the sixteenth century pretended did not exist even while it completely overshadowed the commedia erudita. Exactly, agrees Argomento, snapping the trap: "Piacerebbero forse anche più le loro commedie gioiose e liete, che non fanno queste vostre savie e severe" ("Perhaps, too, their merry and joyous comedies would please better than do these, your judicious and severe [plays]") (186–87).[35] The allusion to peasant style is picked up in the play proper, when the comic servant to a comic master anatomizes the master's outlandish costume and concludes that his face is "alla fiesolana" (206). It is a small guidepost to the fusing art of the play.

As Sanesi observed, Grazzini, the acerbic critic of the incredible kidnappings and discoveries of classical comedy, never strays far from its customary solutions through coincidence and discovery: we do well to remember Valori's identification of Grazzini as the new Terence. And in no comedy is Grazzini closer to the old ploys rejected by his own Argomento[36] than in *La strega*. A shipwreck, a lost son feared captured by Turkish pirates, a girl who has been saved from kidnappers, a mother recovering her lost daughter in a strange city while a father recovers a lost son in a strange city, a lost virginity restored because the erring lovers, upon being discovered by the community, are wed by their parents' wishes as well as their own—these are the play's elements. But upon all of this is superimposed the most detailed Florentine setting, the most numerous *fiorentinismi*, to be found in Grazzini's comedies. After the debate of the induction one cannot comfortably posit a mere lapse of memory: the absurdity of the New Comedy formulae is being thrown into relief by their persistence in a realistic setting where they are palpably anachronistic. As in *Abraam cacciò Agar*, the illusion of reality is simultaneously maintained and destroyed in the interest of pressing home a longer perspective in which the perennial "argument of comedy" —return, regeneration, a restoration and beginning again with the new which restores and re-enacts the old pattern—rises through the surface of the comic illusion. In the transaction between audience and author, Ortega's "double space" of the theater has been acknowledged. Florence has been accepted as milieu in the mirror of Grazzini's stage world in order that it may displace its self-image into metaphor and place itself in the tradition of the New Comedy pattern lying behind the absurd adventures: Athens is Rome is Florence because the comic *mythos* is regeneration, renaissance.

So much for the surface interplay of illusionism and traditional arts in *La strega*. But Grazzini's hold upon tradition has deeper roots, as we might expect of a self-consciously "popular" writer intent upon preserving the voice of the *popolo Fiorentino* in every variety of expression from *canti carnescialeschi* to comedies.[37] The body of *La strega*, like the induction, forces the imagination to accommodate not only two worlds, the classical and the modern, but a third: that of the *zanni*, the commedia dell'arte.[38] This is the world of two characters, Taddeo Saliscendi ("up-and-down") and his servant Farfanicchio. Grazzini's earlier comedy *La spiritata* involved masking during carnival season by the *juventus* intent upon public acknowledgment of his secret wife, but the servant of his conspiratorial friend brought the wrong masks, diabolic grotesques ("io non vo' maschere da diavoli")[39]—the masks, in short, of the *zanni*, of *Arlecchino* with his daemonic origins in a popular tradition which antedates the *commedia dell'arte* by centuries.[40] With this mistake, the *commedia dell'arte* and the associations of its masks with a release from order in such ritualistic holidays as carnival is noted without a change in the dimensions of the plot. An anti-classicist thus reminds his rather sophisticated private audience of the cross-fertilization of plot and types which was gaining momentum as the great *commedia* troupes began to establish themselves firmly at mid-century.

But in *La strega* the *commedia dell'arte* characters and manner are allowed to exist alongside of and, ultimately, to triumph over the apparent *commedia erudita* absurdities which Grazzini so elaborately develops in the teeth of his Argomento's criticism. In short, the real unity of *La strega* is not in the plotting of the narrative but in the re-enactment of the critical debate of the induction by the play proper, a play which is an essay on comedy.

The *commedia dell'arte scenari*, of course, often differ little from the love intrigues of the formulaic New Comedy tradition except that, juxtaposed to the romantic *inamorati* and blocking *senex* are the acrobatic *zanni* in their black leather animal and demon masks, or the *miles gloriosus* reduced to the rag-tag captains of Callot's drawings for *I balli di Sfessania*, carrying on a carnival of hyperbolic and obscene activity in word and deed. In *La strega* Farfanicchio is such a figure. Taddeo is a simpleton who, disappointed in his suit for a widow, arms and dresses himself extravagantly to go to the wars. When he is dissuaded, he next determines to be a statesman and dresses accordingly in a great cape and a citizen's cap, but becomes a figure of farce rather than satire when he adds a tambourine, to which he capers and sings his way to success. A good share of the play is given over to his folly, with comic *lazzi* such as his struggle to get his head out of a helmet while the sadistic Farfanicchio looks on, laughing and mocking. Everywhere, of course, he is laughed at. At one point he notices this and attributes the laughter to Farfanicchio's mockery. The servant pleads innocent and says it is caused by Taddeo's mixed dress: a German cap, a French cape, a Spanish ruff, a plume like a cavalryman, and, as we have noticed before, a face like a Fiesolano. We would agree and miss the point of Taddeo's vexed cry of "Who the devil are they laughing at" ("O di che diavol ride?" [205]) had not Grazzini printed a special stage direction before the text. Here, along with details of Taddeo's dress, we learn that "Farfanicchio his boy must have a terrible mask with a deformed and ugly snout which is attached behind with a hook, . . . which he puts on and takes off, but dexterously, so that Taddeo cannot notice; this he does the first and second times he comes on stage."[41]

Precisely as the innocent Taddeo unwittingly realized, the people are laughing at a "devil," at the antics of the (to recall that popular English word for this type and behavior) zany, Farfanicchio, in his grotesque demon mask. Structure is interrupted, sentimentality in romance is mocked, realism submerged in this solvent from the under-world who reminds us that the regenerative argument of comedy origi-nates in ritual, in celebration of the indomitable forces of a nature whose hyperbolic energies have always been represented by such a figure, half-man, half-spirit. It is an energy, after all, only wanly echoed in society and sentiment and the semblance of order which rationalizes it as New Comedy.

In *La strega* Grazzini has made a daring experiment. He has offered the sort of mirror illusion of reality which Castelvetro would have ap-proved and which the modern scenic perspectives invited ("la scena si conosce benissimo esser Firenze; non vedi tu la Cupola"). Then he has teased the audience into recognizing that it is not life but art, the old art of the New Comedy. If some will be as disgusted as Hippolyta, crying "this is the silliest stuff that ever I heard," others will see the point: all comedy is both more and less "real" than Prologo's Ciceronian for-mula of an "example of manners and a mirror of life." The present (and, therefore, all pasts) is always only metaphor for some continuity called tradition and the actors always only metaphors of *that* metaphor, unless we enter the dramatic transaction from beyond the stage with Theseus and admit that "the best in this kind are but shadows, and the worst are no worse if imagination amend them." Having offered and thrown away illusionism in the interest of a metaphoric plot, Grazzini then risks throwing away the plot itself with the emergence of Taddeo and Farfanicchio. One more adjustment is demanded: not only must the audience aid the actors with their imaginations, but they must aid the author, too. If Grazzini is writing a play about his prologue, testing the bases and functions of comedy, he can succeed only if the audience does not fail in accompanying him. They must discern a movement from the apparent uniqueness and randomness of the mirrored quotidian, to the traditional order giving that appearance its pattern, to the more primi-tive disorder in which both share their origins and meaning. Apparently he failed. There was no audience for it at the time, and modern critics have de-scribed the juxtapositions which constitute the structure of *La strega* as lapses. But in another sense perhaps he succeeded, for the spirit of his effort was perpetuated while the letter was ignored. Or, looking back across the decades which separate *Abraam cacciò Agar* and Ficino from Grazzini, perhaps *La strega* was only a brilliant reflection of Florentine tradition. On the causes and effects we can never be clear; on the tradi-tion and its history we can.

I have mentioned Grazzini's adoption of the pseudonym *Il Lasca* ("the roach") as a member of the Accademia degli Umidi, a small group of literate young men who gathered to discuss Florentine literature of past and present, a modest and unpedantic ripple on the ocean of ink concerned with the *questione della lingua*. The group first met on November 1, 1540, in the home of the eccentric well-known bibliophile Giovanni Mazzuoli, self-styled *Stradino*. Humorist, actor, and antiquarian, Mazzuoli was not only host and Maecenas but spiritual leader, *padre Stradino*, to the Umidi and most particularly to Grazzini, who in 1549 wrote a moving, if unsentimental, dream vision poem on *Stradino's* death. Both mocking and lauding himself in the style of an in-joke, Grazzini in *La strega* has Farfanicchio suggest to Taddeo that he should read a lecture at an academy, and Taddeo replies: "egli è un tempo che io ne sarei stato, se io avessi voluto: lo Stradino mi pregò cento volte che io volessi entrare negli Umidi" ("there was a time when I could have done it if I had wanted to; *Stradino* begged me a hundred times to join the Umidi") (199). The complication lies in the fact that the Umidi lasted only until March of 1541, when, over the objections of Grazzini, the group was taken under the patronage of the young Medici Grand Duke Cosimo I, its membership was broadened by the addition of numerous academics, and its name was changed officially to the *Accademia Fiorentina*.[42] Grazzini felt displaced and embattled by this shift in emphasis: by 1547 he had withdrawn and did not return for twenty years. With this bitterness in mind we understand a brief epicycle in the prefatory exchange between Prologo and Argomento to *La strega*, wherein the latter suggests that poetry has fallen into the hands of pedants and taunts Prologo into silence when he offers "l'Accademia Fiorentina" as an antidote (186). It is the satire of a man nursing his own special bitterness, of the practitioner trapped amongst theorists. It is to one of those theorists that we now turn, but one to whom Grazzini would have been sympathetic had he lived to hear his lectures.

I have drawn attention to *Abraam cacciò Agar* and *La strega* in order to suggest a tradition of Florentine sophistication in manipulating the transactional process relating drama and reality, art and audience. As suggested earlier in this chapter, such complex practice was thriving in defiance of an incompatible illusionistic theory which reached maturity in Castelvetro's *Poetica* in 1570. It was inevitable that theory would eventually accommodate itself to practice, and it did so in the closing years of the century through the work of two important critics, Jacopo Mazzoni and Francesco Buonamici. The work of both suffers from recurrent confusion of past and present practices, Mazzoni because he was defending Dante, Buonamici because he was challenging Castelvetro's reading of Aristotle. But ultimately each is drawing upon contemporary dramatic experience as his shaping norm, Mazzoni concentrating upon the imagination, Buonamici upon imitation. Both Mazzoni (whose theories will be examined for dramatic relevance in a later chapter) and Buonamici were committed to the currents of Florentine Platonic philosophy which have emerged in the earlier discussion of Ficino. Buonamici's contribution came through eight *Discorsi poetici* delivered in the Accademia Fiorentina, presumably in the months just preceding September 19, 1587, the date of Buonamici's dedication letter,[43] but still influential enough to merit publication a decade later.

Before looking at the *Discorsi*, we should ask who was Francesco Buonamici, and what was the historic role of the Accademia Fiorentina in Florentine intellectual history. Buonamici was a Florentine gentleman and physician who died at an advanced age in 1604, having taught at the universities of Florence and Pisa for forty-three years as professor of philosophy in all its phases, as evidenced by his numerous commentaries and treatises on meteors, medicine, pharmacology, logic, etc. He was a long-standing member of the Accademia Fiorentina and a man favored and patronized by the Medici grand dukes throughout a lifetime, as Ficino had earlier been.[44]

A learned Aristotelian who allegedly had read through the Thomistic corpus twice, he was also a Florentine *letterato* who in 1569 read before the Accademia Fiorentina one of those Platonizing explications of Petrarch which were the staple of so many meetings at this as well as other Florentine academies, providing one loose but continuous link between the generation of Lorenzo de' Medici and those of the next century.[45] And if the *Discorsi poetici* constitute a learned Aristotelian's "defense of Aristotle" against Castelvetro's errors, "the ghost of Plato nevertheless hovered close and nudged the hand of Buonamici," as one learned critic of critics reminds us.[46] We are not surprised at the implied syncretism when we remember that Tasso was recalling a rich tradition from the *De ente et uno* when in 1576 he wrote to Scipione Gonzaga, "if to Pico della Mirandola and so many others it has been legitimate to bring Plato and Aristotle into accord in things wherein they manifestly disagree, why . . . should not I be permitted to conjoin . . . the poetic principles of Aristotle and Plato?"[47] But it is no accident that the *Discorsi* should have been written by a professor at Pisa under the auspices of the Accademia Fiorentina. It was a Platonic garden officially cultivated by the Medici grand dukes at least in part to advertise the rebirth in their own day of that great Platonic triumph in which Ficino and the earlier Medici patrons had joined in scholarly and political reknown throughout Europe.[48]

The University of Pisa was the principal academic showplace of the Medici; they introduced there the chauvinistic Florentine identification with Platonism when Grand Duke Francesco I in 1576 authorized Francesco Verino il Secondo to offer an extraordinary course in Plato. This proved the most enduring Platonic foothold within the universities, and the mutual influence of Buonamici and Mazzoni is suggested by the fact that the latter was called to Pisa in 1588, where he took over or reinstituted the course in Plato.[49] The cause of Mazzoni's appointment, aside from his early 5,197 theses toward reconciliation of Plato and Aristotle and his reputation as the most learned polemicist in Christendom, was his dedication of the expanded *Difesa della Comedia di Dante* to Cardinal Ferdinando de' Medici on February 21, 1587. Ferdinando, for years a bitter rival of his brother, Francesco I, became Grand Duke of Tuscany upon Francesco's death in October, 1587, and Mazzoni was one of the first beneficiaries of his patronage, being installed at Pisa in November, 1588.[50]

It was not the university, however, but the Accademia Fiorentina which housed, symbolically and historically, the spirit of the Careggi circle of Platonists. I suggest that, just as Grazzini's dramatic sophistication was in the tradition nurtured by the *sacre rappresentazioni* popular in the time of Lorenzo il Magnifico, so Buonamici's criticism was dependent not only upon his knowledge of this tradition but also upon a continuous heritage from Ficino, who also knew how perspective and dream both depended upon the creative cooperation of the spectator's imagination.

If the first Florentine academy was informal—Socrates' symposium revived in the gathering of friends and disciples at Careggi—the second was more formalized under the leadership of Ficino's student and successor as the modern Plato, Francesco da Diacceto.[51] Diacceto went to the University of Pisa in 1491 as a young man, returned to study with Ficino in 1492, and after the latter's death in 1499 served as a rallying point for his followers. He became a professor at Pisa in 1502, a post he held for twenty years, during which the university was, in fact, functioning largely in Florence. He participated in the gatherings of the Orti Oricellari, but what was most important was that he was a leading force in the Accademia Sacra established by the Medici in the second decade of the sixteenth century to promulgate Dante worship, *campanilismo*— as the Florentines call their civic pride, and a cultural image of continuity for the heirs of Ficino and Lorenzo de' Medici alike. With Diacceto's death and the third anti-Medici revolt in 1527, the Accademia Sacra also died, but the Florentine bond to Ficino and the concept of a Platonic academy survived through Diacceto's pupils and friends. One was Giovanni Corsi, first biographer of Ficino.[52] Another and perhaps the most important link between the early and late eras of the century was the classical philologist and diplomat Pietro Vettori, who died only in 1587 and whose formal and informal circles of students included

Baccio Valori, to whom Buonamici dedicates the *Discorsi poetici*, and Benedetto Varchi. Varchi for our purposes is most important as Diacceto's biographer, Grazzini's friend, and author of the Terentian comedy *La suocera* (1546), in which tribute is paid to *Stradino* as "il migliore uomo di Firenza."[53] It was Varchi who was the guiding spirit of the third and most formal Accademia Fiorentina until his death in 1565. What weight was given to the direct historic links of this last academy with Ficino's own is suggested by the observation of its eighteenth-century historian that the first *Consolo*, or director, Lorenzo Benivieni, was chosen because of the prominence of his ancestors Domenico and Girolamo in the academy of Ficino.[54] The context of the *Discorsi poetici* of Buonamici, then, is a society of letters which numbered among its members active playwrights and which was self-consciously Platonic in its history and image, and Buonamici's aim was to rescue Aristotle and the theater from the shadow of Castelvetro's darkness (the *Discorsi* concentrating heavily upon drama).

As I have said, Castelvetro's ideal of drama is coercive, creating an alternative objective world into which the viewer is drawn out of his own. The theater becomes a world, but woe to the dramatist who permits an audience to remember the theater of the world in which they, too, play their parts. It is Castelvetro's demand for this impossible split in the psyche which the *Discorsi* are basically concentrated upon exposing and rebutting. Francesco Buonamici is the Ortega y Gasset of the Renaissance; he seizes more clearly than any other critic upon the inevitable doubleness of the theatrical experience and its epistemological consequences. He, too, Platonically oriented, assumes that in drama as in life man seeks a journey of the imagination "ultravida."

The lesson is not easy because Buonamici's prose is difficult, but it is difficult because of his effort at precision, as an early historian at Pisa observed: "he became ever more obscure because he went over his lectures, retouching them, cleaning them up; and since he understood them, he supposed the same of others, until gradually he rendered them almost unintelligible. Nonetheless, basically they are always solid."[55] It seems a judgment for posterity.

An additional difficulty has been mentioned earlier: defending Aristotle, Buonamici oscillates between historically resurrecting Aristotle's milieu and reacting to modern drama. But that his principal aim is to reflect what he sees working successfully in the theater of his own day is made clear in his recognition that descriptive synopses of practice tend to become prescriptive by a natural momentum (pp. 21–22), as Castelvetro and others had made Aristotle appear to be. Buonamici asserts that Aristotle's *Poetics* was only the first of planned twin works.

The *Poetics* is descriptive of the poem; the other planned work was to be on the *poet's* art, and this (with help from Horace) is what Buonamici is supplying in his *Discorsi* (8).

Verisimilitude, so important to Castelvetro, is the starting point. History is verisimilitudinous through a cause-and-effect logic. But history is not treated in the *Poetics* (9) because this logic differs from that of poetry, or the *arte rappresentativa*. Castelvetro's failure to understand the distinction was what led him into the absurdity of basing his prescription for unity of time upon the physical stamina of an audience (103–4, 110). Buonamici makes a clear distinction in length (*grandezza*) between represented and representation, between *il segno* and that *di cui è segno* ("of which it is a sign") (105). The introduction of this distinction and the term *segno* takes us in two directions which together constitute the principal significance of Buonamici's treatise. By one path they lead us toward clarification of his Platonic notion that all true poetry is allegorical in the sense of shadowing universals through particulars, and by another they lead us back to the acknowledgment that drama is always an imaginative transaction between worlds which refuse to be clearly divided.[56] Not to observe this, Buonamici discerns, is to reduce the poet to a species of historian "who limps along behind what has been," which "would denigrate and diminish the divine genius of the poet, who must be a maker and rediscoverer of things, not a mere recorder."[57]

How does the poet avoid "limping along behind," however, if his is a representative art and all representation implies a thing represented? The answer lies in the Platonic word "participation." In a special way history *is* prior to poetry: "history is like the thing represented, and like the Idea; poetry is like the thing representing and participating."[58] History, the "existent" (and at this point it is not the art of history, but the totality of the past that Buonamici includes under the term), plays the modeling role of the Platonic Ideas in which the artist has the power to participate. If I correctly interpret him, Buonamici has utilized Aristotle to vault the poet into a prominence Plato denied him in the discussion of poetic imitation of imitations in the *Republic*; the artisan's imitation has been rhetorically removed to the realm of Ideas and the poet's imitation has been exalted into participation in those Ideas. But this analogizing of history and the Ideas is an alignment only for the moment. Later Buonamici inverts the relationship between history and poetry (now meaning history as an art) in order that we may see *how* the poet does, indeed, participate in the Ideas. He does so by raising the particular to the new dimension of the universal, or, in modern phraseology, by creating a concrete universal.[59] The poet "supposes a particular, but in it he considers the Idea, which is universal, inasmuch as he does not describe him exactly as he is, and describe precisely that which he does, but raises the actions and character to the highest grade of which human nature is capable . . . so that imitating in this subject this or that particular fact, such as a pious act of Aeneas, he treats and imitates the particular, but raising the action to a higher degree than it was in effect . . . he comes to consider it according to his Idea, abstracted from the material, and universally; so it is that he considers the particular universally."[60]

The poet's imitation of nature turns out to be imitation only in a paradoxical sense, as—inspired by his melancholy furor—he climbs past the shadows on the wall of Plato's cave (along with Ficino's contemplative philosopher) to rediscover the midday sun of the Ideal. And he does so by remembering that all particular men are figures of the real, containing that metaphoric doubleness which Ortega also recognized in the actor and in the nature of man's relationship to his own particularity and the "ultravida."

This sense of man as symbol leads Buonamici, as it led Ortega, to give special consideration to the theater, in which the poet shares his function with actors and audience. The end of drama is a balancing of the passions, by which Buonamici means the instilling of compassion in a fiery soul, gaiety in a melancholiac, etc. This is possible only through a species of suspension of disbelief.[61] But the dramatist is not wholly responsible for establishing this state. In the first instance, he shares responsibility with the actors. The plot is to be judged as poetry only in the light of its potential for presentation, independent of every actual presentation. But as a representation "composed of verse, speech and dancing, in which the actors alone are involved, the poet has no role" in the drama.[62] Indeed, the prologues against which Castelvetro inveighed, insofar as they are theatrically allusive crossings of stage boundaries, are not the responsibility of the poet but of the actor representing himself as the receptacle of a knowledge about the plot which is either supernatural or the result of his natural prescience as an actor (96–97). Audience purgation itself is not the responsibility solely of the poet, but also of the actor, since the spectator's inner emotions are swept up by the performer's "extrinsic" ones, as Hamlet had too good reason to know: "if the actors are moved, we also are moved and would weep with them, laugh with them. . . . so it is that purgation depends upon this motion made by the 'representing' poet with his plot along with the actor's contributing gestures and presentation of the plot."[63] This is as close as any sixteenth-century critic came to following up Robortello's earlier approving elaboration of Plato's view that the poet's inspiration passes, chain-like, through the actor to the auditor (*Ion.* 535e).[64]

Buonamici's fullest account of the imaginative interdependence of all parties to the dramatic transaction covers pages and grows out of his criticism of Castelvetro's mimetic basis for ruling upon the unity of time.[65] Having made the above-cited distinction between the size of the sign and of the thing signified, Buonamici points out that a little light entering at a window can signify a light one hundred and seventy times the size of the earth, and correspondingly one can signify long durations of time briefly because "il tempo nella mente nostra è imagine del tempo" ("time in our mind is an image of time") (110). Indeed, he continues, do we not in theatrical practice always accommodate to such imaginative compression: "this inequality of size is recognized in the signs which are the actors, because if one will represent a king, who dresses in purple and pearls of great price, he will represent him in a garment of damask" and will signify his troops and courtiers with a handful of actors (110).[66] There is, indeed, nothing wrong with compressing a play into the twelve hours of Castelvetro's artificial day if it is compatible with a convincing and pleasing plot, but the basis of decision should lie in the plot, to which Aristotle was referring, and has nothing to do with actual presentation, to which Castelvetro turned his attention when he sought to delimit a play by the endurance of the audience. One must recognize two kinds of verisimilitude in the theatrical art. One is in the thing represented, the action; the other in the representation. The former verisimilitude belongs to the art of the poet: "in the poet is the behavior, the diction; [but] the costumes, the gestures are in the actors and external to the poet," and these latter constitute the verisimilitude of the representation (111).[67] At this point the whole Castelvetran notion of a verisimilitude so effective that it will coerce the viewer is thrown out on the grounds of experience, and the creative imagination of the spectator is drawn in, along with that of the poet and actor, as third party to the fluid theatrical transaction: "In things represented verisimilitude stands in the parts of the action being connected, in such fashion that they incline the mind of the spectator to believe that it should have been just so: but, nonetheless, verisimilitude is never able to work in the spectator so thoroughly, if he is not a dolt, that he will take the representation for the thing represented, as silly country girls do on Good Friday." And the reason such verisimilitude is impossible, and unnecessary, is that spectator's awareness of the actor's doubleness which Ortega theorized to be the quintessential nature of the relationship between the stage and reality: "And we know full well that we are at a comedy, and that that is the Prologue who has learned the comedy, and how he is giving a brief exposition, and that that is Roscius, that other Callipides, not King Agamemnon or *Stradino*, and we recognize the perspectives, the seats, the drapes, the chorus, and seeing that young man dressed in white with a lighted torch in his hand, we know that he is that Panfilo the *inamorato*" (111).[68] It is a mysterious communion in which the art of the art is to fuse life and make-believe imaginatively without ever confusing them as Castelvetro did. Buonamici came to understand and articulate the interaction, however, not through reading Aristotle, but through attending the plays of Grazzini's and Varchi's Florence. *Panfilo e Filogenia*, an unpublished little Florentine morality comedy, was presumably one of them.[69] The allusion to *padre Stradino* is more difficult. In Varchi's *La suocera* he is not represented on stage, only spoken of, and I have discovered no other Florentine play in which he appears; if Buonamici means us to understand that he was himself the actor whom we recognize for himself, the allusion probably represents a tradition about Stradino being perpetuated in the Accademia Fiorentina, where he had become a myth.[70] In any case, it is an appropriate symbol for that interaction between life and art which takes so many forms in Florence from Ficino to Buonamici. What the latter did was to take up Ficino's metaphor of the world as theater and turn it into theory. Later we will find Mazzoni taking up the twinned metaphor of life as dream and turning that into a theory akin to, but even more sophisticated than, Buonamici's own.

Through what channels, direct and indirect, such theory came to England we probably will never know in much detail. It is enough to know that it describes better than any other critical analyses of the Renaissance a new form in English drama which was emerging at the time. One version of that form we have seen in Chapman's major tragicomedies, and others will be explored in ensuing chapters. But before proceeding to major plays, it is wise to recall the impact of a parallel phenomenon which undoubtedly contributed to Elizabethan as well as Florentine views on dramatic form: "improvised" comedy and its relationship to stage spectacle.

CHAPTER IV The Actor and the Artist in the Audience: Early Versions of Improvisation as Structure

An effective warning against interpreting the *commedia dell'arte* as merely one stage of a continuous Italian tradition of improvisational playing which reaches back to the Roman and Atellan mimes is provided by the parallel development of English secular comedy at the beginning of the sixteenth century. Scholars have noticed the emergence of highly influential performer-playwrights such as Cherea and Ruzzante in the Veneto around 1500 and have noticed how these men followed the lead of public mountebanks such as Zan Polo and his son Cimador from the ruder scaffoldings of Piazza San Marco into the private banquet halls of the Venetian palaces.[1] It is precisely this time that saw the independent development of secular comedy in England, a moment which has never been more succinctly described than by Chambers: "The drama which had already migrated from the church to the market-place, was to migrate still further, to the banqueting-hall. And having passed from the hands of the clergy to those of the folk, it was now to pass, after an interval of a thousand years, not immediately but ultimately, into those of a professional class of actors."[2]

This transition from the piazza to the palace paradoxically was responsible for creating a public drama: it first gave the players a new prestige as private performers—retreating to their more sophisticated base of operations in the hall, they would soon re-emerge permanently strengthened as the companies of the *commedia dell'arte* and the licensed and liveried players who created the Elizabethan theater in London.[3] What concerns us here, though, is that transitional period within the banqueting hall, before the corporate consolidation of the companies. Certain of its most significant aspects have been described by M. C. Bradbrook with admirable clarity as follows:

Roughly, for the first half of the sixteenth century the theatre of the Hall predominated, where traditional arts mixed with sharp and novel controversy, and dialogue was eventually to challenge display. This, however, was not only the Hall of the great lord, but also of the school, college, or lawyer's Inn. The interlude developed as part of the feast. . . .

The sudden intrusion of players with a cry of "Room" for the Vice, the apparent irruption of members of the audience into the play, aided the real improvisation to which players must often have been driven. . . . It was the common fate of plays given at feasts to be interrupted by spectators' change of plans; and hired players might be turned off and on again like gramophone records. Nevertheless, the kind of attention that can be given in a closed building is always more concentrated than is possible in the open air; sharp debating-points must have been followed keenly by trained listeners. Spectacle became a secondary matter.[4]

This summary of the conditions under which the drama integrated itself into the banquet, or underwent, we might say, a kind of interiorization, brings us once again to the problems of perspectivism and epistemological theater raised in the opening chapters.

The first point to be noted is both inevitable and somewhat surprising, namely, that "spectacle" tends to become subordinate.[5] It seems obvious from our vantage point that "spectacle" is much more manageable within the enclosed confines of a "hall"—obvious not only because of the development of the early scenes and machines into the perspective box theater of the seventeenth century but because of the increasing elaborateness of production in the Italian *intermedii* and English court masques, which were not only the most direct heirs of banquet hall playing but the most scenically spectacular of contemporary performances. Both genres had their triumph, of course. The *intermedii* so far surpassed in interest the comedies for which they had originally served as intervals that before the century was out in Florence they gave birth to that most spectacular of dramatic genres, opera.[6] The masques of Jonson simultaneously were giving literary and social rarefication to a type which both before and afterwards served as the plot-pawn of playwrights in search of a revenge mechanism or as the park and garden mythology of a Miltonic afternoon at Bridgewater.[7] But both *intermedii* and masque were short-lived in pure form, for an obvious reason. Spectacle in itself, as the visual incorporation of the world into the theater through the development of the modern machines, was too simple in its basic equation; demanding audiences would not long be satisfied with the limited reflection that the world itself, this goodly frame, all beneath this majestical roof, is merely a larger theater of scenic wonders. In Italy we have the eloquent if late evidence of Bernini, who realized that his magnificent scenic machines had to be incorporated into an anti-spectacular and ironic context before they could take on any of the potentially epistemological force of the *commedia dell'arte scenari*. In England there was no Bernini, but on the whole the dramatists learned the limitations of the simple theatrical trope, visual or verbal, perhaps even earlier. A universal *memento mori* was presented every-where by a world which must many times have seemed quite literally to be a theater, a world in which the royal progresses, the parvenus with fortunes upon their backs and bran in their codpieces, the lord mayor-alty pageants with their conduit scaffoldings, and the courtly masques themselves came and went, while apparently inexhaustible, restless ener-gies were expended to produce a kaleidoscope of spectacle. And yet, as one historian has wisely observed, "after the day of the spectacle had passed, these same citizens saw the razing of the structures."[8]

At this level, the trope passed into the pompous circumstance which surrounds Shakespeare's kings, from Henry VI to Henry Bolingbroke, with all of their rhetorical sense of man in the costume of his earthly progress. "I did keep my person fresh and new," Henry IV tells his son.

> My presence, like a robe pontifical,
> Ne'er seen but wonder'd at: and so my state,
> Seldom but sumptuous, showed like a feast
> And won by rareness such solemnity.[9]

But, as we have seen in the mirrored Florences of *Abraam cacciò Agar* and *La strega*, the perspectives of the external theater tend to become merely metaphors for the imaginative "placing" of oneself in a shifting world which raises the internal epistemological question. If one's presence is like a robe pontifical, one may perform in a spectacle, but that leaves the almost explicit question very near the surface: does the robe express an essential presence or is that presence as evanescent as the pageant within which the robe assumes its moment of significant definition? The world is a theater, but Cusa had said that man knows himself through seeing and being seen—as spectator and spectacle, as audience and actor at once. It was this probing concentration upon the actor rather than the action which was responsible for the fact that the "hall" drama of the first half of the sixteenth century neglected specta-cle for speculation. The most successful results were two minor master-pieces, ambitious experiments of the "hall" proper—the one from the hall of a cardinal, the other from that of a college.

The earliest purely secular English comedy surviving to us is the interlude of *Fulgens and Lucrece*, "compyled," as the title page asserts, "by mayster Henry medwall. late chapelayne to ye ryght reuerent fader in god Johan Morton cardynall & Arche ebysshop of Caunterbury." And the most pertinent background to this play seems to me to be the account by his son Roper of Sir Thomas More's youth as a page in the household of Cardinal Morton, where "would he at Christmas .tyd sodenly sometymes stepp in among the players, and never studinge for the matter, make a parte of his owne there presently amonge them."[10] Prepared to envelop two parts of a grand state banquet at the Cardinal's palace, *Fulgens and Lucrece* is a pastiche of semi-dramatic genres in which a contest between a virtuous bourgeois citizen and a costume- and title-conscious patrician for the hand of the Roman virgin Lucrece is paralleled by a double plot which traces the less exalted struggle between two unscrupulous floaters for the favors of Lucrece's maid Joan.[11] But this pastiche has taken on in Medwall's hands a new, one might say a self-defining, form: *Fulgens and Lucrece* is a play which describes the origins of its own genre, a play about the origin of a play in a historic as well as formal sense.

It is clear that the secular interlude of the early English Renaissance grew up as an adjunct to courtly festivals, to the great banquets where players had to vie with dancers and musicians and roast beef and the effects of a good canary. And in such an atmosphere the banquet, not the play, is the thing, so that inevitably the actors had to adjust their efforts to the intrusions of the audience—at best a young Thomas More insistent upon improvising a part for himself; at worst the mercurial imaginations of a drinking, heckling, and yet powerful set of table companions. Medwall solved the problem in such a way that the intrusions of the audience became at once practically improbable and theoretically impossible: he installed his actors within the audience and made their "intrusions" the very structure of his play. The *débat* which is the surface subject and which is decided in favor of the self-advanced plebeian has been much discussed,[12] but the truth is that it derives from a text almost a century old wearied by popular translations into the vernaculars (including an English version twenty years older than Medwall's interlude) which was doubtless adapted simply to aim a compliment at that mighty host risen from the masses, Cardinal John Morton.

The real substance of *Fulgens and Lucrece* is the sliding structure which permits the two opportunists, properly nameless and labeled A and B in the script directions, to be everybody and nobody, to exist as a part of the audience and as a part of the play, to be totally confused about their relations with either, and yet somehow to make their own confused mistakes into new realities.[13] By improvising parts for themselves, even as More had done at the Christmas festivities in this same great hall, A and B rewrite the play of *"Fulgens and Lucrece."* This serves as more than a technical trick—a device to entertain the audience with a rougher level of play (as the jigs with their *fabliau* fun would vary the fare for Elizabethan theatergoers) and also to forestall its potential interruptions: this rewriting by the actor in the audience raises the question of values in the theatrical world which the banqueters themselves inhabit.

If the *débat* proper is only a convenient vehicle for subdued recollection and approval of the Cardinal's antecedents and efforts, the terms of presentation drive deeper into the heart of the matter. Publius Cornelius, the patrician suitor, is a familiar figure in the noble circles of the court, many of whose members sat watching the Cardinal's Christmas interlude. As his servant B tells us, Cornelius "were worthy to be a kyng for liberall expensis in all his dealing," but most especially in costume—in the robe almost pontifical.[14] The stockings are so costly they seem of "sylke and golde";

> they moste be strypide all this way
> with small slypes of coloures gay;
> A cod pece before, allmost thus large;

the gowns "have whingis behynd redy to flye, / And a sleve that wolde cover all the body." And, further, "There is never a knave in the house save I / But his gowne is made in the same wyse" (I, 725–61). This very Elizabethan Roman is dressing for a very particular role: "All is done for lucres sake" (769). A and B are confused about where the play begins because its society, like that of the hall whence they emerge, is a costumed, masking players' society; when B described Cornelius' slashed stockings, many of the guests must have stolen a furtive glance at their own legs. And all the more so because A and B foist their fictive confusion upon the auditors even before they themselves feel it.

When A enters to commence the play, he is no part of it. He is, rather, a servant in the cortège of Cardinal Morton who both taunts and invites the guests. They "are welcom eche oon / Unto this house withoute faynynge" (12–13). But A seems surprised at their lack of inventiveness ("There is no worde amonge this presse, / Non sunt loquele neque sermones" [17–18]) and at the host's failure to provide the prototypical entertainer, some "pretty damesell / For to daunce and sprynge" (23–24). Then B comes in to scorn such mountebank stuff and announce a "play." A looks him up and down and concludes: "I trowe your owyn selfe be oon / Of them that shall play" (44–45), a conclusion which B rejects with an ironic *tu quoque*: "I thought verely by your apparell / That ye had bene a player" (48–49). In accepting the mutual "mistakes," A implicitly sets the theme of the evening's entertainment by summarizing the society and the structure of the play: "I cry you mercy," he apologizes,

> Ther is so myche nyce aray
> Amongest these galandis now a day,
> That a man shall not lightly
> Know a player from another man. (51–56)

B, who has been told the "argument," recites it to the audience and to A. As B outlines it, the argument is taken from the source debate in that it closes upon Lucrece's appeal to the Senate for a matrimonial choice. This account, however, becomes a structural pivot in the improvisational modality which is the play's *raison d'être* inasmuch as Lucrece ultimately does not follow the source—or the "plot" as it is outlined by B: the Senate never enters the case, and the choice of Gaius Flaminius over Cornelius is her own—conditioned in part by the interference of that very B who at the beginning seems to know the "outcome" of that play whose order he will enter and subvert. The players enter, and B directs A to a vantage point from which to watch the performance. All goes on apparently according to plan for quite a time. The "Romans" enter, enact their rivalry, and the two "inductors" stand aside, much in the way of Christopher Sly slumping silently over the balcony when his clever confusion has gotten the story of Kate and Petruchio under way. Then all flies asunder and chaos becomes structure when Cornelius decides he needs a confidant-servant to expedite his suit to Lucrece. He faces the audience with an invitation to the budding aspirants for Thomas More's mantle of improvisation

> (So many gode felowes as byn in this hall,
> And is there non, syrs, among you all
> That wyll enterprise this gere?) (354–56)

and finds B so forgetful of the fiction that he leaps at the chance. A would hold him back, crying: "Be god, thou wyll distroy all the play"

(363), but *B* has changed the dimensions: "Distroy the play, quod a? nay, nay, / The play began never till now" (364–65). Illusion is infectious; *A* forgets as quickly as *B*, and tugs him at the sleeve to stay "out" of the play, whining "What shall I do in the mean while?" (369). *B* is rewriting the plots faster than he can think. "Marry," he reassures his companion, "thou shalt come in anone / With another pageant" (370–71). Before *A* has time to object, *B* is altering everything and plans to arrange Cornelius' marriage himself—suddenly turning back to *A* with a furtive warning to

> Hold thy pece, speke not so hye!
> Leste any man of this company
> Know oure purpose openly
> And breke all oure daunce
> For
>
> . . .
> This gere shall vs both avavnce.   (387–93)

From the shifting perspectives of *A* and *B* the audience and the play have first reversed reality quotients and then fused—and one can see the point as well as sympathize with the confusion, for what would-be servant of Cornelius with his flared sleeves and slashed stockings could manage for very long to distinguish his lord from the peacocks at the festival boards?

Next it is *A*'s turn to make the leap from England to Rome, and if he has been more careful about preserving the defining boundaries of play from the inundation of the living hall than has *B*, when he makes his decision it is an even more total, daring commitment than that of his friend. Accosting Gaius Flaminius for employment, he convinces the Roman that they have known each other previously and alters the plot of the inner *"Fulgens and Lucrece"* which he has been watching not only in the future—as *B* had determined to do—but in the past: he simply lies his way into Gaius' service by inventing an interview between Cornelius and Lucrece which never occurred, accusing the lady of double-dealing, and promising to win her for the plebeian suitor (575–685). And so the audience-actors plunge onward, the remainder of part I of *Fulgens and Lucrece* being the slapstick contest in which they vie for the affection of Lucrece's maid Joan. It is a contest possible only because they have entered a "play" in which Joan is merely an actress, and having overturned its proper progress while they woo and bumble and lie, they also have projected upon Joan their own confusions so vividly that pretense is forgotten and her role reforged into reality by their imaginations. And yet when all has been remade, *A* and *B* make another unexpected shift: they announce that Lucrece's decision will be made the next day, not only before the "characters" but "besyde this honorable audyence . . . so many as here be present" (1315, 1331). They then separate (rather than further incorporating) the audience from a play whose illusion is totally broken when they decide they must have an intermission because of "these folke that sitt here in the halle":

> Thay haue not fully dyned;
> For and this play where ones ouere past
> Some of them wolde falle to fedying as fast
> As thay had bene almost pyned;
> But no forse hardely and they do,
> Ussher, gete them goode wyne therto. (1417–22)

Nothing could be simpler than this epilogue speech, in which the actor steps out of both worlds, that of the play and that of the audience, to close the one and to revive the other to itself, to restore the more pragmatic, quotidian self-recognition of the spectator who through the illusion-glass of drama both discovers and forgets himself. Yet for those who have listened closely another problem has been raised concerning the power of that very imagination which is being deliberately disenchanted that the banquet may proceed. When the whole confusing performance began so simply with the two inductors mistaking one another for the actors they really were, it was B who knew the play and recited the "argument" to the audience and to A. But as part I closes, A's sheer engagement in the illusion has mysteriously transcended ignorance by restructuring the data. As an auditor he had been reluctant to compromise the play's progress. Once engaged, he is not only an actor and auditor simultaneously, but creator as well. B asserts Cornelius' social superiority, his riches, his blood, and A rejects them out of hand, assured that Gaius will win Lucrece. Indeed, he *knows* the outcome: "but come hether sone to the ynde of this playe," he tells B, "And thou shalt se whereto all that wyll wey, / It shall be for thy lernynge" (1386–88). There is no *way* for A to know, but he knows; through accepting the reality of his own imagination, A *has* remade it all. When B outlined the plot of "*Fulgens and Lucrece*" which had been retailed to him by the players, he was, as we have seen, mistaken: the decision does not go to the Senate. It is Lucrece's decision, and it will be as A imagines it, in Gaius' favor. As part I closes, then, it is justifiable to say that even while the illusion is being most violently broken, *Fulgens and Lucrece* is quietly arguing the power of illusion. In defiance of the laws of "reality," A's imagination has become an instrument of real knowledge; confusion has been translated into a mode of perception.

Part II is a less interesting effort. The banquet over, *A* returns to summarize the earlier action and to admit that he is himself a player, while the improvisational mode is kept alive by obvious and unpromising devices: the other players are late in arriving, and *A* self-consciously worries about the possibility that they will not show up. Then the player of "Cornelius" arrives to report that he was delayed because he was arranging a mummers play-within-the-play-within-the-play, a report interesting only because he has acted outside the script in the character of the suitor he acts within the script (61–140). Or at one point *A* turns to the audience directly when he has lost a letter with which he has been entrusted and inquires: "Syrs is there none there among you / That toke up suche a wrytyng?" (326–7). There is, indeed, only one moment at which the intricacy of part I is touched. That is at the close. Lucrece makes her decision in Gaius' favor and turns to the largely patrician audience to assure them that it is no denigration of "blood," but an individual choice: "I pray you all syrs as meny as be here / Take not my wordis by a sinistre way" (766–67). *B* pounces to her side in a double role, on the one hand as part of that audience to which Lucrece has just addressed this petition for moderate judgment, on the other as the servant who was once certain he could sway the "known" outcome of the plot. *B* refuses to accept Lucrece's *apologia*, insists that she has chosen "a chorles son" over a "gentilman bore," and flatly refuses to carry the decision to Cornelius: "Shall I do that erand? nay let be, / By the rode ye shall do it yourselfe for me!" (808–9). But the point of this performance is too transparently occasional: what humorless patrician at the tables would be so blindly proud as to hiss Lucrece's choice off the stage if, in doing so, he had to emerge from anonymity to join the waspish *B* as a spokesman for tradition? Lucrece is gone, and *A*, *B*, and the audience stand once again alone as they had at the beginning. "Why than is the play all do?" queries *A*, and *B* assures him that "and we were ons go / It were do streght wey" (875–77). Yet even at the end, when the actors have been put back into their greenroom and the banqueting hall turns to the wine and the dancing and perhaps even the "pretty damsel" tumbling whom *A* had expected at the first, the play itself is left open at one end—that which fuses it with the spectators. Before *B* leaves the hall he presents the author's apology for his work, and suggests:

> glade wolde he be and ryght fayne
> That some man of stabyll brayne
> wolde take on hym the labour and payne
> This mater to amende. (915–18)

Fulgens and Lucrece is not a complex play and does not seriously develop the questions it raises. But it does raise questions which will be probed later, and what is important is that it raises them structurally rather than discursively. The invitation to the audience to become playwrights at the close is a faint, almost indiscernible tracing of the plan from which *The Knight of the Burning Pestle* would be elaborated.. But the idea of drama and society as cooperative and mutually reacting faces of the imagination, of the spectator as improvising actor, has been launched, in the first comedy so independent of church and classics that it bespoke the arrival of the Renaissance upon the great stage of England.

 The other example of "hall" drama which will repay attention in our context is the anonymous mid-century school interlude *Jack Juggler*.[15] Here the actors do not emerge from the audience, and they are not, like Medwall's *A* and *B*, confused about whether their real status is within the play or outside it. But there are much deeper channels flowing through the structure of the interlude which forcibly engulf the audience.

The first thing to observe is that the apparent attitude of the players in *Jack Juggler* is almost antipodal to that of *A* and *B*. Where Medwall's are blustering—with a sort of inverted coyness in their early denial that they are actors—and thoroughly confused when they once enter into the action of the inner *"Fulgens and Lucrece"*—the Prologue to *Jack Juggler* is insistent upon the theatricality of the evening's entertainment and both overwhelming and confusing in his torrential initial *apologia* for comedy. Whereas the audience is subsumed into *Fulgens and Lucrece* only to demonstrate that the "players" have forgotten the measure of imaginative distance between them (as in *A*'s sudden query as to who among the banqueters might have stolen his letter), in *Jack Juggler* they are continually being confronted and addressed as an audience rather than as presumptive participants in the play.[16] The tricks are explained carefully by Jack before he perpetrates them, the characters are described before their arrival, the interstices are filled in with exposition which is unabashed, and a lengthy epilogue is supplied suggesting the significance of the fable—in part. In short, neither players nor audience are permitted for a moment to enter into the illusion that drama is generally supposed to achieve: the spectator is outside an artifice engendered for his pleasure and pastime. And this brings us to the argument on comedy evolved by the Prologue.

The first point is medical: comedy provides that relaxation for the mind, that "honest mirthe" which is "requisite and necessarie," as so many ancients attest.[17] The second stage of the Prologue's defense, however, seems so different as to appear contradictory: relaxation gives way to didacticism. Cicero commended "old cōmedie" (the term is not historic here) because it was "replenished with precepts of Philosophie," because it contained "mutch wisdome" and taught "prudent pollecie." "And in this maner of making Plautus did excell, / As recordeth the same Tullius, cōmending him bi name." Plautus, then, is a philosophic playwright, a preceptor of the stage, and it is precisely Plautus whom "the maker" of *Jack Juggler* elects as master, in order "too folow his arguments, and draw out the same" (51–60).[18] Yet somehow the resultant play is "not worthe an oyster shel," is "a trifling matter." But all of this is of a piece with the exaggerated insistence upon theatricality throughout, in that its confusion is so manifest as to demand attention. That attention is rewarded at the close of the Prologue's address for those who hear the sentence which coalesces the apparent contradiction involved in defending the comedy as both philosophic and trivial: "You may report and saye ye have hearde nothing at all" (72). "Nothing"; that is what the play is about. And it is a nothing into which existent entities have been annihilated in just the way of the Prologue's structure—through the combustion of simultaneous contradictions. It is a nothing whose contradictions emerge from manipulating just the dichotomy which the play insists upon: actor and audience, player and "real" observer. And it is further a nothing which is ontological in that it implicitly represents the doctrine of transubstantiation and explicitly represents what remains when the question is reduced, by sheer power, to contradiction.[19]

Jack appears on stage following the Prologue's exit, greets the audience with all the intimate aplomb of a music-hall entertainer, and reminds them that they have come to see a *play*, and a play by boys at that. Then he settles down to the business of exposition: "I am called Jake Jugler of many an oon / And in fayth I woll playe a iugling cast a non" (108). He has had trouble with a fellow servingman, one Jenkin Careaway, and his whole intention is "to make Jenkine bylive if I can / That he is not him selfe but an other man" (180–81). In the midst of this account, Jack interjects an oath which seems casual only until we realize that it sets the stakes for the entire *fabliau*-like plot at the same desperate level suggested by the "nothing" of the Prologue. If he does not succeed with Jenkin, cries Jack, "leat me lese my name for euer more" (111). Someone must sacrifice his identity, must be reduced to nothing. The plot vehicle is venially negligible, but the whole complex of Prologue and exposition has announced that it exists as vehicle, not as end.

Jack's mode of operation is simple—but again so outrageously neglectful of probabilities, so determined to be theatrical from a perspective internal to the plot, that it must re-emphasize the theatricality of the interplay between spectator and player. What Jack does is to follow Jenkin about, watching his petty gambling and stealing and general neglectfulness in order to have the historic data which will verify the external assumption of Jenkin's person

> (This garments cape, and all other geare
> That now you see apon me here
> I have doon oon all like unto his
> Fo the nons). (176–79)

Careaway enters (ironically, himself inventing a set of lies to cover his failure to carry out Master Bongrace's orders to escort Mistress Bongrace to a supper) and is soon accosted at his own gate by Jack Juggler. Juggler beats him off as an interloper while claiming Careaway's identity and post, and the unfortunate Jenkin first turns to the audience for help ("saue my life maisters for ye passion of christ" [509]) and then plays Kate to Jack's Petruchio: he will be, he says, "whom please you," but, he pleads, "giue me a new maister, and an other name" (538). The capitulation is only a temporary reaction; a moment later he cries boldly: "beate on me, tyll I stinke, and tyll I dye / And yet woll I stiell saye that I am I" (564–65). The only circumstance that can convince Jenkin is an intimate account of his own recent history ("Reherse me all that with out anye lye / And then I wol confese that thou art I" [599–600]). This, of course, is just the eventuality for which Jack has been prepared. The history is repeated, Jack's disguise is so absurdly good that he looks more like Jenkin than Jenkin himself, and the victim finally is reduced to inserting in the audience a sort of existential lost-and-found advertisement: "I besiche you hartylye take the paine / Yf I be found in any place too bringe me to me againe" (681–82).

He berates himself in the most uncompromising terms when Jack leaves (making clear that this time the loss of self is internalized, rather than that mere lip-service to Jack's potent presence which Jenkin had earlier provided), then goes to Mistress Bongrace to report the existential theft:

> by the waye I had a gret fall
> And my name, body shape legges and all
> And meat with one that from me did it stelle. (825–27)

The turn arrives when Jack reappears alone to petition the audience's direct approval for his success at turning Jenkin inside out, that is to say, making him believe that his outward appurtenances of form and history are more real than his psychic continuity. Discarding his costume, he cries, "Now let Careawaye be Careawaye agayne" (882). When Jack leaves, it is to be succeeded on stage by Jenkin and Master Bongrace, the latter incredulous at Jenkin's own credulity at things "no wyse possible for to bee" (889): would you have me believe, demands the clearly anti-transubstantiational master, "that on man may haue too bodies & two faces / And yt one man at on time may be in two placys"? (901–2). For Bongrace it is an impossibility or at best a dream,[20] for Jack a juggling trick to his own ends, for Jenkin a reflex of power:

> Nor I wold myne owne [e]yes in no wyse belyue
> Untyll that other I beate me soo
> That he made be belive it whither I wold or no.   (954–56)

From here onward there is not much to the play proper. Jenkin Careaway will never be careless again: he is totally confused, a confusion which is translated into stylistic oversimplification when he seeks Jack in the audience (989–91) and is reduced to incorporating his dichotomized being into the pronouns: "I maruayll greatlye . . . / How he I escapid I me beat me thus" (1061–62).

The play, the Prologue warned us, would be *nothing*; Jenkin has been reduced to nothing by the paradoxical doubling which is acting; transubstantiation is reduced to nothing by demanding what the audience (and Bongrace) realize that the juggling Jack has demanded of Jenkin ("to believe that one man at one time may be in two places"); and the audience itself is warned that every man stands in danger during these difficult times. "I praye god geve you all good nyght," says Jenkin in closing the play proper, "And send you better hape, and fortune / Then to lesse your selfe homward as I have don" (1140–42).

This is a disturbing *envoi* which is picked up and generalized by the Prologue-become-Epilogue who succeeds Jenkin upon the stage. "This trifling enterlud . . . / May signifye sum further meaning if it be well serched," he suggests. And here we are returned to the point of departure in the more apparent than real contradictions of the Prologue, who asserted that the play's tradition was philosophic even while it was an absurdly trifling, farcically "dramatic" play about a man who robs another man of his being with a robe and a few secrets, reduces him to nothing. The superficies of *Jack Juggler* are trivial sketchings only until we perceive them as metaphoric vehicle for a tenor which may be defined as theological, epistemological, or ontological. One is allowed to draw the limits where one wishes to stop only by blinking the inter-relationship between one's religion and one's philosophic grounds for measuring the essence of individual existence because the Epilogue's simile becomes scientific in a strict sense:

> Such is the fashyon of the worlde now a dayes
> That the symple innosaintes ar deluded
> And an hundred thousand diuers wayes
> By suttle and craftye meanes shamefullie abused
> And by strenth force, and vyolence oft tymes compelled
> To beliue and saye the moune is made of agrene chese
> Or elle haue gret harme, and percace their life lese. (1150–56)

In this school play of the 1550s space, like individual identity, is simile rather than adventure, and only the obscure hints in the ha-rangues of Prologue and Epilogue reveal that the audience is itself the substance of which this "trifling" play has been the monitory image. But the suggestions have not been too subtle. The attentive spectator would have heard that his witness was sought by Jack and by Jenkin, that what he was about to see was simultaneously entertainment and education—in short, because *Jack Juggler* was so artificially dramatic internally and in relation to the spectators, he was warned that reality could become a cheap drama at the altar as easily as drama could be-come cheaply transparent to those watching, while being desperately demanding of those who played.

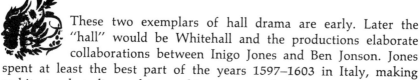 These two exemplars of hall drama are early. Later the "hall" would be Whitehall and the productions elaborate collaborations between Inigo Jones and Ben Jonson. Jones spent at least the best part of the years 1597–1603 in Italy, making architectural studies and it was his contact with the musical mythologi-cal spectacles of the great courts, the *intermedii*, which qualified him so thoroughly to join talents with Jonson to create the full-blown Jacobean court masque when the new queen requested a spectacle in which she and her ladies could arrive in splendor in the old Banqueting House in 1605. While we have little detailed knowledge on Jones's Italian stay except that part of it associated with Venice, his most recent biographer and critic is doubtless correct when he argues that "Venice, though ob-

viously of great importance to Jones, does not supply the courtly pattern which his own career was to follow. That is more probably to be found in Florence. There the Medici court under Ferdinand I was one of the most decorative and artistically productive in Europe. The court entertainments were the source of the masque in its most ambitious forms and Jones must certainly have had deep acquaintance with the masques produced at the Palazzo Pitti and the Palazzo Vecchio."[21]

The machines and even costumes for the masques designed by Jones echo Italian originals long in use,[22] and one wonders whether the influence did not go further. In the *Masque of Queens* (1609) the hags are suddenly stopped in their wild dance by a blast of music, at which "not only the *Hagges* themselves, but they[r] *Hell*, in w[ch] they ranne, quite vanished; and the whole face of the *Scene* altered; scarse suffering the memory of any such thing."[23] It is difficult to imagine that a man studying the outer and inner aesthetic of Italian courts would have missed going to Florence in October, 1600, to see the magnificent series of spectacles in honor of the marriage of Maria de' Medici and Henry IV of France. If he did so, he might well have described to Jonson a few years later the effectiveness of the stunted and leaden forest of Hades which suddenly replaced the pastoral wood in Jacopo Peri's *Euridice* in the Palazzo Pitti, only to vanish itself, "scarse suffering the memory of any such thing," when "si rivolge la scena."[24] Whether such speculation has any ground in history we are not likely to discover. But either collaborator could have read of the effect in Michelangelo Buonarroti the Younger's *Descrizione delle Felicissime Nozze della Cristianissima Maestà di Madama Maria Medici Regina di Francia e di Nauarra* (1600). In any case, the indebtedness of Jonson, Davenant, and other masque writers to the illustrated descriptions of such Florentine *intermedii* has been demonstrated in great detail by Enid Welsford.[25] The particulars do not much matter. What does is the immense overall shaping power of the Florentine spectacles upon the English court masque and yet the equally remarkable difference between the two forms. In Italy the *lazzi* and *zanni* were borrowed from the *commedia dell'arte* repertoires by the authors of *commedie erudite*, from Dovizi da Bibbiena's *La calandria* at one end of the century to Giordano Bruno's *Il candelaio* at the other, and since the *intermedii* originated as *entr'acte* entertainments at such comedies, one might have predicted crossbreeding. But, in fact, comedy and mythology went their separate ways, and the *entr'acte* became, as I have suggested, first the rival, then the destroyer of comedy. *Intermedii* expanded into the ubiquitous *melodrammi* of the *Seicento* against which Goldoni and others reacted when the Renaissance had become only a distant ghost. In the English court masque the worlds of familiar comic play and Platonic mythological spectacle[26] do meet in Jonson's anti-masques. But the anti-masque, if necessarily grotesque, is not necessarily comic. It becomes so rather late in the career of the Jonsonian masque and in great part as Jonson's defense against Inigo Jones's growing power to make fantastic spectacle too convincing an illusion.

Jonson's masques function, as Stephen Orgel has carefully argued, to incorporate the mythological world and that of the Jacobean court, the reveller-participants who are also audience, into an untranslatable vehicle-tenor relationship.[27] Orgel also believes that after the initial, obviously Italianate, efforts Jonson and Jones came to an understanding of their mutual aim and to a fusion of techniques which, if unappreciated at first, led to the popular anti-masque and to the later acceptance of a perspective stage (with proscenium) in England.[28] As he traces it, the first stage of the collaboration was one in which spectacular scenic effects (such as that of the disappearance of Hell in the *Masque of Queens*) reflected an emblematic mode of expression for Jonson's ideas, a mode learned in Italy not only from the *intermedii* but, we may remind ourselves, from the emblem books and mythographers.[29] Between that masque and *Pleasure Reconciled with Virtue* (1618) "poet and architect are moving toward a significant redefinition of the form."[30] The redefinition, insofar as the designer is concerned, is away from spectacular vertical effects toward a horizontal or perspective stage axis: toward increasing use of inserted flats, the *scena ductilis*. This decreases the opportunities for spectacle, reduces the dominance of the symbolic metamorphoses possible through the *periaktoi* and pulleys, and presents a world which is, "however idealized," "a version of the spectators' own world." This moved the Jonsonian masques in the direction of drama. But in realism there is paradox: "Jones is starting to conceive the stage as a unified machine, not as a series of individual effects; this is a revolutionary idea in the English theater. . . . But ironically, this is also the first step toward the poet's becoming superfluous."[31] As Orgel has argued, Jones was becoming increasingly successful with techniques which demanded the "collusion" of the spectator in projecting illusions that had enough "meaning and moral force" to transform the scene into an image of a Platonically idealized courtly life.[32] Misunderstanding or resenting Jones's vision of an ideal vision, Jonson in his own less ambitious way also set out to protect this interaction within a genre which was written for its participant royalty, not only at a philosophic but at a dramatic level. Having subjugated the fabulous machines to realism, Jonson was faced with a surprise: it seemed to him that they rose up again over the years to reassert their power over the imagination. As a result of this gradual realization, he not only broke bitterly with Inigo

Jones but also inserted himself as writer into the masques as a persona to stick the machinery back into its place.

In a later chapter we will note the effectiveness with which Jonson utilized his own image and a series of alter-egos in *Every Man Out of His Humour* at the end of the sixteenth century, as he would do in the series of poems celebrating "Charis" a quarter of a century later. When the popularity of the masques, jointly created with Jones dwindled into a murmur of courtly discontent, Jonson realized the special value such a device might have in the spectacular, but nonetheless social, genre invented for the royal family and their intimates.

The earliest instance is a self-conscious defensive maneuver. *Pleasure Reconciled to Virtue*, performed in January, 1618, had given the court its first view of the young Prince of Wales as a masquer, and the court was unanimously disappointed at Jonson's failure to create an exciting vehicle. But since the Queen had been ill and missed the performance, it was soon repeated, this time with considerably greater success because Jonson added a new anti-masque, *For the Honour of Wales*.[33] Into the addition Jonson introduces some Welsh gentlemen, supposedly just arrived at court, who proceed in a direct address to James to express their amazement that "you ursippe would suffer our yong Master *Sarles*, your 'ursips Sonne and Heire, and Prince of *Wales*, the first time he ever play Dance, to be pit up in a Mountaine (got knowes where) by a palterly *Poet*" (VII, 498). The discussion carries on for some time at the poet's expense, until finally the Welshmen are so delighted with the new Welsh additions that one excitedly turns to his cohorts to award the masque a laurel: "I pray yow now, and yow s'all see natures and propriedies; the very beast of *Wales* s'all doe more then your men pyt in bottils, and barrills, there was a tale of a tub, y'faith" (VII, 507). The Welshmen of the earlier masque are cutting through the boundary separating dramatic pretense from reality, and the "palterly *Poet*" can be mistaken in his person by no one. Add to this the fact that Jonson was so well known to many of his audience that Nathaniel Brent, disappointed at *Pleasure Reconciled*, wrote: "ye poet is growen so dul y^t his devise is not worthy ye relating, much lesse ye copiing out. divers thinke fit he should retourne to his ould trade of bricke laying againe" (X, 576), and one realizes that the references would have brought the author vividly into the viewers' imaginations. It is a mark of his personal distortion of the usual humility of Renaissance poets when addressing their great patrons that Jonson should enjoy thus becoming mock-critic of his own work. *The Masque of Augures* in 1622 opens with Peter Notch the brewer's clerk arriving at court with "some pretty presentation" because he has heard that "the Christmas invention was drawne drie at Court; and that neither the KINGS Poet, nor his Architect had wherewithall left to entertaine so much as a Baboone of quality" (VII, 632). And only a few months before, the Epilogue to the very popular *Gypsies Metamorphos'd* had admitted that the means of the metamorphosis was "a thing not touched at by o^r Poet; / Good *Ben* slept there, or else forgot to showe it" (VII, 615).

A more extended instance appears in *News from the New World Discover'd in the Moone*, the Christmas masque for 1620 (X, 596). In the summer of 1618 Jonson set out on his walking trip into Scotland; there he not only stayed with Drummond but was publicly feted at Edinburgh. Upon his return in the winter or spring of 1619 he was welcomed back to court warmly, especially by James, who was interested in his proposals for a Scottish poem (I, 77–82). Having missed the Christmas masque in 1619 because of his trip, Jonson took full advantage of the 1620 masque to welcome himself back, to commemorate his journey, and, incidentally, to place the pedestrian reality and the lunar voyage fiction in an ambiguous juxtaposition tantalizing to the imagination. Two heralds, a printer, and some like characters are discussing the discovery of the new inhabited world by a poet:

Printer. How might we doe to see your Poet? did he undertake this journey (I pray you) to the Moone o'foot?
I Herald. Why doe you aske?
Printer. Because one of our greatest Poets (I know not how good a one) went to Edinburgh o' foot, and came backe; marry, he has been restive, they say, ever since, for we have had nothing from him; he has set out nothing, I am sure.
I Herald. Like enough, perhaps he has not all in; when he has all in, he will set out (I warrant you) at least those from whom he had it, it is the very same party that has become i'th' Moone now.
Printer. Indeed! has he beene there since? belike he rid thither then.
Factor. Yes, post, upon the Poets horse for a wager. (VII, 518–19)

Such gamesome injections of himself into extravaganzas in which thousands of pounds were spent to the greater glory of the world's mighty perhaps seem more indecorous than they were in fact. It was the nature of the masque as a genre to involve its audience, even in Milton's culminating performance in the form, and Jonson as the king's own poet was an important figure in that audience. It must have been no little part of the pleasure of the performance for his velveted and bejeweled neighbors to turn and chuckle at the joke with the man who had put his own praises and apologies in the mouths of sometimes noble players. This is only a single instance of Jonson's habitual projection of himself into his works, as will become apparent in a later examination of *Every Man Out of His Humour*. It is more important to notice here, however, that once again it placed the emphasis in hall dramatics upon the audience interacting with actor and author, where *A* and *B* had placed it at the beginning in *Fulgens and Lucrece*. From that early, complex acknowledgment of Morton's rise from the ranks of commoners through *Jack Juggler* to the Jacobean masques, the point was not to help the spectator escape into another world but to tease him through the amazing looking glass into a recognition of the complexity of his own. Life can be fully realized only through artifice, as Ortega y Gasset argues in *Idea del teatro*. But if that artifice is to a remarkable degree mimetic, the mimesis must be kept within the limits of the charged dual awareness of which Ortega and Francesco Buonamici speak. That bridge must be maintained and the artificial perspectives of the "other" world ultimately dissolved into permanence in and through the imaginative growth of the spectator, who shares the creative act by taking it back into that world on his side of the stage.

There was one late Renaissance genius of the theater who realized this necessity more fully, perhaps, than any other. Gian Lorenzo Bernini incorporated in himself the roles of Jonson and Jones; as playwright he paradoxically subordinates, by exalting, Bernini, the grand artificer of stage machines. Probably no one has ever been more wholly responsive to the changes to be rung upon the trope of *theatrum mundi*. As a recent commentator observes: "Bernini was not only an actor when he mounted the stage and taught the others their parts, but was always an actor, in every moment of his days when he felt himself watched or pretended to."[34] But he was, moreover, very much on stage in the professional sense, as we know. The young John Evelyn reported from Rome how "the Cavaliero Bernini . . . gave a Publique opera (for so they call those shews of that kind) . . . wherein he painted the sceanes, cut the Statues, invented the engines, composed the Musique writ the Comedy, and built the Theatre."[35] Even if exaggerated, this account of his theatrical talents would not have satisfied Bernini, we can speculate, because it makes no mention of him as the Roscius of his age, who, Baldinucci reports, "played all parts admirably, serious or ridiculous alike, and in all dialects which had been presented on stage to his times." Indeed, he continues, "sometimes he needed an entire month to play all the parts himself to teach the others."[36]

In all of this activity, however, it was primarily as a producer of scenic stage effects that Bernini was admired and discussed in Rome and in Paris. The plays were written and attended with an eye to the realistic effects which Bernini was capable of manufacturing—the Roman flood, the crumbling building, the fire-within-the-theater—from all of which the audience started away in terrified conviction, or the double audience of the famous mirror play of 1637. Yet the very fact of their popularity raises one of the innumerable paradoxes surrounding Bernini: these "novelties" were hoary old traditions and must certainly have been raised to the scaffoldings from the diagrams and descriptions of Sabbatini's contemporary *Pratica* all too often in these years.[37]

The factor which dictated Bernini's striking appeal was, I believe, an extraordinarily total, organic commitment of all his individual theatrical talents to tradition.[38] His uniqueness (if we may phrase the paradox another way) lay in focusing his engineering and his literary abilities upon a single point—one so often made that it had been obscured by repetition.

Let us begin with the scene. There is a dimension in Bernini's understanding of theatrical machines which sets him apart from Sabbatini, whose stage designs paralleled and prepared for his own. Bernini recognized that the role of the machine, like that of the actor, was nothing so simple as the establishment of an illusion.[39] Baldinucci tells us that he "disdained having horses or similar realities appear on stages, saying that art consists in making everything of pretense, yet so that it appears to be real."[40] Something of this pride in the very artificiality of that which is constructed to create an illusion is revealed in the anecdote of Bernini's response to Louis XIII when the latter asked to be sent a famous machine for a sunrise, "which Bernini sent at once, with precise instructions; but as a coda he wrote, characteristically, these words: *it will work when I also send you my hands and my head.*"[41] This insistence upon a simultaneous awareness of the verisimilitude of effect and the artificiality of cause was itself once proposed by Bernini as a stage subject: "He said he had a great idea for a comedy; in which all the mistakes that happen in managing [stage] machines, with their corrections, might be revealed."[42]

We were limited to such comments until D'Onofrio's discovery of the manuscript draft for one of Bernini's plays—nameless, not quite completed, probably a detailed *bozza* for the Roman *carnevale* of 1644.[43] It employs old complications between servants and masters and the mixed dialects and masks of the *commedia dell'arte* tradition. Like *Jack Juggler* it boasts of its triviality, and like *Fulgens and Lucrece* it commands participation.

The clever *zanni* Coviello is the flywheel of the entire movement. His young master Cinthio cannot marry Angelica, daughter of the playwright-producer Gratiano, because he is poor, but Coviello suggests that a lavish display of coaches and banquets for a few weeks will dispose of the objection (thus giving us the first clue that artifice controls Gratiano's reality). The salt of the plot will be that Gratiano will bait his own trap. Cinthio is instructed in playing a double game: through his influence with the Prince he is to induce a bearishly reluctant Gratiano to write and produce a court play. Coviello is in contact with a foppish painter-actor-playwright Alidoro (quite possibly, as D'Onofrio argues, a satiric depiction of Salvator Rosa) who will pay handsomely to learn the secrets of the stage machines which lend splendor and fame to Gratiano's spectacles. Gratiano, caught, is seen writing the play script with the aid of Rosetta, his chambermaid, of whom he is enamoured, and directing servants in one door and out the other. There is a farcical deluge of preparations with carpenters, painters, and the rest of the crew who will prepare the machines. Through a chain of intrigues, the imported French painter Cochetto, in charge of scenic preparations, is persuaded to allow Alidoro to enter the secret workshop in the disguise of an apprentice workman and view the mysteries of Gratiano's machinery. So it is that Gratiano is betrayed—and at this point the manuscript abruptly ends.

It will be clear that Gratiano is a wry caricature of Bernini himself not very different from those which Jonson worked into the masques, poems, and *Every Man Out of His Humour* and that the play is about itself: the audience with Alidoro, watching the master's scenic wizardry (and its display doubtless would have provided the bulk of the entertainment), is meanwhile listening to the history of how and why that mastery had been practiced—watching machines which have become both subject and substance of the play. Further, Bernini has chosen the most "artificial," least "personal," dramatic tradition, that of the fixed *maschere* of the *commedia dell'arte*, to implement a play whose chief comic effects lie in its quite personal satire.[44] Leaving the identity of Alidoro aside, the audience knows Bernini, knows him to be "Signor Gratiano," and laughs because the artifice is so transparent that it redoubles every ironic touch—and there are many. After all, Bernini-Gratiano is the victim in his own plot; further he is the aging *padrone* whose advances are lightly parried by the maid Rosetta; he is the author of the fulsome flattery of his wheedling parasites ("Passano de secoli signor Gratiano avanti che la Natura dia al mondo de pari suoi, e però hoggi che abbiamo questa fortuna bisogna che tutti cerchiamo di conservarlo" [44]). But if Gratiano who receives the flattery is Bernini who invents it, the courtiers who flatter him are that very sophisticated *carnevale* audience which is laughing at him while he laughs at himself—and at them.

The machines' artificial insides must be made to "astonish," and when Gratiano explains the formula it is simple: "Faria che l'imitasse 'l naturel" (74). The technique for the machines and for the double structure of a plot which is as traditional as it is topical is summed up in the clearest terms by Gratiano's servant, in a maxim familiar to the Renaissance, from Tasso's Ficino ("Il Ficino, ovvero dell'Arte") to Shakespeare's Polixenes: "Infatt dov'è naturalezza è artifitio" (60).

But Bernini has further prestidigitations, for if Gratiano flows from the stage into the life of an audience which knows Bernini, at one point all seems to retreat into a corridor of mirrors focused somewhere behind the stage action. Gratiano, lusting itchily for Rosetta, calls her to him when he begins writing the command performance. The first character will be named "Gratiano." Rosetta at once recognizes the ironic shadow of tradition and cries "Ci sarà 'l Gratiano eh? e Pantalone?" Ignoring this, he goes on to explain that "Gratian lè inamorà de la sò serva" (a situation realized in the play because it is so traditional in the comedy scenari, one of which Gratiano and Bernini are writing). Rosetta titters when the name of "la sò serva" inevitably is "Rosetta." But as the plot unfolds from Gratiano's pen as a plan to keep this Rosetta as mistress until the aging wife dies, she cries out (with an objection which more than one Roman voiced to Bernini's plays): "Ohibò . . . everyone will immediately say that this is a gross, unnatural comedy." Anything but, Gratiano indignantly (and slyly) responds, and sets to continuing Gratiano's lines. At this point the script talks back: the Gratiano whom Gratiano is trying to invent walks out of the wings and the role, rebels against his would-be author, and simply refuses to have any part in such goings-on: "Signor, if the world is only a comedy, Gratiano wrote the plot. Pugh, shame . . . the heavens don't allow such wretches to enact their filthy fantasies" (65–66).

As Bernini mocks himself in the figure of Gratiano the playwright, Gratiano the creation mocks this playwright Gratiano. And if in the machines artifice mocks nature, in the play-within-the-play nature mocks artifice; the character refuses to be shaped by his author's intentions. But this is an uncontrollable "nature" outside the social order of the drama's conventional contract. It is the nature of a world that is self-inspired and that, in this sense, shares some daemonic region with the imagination through which the spectator agrees to expand and overleap his "reality," as Ortega phrased it, a region ultravida, ultramundo.

Bernini's play, like Jack Juggler, can insist upon its surface triviality made from the stuff of hackneyed convention because it is raising epistemological questions of how and whether one can know the nature of things which seem to shift levels of meaning as swiftly and deceptively as the machines shift scenes, as the actors shift identities. In such a world surface and sapience are disturbingly, but necessarily, laminated: "dov' è naturalezza è artifitio." But Bernini's play also demonstrated, to the noble Roman revelers, as *A* and *B* had demonstrated to the guests of Cardinal Morton and as the Welsh gentlemen come to Whitehall for the revival of *Pleasure Reconciled to Virtue* had demonstrated to James's courtly guests, that where there are artists there is also nature. The actor is always waiting to break through the artist's carefully confining plot from his wild world of contingency. We are made in the likeness and image of God, that first poet, first playwright for the *theatrum mundi*. But even the playwrights of the Renaissance at their best came to understand the limits of the analogy. It was becoming apparent that it is only as actors on this great stage of fools that we can become artists and rewrite the traditional morality script in the image of our own mysteriously metaphoric destiny.

CHAPTER V Seventeenth-Century English *Commedia Improvvisa:* Art over Nature

Near the opening of John Ford's *Lover's Melancholy* (1628) Menaphon, newly returned from his grand tour of Greece and Italy to his native island of Cyprus, recounts an extraordinary Thessalian adventure (classical in provenance and inevitably popular in the seventeenth century). Early one morning in a wood he heard "the sweetest and most ravishing contention / That art and nature ever were at strife in." A young man (who enhances the theme later by turning out to be a young woman disguised) is playing the lute so sweetly in his solitary corner of the forest that the "clear quiristers of the woods, the birds" all sit silently in wonder—all but one, "A nightingale, / Nature's best-skill'd musician," who undertakes the challenge to match every note. The contest is equal; the handsome pastoral youth "could not run division with more art" than the nightingale "did with her various notes / Reply to," until the boy

> grew at last
> Into a pretty anger, that a bird,
> Whom art had never taught cliffs, moods, or notes,
> Should vie with him for mastery, whose study
> Had busied many hours to perfect practice;
> To end the controversy, in a rapture
> Upon his instruments he plays so swiftly,
> So many voluntaries and so quick,
> That there was curiosity and cunning,
> Concord in discord, lines of differing method
> Meeting in one full centre of delight.

121 §

Under this onslaught of technique the bird

strove to imitate

These several sounds; which when her warbling throat
Fail'd in, for grief down dropp'd she on his lute,
And brake her heart.[1]

Nature gives to art the homage of imitation, and fails. It is little wonder, of course, in that this art is half-divine, rapture imped with practice— an art which recalls the image of Ficino plucking his ecstasy upon the Orphic lyre in Florence, or the omnivoyant portrait of Cusa's god in Ford's visual metaphor for the musical *concordia discors*.

An art which triumphs at the expense of nature; this is the burden of the pretty little Claudian vignette which Ford adapted, and which may serve as emblem for the thematic bass upon which the plays examined in this chapter sound a rich array of changes.

JOHN FORD: *PERKIN WARBECK*

John Ford was a careless architect, even by Caroline standards. It is, in fact, only in *Perkin Warbeck* that one can discern his power as a dramatist whose fidelity to theme is strong enough to elaborate a coherent structure in spite of his tendency toward tangential rhetoric and melodramatics. And *Perkin Warbeck* is the chronicle of a man who began as a pretender, in every sense of the word, only to finish as a royal martyr—of a man who acted his way into his own actuality. As we will have occasion to observe in the next chapter regarding the comedies of Heywood and Beaumont, one seems to be confronted with the almost autonomous force of a tradition shaping individual talent against its normal tendency. In the case of Ford, one might justifiably conclude, I judge, that the tradition shaped for an able poetic melodramatist his one true claim to the title of tragedian.[2]

Perkin Warbeck, says the Earl of Crawford, is a man whose "witchcraft of persuasion" powerfully

fashions

Impossibilities, as if appearance
Could cozen truth itself.[3]

(II, iii, 3–5)

And King Henry himself hopes to "have a charm in secret that shall loose / The witchcraft" (III, i, 33–34) with which the pretender keeps a topsy-turvy world enthralled. Such suggestions of magical forces engaged in inverting the roles of prince and pretender legitimate our recalling the popular "pretended-prince" plot of the *commedia dell'arte*, which happens to be the source of our one direct English expansion of a *commedia scenario*, Sir Aston Cokayne's *Trappolin creduto principe: Or Trappolin Supposed a Prince* (and it is interesting to notice that although *Perkin* is difficult to date, both plays clearly come from the thirties and are generally placed in 1633–34[4]).

A fine, slapstick mélange of devils, magic mirror rings, and powders for changing identities with onlookers, *Trappolin* is a play in which a pimping *zanni* is exiled but takes on the person of the temporarily absent Duke of Tuscany, while foisting his own identity upon the Duke, all of this through the machinations of a magician who in the end turns out to be Trappolin's "natural father, twenty years since banished ten years from Florence," a magician who—all confusions spent, Trappolin again Trappolin, and the Duke again the Duke, the young lovers on the plot perimeter joined safely and all in a harmonious mood—cries, "From henceforth I abjure my wicked art."[5] As the confusions heighten with the return of the true Duke, who appears part of the time enchanted, in the guise of Trappolin, part of the time in his own form, this Duke cries in bewildered dismay:

> Perhaps some fiend,
> Permitted by the heavens, assumes my shape,
> And what I do undoeth. (192)

It has been an educated guess, and only at the close does the gyrating devil's disciple sigh, "The weaker side must yield unto the stronger, / And Trappolin's suppos'd a Prince no longer" (203).[6]

It would be easy to see the background of *commedia* conventions out of which *Trappolin* emerged as also the chief motive force behind what is Ford's best and least typical play.[7] And no doubt the general "metamorphic" orientation which the coincidence of their appearance implies and which we have explored in earlier chapters did at some level of awareness influence Ford's choice of subject for his history play. After all, the chronicle as a genre had been out of fashion since the beginning of the twenties (Professor Ribner lists only five histories after 1623, even using a rather elastic definition, and one of these was never published[8]). But Ford grasped that this episode from the historians' chronicles of England was itself focused in that very theatricality which had become the stage's self-reflexive motif, and grasped, too, that in Perkin's struggle with Henry VII this theatricality was implanted in a sweeping context which demanded that questions of personal identity be argued upon the great stage of the political world. The chronicle writers had even provided the pattern of traditional metaphors with which we have become familiar, so that Ford did not have to invent either fable or figures or tone. What he did have to do was to give these all the meaning which they never quite attained in the accounts of the historians, and this he accomplished by combining them into a paradoxical paean to man's power of falsehood, to the art that mends nature.

William Rankins, a puritan critic of the theater, objected against actors in Elizabeth's heyday that "for a mean person to take on him the title of a prince, with counterfeit port and train, is by outward signs to show themselves otherwise than they are, and so within the compass of a lie."[9] It is as though Ford, in developing a Perkin Warbeck specifically so similar to the pretender met in the chroniclers and yet so infinitely different in substance, had seen in the subject a symbol of the great debate on man as an actor in the world of the theater and in the theater of the world. It is as though he were asking of Rankins and the multitude of critics for whom he spoke whether Augustine's ancient justification of drama might not be applied to the larger theater as well:

On the stage Roscius in will was a false Hecuba, in nature a true man; but by that will also a true tragedian. . . . From which now arises a certain marvelous thing . . . that all these things are in certain aspects true, by this very thing that they are in certain aspects false. . . . how could there be in a mirror a true image of man, were it not a false man? Wherefore, if it avails some things that they be somewhat false in order that they may be somewhat true; why do we so greatly dread falsity, and seek truth as the greatest good?[10]

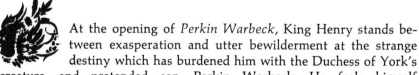 At the opening of *Perkin Warbeck*, King Henry stands between exasperation and utter bewilderment at the strange destiny which has burdened him with the Duchess of York's creature—and pretended son—Perkin Warbeck. He feels himself "frighted with false apparitions / Of pageant majesty," and yet paradoxically is himself reduced by this incubus "as if we were a mockery-king in state" (I, i, 2–4). In short, the drama opens as a species of actor's agon: the question it puts is one of negative identity; that is, who is

the player-king, the mocking lord of misrule who shakes a Falstaffian sword of lath? When we watch Perkin at the court of Scottish King James, and are made through the eyes of the Earl of Huntley

> to see the gambols,
> To hear the jigs, observe the frisks, b' enchanted
> With the rare discord of bells, pipes and tabors   (III, ii, 2–4)

which form his milieu, it seems apparent that this is a carnival king whose moment of pageantry must fade with the holidays. And clearly this is Henry's view as Perkin ultimately faces disgrace and death. Certain now in his own majestic superiority, he overrules the outrage of his followers at Perkin's haughty insults:

> let him range:
> The player's on the stage still, 'tis his part;
> A' does but act.

As Perkin continues his Yorkist version of history, Henry himself finally interrupts, however, to comment:

> Thus your aunt of Burgundy,
> Your duchess-aunt, informed her nephew; so,
> The lesson prompted and well-conned, was moulded
> Into familiar dialogue, oft rehearsed,
> Till, learnt by heart, 'tis now received for truth.

When Perkin objects that "truth in her pure simplicity wants art / To put a feignèd blush on," Henry loses all patience and brusquely orders,

> Sirrah, shift
> Your antic pageantry, and now appear
> In your own nature.[11]   (V, ii, 67–89)

The "antic pageantry," the testing and contesting of player-kings in their grimly festive rhetoric, certainly owes its debt to the pretended-prince *scenari* which eventuated in *Trappolin,* and yet these particular phenomena themselves must be embedded in the larger movement by which comedy gradually emerged from the folk rituals of the May game or the *carnevale.* And all of these forms we wish, in turn, to envelop within the still broader tendency toward epistemological perspectivism— toward viewing the world as a theater in which man is a Protean performer who seeks his place endlessly among the credits, now as player, now as playwright, now as director of the whole and even—with Bernini in mind—as artificer of the scene itself. As is so often the case in measuring the interaction of cultural forms, the more local case, the particularized circle of influence which seems logically and obviously most germane, becomes the most difficult to define. For example, we have noticed that *Perkin Warbeck* almost immediately introduces an ambiguous note of witchcraft around Perkin's amazing success, which is also an inevitable component of the pretended-prince *scenari* and which we see exploited shamelessly in the magic properties and the exiled magician who dominate the plot movement of the English *Trappolin*. The conclusion seems obvious until we turn over the leaves of that sourcebook by "a late both learned and honourable pen" which Ford himself takes note of in his dedicatory letter printed with *Perkin Warbeck*, Sir Francis Bacon's *History of the Reign of King Henry the Seventh*.[12] When we do so, we find that Bacon's account of Perkin's incursions upon Henry's peace begins: "At this time the King began again to be haunted with sprites; by the magic and curious arts of the Lady Margaret; who raised up the ghost of Richard Duke of York . . . to walk and vex the King" (VI, 132). Perkin, Bacon relates, "was a youth of fine favour and shape; but more than that, he had such a crafty and bewitching fashion both to move pity and to induce belief, as was like a kind of fascination and inchantment to those that saw him or heard him" (133).[13]

Much more important is the case of the player-king motif itself. For Speed the whole of Perkin's attempt was seen as drama, although it seemed to many "almost incredible, that such a bloudy play should meerely be disguised and fained" (750). As a prince, Perkin was never "in any point wanting to his part" (750), but when he fell, the show was closed. Sitting in the stocks to read his public confession, first before the gate of Westminster Hall, later in Cheapside, he concluded a play whose plot had become too repetitious and confusing for the masses: "From having thus beene made a publique spectacle, till all eyes were wearied with the view, and imaginations tyred with thinking; hee is convaied to the Tower of *London*" (757). Such brief emergences of the metaphor implicit in Speed's whole account grow into a dominant surface vehicle in Bacon's elaborate expansion. As Perkin first appears in *The History of the Reign of King Henry the Seventh*, it is as one who "could make his own part, if at any time he chanced to be out" (132). The Duchess, Lady Margaret, taught him to mix truths with pretense, "but still making them to hang together with the part he was to play" (135). "Perkin, by playing the Prince" (157), learned the discipline of a commander; "acting the part of a prince handsomely," he even remonstrated with his Scottish protector King James about plundering "his" English subjects. If Henry's representatives could scornfully upbraid the Council of Flanders that it was shameful their "country of all others should be the stage where a base counterfeit should play the part of a King of England" (145), yet much later, when James of Scotland had "begun to suspect him for a counterfeit . . . Perkin, not descending at all from his stage-like greatness, answered the King in few words; That he saw his time was not yet come; but whatsoever his fortunes were, he should both think and speak honour of the King" (187). Surely both player and plot were changing; before discovery came the reversal. And Bacon assures us, with the reversal, climax and denouement cannot be far behind: "Therefore now, like the end of a play, a great number came upon the stage at once" (191). With them came the capture of Perkin: "But from his first appearance upon the stage in his new person of a sycophant or juggler, instead of his former person of a Prince, all men may think how he was exposed to the derision not only of the courtiers but also of the common people" (194–95). Reversal upon reversal, but perhaps inevitable under the circumstances, since "it was one of the longest plays of that kind that hath been in memory" (203). Even as Ford's version opens with Henry feeling himself almost "a mockery king in state," so the historic Perkin laid down a proclamation of challenge to Henry VII, lord of that "misrule and mischief now reigning in England" (169).[14] But as the reversal of hopes came, so came the reversal of roles; Henry begins to act as though Perkin's designs are "but as a May-game" (161), and in the end he proves right: "As soon as he was comen to London, the King gave also the City the solace of this may-game. For he [Perkin] was conveyed leisurely on horseback, but not in any ignominious fashion, through Cheapside and Cornhill to the Tower, and from thence back again unto Westminster, with the churmne of a thousand taunts and reproaches" (195). With his public confessions, the player-king has become juggler; with his execution, the Saturnalian Lord of Misrule has become carnival scapegoat. It is Henry's opinion, and Bacon's.

This coursing of Bacon's running structural metaphor for his history of Perkin Warbeck's career encourages confidence in the juxtaposition of forms and sources under the rubric of "history." We can readily discern two "direct" historic sources for the form of *Perkin Warbeck*,[15] the pretended-prince plays, which explain why Ford chose an uncharacteristic subject in a no longer popular genre, and the historic chronicle from which he drew his plot. Both sources account for the general structure of *Perkin Warbeck* and for a multitude of detail in incidents and imagery; and if *Trappolin* (not to mention the Venetian performances on which it was based) was written by Cokayne at almost precisely the same time as *Perkin Warbeck*, this coincidence is counterbalanced by Ford's implicit dedicatory acknowledgment of Bacon's *History* as his preparatory reading. The obvious conclusion is that even the most certainly "historic" connections may, paradoxically, assume valid significance only when merged in larger cultural patterns; it would be foolish either to affirm or to deny that the player-king motif which structures *Perkin Warbeck* is a reflection of the ritual origins of comedy, as it would be equally foolish to affirm or to deny that it is a reflection of Bacon's *History*. What is encouraging is the coincidence which suggests that the play metaphor may have impressed itself upon Bacon's *History* less because of the hints in Speed's *History of Great Britain* than because the Renaissance was polarized, as I have argued, toward the conceptions of the world as a theater and as a dream. Turning to this latter pole as it is present in *Perkin Warbeck*, we are drawn back to our second, more restricted, observation from a reading of Bacon's *History*: what Bacon recounted in dramatic terms as a strange artifact of history, almost a by-blow in the reign of a clever monarch, Ford grasped as a tragic paean to man's Protean ability to create himself in the image of his own imagination. In the Restoration, William Wycherley would lament that

> most Men act Parts which are least their own.
> The dull grave Fool will ever act the Wise,
> The Coward be a Bully in Disguise.[16]

Ford would have read this as prologue to a truth: the fool and the coward learn wisdom or courage through the universal actor's art. The mask is maker of the man.

On a smaller scale Ford plays across *Perkin Warbeck* a harmonic undertone to the player-king agon of identity, an undertone heard in the imagery of evanescence. Henry, annoyed and frustrated, immediately realizes that Perkin is a "smoke of straw . . . packed from France . . . / T'infect some grosser air" (I, i, 115–16); he has followed every moment of his ominous history

> since this meteor,
> This airy apparition first discradled
> From Tournay into Portugal, and thence

Advanced his fiery blaze for adoration
To th' superstitious Irish; since the beard
Of this wild comet, conjured into France,
Sparkled in antic flames in Charles his court;
But shrunk again from thence, and, hid in darkness,
Stole into Flanders.

(I, iii, 35–43)

And yet the King is confident that "these clouds will vanish, / The sun will shine at full; the heavens are clearing" (I, i, 140–41).[17] His hopes seem at long last justified when King James of Scotland reminds Perkin of "how windy, rather smoky" his promises of armed forces have become (IV, iii, 71) persuaded not only by events but by the Bishop of Durham's judgment that Perkin has proven himself "but in effect an apparition, / A shadow, a mere trifle" (IV, iii, 13–14).

Henry cries out against reality: "Why, Clifford stabbed me, or I dreamed a' stabbed me" (I, iii, 90), when Sir Robert Clifford reveals to him that Perkin has infected even the King's closest confidant with treason. And King James of Scotland, accepting Perkin unconditionally, "be whate'er thou art," cries,

Come, we will taste a while our court delights,
Dream hence afflictions past, and then proceed
To high attempts of honour.

(II, i, 105–13)

It is an ironic invitation, for no one more than James himself has demonstrated the universal validity of the Earl of Crawford's observation that "this young Phaëthon" Perkin can so work upon people that "the meanest of 'em / Dreams of at least an office in the state" (II, iii, 16–19).[18] But Henry, triumphant, finally turns to his supporters with a sigh, to affirm:

Your king may reign in quiet. Turmoils past,
Like some unquiet dream, have rather busied
Our fancy than affrighted rest of state.[19]

(V, ii, 7–9)

Yet there is an unpredictable reversal, even within the King's own garrison, once Perkin is made prisoner; as the loyal Lord Dawbeney informs Henry, upon initiating the first face-to-face confrontation of the two "kings,"

I here present you, royal sir, a shadow
Of majesty, but in effect a substance
Of pity.

(V, ii, 32–34)

This transformation from shadow to substance, from scorn to pity, injects the disturbing possibility of autogenesis, the possibility that Perkin may have willed himself into reality.[20] The audacious hint that pretense can create comes full circle when, preparing for death, Perkin confronts his less talented predecessor in fraud, Lambert Simnel, to turn upon him the imagistic stigmata which had originally been his own:

> So a puddle
> By virtue of the sunbeams breathes a vapour
> To infect the purer air, which drops again
> Into the muddy womb that first exhaled it.
> . . . .
> But, sirrah, ran there in thy veins one drop
> Of such a royal blood as flows in mine,
> Thou wouldst not change condition to be second
> In England's state without the crown itself.   (V, iii, 59–68)

 The imagistic patterns of theatricality and evanescent dream focus the action not upon "history" but upon the question of "reality." But this is a question which is also put directly; and, in the end, reality, like the theater and the dream, becomes neither more nor less substantial than belief. Thus conviction does put crowns upon us all.

The first direct statement concerning identity is Perkin's, and in it he denies himself. Appearing before King James, he rhetorically opens all schematic stops in recounting how he was victimized as a child,

> How from our nursery we have been hurried
> Unto the sanctuary, from the sanctuary
> Forc'd to the prison,

and on in such a vein, until he turns to the story of how—once escaped —he was "fostered / By obscure means, taught to unlearn myself" (II, i, 49–69). Selfhood is lost in role; but the irony is that Perkin's account of his false history is the truth in reverse. He relates it as part of an assumed role, and yet it is more real than the role itself. Ends and means have crossed paths from opposite directions and continued on their respective ways.[21]

This confusion become fusion, a renunciation of truth that truth may be reformed, must be read in the light of the willing suspension of disbelief which Perkin activates in both King James and in his future spouse Lady Katherine Gordon, reactions which Ford has made follow immediately upon Perkin's autobiographical account. James affirms:

> Be whate'er thou art,
> Thou never shalt repent thou hast put
> Thy cause and person in my protection.
> . . . Dream hence afflictions past, (II, i, 105–12)

and Lady Katherine, as we have seen, sighs "I should pity him, / If he should prove another than he seems" (II, i, 119–20). Their active desire that Perkin should *be* the prince because he acts the role so superbly is glossed by Henry's comment on the traitor-friend Stanley: "I could see no more into his heart / Than what his outward actions did present" (II, ii, 31–32). Hence it is in the nature of things that Crawford will soon find that Perkin's conduct in Scotland

> fashions
> Impossibilities, as if appearance
> Could cozen truth itself. (II, iii, 3–5)

There is another face to this observation, though, a profounder realization of the entire psychic situation evoked by Perkin's development from ambiguous into ambivalent character, which is made explicit when Katherine, who has come before the condemned Perkin, brushes away all debate:

> when the holy churchman joined our hands,
> Our vows were real then; the ceremony
> Was not in apparition, but in act. (V, iii, 113–15)

"Act" has taken on a double sense in *Perkin Warbeck*, and, taken together, both senses legitimize the extension of reality beyond the confines of verifiable history. The drama *Perkin Warbeck* is, in a double sense, transcending its historic sources.

"How like a king a' looks" (II, iii, 73), King James admired when the "Plantagenet undoubted" first arrived at his court, and shortly after, when Stephen Frion advises Warbeck

> if you will
> Appear a prince indeed, confine your will
> To moderation. (IV, ii, 20–22)

Perkin reveals that he has converted himself:

> If, if I will appear!
> Appear a prince! Death throttle such deceits
> Even in their birth of utterance; cursed cozenage
> Of trust! Ye make me mad; 'twere best, it seems,
> That I should turn impostor to myself,
> Be mine own counterfeit. . . .   (IV, ii, 23–28)

The peace between the two is never clarified; Frion objects and Perkin apologizes—but in the psychically noncommittal terms of "speak what you will."

From this point onward, as Perkin's "historic" fortunes descend on the western turn of the wheel, his regal actions and internal actuality seem to rise together. If he has convinced a wife and a king of his claims upon entering Scotland, when he must leave in exile he exits to the universal cry of the multitudes, "a prince, a prince, a prince!" (IV, iii, 120). When he arrives in Cornwall to gather force, Perkin now echoes another player-king (but, with confusing irony, one whose claims were "real"), Shakespeare's Richard II, when he greets England with expectations of providential aid:

> we are safe arrived
> On our dear mother earth, ingrateful only
> To heaven and us in yielding sustenance
> To sly usurpers of our throne and right.
> These general acclamations are an omen
> Of happy process to their welcome lord   (IV, v, 3–8)

This is the role which will not, *cannot*, be rescinded. A royal St. Genest, Ford's Perkin has become—as even King Henry recognizes after his capture—his role: "The custom, sure, of being styled a king / Hath fastened in his thought that he is such" (V, ii, 132–33).

The seed of this conversion had been implanted in Perkin's chroniclers. Speed had noticed that "as it is so observed of some, that by long using to report an untruth, at last forgetting themselves to be the Authors thereof, beleeve it in earnest, so these honours making our *Peter* to bury in utter oblivion his births obscurities, he seemed to be perswaded, that he was indeed the selfe partie, whom hee did so exactly personate."[22] And Bacon had affirmed the judgment, saying that "himself with long and continual counterfeiting and with often telling a lie, was turned (by habit) almost into the thing he seemed to be, and from a liar to a believer."[23]

But the historians had withdrawn all imaginative meaning from their observations—as their genre had insisted they must do—by going forward to recount Perkin's confession of fraud, repeated in public disgrace in the stocks.[24] Ford was under no such obligation. His Perkin, too, would appear in the stocks, a grotesque carnival king on his way to death. But he would appear not as one of history's curiosities, a great pretender, a confidence man who had overplayed his hand; he would appear, rather, as the dignified symbol of man's ability to design his own inner destiny. Perhaps in the decadent 1630s the great Renaissance affirmation of the dignity of man was finally satisfactorily written, the history of a Faust whose imagination simply outgrew the worlds he thought he had compromised himself to conquer. Ford's Perkin makes no confession, and his persistence in the face of threatened death draws a confession of conviction even from the voice of Christianity, the chaplain, Urswick. At the close, he is convinced of what Henry had believed at the beginning: Perkin is a creature of diabolical magic:

> Thus witches,
> Possessed, even to their deaths deluded, say
> They have been wolves and dogs. . . .
> . . . .
> . . . the enemy of mankind
> Is powerful but false, and falsehood confident.   (V, iii, 104–10)

But it is at this point that Lady Katherine is brought to remind him that her husband is real, "the ceremony / Was not in apparition, but in act." If it has been magic, it has been of this world. And if, in some sense, Perkin has been deluded, been enchanted, dreamed, it has been a dream which has left this world less solid than the actor who has insisted upon making it the stage of his own imagined possibilities. As Perkin walks to the gallows, he turns for a moment upon us all, from his imagination's heights admonishing our substantiality:

> Death? pish, 'tis but a sound, a name of air,
> A minute's storm, or not so much. . . .
> . . . .
> Spurn coward passion! So illustrious mention
> Shall blaze our names, and style us KINGS O'RE DEATH.
>   (V, iii, 199–207)

It is this triumph of Perkin the artist over life and death which Ford was pointing to with the unique generic subtitle for the 1634 quarto: "A Strange Truth."

RICHARD BROME: THE WORLD AS ANTIPODES

Chapman and Ford in their various ways explored the terrible and triumphant power of the imagination as a faculty of total re-creation, blowing away fact and reason, principle and plot, as insubstantial bubbles. If, stretched on the tenters of absolute chronology, Ford was a Caroline, in his simultaneously somber and garish temperamental landscape, in all of his rapports and formations he was, like the others, a Jacobean. There is no need here to rehearse once more the factors at work to alter the mood of England under Charles. But perhaps our method of writing an unhistoric history by means of juxtaposition can in itself say something pertinent about an important vector of that alteration by setting against *Perkin Warbeck* the "pretended-prince" plot as it was developed by Richard Brome, Jonson's protégé—as servant, secretary, actor or all three[25]—and in every sense a Caroline dramatist.[26] Such a juxtaposition, too, teaches us where to look for the principles which order his best plays and—somewhat surprisingly— makes clear the fact that Brome is the most accomplished and serious dramatist between the Jacobean masters and Dryden.

It is useful to look first at *The Queen's Exchange*, a play not printed until 1657 but dated usually in the early 1630s on the basis of a variety of echoes and allusions;[27] the date may seem even more probable in the light of our earlier discussion because this constitutes Brome's first experiment with the "pretended-prince" theme.[28] The play centers on the political marriage projected between Osric, King of Northumbria, and Bertha, Queen of the West Saxons. For opposing the marriage, the late Saxon king's old and honest adviser Segebert is summarily exiled. This figure (patterned transparently on Shakespeare's Gloucester) has a patricidal son, Offa, and a loyal but distrusted son, Anthynus, the latter of whom shares his exile. Leaving Saxony, Segebert determines to go directly to Northumbria to try to dissuade Osric himself from the politically unsound marriage.

Osric, meanwhile, has his own complications: his ambassador to Bertha and closest friend, one Theodric, has returned not only with Bertha's picture and promise but also with a portrait of Segebert's daughter Mildred, whom Theodric had wooed for himself during his embassy. Mildred's picture overturns the King's reason with a sudden love which betrays both his betrothal to Bertha and his loyalty to his friend; he is so powerfully affected that he literally falls at Theodric's feet, sick in heart, body, and mind. As he falls, Theodric cries: "Call the Kings Physitians!"[29] and Brome has introduced for the first time the psychiatric manipulation of reality which is one of his most persistent— and revealing—concerns.[30]

The first treatment is attempted by one of the lords of Osric's Council, who comes upon Jeffrey, a country natural whom he takes to court: "The Kings disease is melancholy, and thou mayst do him more good then a whole Colledge of Physitians" (484). This Fool parades with bawdy and some satire through the court but in the end is never integrated into the King's problem, as is his prototype in *Lear;* his appearance is so forced and his impact so futile that one may read him as Brome's gesture of rejection toward old symbols that have become too simple and too magical for a world with more complex surfaces and less profound roots in the ritual past from which the Fool's traditional power was drawn. One may read Jeffrey so, or one may choose to conclude that Brome was still glueing together a pastiche of old pieces of business without matching the joints. At any rate, by act III the courtiers are more at a loss than ever and the infection has spread: he is "sick enough to be pray'd for," and they are "sure 'tis a disease / Both to himself and all that come about him." He is

> brain-crack'd, lunatick and Frantick, mad,
> And all the Doctors almost as mad as he,
> Because they cannot find the cause. (497)

The doctors cannot cure Osric because in this play melancholy has come through a benevolent if involuted destiny, and its cure will be worked out in the parallel and crossing patterns of dream inversion by which that destiny works. The dream motif is introduced at the beginning of act III in the tale of how the King takes his rest:

> Troth as mad mortals do; we cannot tell
> Whether he sleeps at all or not. Sometimes
> He seems to sleep, but then his troubled thoughts
> Expresse themselves in sighs, in suddain starts,
> In groans, and sometimes speech of od confus'd
> And indigested matter; then he leaps
> From off his bed, calls for his horse and Armour
> Swords, Spears, and Battleaxes. But anon
> Bids all be let alone; and calls for books,
> . . . .

> ... then walks forth
> Into the Groves and Thickets ...
> ....
> In those obscure Meanders which his melancholy
> Has led him to. (498–99)

If the world has become merged with nightmare, the King has tried to cure himself by costume and pose. By symbolically acting an emblematic charade with love he has hoped without success, he tells us, to subdue the dreamer with the actor:

> To be completely arm'd from head to foot,
> Cannot advance the spirit of a King
> Above the power of love, nor to be clad
> In poorest habit of humility
> Can mortify the least of the desires
> That love enflames man with. No outward dress
> Can change or make affection more or lesse.
> I have tried all the ways I can to conquer
> Or to humiliate my raging passion. (500)

There is fine irony in the King's effort, for it is precisely acting which *will* invert the dream again and restore a reality with which reason and passion can both live at peace, but it is not the King himself who can write the plot.

To see how this plot develops one must look back to the exiles. Segebert is wounded by bandits (led by his son Offa) and, while Anthynus seeks help, is carried off by a hermit; this hermit in the end proves to be his old enemy and ultimate savior, Alberto. When Anthynus returns and discovers his father's disappearance, he is seized by a mysterious, prophetic sleep accompanied by the sound of recorders: "Ha! do I hear or dream? is this a sound, / Or is it but my fancy?" he cries as he sinks under to behold a vision of Saxon kings whose dance seems to imply his own succession; and after the vision Anthynus cries again:

> Am I
> Alive, or dead, awake, asleep, a man,
> Or airy ghost? Or did I see or dream?
> ... It were more idle then a dream can be,
> For me awake to think it possible
> I should become a King
> ... it must
> Be then a dream. (505–6)

But waking into this dream, Anthynus at once sleeps again, only to be discovered by Northumbrian courtiers, who mistake him for Osric, with whom he is identical in appearance. These lift him sleeping and transport him to the palace with the hope that "when he has slept it out, he will perhaps / Be cur'd" (507). Destiny goes by dreams, and this principle ties the fates of Osric and Anthynus in a bond of mystery which (like the aborted function of the Fool, Jeffrey) seems aimed only at frustrating conventional expectations. Even as Anthynus is being carried to Osric's palace asleep, Osric with his confidant is himself preparing to sleep—perchance to dream:

> But not to take a thought unto my fancy
> By my soft dreams, but of my beauteous *Mildred.*
> Nor will I in sleep or waking think of any
> Other adventure. (507)

When the sleeping Anthynus arrives before the King—amidst slapstick confusions and surprise no more exalted in tone than those in *Trappolin* —Osric decides to have the fortuitous and timely guest take his place while he goes incognito as a pilgrim to woo Mildred: "I'l give him all I have during his stay. / Exchange myself with him and be beholding" (513). It can be done because "all his dimensions bear the same proportion / To outward seeming as your Royal Person" (512), in the observation of one courtier. Surely, we assume, here in this mysterious physical identity, reinforced by the psychic sympathies which draw both men simultaneously to sleep and dreams of future delights, we can recognize the preparation for one of the almost inevitable tragicomic tropes, that of the lost and recovered royal son. But in *The Queen's Exchange* the old mechanism is not activated; Anthynus is not Osric's son, but a stranger whose resemblance to the point of identity is not even rationalized by the crude magic of Trappolin's mirrors and powders. Anthynus is simply an antipodal mirror image of Osric—identical to the eye but moving in an opposite direction.

Osric's rather smug mock-generosity to the pretended prince is unwittingly prophetic. When the King has silently departed for his pilgrimage of love, courtiers uninitiated into the scheme discover Anthynus bound to his bed, mistake him for the King, and attack the latter's confidants with all variety of accusations. Only Anthynus—like a Saxon Segismundo here as in the denouement—is awake to the reality of his own identity, and, paradoxically, his insistence upon the truth draws the physician to advise sleep:

> such fancies fall
> Naturally into this disease, which now
> Is almost a wild Phrensie, that will seldome
> Suffer the Patient think himself to be

The person that he is . . .
. . . could I fasten but a slumber on him.   (526)

It is a romantic comedy of errors which continues until a "Genius" (whence and why one never learns) appears to whisper to Anthynus who, as he awakens, "taught / By hidden inspiration" (528), realizes that he can instrument the earlier dream prophecy of his own rule over West Saxony by impersonating Osric in confrontation with Bertha. But even with this union of supernatural inducement and rational plan Anthynus is bemused: "yet me thinks / This is so like a dream" (529).

The marriage of Anthynus and Bertha is celebrated in dumb show, and the last act develops in a pattern of mistaken identity compounded. The disguised Osric arrives in Saxony, is immediately taken for Anthynus, and is imprisoned for the supposed killing of the missing Segebert; as one courtier here sums up the confusion so patently antipodal to that we were shown earlier in Northumbria,

If I am I,
If you are you, if any thing be any thing,
It is *Anthynus*.   (532)

And it is not. Action and ambient tone alike in this wild complication are familiar from dozens of similar frenzies in the *commedia dell'arte scenari*. In *Trappolin*, to return to that useful touchstone, the Trappolin-Duke reversals of identity mount to shameless farce in the final act, and the inherent farcical note is allowed free development in Brome's play. Indeed, he makes every effort to emphasize it by interlacing the rapid shifts in mistaken identity with a complex and changing series of lies about the blood relationship of Mildred and her lecherous brother Offa, told by a nurse intent on warding off incestuous rape, and by introducing a wild skit in which starving bandits are resurrected from a trap— with their teeth firmly set in the buttocks of their clowning, terrified rescuers.

This is not another *commedia dell'arte* plot expanded in the manner of Cokayne's *Trappolin creduto principe*. Over all the broad comedy situations and flourishes Brome has cast the tragicomic shadow of a desperate melancholy to be "cured." But this "cure" is not conceived in the old terms, as a merely outward symbolic gesture of the individual's reabsorption into the harmony and order of a total situation, like the cure of Duke Alphonsus' madly mistaken love at the denouement of even so serious a play as The Gentleman Usher, for example. Brome's "cure" is conceived of less as a return to reason—in this generalized sense of completion of a universal harmony—than as a return to reasoning as an individual means of control over one's journey toward desired ends. When Osric is told of Anthynus' successful, although allegedly mad, maneuvering, he himself is wryly rational: "It seems he was not so mad, but he could take / The Queen into my bed" (541). And when, all confusion spent, Anthynus as a true king steps out of his assumed role to confront Osric, he triumphs without apology:

> [I] will no longer personate him;
> But now be it known to you that I am no *Osriick;*
> But he that warns you call me so no more.   (545)

When imagination could knock men's heads against the stars in that tradition of mysterious affinities and inspired enthusiasms some of whose philosophic and critical manifestations we have examined, Perkin Warbeck could use it to transcend reality, and, as actor, defy the little world of reason. But Anthynus is a man of a different school, where the discipline is subtler and one must study the script with attention. Perkin acts that he may lose himself in the role, Anthynus that he may hide himself. The one welcomes and scorns death because he has lived a mystery that makes him too large for the theater of the world; the other wins a throne because he is the best actor in a world where all men are actors, dissimulating their ends and implementing them by disguise and by that design which in the political life of the seventeenth century came more and more often to be designated by the very theatrical term "plot."

In these two plays written almost simultaneously, one with the voice of a world dying and the other of a world not yet formed in its society and sensibilities, the antipodal conceptions of the trope that man is an actor are clear and real. Still, Anthynus is not a Restoration protagonist, and when *The Queen's Exchange* closes and Segebert is revived to greet his now-royal son, his reaction to the strange logic of events seems appropriate in the face of all the rationalism: "If this were real now, and not a Dream" (547). For Brome has allowed us to glimpse one world only through the thin but distorting fabric of another which he has superimposed upon it. The latter is the world of absolutely incredible coincidence and supernaturalism about which Brome is so insistent precisely because he refuses to justify it. Anthynus is not Osric's son, just a fortunately and fortuitously placed mirror image. He is sent to sleep by a power he cannot withstand and given not only a dream vision but its interpretation by a "Genius" ("I *hope* by some good Angel," he casually says in accepting the advice). This is a magic with obvious affinities to Lord Strozza's Platonic dreams rather than to the wizard in

Trappolin and his *commedia dell'arte* ancestors, yet with less rationale than either. *The Queen's Exchange* presents us with a game in which all the procedures are rational and the premise from which they must move absurd. It seems historically significant that, different in all other respects from Brome's play, the heroic drama might equally accurately be described by the formula I have just used in analogy, for that genre would be born primarily out of the simple and awesomely stringent rationalizing of the absurd conventions of tragicomic romance. Brome inherited dichotomies, I am suggesting, from history, from the fact that he *was* a Caroline dramatist. It is a tribute to his instinct as a playwright and to the strength of the tradition this book is tracing that he never tries to resolve them or to force an impossible choice. Rather, the elements which confront one another in *The Queen's Exchange*—dreams, dramatics, and that toward which both in their ways tend, therapeutics for the ruptured or raptured reason—remain the burden of Brome's explorations. As was proper to a sensitive Caroline he turned his back upon harmony for the harder way of dialectic. It is a path worth following in three late plays: *The English Moor, The Antipodes,* and *The Jovial Crew.* The first is prologue, the last a lovely epilogue to *The Antipodes* which, perhaps better than any other drama, summarizes the sophisticated but simplicity-seeking mentality of an age which foresaw clearly neither the civil war nor the Restoration, but glimpsed what both might be.[31]

Amidst contract difficulties and legal haggling with Richard Heton, owner of the Salisbury Court Theatre, where the King's Revels company acted, and with his professional life complicated by his ties to an old friend, William Beeston, whose players at the Cockpit needed a pen, Richard Brome received an aesthetic, if not financial and psychological, reprieve during the long and virulent London plague of 1636–37. If it enforced an idleness among the players, it gave to the playwright an opportunity to formulate and articulate his principal insights in a way impossible under the pressure of continuous writing and production. As a result, *The English Moor* contains the ideas which we have seen emerging in Brome's plays, and they are reworked into a carefully structured expression in *The Antipodes.*[32]

The English Moor, or the Mock Marriage is a complex series of parallel mechanisms which permit two sets of young lovers to surmount the obstacles of fortune and marry. Its central action revolves around a usurer (Quicksands) who has married a young ward (Millicent), forced into this May-December marriage; its central "business" is explicitly, if satirically, borrowed from Jonson's *Masque of Blackness;*[33] and its denouement mocks while imitating with tongue-in-cheek comment the easy disguises of Jonson's late allegorico-Morality method.[34] Still, the play works all of these topical and conventional pieces into the pattern of Brome's long-established concerns.

Quicksands, an old pawnbroker, has managed to gain Millicent through the aid of her guardian-uncle, although she was known to be the fianceé of Theophilus. He, in turn, is the equally hot-tempered son of Rashly and brother to Lucy, who loves and is loved by Arthur. Unfortunately, Rashly and Arthur's father, Meanwell, have created a blood feud by presumably challenging and killing one another over a bowling match—this deception is engendered by the elder protagonists for negligible motives which dovetail with tragicomic aspects of the plot which itself focuses on the aggressively male disguise of Dionisia, Meanwell's daughter. But these are only mechanisms to rationalize the typical Brome situation: Arthur (1–2, 20), Lucy (10, 18–20), and Theophilus (55–56) are all driven into dangerous lovers' melancholy by their untenable situations and must be cured—and this cure must certainly involve the liberation of Millicent from Quicksands. The abortion of this unnatural marriage begins on the wedding night, when the town gallants in debt to the usurer invade his house with a mythological masque of "horns," in which "*Cupid* and *Hymen*" are shown as they "fell at bitter odds" over marriage and so divided: "*Cupid* no more of *Hymens* matches fram'd; / Nor *Hymen* married those that love inflam'd" (15). The result is a show of symbolic horned beasts which so maddens Quicksands that he cannot consumate his marriage (15–17, 23–24), an indication of yet another psychic imbalance to be corrected.

As the masquers dance out, the old man and his young bride agree that he will not make marital demands upon her for a month if she will agree to stay in his household disguised as a Moor. To her disgust, Quicksands then goes up and down the town reveling in the taunts of all those to whom he has given out that he has been abandoned. The climax of this behavior is his announcement of a banquet at the end of the month, to which he invites all the gallants who have mocked him in the masque and in the streets. He plants the rumor that the occasion for the celebration is Millicent's death in the country, a maverick runaway:

I
(To avoid the scandal of Hypocrisie,
Because 'tis plain she lov'd me not) invite

You and your like that lov'd her and not me,
To see me in the pride of my rejoycings.   (54)

His plan in all this self-humiliation is to present a counter-masque
of Moors in which he will display all its weaknesses to his audience, at
the close of which he will triumphantly reveal the major Moor to be
his disguised wife. The masquers enter and present a dream masque:
"The Queen of *Ethiop* dreampt upon a night / Her black womb should
bring forth a virgin white" (65). The legend of the masque is that the
baby was born black and will only turn white upon marriage to a white
man which gives the players the chance to try every gallant and find
him wanting as a match, for embarrassingly realistic reasons (65–67).
The plan goes quite well, but Quicksands has let one of his dismissed
servants know of the existence of his bastard idiot son, hidden away in
the country many years ago. The gallants have learned this morsel of
gossip and have built a counter-counter-masque in which the servant
himself is to act the principal role of the idiot (43–44, 47, 54–55, 62,
67–71).

With the introduction of this semi-impostor, whose value to the
farce is elevated by the solemn fiction that he has made Quicksands
grandfather to sixteen bastards, madness and mockery permeate every
corner of *The English Moor*: theater as masque is countered by masque
which is countered by the convincing—because carefully rehearsed—
"play" of the idiot. When the elder Meanwell and Rashly opportunely
appear to stop all violence and to obviate the feuds (their arrival underlining the theatricality of their original "plot" to disappear by explicitly
pointing to its origins in the "old play-plots" of Jonson), theatricality as
a tool of manipulation has run its course: Arthur and Lucy can regain
their balance through regaining the love the denial of which originally
caused their psychic upheaval—their fathers only pretended to quarrel
and die that they might take a leave of absence to right old wrongs (10,
59, 72–75). Even old Quicksands is brought to his senses and willingly
relinquishes his quasi-bride. And yet there is Theophilus left to show
that manipulation, even with counter-manipulation, is not all. When the
older men appear and it is clear from all the frantic action that he can
have his Millicent, he is "stricken with an extasie of joy" (79). In this
suspended state he cries out the epigraphic summary which attaches
The English Moor to our tradition:

I see, I feel, I hear and know ye all:
But who knowes what he knowes, sees, feels, or hears?
Tis not an age for man to know himself in.

The ecstasy and bemusement are real; they result from and counter all of the carefully or crudely rehearsed masques of management within the play. Theophilus falls into a "slumber"—from which, says his father in typically theatrical terms, he, like all the rest, may be awakened to "conclude all in a comick scene" (80). The awakening comes when the still mute (dreaming?) Theophilus is awarded Millicent by her repentant uncle (85), and the drama closes in a triumph of young nature and elderly disguises converging upon a dream of love. In rapture, Theophilus has inevitably fulfilled the dream prophecy which began as drama: united with him, the English Moor has not only turned white, but become the symbol of how within nature there is

> an art
> Which does mend nature, change it rather, but
> The art itself is nature.

Youth has found youth through a dream masque which in the end became a drama of dream's fulfillment; plot became prophecy in a way no one quite foresaw.

Brome's joke in *The English Moor* at the expense of the "old play-plots" in Jonson's "dotages" points too directly at their central weakness to be entirely benevolent. Its impact is complicated, however, by the improbable return of the older generation to set all right which had gone wrong after their (weakly motivated) disappearance. The simultaneous satirization and employment of disguises—which are flippantly casual and at the same time absolutely impenetrable—shows that Brome understood that Jonson's late use of this device, successful or not, was the embodiment of a clothes philosophy, a probing of reality, rather than a mere mechanism.[35] In *The Antipodes* he made a fresh start upon the point. *The Antipodes* is certainly the most "original" of Brome's plays, if we understand that probably meaningless epithet as indicating the play most characteristic of the author.[36] As we have noted from time to time in this study, Brome was never afraid to adapt old matter to his own purposes, however, and in *The Antipodes* he has turned once again to *The New Inn* as the stuff for his play, perhaps sensing that in *The English Moor* he had cultivated only a very small corner of a ground fertile for his own peculiar invention. In doing so, he for once overmastered his great teacher—which is perhaps accomplishment enough for any career.

The New Inn centers in the two Court of Love sessions, carefully staged and yet *ex tempore* theatrical artifices which are embedded in a nest of disguises and roles both within and surrounding the sessions of Love. The Frampul family all are incognito from one another and from the world. They wear the absurd disguise props, the eye patch, the false beard, the costumes which seem deliberately drawn from the motheaten trunks of a vaudeville burlesque group; the lady's maid Prudence is inverted into the Queen of Love in a gown of her ladyship's which must make do because the tailor's wife is playing countess in the gown that should have been hers for the occasion—all this extravagantly inept shifting is the physical ambient of the amateur play, in imitation of the Caroline court's amateur playing at Platonic Love games. And this all envelops a question of identity formulated when the Host asks: "But is your name *Loue-ill*, Sir, or *Loue-well*?" and Lovel replies: "I doe not know't my selfe, / Whether it is."[37]

The "Host" almost immediately announces the symbolic universality which the exaggerated theatricality aims to establish as the inner identity of the play's action: he describes his own relation to his Inn, a place

> Where, I imagine, all the world's a Play;
> That state, and mens affaires, all passages
> Of life, to spring new *scenes*, come in, goe out,
> And shift, and vanish; and . . . I haue got
> A seat, to sit at ease here, i'mine Inne,
> To see the *Comedy*.   (I, iii, 128–33)

But, as we eventually learn, no one is spectator alone, all watch and all act; the "Host" himself has long been playing a role to disguise his identity as Lord Frampul, and his daughter is more accurate when she asserts that there is no shame in passing on her old gown (itself at the moment serving to costume Prudence) to "the *Players*": "Tut, all are *Players*, and but serue the *Scene*" (II, i, 39).[38]

When the Court of Love game closes and like "an ended Play / Shewes my abrupt precipitate estate" to disconsolate Lovel, he takes his bitter consolation in another familiar trope: "Ile to bed, and sleepe, / And dreame away the vapour of *Loue*" (IV, iv, 280–81), he promises. And when all disguises have been doffed and all identities fixed in the harmony of comedy, his is the last cry of wonder:

> Is this a dreame now, after my first sleepe?
> Or are these phant'sies made i'the light Heart?
> And sold i'the new Inn?   (V, v, 120–22)

These are the inevitable *topoi* which we, like Brome, have met so often in the literature surrounding his artistic maturation. But, quite aside from the external evidence in *The English Moor* for his special interest in *The New Inn*, there are two local details of Jonson's play which are of significance in fixing it as his immediate inspiration for *The Antipodes* because they emerge in the later play as structural beams upon which the whole theater-dream dichotomy leans for support.

First, we may notice an attitude from which I believe the central plot business of *The Antipodes* was drawn, that is, the circling home-travel motif with which Frampul realizes that he has gone the long way about to rediscover himself and his family:

> I am he
> Haue measur'd all the Shires of *England* ouer:
> *Wales*, and her mountaines, seene those wilder nations,
> Of people in the *Peake*, and *Lancashire*:
> Their Pipers, Fidlers, Rushers, Puppet-masters,
> Iuglers, and Gipseys, all the sorts of Canters,
> For to these savages I was addicted,
> And Colonies of beggars, Tumblers, Ape-carriers,
> To search their natures, and make odde discoueries!
> And here [in the inn] my wife, like a she *Mandeuile*,
> Ventred in disquisition, after me.   (V, v, 92–102)

More important to the psychic center of Brome's play is the episode of Lady Frampul's tailor, Nick Stuff, who appears for one fascinating, perverted moment in *The New Inn*. Here theatrical play and that psychiatric concern which forms so large a part of Brome's approach to the imagination are fused, in an adumbration of the elaborate plot of *The Antipodes*. Stuff, commissioned to make a gown for Lady Frampul, appears at the inn with a striking *bona roba* who is eventually revealed as his own wife, dressed in the commissioned finery. Mistress Stuff, trapped and disgusted, volunteers to "tell his story":

> When he makes any fine garment will fit me,
> Or any rich thing that he thinkes of price,
> Then must I put it on, and be his *Countesse*,
> Before he carry it home vnto the owners.

> A coach is hir'd, and foure horse, he runnes
> In his veluet Iackat thus, to *Rumford, Croyden,*
> *Hounslow,* or *Barnet,* the next bawdy road:
> And takes me out, carries me vp, and throw's me
> Vpon a bed.   (IV, iii, 66–74)

As one of the courtiers comments: "He lies / With his own *Succuba*, in all your names" (IV, iii, 80–81).

Brome had glanced toward the matter of psychic impotence not only in the frustration of Quicksands in *The English Moor* but a few years earlier in *The Late Lancashire Witches*, a collaboration with Heywood in which a couple quarrel upon the wedding night, not "for want of bedstaves" but because "a better implement it seems the bridegroome was unprovided of." This failure, though, since he has been "complain'd on, for an over mickle man among the maids," turns out to be "witchery" the instrument of which was "the codpeece . . . gave him at the wedding."[39] In *The Antipodes* the subject not only merges with the travel, or "antipodes," business to shape the action but rises suddenly and ephemerally among the minor characters in a cry which articulates the Jonsonian tailor's own sexual epicycle within the circle of marriage. While listening to his wife chatter with a doctor who practices what a modern recognizes as psychiatry, the painter Blaze—on one hand jealous, on the other jaded—muses:

> How prettily like a foole she talkes?
> And she were not mine owne wife, *I* could be
> So taken with her.[40]

Such things are inherently uncertain, but I would infer that Brome saw the point Jonson was trying, somewhat awkwardly, to sharpen in *The New Inn*, understood the import of the mechanisms and metaphors of his quondam master in the dramatic art, and himself essayed a tangential development of them in *The English Moor*. No more satisfied with the total effect here than in the Jonsonian original upon which he had made his jokes, however, Brome took advantage of the long closure of the theaters because of the plague to try a new, more ambitious and orderly version of the whole complex in *The Antipodes*.

The first thing to observe about this play is that it is not a single protagonist but the whole world that is mad. Peregrine, son to Joyless, has something close to the Quixote syndrome: reading travel books has so far removed him from reality to a vicarious world of exotic places that he has shown no interest in consummating his now three-year-old marriage with Martha. She in turn has become so unbalanced by this deprivation that she thinks and talks of nothing but babies and the making of them—providing some particularly salacious passages under the rubric of innocent ignorance. But Peregrine's anguished father Joyless, who brought him to London to be examined by the famous Doctor Hughball, himself turns out to be irrationally jealous of his symbolically named wife Diana. His city friend Blaze, who recommended the Doctor, assures him that he can also be cured because Blaze suffered from jealousy too until Hughball gave him a suspect cure which smells mightily of horn. When we meet the Doctor, he himself has the usual psychiatrist's sickness: his eye projects psychoses wherever it falls upon a subject. Told of the plight of Peregrine and Martha, he interrupts:

> Come, let me see 'hem Sir, Ile undertake
> Her, too: ha' you any more? how does your wife?
> . . . .
> Ile undertake
> Her too, and you your selfe Sir (by your favour,
> And some few yellow spots, which I perceive
> About your Temples) may require some Councell.   (239)

And then there is Blaze's other friend with whom the Doctor lives, Lord Letoy. He writes plays and keeps players so extravagantly that he has become the scandal of the town, for he goes in "broadcloth" and "look[s] more like a pedlar, / Then like a Lord," while his followers are dressed in the handsomest of clothes (244–45)—a living embodiment, on the visual level, of the "antipodes" theme which will become the burden of his play-within-the-play. If all the world is mad, even topsy-turvy (as is suggested by Letoy's relation to his retinue, or by the lawyer patient who "knew not whether he / Went on his heels or's head" [235]), then only by inverting reality can reality be restored as a norm. Thus *The Antipodes* becomes a title which describes both inner and outer plays.[41]

The inner play is designed by the Doctor and directed by Letoy as a simple extension of Peregrine's travel madness from fancy into action, a calculated projection of an illusion from a mad mind into the paradoxical "reality" of dramatic play in order that it may destroy itself by the logic of extremes. When Peregrine has been thoroughly exploited, Letoy articulates the theory of the double illusion by which a man is to receive his own invented world as a reality which engulfs him rather than emanates from him:

> [The Doctor] has shifted your sonnes knowne disease
> Of madness into folly; and has wrought him
> As farre short of a competent reason, as
> He was of late beyond it. . . .
> . . . .
> So is a mad-man made a foole, before
> Art can take hold of him to wind him up
> Into his proper Center, or the Medium
> From which he flew beyond himselfe.   (316–17)

The "play" plot turns about Doctor Hughball's description of the Antipodes:

> The people through the whole world of *Antipodes*,
> In outward feature, language, and religion,
> Resemble those to whom they are supposite [*sic*]:
> They under *Spaine* appear like *Spaniards*,
> Under *France French-men*, under *England English*.
> To the exterior shew: but in their manners,
> Their carriage, and condition of life
> Extremely contrary.   (251)

Naturally, Peregrine is devoured by the desire to visit the farthest Antipodes—the anti-English land, a desire encouraged by the Doctor, who agrees to take him there. First they pledge their journey in a drugged wine,

> a deep draught indeed, and now tis downe,
> And carries him downe to the *Antipodes*;
> I mean but in a dreame.   (255)

Awakened after some hours, Peregrine finds himself surrounded by Letoy's players "in sea-gownes and Caps," welcoming him ashore in the Antipodes. Amazed at his arrival, at the "eight months" sleep he is told he underwent, at the fulfillment of his yearning for travels, Peregrine's world is a mist without clear focus:

> What worlds of lands and Seas have I past over
> . . . as if all had beene,
> Meere shadowy phantasmes, or Phantasticke dreames,　　　(263)

he muses.[42] Once persuaded that he is in the Antipodes, Peregrine is treated by the actors to a series of inversions of conduct on the part of social types familiar from the satirists: a lawyer who will take no fee from a poet, a gentleman who is scolded by his wife for refusing to live up to a bargain by which he promised to get a merchant's wife with child in exchange for goods, servants who dominate masters, old men set to school again by their children.[43] "Sure these are dreames, / Nothing but dreames," Peregrine cries. "No, doubtlesse we are awake," responds the Doctor (302), and mercilessly drives home the inverted aspects of this new world:

> 　　　　　That's a Schismatick,
> Teaching a Scrivener to keep his eares:
> A parish Clearke, there, gives the Rudiments
> Of Military Discipline to a Generall:
> And there's a Basket-maker confuting *Bellarmine.*

This last glimpse into the emerging world of the Puritans in the civil war is too much for a Peregrine who cries "Will you make me mad?" (307). He has come to the turning point from "madness into folly" which is necessary in Hughball's cure, and the effect is to draw him into the theatrical world whose reality he can no more credit than he can discern its artifice. When he enters, it is in the tradition of Don Quixote among the puppets and, probably quite directly, in that of the stage havoc performed by Rafe in *The Knight of the Burning Pestle.*[44] One of the players breathlessly rushes to Letoy with news of how Peregrine had "got into our Tyring-house amongst us," had

> tane a strict survey of all our properties,
> Our statues and our images of Gods . . .
> Our Helmets, Shields, and Vizors, Haires, and Beards,
> Our Pastbord March-paines, and our Wooden Pies,

and then set to work:

> 　　Whether he thought twas some inchanted Castle,
> Or Temple . . .
> . . . .
> I dive not to his thoughts, wonder he did

A while it seem'd. . . .
When on the suddaine, with thrice knightly force,
And thrice, thrice, puissant arme he snatcheth downe
The sword and shield that I playd *Bovis* with,
Rusheth amongst the foresaid properties,
Kills Monster, after Monster; takes the Puppets
Prisoners, knocks down the Cyclops, tumbles all.   (285)

Then he takes the actors' regal costume, puts it on, and "crownes / Himselfe King of the *Antipodes*," in which role

       he begins to governe
With purpose to reduce the manners
Of this country to his owne.   (286)

And we have arrived again at the "pretended-prince" trope. But before pursuing the course of Peregrine's cure through theatricals, it is important to step back and examine the subtler but wider schisms between perception and delusion which the little inner play serves to draw out of the imagination of the others: of the Joylesses and Blazes who are the really captive spectators to the double play of "*The Antipodes*," and Peregrine's progressive reconstruction of and by that play. The psychiatric Doctor Hughball gave a hint of this quieter but profounder movement when he had assured Letoy that they

Shall all be your guests to night, and not alone
Spectators, but (as we will carry it) Actor[s]
To fill your Comick Scenes with double mirth.   (257)

Letoy seats his guests to watch the play which will cure the vicarious traveler by transporting him to the Antipodes, much to the delight of Diana Joyless, who cries "I never saw a play" (262). This not only sets the teeth of her husband on edge, as he begins to suspect he had best hustle her out of this worldly theater, but also sets the important tone of naïve involvement for what follows. When the "Antipodean" gentleman refuses to impregnate the merchant's young wife, Joyless begins to wriggle uncomfortably in his seat and tries to nudge Diana home. He is hushed by Letoy, but this does not prevent Martha from breaking into the play to inform the gentleman who virtuously wishes to remain home of nights:

If it be me your wife commends you to,
You shall not need to stray from your own house.
I'll goe home with you. (269)

When a beggar comes onto the Antipodean scene offering money to a
gallant, the inexperienced Diana begins to urge her humane (but anti-
Antipodean) observations until the exasperated Joyless again checks
her: "You will not sure, will you turne Actor too? / Pray doe, be put
in for a share amongst 'em?" Diana, semi- or pseudo-innocent, asks
"How must I be put in?" and Joyless closes the turn on his jest:

The Players will quickly
Shew you, if you perform your part; perhaps
They may want one to act the whore amongst 'em. (283)

Peregrine pops his principles into the play, and an Antipodean actor
querulously complains that "he puts me out, my part is now to bribe the
Constable" before the Doctor rapidly ushers him out (299). Then Diana
begins to understand the art which is involved in acting, and applauds
the most talented of the "inner play" players: "Never was such an actor
as *Extempore!*" But just as she slips into a tacit recognition of the art-
life dichotomy, Joyless loses perspective: now he is jealous of her admiration not of the man but of the actor, and bitterly replies: "I could
finde in my heart to Quoit thee at him" (311). "Peace both of you,"
reminds Letoy, "or you'l spoyle all."

It is clear from Peregrine's translation into the distant travels of his
dreams, from Martha's reaching out toward the sexual fulfillment which
has unbalanced her, from Joyless' jealousy of mere masqueraders and
Diana's fascination with a careless, gay actor whose personality is the
reverse of her strait husband's, that for the "spectators" as well as for
the protagonist Peregrine reality is being inverted so that the "play"
world has become an Antipodes which is the imaginative ideal mirroring,
but also therefore inverting, the sick, "mad" world in which each lives.

To understand this involvement is to understand Brome's insistent
discussion of *ex tempore* playing which threads throughout *The Antipodes.* We have earlier noticed that he was cognizant of and interested
in the tradition of *commedie improvvise* among the Italian players and
that his work was probably directly derived in important ways from it,
but the topic was less historic than psychic in this play about players.[45]
Hamlet warned that his players should "speak no more than is set down
for them"; Letoy knows more about the traditions and effects of drama.
"My Actors," he promises,

Are all in readinesse; and I thinke all perfect,
But one, that never will be perfect in a thing
He studies; yet he makes such shifts extempore,
(Knowing the purpose what he is to speake to)
That he moves mirth in me 'bove all the rest.
For I am none of those Poeticke furies,
That threats the Actors life, in a whole play,
That addes a syllable, or takes away.   (256–57)

By-play or, as Diana calls him, Extempore, is the man. And if Letoy
chides him as an "incorrigible," as one who

                        when you are
To speake to your coactors in the Scene,
You hold interloquutions [sic] with the Audients,

he admits that on this occasion his extemporal skill will be allowed and
even valuable, for "the mad Patient," like his stepmother, "never saw /
A Play in's life" (259–60). Joyless is agitated and objects to the whole
proceeding, in which Letoy seems to be constantly interfering

By banqueting and Courtship twixt the Acts
[You] Will keep backe the Catastrophe of your play
. . . And then in midst of Scenes
You interrupt your Actors,   (274)

while Letoy himself ultimately surrenders plotting to plunging:

                    we now give over
The play, and doe all by *Extempore*,
For your sonnes good   (312)

he cries. Extempore, By-Play, is the subject of discussion not only as
actor but as allegory, for this is a play which might be described with
complete accuracy as the history of several characters in search of an
author to rewrite their chaotic lives. Doctor Hughball has recognized in
the case of Peregrine (who is symbolic of the plights of all the others as
well as protagonist of the plot) that fantasy is an inner wheel which,
when turned, at the extreme point comes back to reality. And like
Peregrine, the others too must be extemporal actors, players in spite of
themselves, that they may return to themselves.

    Drama is a cure, but life itself is a series of plots in both the gen-
eral and dramatic senses of the word; it is a series of disguises and de-

signs which shift and alter as they fail in their objectives almost as fluidly as the "extempore" drama which is being staged around Peregrine. The marriage of Peregrine to Martha itself was plotted as a "cure." Finding his mind "all on fire to be abroad," Joyless and his wife

> oppos'd him still in all, and strongly
> Against his will, still held him in, finally wonne
> Him into marriage; hoping that would call
> In his extravagant thoughts. (238)

Far from effecting their aim, of course, the marriage only brought the Joylesses a double problem in therapy as Martha withered into her sexual melancholy, so that to the marriage plot now has to be added the new therapeutic drama of Hughball and Letoy. And if this playlet of "*The Antipodes*" is manifestly medicinal for the young Joylesses, it soon begins to make forays in another direction. Joyless pricks his imaginatively horned ears when he begins to hear the Doctor's sociosexual report on the inverted isles:

> cuckold making . . . is not so abhorr'd here as tis held
>   In reputation there . . .
> As generation were to be maintain'd
> Onely by cuckold making. (253–54)

Diana's theatrical interest is whetted, and Joyless tries at once to sweep her home, but Hughball blocks him with a threat which seems to apply to Peregrine, but in retrospect is obviously meant for Joyless himself:

> She must [stay] if you can hope for any cure,
> Be govern'd, Sir: your jealousie will grow
> A worse disease than your sonnes madnesse else. (254)

Letoy sends Diana a ring by way of the Doctor and becomes suspect until the Doctor explains that not only has he delivered the token, but that he has also instructed Diana "to spurre his jealousie of o'the legges" (257). The ring is discovered by Joyless, Diana balks his urgent new demands to leave Letoy's house and play,[46] and he finds himself virtually a prisoner of the apparently lascivious Letoy, who begins to woo Diana directly with an appropriate dramatic conceit:

> Yes, Lady, this was Prologue to the Play,
> As this is to our sweet ensuing pleasures. *Kisse.*
> *Joy[less].* Kissing indeed is Prologue to a Play,

Compos'd by th' Divell, and acted by the Children
Of his blacke Revelles, may hell take yee for't.   (265)

The play of jealousy is acted out, as we see, within the play—it soon
moves out of "the Antipodes" into the castle. To the accompaniment
of the latter's continued promises "to cure your husbands jealousy"
(317–18) Diana and Letoy disappear, and a frenzied old Joyless paces
the corridors with knife and candle seeking them, mistaking allusions,
and ultimately having to be physically restrained and psychologically
dissuaded, with some effort, from suicide or murder (318–22). Around
this crescendo of Joyless' jealousy is wrapped an older historic layer of
the same theme with the appearance of Blaze, who at the very beginning
of *The Antipodes* had protested too much of how Hughball had cured
him of jealousy. Like Peregrine, he has been medicated by the logic of
extremes: convinced that the horns which haunted his fantasies have
become real, he has nothing to fear. While Joyless roams in rage, Blaze
meets his own wife, Barbara, in another part of the castle, says he has
slept with the butler, and queries with strained nonchalance (for the
point always is the power to control, not to change, the imagination):
"Who was thy bed-fellow?"

> Bar[bara]. You know I was appoynted to sit up.
> Bla[ze]. Yes, with the Doctor in the Bride-chamber.
> But had you two no waggery? Ha!
> Bar[bara]. Why how now *Tony*?
> Bla[ze]. Nay facks I am not jealous.
> Thou knowst I was cur'd long since, and how.
> I jealous! I an asse. A man shan't aske
> His wife shortly how such a gentleman does?
> Or how such a gentleman did? or which did best?
> But she must thinke him jealous.
> Bar[bara]. You need not: for
> If I were now to dye on't, nor the Doctor,
> Nor I came in a bed to night: I meane
> Within a bed.
> Bla[ze]. Within, or without, or over, or under,
> I have no time to thinke o'such poore things.   (322–23)

This show of therapy as life-acting closes with Blaze emblematically
putting the seal upon his role as one who will make no outcry against
infidelity by exhibiting the costume for his role in the inner *"Antipodes"*
—that of "two mutes": "A Mute is one that acteth speakingly, / And
yet says nothing" (323). And no sooner has this scene closed than a new

play begins. Letoy has gotten Diana alone and is shown in a seduction scene modeled on that between Volpone and Celia. He offers wealth, luxury, pleasure, violence—and she rejects all with stiff highmindedness. As a final effort, he turns to the cure of Joyless as a motive, a cure already successful with Blaze:

> But for his yellows,
> Let me but lye with you, and let him know it,
> His jealousie is gone, all doubts are clear'd. (327)

At this peak of outrage, the desperate Joyless enters with the actor Extempore—and the turn comes in that both the eavesdropping husband and the spurned seducer cry out in happy wonder at Diana's chastity. "She is invincible!" shouts Letoy: "Come ile relate you to your husband." But Joyless answers

> No,
> Ile meet her with more joy then I receiv'd
> Upon our marriage-day

and turning to Letoy admits: "O my Lord, / My Lord, you have cur'd my jealousie, I thanke you" (328). This reaction is illuminated when the actor explains that he has placed Joyless where he could witness this trial scene,[47] but when Extempore suddenly reveals that what Joyless has taken for real seduction has been another play—that "my Lord give me order, / To place you there"—Joyless is again confounded. Letoy has been acting; perhaps in that case so has Diana. "Why may not this be then a counterfeit action, / Or a false mist to blinde me with more error?" (329) he cries in renewed agony. And now the peripety and discovery burst over the action to reveal all the plays as part of a larger play, all the cures as part of a larger cure, and the playwright-director Letoy as chief actor in his own psychiatric improvisations.

Letoy cuts off Joyless' new fit of distrust with the assertion that he "try'd and tempted" Diana "for my owne ends, / More then for thine" (329) and offers a jumble of obscure hints about honor, wealth, surprises, and recognitions. "So, so, now he's made," cries Joyless for us all, dizzy in a world which runs on spinning wheels. Now Brome takes the same page of casual, wildly improbable disguise and paternal return and recognition from Jonson's book for *The New Inn* which he had earlier employed for the return of Meanwell and Rashly in *The English Moor*. Diana's father, Truelock, appears from nowhere. Without a blink of reaction from either Diana or Truelock, the latter explains all mysteries at the invitation of Letoy, a "constant friend and thirty years acquaintance":

> [Diana] is yours my Lord; your onely daughter,
> And know you master *Ioylesse*, for some reason
> Knowne to my Lord; and large reward to me,
> Shee has beene from the third day of her life
> Reputed mine.   (331)

But this time, while the mechanism creaks with the same intentional, shameless amateurishness which we have commented on in the coincidences of *The Queen's Exchange* and the disguises of *The English Moor*, it functions antipodally, for one may pun seriously and, I think, accurately. Where before the emphasis was directed toward the mysterious, uncontrollable subsoil of destiny which gave an element of futility to the conscious motivations of men's plots in this theater of the world, in *The Antipodes* the absurd disguise and concealment plot reveal that motivation on which the entire structure is built. The revelation that Letoy has been playing a trial for Diana and Joyless simultaneously demonstrates that he has acted rationally—and that he has been mad:

> Now shall you know what mov'd me sir. I was
> A thing beyond a mad-man, like your selfe,
> Jealous; and had that strong distrust, and fancied
> Such proofes unto my selfe against my wife,
> That I conceiv'd the childe was not mine owne.

His first level of suspicion was laid to rest by his wife's deathbed behavior, and he has passed to the next, which we have witnessed:

>   I then resolv'd
> To see and try her [Diana] throughly; and so much
> To make her mine, as I should find her worthy.
> And now thou art my daughter, and mine heire.
> Provided still (for I am still *Letoy*)
> You honourably love her, and defie
> The Cuckold-making fiend foule jealousie.   (331–32)

"I am confirm'd, / And throughly cur'd," cries Joyless, and the cure has passed from one generation to the next through the seduction scene, which has been but a play-within-a-play managed by a lord of the revels who has made all the world his stage and all his people actors.[48] But the cure must be passed on to the third generation in the persons of Pere-

grine and Martha, which returns us to the playlet of "*The Antipodes.*"
We can now redefine this level as the central action of *The Antipodes*
only in the sense that a pebble makes widening circles in water, circles
which in this case have expanded to reveal the dramatic form of the
universe the play is interpreting. "*The Antipodes*" has been designed to
cure Peregrine of his madness in order that Joyless could be induced to
watch the pretended seduction, not only that he might be cured of his
madness but that Diana could be tested—in order that, ultimately,
Letoy might be cured of his madness. As the perspectives recede from
beginning to close, "*The Antipodes*" finally is recognizable as a play-
within-a-play-within-a-play—all simultaneously enacted. But the complicated perspectivism does not end here, being repeated yet again within
the confines of the innermost play.

Having moved so far into the illusory reality of Letoy's
travel drama as to have taken upon himself the tiring-house
finery and with this imitation "imperiall diadem" to have
crowned "Himselfe King of the *Antipodes*" (286), Peregrine is induced
to join the tradition of Adam Overdo in secretly seeking out the "enorm-
ities" of his domain. "Now sir," urges Doctor Hughball,

> be pleas'd to cloud your Princely raiment
> With this disguise. Great Kings have done the like,
> To make discovery of passages
> Among the people: thus you shall perceive
> What to approve, and what correct among 'hem.

Donning hat and cloak, disguise over disguise, Peregrine readily agrees
with sober-seeming balance: "And so ile cherish, or severely punish"
(295). As we have already seen, he finds little to cherish and is so
stricken by the inverted customs and morality of the new world that he
leaps into the scenes, throws one player after another out of his stride—
like the actor who laments at the justice of the mock-king-in-broadcloth,
"He puts me out, my part is now / To bribe the Constable" (299)—until
he finally forces Letoy's order to "give over / The Play, and doe all by
Extempore." As Peregrine moves "inward," then, becoming so involved
in the "play" as to disguise himself and perform at yet another level of
remove (the fourth play-within-a-play) paradoxically he is destroying
the dramatic order of Letoy's innermost play: illusion, in becoming so

total as to reproduce itself, is also self-destructive, and as its protagonist, Peregrine, begins to "act" his part the play *"The Antipodes"* must become an improvisation.

But the important point is that this shifting relationship has a psychological parallel in Peregrine himself. "Sure these are dreams, nothing but dreams," we heard him cry in amazement at Antipodean conduct. Increasing involvement in the world of the Antipodes is leading him to see it more and more clearly as what it is: the world of his own fantasy. The action of *"The Antipodes"* closes at the point at which Peregrine's double vision of the playlet is at a height of simultaneous illusion and recognition. Casting off his "disguise," he enters the city, an anti-London, to receive the "generall joy your people bring / To celebrate the welcome of their king" (312). Amidst pomp and circumstance, he is met by a parade (emphasizing the fusion of illusion levels, "Letoy enters and mingles with the rest") which brings him Martha, costumed and presented as the daughter and heir-apparent of his predecessor. When he is urged to marry her, Peregrine reaches back to grasp a reality we thought he might have lost: "A Crowne," he objects, "secures not an unlawfull marriage. / I have a wife already." Doctor Hughball answers—doubtless *"extempore"*—that Martha is dead and "her fleeting spirit / Is flowne into, and animates this Princesse." All levels merge, and the theatrical illusion has become stronger than the world in which the actors once thought they lived. Peregrine admits it—"Indeed she's wondrous like her"—and embraces and kisses Martha as Queen; she, in turn, revives in the fiction. "He kisses sweetly," she sighs, "and that is more than ere my husband did." But she, too, carries a hold upon the past which gives her pause:

> But more belongs then kissing to child-getting;
> And he's so like my husband, if you note him,
> That I shall but lose time and wishes by him. (314)

The fusion of reality and play creates its own heat. Urged by all, the couple "marry," and Peregrine joins Nick Stuff of *The New Inn* in being liberated to enjoy his own wife when she comes in the fantastic strangeness, the exalted and exotic guises, of his dreams.

Like the others of older generations, as *The Antipodes* ends Peregrine and Martha are cured—indeed, "was never such a Cure":

> They have bin in th' *Antipodes* to some purpose;
> And, now, are risen, and return'd themselves:
> He's her dear *Per*, and she is his sweet *Mat*.
> His Kingship and her Queenship are forgotten.

And all their melancholy and his Travailes past,
And but suppos'd their dreams.   (333)

But when Peregrine is introduced ("somthing amazed," says the stage direction) into the whole group and the history of events is recounted to him, the fusion goes deeper. He accepts the "reality" calmly because it provides him a pleasant anchor in the sea of mirrors and mirages which his fantasy- and drama-ridden traveler's life had become. But the awakening from a dream has made him aware that he may yet awaken from a dream of a dream: "I am what you are pleas'd to make me; but withall, so ignorant of mine owne condition; whether I sleepe, or wake, or talke, or dreame; whether *I* be, or be not; or if I am, whether I doe, or doe not any thing; for I have had (if I now wake) such dreames, and been so far transported in a long and tedious voyage of sleep, that I may fear my manners can acquire no welcome, where men understand themselves" (336).

When Peregrine "landed" on the Antipodes, the passage of his former life seemed "as if all had beene / Meere shadowy phantasmes, or Phantasticke dreames" (263). Now the playlet of *"The Antipodes"* itself seems the dream. And this is the real point to note in all of the receding theatrical perspectives in which *The Antipodes* works out its fourfold interpretation of reality. Where Perkin Warbeck changed the imagination by agreeing to act its fantasies upon the stage of the world, the outward circumstances of this stage must change constantly to adapt to the therapeutic needs of the cast of curables in *The Antipodes*, who alter those circumstances by acting out their fantasies. There is a world of difference between Ford's and Brome's, between—we may hazard—the Jacobean and the Caroline conceptions of drama and of man's roles in life. But the equation remains stable: art is the mold of reality. Yet the play itself seems a mere dream at the end, a small reminder that Brome had not quite dissolved the debate on art and actuality which no artist *can* honestly dissolve. When he turned to *The Jovial Crew*, the significance of the equation became even more ambiguous.

 A Jovial Crew: Or, The Merry Beggars, written for Beeston's Boys in 1641,[49] was the last of Brome's plays and the swansong of a culture in its eleventh hour. It is appropriate that the last serious play written before the closing of the theaters which also closed the great Renaissance chapter of English drama should sit so firmly in the center of the tradition of philosophical theater; it is a perhaps symbolic act of faith on the part of Brome or of providence that its theme should have been rebirth.

The attractive Squire Oldrents is desperate at the play's opening because of a prophecy made him by an old patriarch of the beggar tribe that never fails to stop at his estate because of the extravagant welcome they receive from his young steward, Springlove. The prophecy has said that both of Oldrents' unmarried daughters shall become beggars although they are co-heirs. The good man is so struck by the prospect that he has fallen into a melancholy out of which his dear friend Hearty cannot cajole him and which has made it impossible for him to look upon his daughters without "sigh, or teares in his eyes," as one of them explains, "tho' we simper never so sanctifiedly" (*Dramatic Works*, III, 371). Melancholy—as in *The Antipodes*—is contagious, as the other daughter notes: "he makes us even sick of his sadness" (371).

But Oldrents has yet another concern weighing upon him. Springlove (so dear to him that Hearty comments, "But that I know the old *Squire's* virtue, I should think *Springlove* were sure his Bastard" [383]) has gotten the estate books in order and comes to remind Oldrents that " 'tis well-nigh *May*," that the nightingales sing, the cuckoo cries, and it is time to leave upon his annual summer pilgrimage across the open countryside. The rub is that two years earlier Oldrents accidentally came upon his young retainer during this time in the guise of a beggar, one with the jovial crew he welcomes so warmly to the estate at his own expense. Mortified and saddened, Oldrents turned the other cheek and not only accepted the young man back into his service but made him steward over all his goods in the hope of drawing him away from his "uncouth practice." This plan worked for one year because of Springlove's deep respect for his master, but is now powerless against "disposition," which "philosophy can[not] render an accompt for" (359). Puzzled by his own wanderlust, Springlove is further bemused when the beggar prophet reads him this riddle:

Thou art born to wealth and Land,
And after many a bitter gust,
Shalt build with thy great Grandsires dust. (369)

Springlove then determines to leave with the beggars in spite of all pleas and offers, while Oldrents' daughters, having seen the merry life of the beggar campers, induce their two gentle suitors to join the beggars with them, both to escape their father's mood and "for a spring-trick of youth, now, in the season" (375). Springlove, appealed to, quickly agrees to introduce them into the good graces of the beggars because he at once sees the therapeutic possibilities all around: "The Sentence of your Fortune does not say, that you shall beg for need; hungry or cold necessity. If therefore you expose your selves on pleasure into it, you shall absolve your destiny nevertheless, and cure your Father's grief" (379). With this double prophecy and flight we have come back to the persistent Bromean theme of cure for the ailing imagination, a motivation which is kept continuously in play, not only by Springlove's attempt, but by Oldrents' own try to cure himself in the way of his decayed but happy friend Hearty's advice and example: in seeking and dispensing every legitimate pleasure, wherever it may be found. "I tell thee, I'll purge my house of stupid melancholly" (386), he declares, as a faithful follower comments in bemusement at life's larger ironies:

> This is right my Master. When he had his Daughters he was sad; and now they are gone, he is the merriest man alive. Up at five o'clock in the morning, and out till Dinner-time. Out agen at after-noon, and so till Supper-time. Skise out this away, and skise out that away. (He's no *Snayle* I assure you). And *Tantivy* all the country over, where Hunting, Hawking, or any Sport is to be made, or good Fellowship to be had; and so merry upon all occasions.[50]   (414)

The relations of Oldrents to Springlove and to his daughters is cut across by a third plot strand, the elopement of neighboring Justice Clack's niece Amy with Martin, the Justice's clerk and nephew to Hearty. This pair encounter the "beggars" quite by chance, and are recipients of their hospitality. Amy's flight, the "spring-trick" of the daughters, and the vagabondage of Springlove all are surrounded with the demand for "liberty" expressed in some key, that liberty which even Oldrents recognizes as the prerogative of the beggars when, deserted by his own, he secretly watches his wandering guests at the feast he has provided them as a sort of merry-melancholy memorial to Springlove:

> What is an estate
> Of Wealth and Power, ballanc'd with their Freedom,
> But a meer load of outward complement?
> When they enjoy the Fruits of rich Content?
> Our Dross but weighs us down into Despair,
> While their sublimed spirits daunce i'th'Ayr.   (388)

This attitude toward physical liberty as a natural good somehow lost or corrupted by discipline and responsibility is fused with or, perhaps better, absorbed into the closely related psychological concept of liberality when Amy and Springlove fall in love almost as soon as she arrives in the beggar's camp. When Springlove encounters Amy and Martin to beg from them, and learns their plight, he immediately makes the ultimate gesture of liberality: "what I have is yours," he vows. Martin, on the other hand, offers a "whole silver three-pence" as recompense for their hospitality, and Amy scorns him as an "ingratefull Miser" while herself showing a freely liberal hand (409–10). Later, confiding to Oldrents' daughters her love for Springlove, Amy accuses Martin (who fled when things got complicated, abandoning her to the beggars) of being "deprav'd by Covetousnesse and Cowardise" (424). This is perhaps inevitable for Clack's clerk, since the Justice himself is a tight-fisted host, always ready to save "the expence of a Renlet of *Sack* the while" (437). Oldrents' servant Randall, who never entirely approves of Springlove's generosity to the beggars, yet knows when he is invited into Clack's buttery that it is to "fill my belly with thin drink to save his Meat," and that he is qualified to say "Shite o' your Master. My Master's Steward's a better Man" (439). Oldrents himself is not too polite to make a joke upon his judicial acquaintance's table: "I love a Miser's Feast dearly. To see how thin and scattering the Dishes stood, as if they fear'd quarrelling." Yes, chimes Hearty, "and how the Bottles, to scape breaking one another, were brought up by one at once" (442). On the other hand, the first thing we learn of Oldrents is his liberality:

Whose Rents did you ever exact? whose have
You not remitted, when by casualties . . .
Poor men were brought behind hand? Nay, whose losses
Have you not piously repair'd?

demands his friend (but no sycophant) Hearty. And when a visitor to Oldrents' estate is offered ambiguous hospitality by the teasing Butler, who first suggests sack, and then by gradations works down to "Household-Beer," the newcomer grimaces knowingly until the man returns with the offering: "Here, Gentlemen, is a Cup of my Masters small Beer: But it is good old *Canary*, I assure you" (417–18). And Springlove seems to have somehow inherited his master's values, for not only is he a free host to the elopers late in the play, but he is first introduced as one who habitually sows largesse where it seems least likely to produce returns— among the beggars themselves.[51]

The "liberty" sought by the young people, the freedom from the societal imprisonment in which Springlove, Oldrents' daughters, and Amy all find themselves at the beginning of the play, is to be found in vagabondage because, as we have already heard Oldrents himself comment, this offers a "natural" life from a primitivistic perspective. Nature also offers its own analogue to the liberality which marks the sympathetic protagonists with that fecundity which Spring both symbolizes and culminates. Springlove is called by the song of the nightingale even as he goes over the accounts with Oldrents (358–59), and from this beginning onward the entire ambience of the play is one of natural sounds and odors, of the springing of the eglantine, the fresh night air inducing sleep in the haystacks, or lust behind the hedges. The beggars seem always at their "high feast," and live by the savor of their own catch:

> Come, come; away: The Spring
> (By every Bird that can but sing,
> Or chirp a note, doth now invite
> Us forth) to taste of his delight. (369)

Harmonizing with these notes of Nature's fecundity is the ambience of the "natural" vagabonds, which at every turn echoes fertility. When Oldrents sends a man to investigate a wild hubbub in the beggars' quarters, he finds it emanating from "a most natural Cause. For there's a Doxie / Has been in labour." Oldrents proposes a month of celebration for the new birth, but is reminded:

> Their Work is done already:
> The Bratling's born, the *Doxey's* in the *Strummel.* . . .
> She'l have the *Bantling* at her back tomorrow
> That was to-day in her belly, and march a footback with it. (386–87)

This vigorous birth is both balanced and echoed by the later wedding of two ancient beggars to the accompaniment of a satiric epithalamium:

> *To the blinde Virgin of fourscore,*
>   *And the lame Batchelor, of more,*
> *How* Cupid *gave her Eyes to see,*
>   *And* Vulcan *lent him Legs:*
> *How* Venus *caus'd their Sport to be*
>   *Prepar'd with butter'd Egs.*
> *Yet when she shall be seven years wed,*
>   *She shall be bold to say,*
> *She has as much her Maiden-head,*
>   *As on her Wedding day.* (425)

The sterility which balances the marital theme in these verses is advanced beyond the physical to encircle a whole mentality when we hear of the unnatural caution with which the groom approached an already sufficiently farcical engagement, of "how carefully he secur'd all to himself, in case he out-liv'd her, being but seven years older then she" (425). Here Martin's or Clack's miserliness is fused with the unnatural ancient marriage to suggest that liberality and fertility have some common root. And this root is implanted deep in the soil of Christian myth: Springlove admonishes the flagging suitors of the daughters that these sisters have realized better than they that the beggars' life has a profound significance: "They have more moral understanding. . . . They know . . . this is your Birthright into a new world. And we all know (or have been told) that all come crying into the World, when the whole World of Pleasures is before us. The World itself had ne'r been glorious, had it not first been a confus'd *Chaos*" (394). In *A Jovial Crew* those elements which demand the liberty of "naturalness" and which make for the generous heart are blood and love, proper guides in a drama which—as the plot and spring ambience tell us—is about generation and generations, but which also—as Springlove's "birthright" allusion warns us—is about regeneration.

 "Nature" in the sense of blood, of one's level of behavior by the natural stratifications of birth, emerges pointedly once the quartet of gentle young lovers have joined the beggars in what is, after all, not their way of life but only a spring trick. What prompts Springlove's admonition to the two suitors, Vincent and Hilliard, is their dismay and discomfort after their first night in the open air and the hay. What had seemed so inviting and free, so splendidly jovial from across the social fence, now has shown them its rough side: "Is this the life that we admir'd in others?" they wonder, having tossed all night under the spring tempest listening to "the Hogs in the hovel that cri'd till they drown'd the noise of the winde" (394). Encouraged by Springlove and by their determination to hold out in the game as well as their loves, they agree to continue the experiment until the girls cry off. But if they or Springlove—with his talk of superior "moral understanding"—could see Rachel and Meriel, the sisters, as they arise from this first night, they might laugh and hie home together. "I am sorely surbated with hoofing already tho', and so crupper-crampt with our hard lodging, and so bumfidled with the straw," laments Meriel, and Rachel choruses: "Think not on't. I am numm'd i'the bum and shoulders too a little. And have found the difference between a hard floor with a little straw, and a down Bed with a Quilt upon 't" (395–96). But all keep to the contest and continue beggars—but what beggars! Vincent and Hilliard, trying out their courtly rhetoric, extravagant demands, and proud hostilities upon some gentlemen, get beaten and whipped. Springlove gets a half-penny from the same men, who warn him not to share it with the others; they are obviously, he is told, "counterfeit Villains" or "Some High-way Theef o'my conscience, that forgets he is weaponless" (397–400). There follows a farcically serious scene in which Vincent very formally "challenges" the passersby who have beaten them off: "You may be pleas'd to call to mind a late affront, which, in your heat of passion, you gave a Gentleman," he begins, and by the time the audacious beggar has convinced his victims that he is in earnest, they are so disgusted at these incongruities that one brushes him away with a counter-offer: "I'll send a Beadle shall undertake you both" (403). The women, meanwhile, are equally absurd in their rhetorical begging, which brings a puzzled query from the man they have approached: "Pray tell me how long have you been *Beggars*"—"How came you to talk thus, and so much above the *Beggars* Dialect." Ironically, their response is true, part of the key to the whole complex of birth: "Our speech came naturally to us" (404). Like the Princess Perdita ineptly trying to serve as harvest queen, these gentle folk simply cannot beg—it is unnatural.

What then of Springlove, who is an artful, successful beggar? It is this question that must be addressed to understand the relationship and significance of all the elements which we have been bringing into relief, for Springlove is the knot which ties nature to society, fertility to liberality. As his allegorical name implies, the call of May is directed to his essential being. If, he tells Oldrents, the latter believed he had given up his pilgrimages of liberty, "You thought I had forsaken *Nature* then." Bitterly, Oldrents replies,

> Is that disease of Nature still in thee
> So virulent? and, notwithstanding all
> My favours . . .
> . . . canst thou, there, slight me for the whistling of a Bird[?]

Springlove, although he is regretful and later even self-accusatory, still knows the only meaningful answer that can be made to his master's line of argument:

> Your reason, Sir, informs you, that's no cause.
> But 'tis the season of the year that calls me.
> What moves her Noats, provokes my disposition
> By a more absolute power of *Nature*, then
> Philosophy can render an accompt for. (359)

Nature calls to nature. Nor can all the effort of art reshape a being to resist it, as Springlove admits when Oldrents has turned away at his apparent ingratitude:

> Nor but by death, can this predominant sway
> Of nature be extinguish'd in me. I
> Have fought with my Affections, by th' assistance
> Of all the strengths of Art and Discipline
> . . . .
> This inborn strong desire of liberty. (361)

Where the others expatiate upon the attractions of the primitive life, Springlove feels that attraction the way Nature itself feels it—in the blood. The call of the blood is left a mystery in nature, but Springlove's almost symbolic personification of that call in his relation to the vagabonds and their spring wanderings is not. "I'll confess all," he tells the other fugitives from comfort and culture,

> In my Minority
> My Master took me up a naked *Beggar*;
> Bred me at School, then took me to his Service.

Grown, "for seven late Sommers," he continues,

> By stealth, I would absent my self from service,
> To follow my own Pleasure, which was Begging,
> Led to't by *Nature*. (380)

His name and nature seem clearly starred in his nativity. All seems clear, that is, until Springlove and Amy fall in love at the close of act IV, at which point all the careful coordination of attitudes toward Nature and genetic natures seems to be overturned by a single, unexpected reaction. The quartet of young lovers, finally ready to abandon the gypsy life they have dabbled in, expect to be chidden by Springlove, but he instead replies: "Know, that I my self begin to finde this is no course for *Gentlemen*. This *Lady* shall take me off it" (432).

 The final act is another play within the larger one; it complicates all of the apparent orders which have been established, but only to reorder them in a pattern closer to what we are now familiar with as Brome's characteristic attitude toward the imagination.

Through the first four acts we have lived among gentry playacting at being beggars; in act V the beggars become actors in an improvised drama about gentry. The development originates around the wedding celebration for the aged beggars. The poet of the group proposes that "we might have a *Masque,* or a *Comedie* presented to night, in honour of the old *Couple,*" and all gaily demand "some Subject now *extempore*" (429). The subject proposed, a utopia populated by just such fallen fellows as make up the extant beggar crew, is an ironic red herring inasmuch as the amateur primitivists who had thought it utopia are about to desert the field.[52] But as the play is being planned, the desertion is balked along with the entertainment: Justice Clack's agents surround and seize the beggars—amateur and professional alike—and carry them to Clack's home. Here they are engaged, on promise of amnesty, to present a play to please Oldrents, Hearty, and the others who have arrived there in the wake of the Amy-Martin elopement.[53]

The impromptu work seems little calculated to please from the first. Hearty is given a list of titles to choose from, and as he reads them off to Oldrents, the latter becomes uncomfortably edgy:

Hearty. First, here's *the two lost Daughters.*
Oldrents. Put me not in minde of the two lost Daughters, I prethee. What's the next?
Hearty. The vagrant Steward.
Oldrents. Nor of a vagrant Steward. Sure some abuse is meant me.
Hearty. The old Squire and the Fortune-teller.
Oldrents. That comes neerer me. Away with it.
Hearty. The Beggars Prophecy.
Oldrents. All these Titles may serve to one *Play,* of a Story that I know too well. I'll see none of them.
Hearty. Then here's *The merry Beggars.*
Oldrents. I, that; and let 'em begin.   (443)

Unlike us, Oldrents was not, of course, in a position to realize that "*The Merry Beggars*" is the subtitle of *A Jovial Crew,* so that he is surprised when the inner play opens with an old beggar giving familiar prophecies: "It begins my Story," he cries, "and by the same *Fortune-teller* that told me my Daughters Fortunes; almost in the same words. I know him now. And he speaks in the *Play* to one that personates me, as neer, as they can set him forth" (445). Act I of "*The Merry Beggars*" is inevitably becoming a re-enactment of act I of *A Jovial Crew* before the living protagonists-become-spectators of the enveloping play. The dialogue proceeds as it had at the first beginning: Hearty appears, he counsels mirth —and then an identification of plays is made as Springlove steps forth to play the role of Springlove asking Oldrents to let him follow the nightingale: *"I've striven with my self to alter Nature in me, / For my good Masters sake; but all in vain"* (446), laments the self-impersonator, soon followed by the four *inamorati* re-enacting their own escape scene.

Springlove has been right in a precise sense: there is little use in trying to alter nature when one's artifice itself becomes solipsistic, when mimesis becomes total coincidence. The play and the past, art and nature, are totally fused as the gentry who had played at being beggars now as "beggars" play at being the gentry they are. On a mechanical level, art is now nature. But unlike the *commedia dell'arte* scripts about actors acting the lives of actors, unlike Bernini's artful playlets on Bernini's Arts, *A Jovial Crew* has been dominated by a concern with Nature and "naturalness." Therefore we are justified in expecting a final turn back toward this old emphasis. It comes when Oldrents interrupts the inner play to question the actors.

The Patrico of the beggars steps out as spokesman:

> Since you will then break off our *Play*:
> Something in earnest I must say;
> But let affected *Riming* go.
> I'll be no more a *Patrico*.
> My name is *Wrought-on*. (447)

With a stroke he clears away everything and restores the "natural" dominance. Wrought-on's sister was "among the Race / Of *Beggars* . . . the fairest." But one gentleman ("whether," surmises Wrought-on, "it were by her *Affection*, or / His *Fate*, to send his Blood begging with her") begot a son. The son is, inevitably, Springlove, begotten by Oldrents in his careless youth (448). Oldrents is then deluged not only by the appearance, *in propria persona*, of his daughters but of a redefined Springlove, a son no longer in will alone but in fact.[54] "[I] applaud," he cries, "great *Providence* in both." Hearty closes the fiction truer than truth: "The *Play* is done."

Springlove is really a natural beggar, and really a natural gentleman by blood, by Providence. And if the gentility wins out, it is not only because it is upon the paternal side of the scutcheon, but because in the blood lines of the distant past the Wrought-ons, too, were fallen gentry, now recovered in this distant son.

We should be prepared to hear yet deeper echoes emanating from

Springlove's promise to the young gentlemen when they take up beggary: "this is your Birthright into a new world." For when all is done, Meriel and Rachel have fulfilled their prophecy and found their men, and Amy has found a gentle husband among beggars, where Oldrents has found a son, not born, but reborn: "A Gentleman, my Son," he exults. In *A Jovial Crew*, Nature has triumphed. But it has triumphed precisely through Art—the art of the drama.

CHAPTER VI Seventeenth-Century English *Commedia Improvvisa:* Nature over Art

A NOTE ON RITUAL

We have seen how George Chapman staged Platonic myths, and in doing so deployed his plots between the antipodal metaphors for life as theater and as dream. But not all of his contemporaries who worked the stuff of mythic tradition were so directly Platonic, so philosophically derivative, as Chapman. Others used the traditional schemes of mythic structure with more complexity just because they were less committed to a systematic view. Their sense of theatricality as a fusion of form and flux derived not from Ficino but from that mixed, oscillating sense of the role of form as process which is a common quality of *commedia dell'arte* performances and of Buonamici's *Discorsi poetici.*

I choose two plays to represent another variant on our pattern because they are the best of their kind (a kind first worked out, I think, in Peele's earlier and simpler *Old Wives Tale*), tapestries of interwoven patterns and anti-patterns superbly ordered while open, in the widest sense, to the world beyond the stage. I choose them, moreover, because they neatly balance one another to make another point. Thomas Heywood's *Love's Mistress* is a court play, a play that even pretends to be a "masque," but one written by a city poet. Beaumont's *Knight of the Burning Pestle* is a city play, which conveniently satirizes city tastes by laughing at Heywood himself. But it was written by a man who at the time was thoroughly identified with private and court theater. And both plays are—as one might expect—completely anomalous, unique in the canons of their respective creators. Have we not in these facts another clear evidence that our concern is indeed, to repeat Lionel Abel's phrase, with "the great tradition of Western dramaturgy," a tradition which flows around and absorbs into itself even the most unlikely talents and —as in the case of Heywood—can raise them beyond their individual potential?

Before proceeding to read these strange twins, which seem almost autonomously created from an ambient their authors could not resist,[1] however, I want to make a claim for them which may seem pretentious, but which it is necessary to discuss because it simultaneously displays their *raison d'être* and their "form." Baldly put, the claim is that these are "ritual" plays.

"Ritual," I take it, is a ceremonial order of acts which at its first level imitates; that is, it re-enacts a pre-established pattern. But at its second level of definition, ritual demands that this commemorative re-enactment be really efficacious, effective in its repetition as it was in its origin. Thus ritual is a present act which historically recalls the past for the purpose of reordering—even predetermining—the future. But that present moment of re-enactment merges into the future, and so makes the efficacy of a predictive action inevitable as its pattern evolves from contingency into control. In short, ritual is a prediction which, completed, fulfills itself.

It has become customary for properly cautious practitioners of ritual (or the closely allied "archetypal") readings of drama to hedge their bets with elaborate reminders that drama is not ritual. One may take as exemplary in every sense C. L. Barber's conclusion to his important analysis of the *Henry IV* plays, since even here, where it is clear that older ritual patterns somewhere underlie dramatic structure, the critic carefully clarifies this distinction:

The persons of the drama make the customary gestures developed in ritual observance, and, in doing so, they project in a whole-hearted way attitudes which are not normally articulated at large. At the same time, the dramatization of such gestures involves being aware of their relation to the whole of experience in a way which is not necessary for the celebrants of a ritual proper. No one need decide, therefore, whether the identifications involved in the ceremony are magically valid or merely expressive. But in the drama, perspective and control depend on presenting, along with the ritual gestures, an expression of a social situation out of which they grow. So the drama must control magic by reunderstanding it as imagination: dramatic irony must constantly dog the wish that the mock king be real.[2]

These are salutary words when applied to Falstaff and restate the distinction which Barber made early in his book by denominating Nashe's *Summer's Last Will and Testament* a "pageant" as distinguished from a "drama" proper.[3] But every reaction has its inherent excesses, and if we are correct in refusing to find ritual in every drama of the Renaissance from which we can extirpate a structural skeleton with ritualistic origins, we can lose our bearings again by making the generalization that historic origin and later manifestation never coincide in a shared end. Barber's point is proper in his own context but is too simple to cover all the professional plays of the Renaissance, and it has been so extended by those critics who have denied that drama, and particularly comedy, can have a ritualistic status. Robert J. Nelson may serve as a focus, since he has reexamined Francis Fergusson's conclusions in his own study of "the play within the play" in France.[4] There Fergusson is indicted for concentrating "attention on the function and not on the effect of the play." The difficulty, Nelson feels, is that a ritualistic conception of drama—nurtured by Fergusson's tragic (which is to say Aristotelian?) focus—omits the quality of "play": "A play pleases. A play, in part, is play, action which is self-contained, directed to no end beyond itself, its aim being achieved in its very performance." Tragedy invites us to identification, naturally, and this involves the spectator in the "play." Here Fergusson stops, Nelson believes. But this, he argues, omits the role of the spectator in comedy, where he "plays or 'makes believe' with the actor through the complementary mechanism of dissociation: the spectator enjoys the play because it is an illusion. . . . Thus there are two ideas in 'the idea of a theater': reality and illusion, or . . . doing and playing. A play does not mean what it says because it is the simultaneous operation of these two ideas." Such criticism reduces us—with Rousset —to a level at which comedy can never be understood as more than "sport" corrupted into spectacle, a game in which the outcome is preordained by agreement on all sides. But we have already listened to the effective reply to such talk in Ortega y Gasset's *Idea del teatro* or in Artaud's *Le théâtre et son double*: the theater by means of its essentially double existence takes men—audience as well as actor—into that desirable realm beyond the world, beyond reality, not as *homo ludens* but in the reformative, effective sense of ritual.

If this is true, then a play not only about play but about the cooperative action of audience and author in the object-as-process which is a play must be in itself a staged ritual. If author, actor, and audience all share the burden of action in such a play, all share its efficacy. When it is over the world has been moved a little nearer to the heart's desire in a strict sense of what we understand by ritual. To recall Gasset's words, "not only the drama, but also the auditorium and the entire theatre end in becoming a phantasmagoria—beyond life."

THOMAS HEYWOOD: *LOVE'S MISTRESS*

Thomas Heywood appears quite properly in the histories and handbooks as a city poet in every sense of the word. Author of London mayoralty pageants, his drama was largely written for city middle-class tastes and was usually about London citizens at home and abroad. Yet his development of domestic tragedy suggests a wider range of gifts, for if the much-praised *Woman Killed with Kindness* is an archetypal success in the "city" genre, his *English Traveller* is superior work because it alternately builds up and frustrates every expectation for that type.[5] Clearly, such a work demands an awareness of the values inherent in making dramatic illusion itself a tacit subject and sounding-board against which to project the action. Such complexity of response is seldom demanded by Heywood, who is usually content with a wink at the audience in the style of the Vices of the medieval morality and who could scarcely be accused of posing as a "philosophic" dramatist.

Yet Heywood did leave two works which show his awareness of his age's awareness of the epistemological potential of the theater as genre. The first is his *Apology for Actors* (1612). Here the prefatory verses ("The Author to his Booke") revive the honored commonplace:

The world's a Theatre, the earth a Stage,
Which God, and nature doth with Actors fill,
. . . .
If then the world a Theatre present,
As by the roundness it appears most fit,
Built with starre-galleries of hye ascent,
In which Iehove doth as spectator sit,
. . . .
He that denyes then Theatres should be,
He may as well deny a world to me.

Facing his puritan antagonists, Heywood proceeds to demonstrate how life and the drama interact by retailing a series of anecdotes concerned with "strange incidents" occurring at plays which brought to light murders and invasions.[6] The theater, then, has real efficacy, intervening in the events of "life" beyond the scaffolding. This mysterious relationship between the great and little theaters is further emphasized by the author's framework for the whole apology. Melpomene comes to Heywood in a dream to teach him the defense of drama.[7] Much of that defense is distressingly apologetic, as the title warns, and wanders into catalogues of anecdotes and arguments popular from the age of Tertullian to that of Jeremy Collier. But there is one moment of the *Apology* which moves toward a categorical exaltation of Melpomene among the Muses: "A Description is only a shadow receiued by the eare but not perceiued by the eye: so liuely portraiture is meerely a forme seen by the eye, but can neither shew action, passion, motion, or any other gesture to moove the spirits of the beholder to admiration: But to see a soldier shaped like a soldier, walke, speake, act like a soldier. . . . Oh, these were sights to make an Alexander."[8] The eye and the ear here interact to impress the motive force of the dramatic action upon the world, that "Stage, which God, and nature doth with Actors fill." It might be passed over as nothing, a loose and shallow extension of *ut pictura poesis,* had not Heywood at his most inspired moment glossed it with *Love's Mistress,* a serpentine maze of plots which coalesce as a single action in which eye and ear are made the instruments to help us realize that poetry is a ritual of resurrection and rebirth.

As I have observed, Heywood's intrusions upon his own illusion are generally casual, as one might anticipate in plays chiefly devoted to romantic adventures. On occasion, when these adventures become too demanding for the scenes and machines of his theater, he follows in the traces of Shakespeare's Prologue to *Henry V* and narrates vast developments in his continent-spanning plots while pleading with the audience to participate in creating the illusion.[9] But in one group of very successful plays, the "Ages," in which Heywood turned from London scenes and London travelers to stage the cycles of classical myth from the gigantomachia to the Oresteia, the relations are more evocative, precisely because the "chorus" and presenter is Homer, the poet who claims the right to present the history for the startling reason that he himself invented the immortality of the gods.[10] He is, in short, a poet whose characters have taken on an autonomous status, and he claims his patrimony in their actions to employ them in a play based on the poem from which that autonomy emerged. And yet the audience must cooperate in an action which at times seems an "occasionalist" definition of art: the gods of the gentiles have obtained their apotheosis at Homer's hands (of his euhemerism, more below), but not only the poet-turned-playwright but the deities turned actors must beg the imagination to aid in reaffirming, in this smaller theater than the world, their "real" status.

"Your suppositions now must lend us ayd," admits Homer in presenting a Jupiter now become a deity, "that he can all things (as a God indeed)."[11] I do not want to exaggerate; the "Ages" as a whole are rather straightforward mythological plays, and Homer's role gradually disintegrates because of Heywood's preoccupation with getting the long, complicated history told, in moods which are now satiric, now romantic, now simply lyric or expository. But the question of the poet, the audience, and the act of poetry does ripple just under the surface of these plays. When Heywood came to dramatize another myth, that of Cupid and Psyche, the roles of Homer and his matter are reversed: it is not the myth—so often reworked in the Renaissance in dozens of guises whose extremes are represented by Calderón's *auto* and Shadwell's Molière—that is important, but rather its author. *Love's Mistress* is not primarily about Psyche, but about Apuleius.

The first hint is contained in the subtitle: *The Queen's Masque.* This is a proud reminder, of course, of the work's great success at court in 1634 (the original entry was even more emphatic: *The Queenes Maske or Loues Mistresse*[12]). But it also emphasises the masque-like character of the action, which is a myth set off by comic dances and song sequences that can only be called "anti-masques" and which (more importantly) is interlaced with innumerable discussions on the taste and participation of several audiences: the audience in the theater, the audience in the mythological site of Apuleius' poetic act, and the audience within the Arcadia which springs up (at once a stage and a "real" place) out of the differences debated between Apuleius and Midas.[13]

To recall the sequence briefly, Apuleius enters holding the ears which are his remembrancer of the asinine metamorphosis from which he has just recovered. He reports how he has suffered his disgrace for aspiring to hidden mysteries "Beyond the Moone"—ambitions which the Renaissance called vain curiosity. But no sooner has he explained this than he turns to the audience for directions toward Helicon. Receiving none from this source, he immediately encounters an acerbic Midas who scoffs at poetry. Apuleius decides to convert him by presenting "a story of mine owne, / Of *Cupid's* love to *Psiche*" (V, 93). The beginning of the Psyche myth follows—Venus' anger at the worship which Psyche has unwittingly distracted from the Cyprian altars, her attempt to humiliate Psyche, and Cupid's love and traditional counterplot. Midas is unimpressed and is about to leave, but Apuleius pacifies him with a satiric anti-masque of assorted human asses, which reads like a catalogue of types from the nineties, from Guilpin or Davies; it concludes with Midas' own mirror image in the person of the "Ignorant Ass." All dance

out, and Midas turns the attack by asking to see the "Poet Asse," who
would bring

> heere on the stage
> A young greene-sicknesse baggage to run after
> A little ape-fac'd boy thou term'st a god. (106)

This literalmindedness occasions Apuleius' first allegorical explication
upon his own plot: Psyche is the Soul, Cupid immortality, etc.[14]

Act II continues the Psyche legend with the first visit of her sisters,
but it is interrupted by the appearance in "Arcadia" of a clown (who is
"Midas' bastard") with a group of country swains. The clown is a cynic
like his father; he ridicules love—both in the person of Cupid and in its
effects—and poetry, reducing the *Iliad* to a cudgeling quarrel between
primitives. Cupid overhears this heresy and has a quick answer: a literal
birdbolt which is still sufficiently metaphoric to metamorphose the
doubter into a rhyming slave of Amaryllis. The Psyche story naturally
displaces his discomfort until Midas again interrupts and insists upon
presenting his own production of a country dance. Then Psyche returns,
disobeys, and loses her love, a sequence which is followed by the musical
encounter between Apollo and Pan with Midas as judge. This meeting
is woven into the Cupid-Psyche story by several devices, the most important being the parallel burden of the ass's ears for Midas and the
substitution of the now-converted clown as Pan's singer. In short, the
second myth has become an occasion to (1) assert the powerlessness of
even Midas' son against the attractions of love and poetry, and (2) to
demonstrate the mutual insistence of father and son upon reducing even
these divine sciences to the level of their own taste. It has, however,
accomplished something more. The Psyche legend re-emerges, as the
angry Boreas bearing the sinning Psyche disperses the contestants—and
thus Midas assumes a double role as audience and actor in the same
mythic masque. The Psyche legend continues, the allegory is explained
again to Midas by Apuleius, and when it does not please him, Apuleius
presents yet another satiric anti-masque in the way of a dance by "Love's
Contrarieties": "A King and a Beggar, a Young-man and an Old woman,
a Leane man, a Fat woman" (133). The Psyche myth then transfers its
action from Arcadia so that Vulcan can liberate the manacled Cupid and
is interrupted only at length by a return to the clown in Arcadia, that
we may learn from his own lips how thoroughly he has been converted
into a disciple of poetry. Midas himself reluctantly echoes this attitude
when he appears to ask Apuleius for further allegorical explications of
a story which now interests him. The final act sends Psyche to Hell for

Pandora's box of beauty. The two inner stories are fused when the clown steals the box in the hope of making his mistress more beautiful, and both are chastised and forgiven. Psyche's apotheosis comes in the context of a new mythic level: that of the annual return of Proserpina from Hades, which has grown up around the narrative of Psyche's own visit. Thus conclude myths and masques. Midas turns to the creator, Apuleius, still grumbling, and Cupid intervenes to close the play. He gives the ears to Midas and a garland to Apuleius, and emphasizes the broad fertility context of the Proserpina myth in a direct prophecy for the audience in the theater: "The Spring comes on, and *Cupid* doth divine, / Each shall enjoy his best lou'd Valentine" (160).

Any question that *Love's Mistress* might be merely another relatively direct recounting of a familiar and popular mythological theme, to which Heywood added a spice of tantalizing depth through an author-narrator, as he had done in the "Ages" plays, is dispelled by the insistent presence of Midas. Himself an actor in the mythic play, Midas, rather than the external spectators, is the object of Apuleius' attention throughout the drama, as the summary outline above indicates, and his very obtrusive, even abrasive, presence demands explanation. Why Midas? He has no traditional relationship to the Cupid-Psyche legend, and his own history certainly offers no opportunity for a parallel "thematic" development.[15] Indeed, there is nothing at all to link the two classical legends except the Apuleian framework for the Psyche story with the narrator's metamorphosis—like Midas'—into an ass. But in Heywood's play the parallel of the symbolic ears is maintained on a solely mechanical level: he does not try to reshape the stories in order to make their symbolic import similar.[16] Midas' very presence constitutes an extension which shifts the focus from narrative to audience. When the author Apuleius stands forth as recipient of the garland, the movement is completed: author as well as audience are to be placed in relation to that dramatic act which is their mutual responsibility and achievement.

Two dominant elements maintain the fluid interaction between the creators and their stage narrative, as well as the equally fluid internal relationships of the narrative itself. The first of these is less insistent, since it forms a motif to which the other gradually gives depth and significance. It is the employment of ascending and descending motion as an image of man's curiosity and knowledge. The drama begins upon this note with Apuleius' entrance:

I had a brayne aym'd at inscrutable things,
Beyond the Moone; what was sublunarie,

Me thought was for my study all too meane;
Therefore, I therefore [sic] was I thus transshap'd:
That knowing man who keepes not in his bounds,
But pries into Heavens hidden mysteries
Further then leave; his dulness is increast,
Ceaseth to be a man, and so turnes beast:
And thus I fell, yet by the selfe same power
That calls all humane wisedome foolishnesse,
Am once more to my pristine shape restor'd;
Onely to shew how vaine my ambitions were,
This follies crest I still about mee beare.   (91)

The language of humility, which drops down from its flight at the rhetorical and visual turn supplied by the word "fell," seems familiar, evoking
a Christian setting for our consideration of pride, fall, and redemption.
But at once, with a syntactical abruptness which reflects the entire
change in mood and milieu, the direction alters, the lesson learned seems
strangely forgotten, and Apuleius is once again climbing, as he demands
of the audience: "I faine would know the way to Helicon, / Can none
heere tell mee?" The response is silence, Midas enters, and Apuleius renews his request to him: "Reverend father, / How lies my journey to the
Muses hill?" (92). Midas grumbles and shrugs off such foolishness in
order to tell his own tale of metamorphosis. By his golden wish he too
became less than man. Pointing to his Phrygian cap, he almost echoes
Apuleius' language:

And where before I was a King of men,
To flie the harshness of fooles bitter jeasts,
I made this wooll crowne, and am King of beasts.   (93)

With this, the talk turns to poetry, and Apuleius settles down to present "Cupid and Psyche" for his recalcitrant spectator. But it should be
noticed that Apuleius, while still an aspirant for the ascent of divine
places, has been thoroughly "retransform'd," as he puts it, while Midas
acknowledges his perpetual role as king of beasts.

If the imagery of ascent seems to be forgotten by Apuleius as he
turns playwright and polemicist in Midas' company, it is only because
he has displaced it from his own history into the action of his dramatic
narrative. At the Delphic Oracle Psyche's family has requested both
prophecy and aid in ending her prolonged virginity; they are instructed
to "leave her on a hill" where she will meet a husband described by
Apollo as having a disturbingly paradoxical nature (95). This hill dominates the entire first section of the "Cupid and Psyche" myth within

Love's Mistress. Cupid, enamored, betrays Venus' command by re-
questing Zephirus to "mount to the top of yonder rocke and Conuey
her gently down" (99); Psyche, meanwhile, rejects the proffered aid of
her brothers-in-law in pious deference to her destiny. "I will ascend
alone," she insists, because "alone said hee [Apollo], / Distressed *Psiche*
shall climbe up yon hill" (100). The staging is complicated, and is certainly one of those moments upon which Heywood gratefully compli-
mented Inigo Jones, "who to euery Act, nay almost to euery Sceane, by
his excellent Inuentions, gave such an extraordinary Luster; upon every
occasion changing the stage, to the admiration of all the Spectators."[17]
Psyche makes visual the movement which has been only verbal, as we
learn from the stage direction, "Shee climbes up the Rocke." And even
as she is ascending over the *pietra scenica* of Jones's masque machinery,
Psyche's relatives stand below counterpointing her efforts with descriptive commentary:

> *Admetus.* What paines that poore girle takes, see how shee strives
> Against the swelling bosom of the hill.
> *Mentius.* See the kind brambles, as enamor'd of her,
> Circle her beautie in their catching armes,
> Woeing her to come back; as who should say,
> Thou run'st too fast to death, sweete *Psiche* stay.
> *Admetus.* But all in vaine, shee now hath climb'd the Rock.   (100)

When Psyche has arrived at the summit, the family leaves her to her
destiny. Jones's efforts once more come into play as Zephirus gently
lowers her to a divine banquet where she is joined by Cupid. But the
verbal-visual ascent is reviewed at the close of the first act, when Midas
insists upon the allegory and Apuleius explains that the scene

> shewes how many strong adversities,
> Crosses, pricks, thornes, and stings of conscience,
> Would throw the ambitious soule affecting heaven,
> Into despaire and fainting diffidence,
> Which Psiche must passe through; the Soule must flie
> Through thousand letts, to seeke eternitie.   (107)

Apuleius' ascent had been introduced amidst Christian echoes which
rapidly gave way to classical settings; Psyche's classical myth presents
the obverse, an ascent which is glossed in the vocabulary of Christianity.
It is a vocabulary which recurs at the crucial moments of her history.
When she has disobediently discovered, burned, and so lost Cupid, he
curses Psyche and calls Boreas not only to bear her away but to blast

the place of sin, to "make this Paradise a den of snakes; / For I will
have it uglier then hell" (123).[18] Paradise lost, Psyche must descend as
had Apuleius, but her descent is the necessary purgative for an apotheosis—and correspondingly profound. Commanded by the vengeful
Venus, Psyche is sent into the underworld to bring back the box of
beauty and, as myths merge deliberately in this last phase of the play,
the classical and Christian become inseparable, narrative and allegory
fused. "No damn'd spell / Shall keepe mee from my wrath, thy soule
from hell" (140), threatens Venus. From this point to the close of the
play the soul's damnation for the sins of pride and vain curiosity merges
with the resurrection of Proserpina in a rite of fertility, but it is a rite in
which the deified Psyche makes her last appearance as an humble Christian saint who has learned that great lesson of torment we have seen
taught Chapman's Strozza. Kneeling in the closing tableau, Psyche begs
forgiveness for her sisters:

> Have pitty on them Father, gentle husband,
> Remember not their frawd in tempting mee:
> You gods, and goddesses, with *Psiche* joyne
> To begg their pardons, all you Arcadians kneele;
> For had they not my happinesse enuy'd,
> My Love and Patience had not so been try'd.

Clearly there is a Christian gloss upon this classical myth,[19] and one
which is urged over the claims of the myth itself, in which Psyche
avenges herself by tricking her sisters into a death trap (*Metamorphoses*
V.26.7; Adlington, *The Golden Ass*, pp. 155–56). But the gloss is subdued at the close. Apuleius refuses to supply the allegory again for
Midas; the relationships should now be clear:

> there's an understanding that hath depth
> Beyond thy shallow non-sence; there's a wit,
> A braine which thou want'st, I to that submit.   (159)

The cause for this refusal is both structural and thematic. The Christian
myth of overweening aspiration, fall, and resurrection has been sufficiently recalled in the language at the turning points, and it is not part
of Heywood's intention—whatever Apuleius's aim may be—to allegorize
classical myth with the simple fecundity of an Alexander Ross. The end
overshadows the Christian element by bringing to the foreground not
only the Cupid and Psyche legend but the new parallel action of the
Proserpina myth. *Love's Mistress*, one must insist once more from this
new vantage point, is not allegory but enactment.

The fifth act opens with Mercury's arrival before Pluto and the council of Hades to bring Ceres' request for Proserpina's seasonal return to the upper world. The return is delayed only until Psyche can undergo the series of trials which ultimately permit her to receive the requisite box of Beauty from Proserpina's hand. This done, Pluto and the others join in urging Proserpina to plead Psyche's case before Venus when she arrives in the upper regions. They then bid a temporary farewell to "Queene *Proserpina*": "all hell shall mourne / With hiddious cries, till my fair love returne" (151). This is the context for the final scene of the play: Venus, Apollo, and the deities are gathered, Proserpina greets and is greeted by all with joyous recognition, and immediately upon Venus' question "saw you not *Psiche* there" (in hell) Cupid enters with his bride, explaining that

> Great *Iove* himselfe
> Call'd for a cup of Immortallitie,
> Dranke part to her, and *Psiche* quaff't the rest,
> At which, deformitie forsooke her quite,
> . . . .
> *Iove* vowing, shee should now be deifi'd.   (157–58)

Psyche kneels, the last masque element is played out as she is drawn into the ceremonial dance of the gods and goddesses, and Apollo closes the whole upon a note which merges the mythic descents and resurrections into one:

> Now circle *Psiche* in a fayrie ring,
> Whil'st I and *Venus* grace her with this Crowne;
> This done, to feast .with *Ceres*, and the gods,
> And next unto the Pallace of the Sunne,
> To end those sacred rites wee have begun.   (159)

 The vertical movement of *Love's Mistress* is, then, symbolic; but if this is clearly so, it has left the role of the playwright-protagonist Apuleius strangely suspended. As I suggested earlier, the full significance of the symbolic movement is realized only through its interaction with another dominant organizational structure which must explain and resolve Apuleius's ambiguous presentation as one who has learned the folly of pride, yet continues to aspire. Let us turn, then, to Heywood's analysis of sight and sound, the eye and the ear, as the instruments of man's knowledge, and remind ourselves, in so doing, that it was just the combined power of these organs which constituted the triumphant power of drama in the argument of his *Apology for Actors.*

The narrator's transmogrification into an ass in the *Metamorphoses* is the first note emphasized by the playwright-actor Apuleius in *Love's Mistress.* As we meet him, Apuleius retains the ears, but he retains them voluntarily, carrying them about as a *memento moriae* "onely to shew how vaine my ambitions were."[20] Just in the manner of his account of overambitious ascent, Apuleius' ears simultaneously establish a symbol for vain curiosity and exonerate the speaker himself from that taint.[21] The interlocking imagery of ascent and asinine ears constitutes a stroke of brilliant economy in sounding a prelude to the entire play for those of Heywood's spectators who recalled the *Metamorphoses* even vaguely; they would know that Lucius is transformed because he attempts bird-like flight through the agency of forbidden witches' magic[22] and is changed back into a man when he has learned his sublunar limitations—specifically, when he has vowed obedience to the goddess Isis.

Like the symbolic ascent, insistent patterns of sight and sound are at once transferred from Apuleius to his play of *"Cupid and Psyche."* The new scene opens to the music of recorders, upon which Psyche's father, King Admetus, immediately comments:

> Listen, oh listen, for these sounds that guild
> The aires light wings, fanning through all our eares
> Immortal tunes, tell us wee are arriv'd
> At sacred *Delphos.* (94)

Thus led by Apollo's divine harmony,[23] the Thessalian family reaches the oracle, which treats the eye as an instrument of terror. On the hill, Apollo predicts, Psyche will meet a husband

> whose flaming sight doth kill,
> And yet wants eyes; his serpents face
> If shee behold, she must see hell.[24] (95)

And if the husband is a blind (or blinding) vision of the unknown, Venus insists that Cupid play the Puck, strike Psyche with a "dull leaden shaft" to "Make her in Love, but let her proud eyes doate / On some ill-shapen drudge, some ugly foole" (98).[25] Unable to resist his own love, Cupid cannot bring himself to make a victim of Psyche, a fate which he reserves (with his leaden shaft) for the clown who is Midas' bastard, the satirist upon love and poetry alike until he is pinked and converted by the angry deity, after which he plays not only Titania but Bottom.[26]

When Psyche has been left alone upon the summit, Cupid persuades Zephirus to bring her to *"Cupid's* Paradise," where "Musicke with ravishing tones [will] inchant her eares" (101). The music turns out to be the disembodied voices of the Echoes, who offer her a banquet, which continues until Cupid, equally invisible (as in *Metamorphoses* V.3.15), arrives. Psyche is immediately in love, and cries: "To this sweete voice, could I enjoy the sight, / I should my selfe then stile Queene of delight" (103). But Cupid warns that this is just the prohibition of paradise, the eye sin: "Doe not perswade me to disclose my shape, / Attempting that, thou loosest this high state" (104).

We are ready to discern another verbal and structural link in Heywood's thematic chain. Apuleius had fallen because he, a Platonist as well as a traveler, had pried "into Heavens hidden mysteries / Further then leave." When Midas regrets not having seen the Echoes, Apuleius makes explicit the allegory once again:

> With a mortall eye
> None can; in them is hid this mistery;
> Celestiall raptures, that to allure the sight,
> Are seene no more then voices being on high,
> Subject unto no weake and fleshly eye.

But why, insists Midas, did Cupid wish to hide himself from Psyche? And Apuleius' reply is simplicity itself, the single all-important lesson his own metamorphosis has taught him:

> Oh who dares prie into those misteries,
> That heaven would have conceal'd; for this shee's charg'd
> Not to see *Cupids* face.[27]   (120)

It is useful to recall the double plot of the *Metamorphoses*: Apuleius-Lucius is transformed into an ass for peering into the forbidden mysteries of the witch's laboratory, while in the inner tale Psyche loses Cupid, just as she does in Heywood's version, through her insistence upon seeing his forbidden beauty. Apuleius, giving an aura of Platonic mystery and oracularity to the whole, frames the Cupid and Psyche legend as a tale told to a kidnapped young bride by her keeper, a Diotima figure, a half-demented old woman who talks of dreams.[28] In the parallel fates of the Apuleiuses and the Psyches—those who seek forbidden mysteries in the pride of human possessiveness, but seek it in such different contexts as their narratives offer—it becomes clear that Knowledge and Love, the True and the Beautiful, are one in *Love's Mistress* as in the *Metamorphoses*.[29] As Apuleius explains to Midas, the eye is mortal but the ear is the eye of the soul:

> Celestiall raptures
> . . . are seene no more then voices being on high,
> Subject unto no weake and fleshly eye.

Thus it seems proper, even inevitable, that Psyche should be most blind at the moment of her fall, the moment in which she deludes herself into triumphing in her new-found sight. As she gazes upon the still sleeping and inert Cupid in that brief vision before the end of paradise, she gloats, "Churle beauty, beautious nigard, thus Ile chide, / Why did'st thou from mine eyes this glory hide?" (121). Here eyes are opened only to her own nakedness. Stripped and deformed by the bitter Cupid, she would shun sight: "Where shall I hide me; let no human eye / Behold me thus disfigured, and asham'd" (128).[30] The vision of beauty has bought ugliness, and the avaricious eye would now be closed in darkness, for the oracle has already been fulfilled on the psychic level: "she must see hell."

Certainly one hears the voice of a more ancient tradition behind the voice of the Platonic novelist Apuleius in Heywood's adaptation of Cupid and Psyche: "And when the woman saw that the tree was good for food, and that it was pleasant to the eyes, and a tree to be desired to make one wise, she . . . did eat, and gave also unto her husband. . . . And the eyes of them both were opened, and they knew that they were naked." The Christian myth is again fusing with the classical as *Love's Mistress* adapts the heritage of ironic vision, the glass eyes and inner blindness of Genesis and of Oedipus, of Lear and of Milton.[31] Yet, appropriate as this heritage is, its invocation raises disturbing questions. Cusa may have said that man was made by hearing the voice of God speaking, Ficino may have exalted the Orphic lyre, but their emphasis—the emphasis of Renaissance Platonism as a whole—was clearly upon the primacy of vision.[32] If Heywood was no Platonist in the sense that Chapman was, it is clear that he has chosen for his author-actor a historic Platonist well known among his contemporaries. It is true also that Apuleius' Platonism, like the Christian parallels, is allowed to remain largely submerged, its presence indicated only by a few small suggestions in the drama. But one can set aside entirely the historical milieu evoked by the character Apuleius (as one could not set aside Ficino in understanding Strozza) and still be surprised and disturbed to find that

the author of *An Apology for Actors,* who had exalted the drama precisely because "to see a soldier shaped like a soldier, walke, speake, act
like a soldier . . . these were sights to make an Alexander," rejects vision
in his play about plays. We must seek a counter-balance, then, if we are
to attribute a serious import to the visual imagery which seems to develop so carefully in *Love's Mistress.*

The ear is the eye of the soul, but it is also the symbol of folly, and
the ass's ears which Apuleius bears on stage at the opening as a sign
are given life in the first anti-masque, occasioned by Midas' dissatisfac-
tion with the story of the love pact of Cupid and Psyche. Apuleius determines to cater to Midas' debased taste by showing the types he
"commerst withall" in his bestial shape and parades across stage the
usual group, the usurers and courtlings, the prodigals and drunkards,
but all "with eares." And no sooner has this satiric interlude been concluded than Psyche's story exhibits the first visit of her jealous sisters
to Cupid's paradise. Here they learn of her unseen servants, hear the
music of the echoes, and then begin the temptation to vision: they would
see the singers, they would see her secret husband. Psyche's fall has
already begun, and in desperation she summons more music and cries
"I needs must stop mine eares when Syrens sing." (109).[33] She should;
Cupid had warned her of these tempters: "shun their sight and speech"
(103). But she listens to the voices of discord, hears them project upon
Cupid the description of their own serpentine betrayal:

> Dulling thy taste with sweetes, thy eyes with shewes,
> Thy eares with musicke, and sweete lullabies,
> Hee will in time devoure thee. (117)

Sinned against, Cupid turns paradise to hell, the invocation ironically
fulfilling the twisted prophecy of the sisters: "Musicke, be turn'd to
horror" (122).

Once Psyche has fallen, every aspect of what had up to this point
appeared to be a relatively simple masque develops internal complications. Apuleius, for the first time, does not supply Midas with a commentary, for the very good reason that Midas is now a character in the
Psyche story rather than merely its spectator. Psyche is hunted from
Cupid's bower by a storm, and the clown appears with his sweetheart
and cronies to announce "musicall news, and therefore worth your
eares." Pan and Apollo (whom Venus called to Arcadia to solicit aid
against Psyche [97–99]) will contest "whether his Pipe or *Apollos* Harpe
could yeeld the better Musicke" (123). In this contest Midas' bastard
himself will sing the accompaniment to Pan's tunes, while Midas is

chosen as arbiter when Psyche's father Admetus refuses the task.[34] Of course the power of Apollo, master of the Muses, has already been demonstrated and tacitly judged by the conversion of the clown himself through Cupid's arrow. Now music will offer a parallel to spectacle, and as Midas preferred the country dance and the satiric thrust to Apuleius' mythological masque, so he prefers the piping of Pan to the diviner harmonies. In his choice he acquires the asinine stigmata which the poet Apuleius has purged from himself. Apollo gives the fiat which cross-breeds grex and myth:

> Henceforth be all your rurall musicke such,
> Made out of Tinkers, Pans, and Kettle-drummes;
> And never hence-foorth may your fields bee grac'd
> With the sweete musicke of *Apollo's* lyre.

Having cursed Arcadia with that earned cacophany with which Cupid has blasted the paradise of love, Apollo then turns directly upon Midas: "for thee, may thy eares longer grow, / As shorter still thy judgment" (127).

Ear and eye, then, no longer are set in polar opposition as right and wrong instruments for knowing; wrongly used, they are juxtaposed as emblems and instruments of man's sin against his eternal longings, the sin of impatience which proves, as Apuleius puts it in gazing upon the smug ass Midas, that "thou art all earthie, / Nothing Celestiall in thee" (133). And so these twin symbols enter the mainstream of Renaissance orthodoxy: it is not the subject but the spirit of the ego which makes knowledge a forbidden mystery.[35]

It is a point epitomized in Venus, a proud deity who sees with the outward eye. She beats and tortures the fallen Psyche with impossible tasks because, in her prelapsarian image, Psyche had confused the eyes of men:

> Iust of my height, my state, and my proportion;
> And were her pristine beauty lent her backe,
> Might in the rabbles judgment rivall mee.   (131)

But, as Apuleius explained in first elaborating the allegory:

> By *Venus* heere is meant intemperate lust:
> Lust woes her sonne *Desire*, to inflame the soule
> With some base groome, that's to some ugly sinne;
> *Desire* is good and ill: the evill sweares
> To obay his mother *Venus*, and vexe *Psiche*:

But *Cupid* representing true desire,
Doates on the Soules sweete beauty, sends his seruant
Zephirus; In whom, Celestiall pleasur's meant,
To entice his love, the Soule, to his chast bed,
Giving her heaven for her lost maiden-head.   (107)

Venus is reduced to a figure resembling Pico's *Venere volgare*, who knows only the senses—and correspondingly sees only Psyche's outward state, mirror of her own circumscribed inner nature.[36] But Desire is good and ill—like music, like the eye, like the ear, like man himself. And so it is that love can send Psyche both to hell and heaven. And so it is, further, that hell itself has a double nature, according to its use. *Love's Mistress* in its final stages must explain and justify the Apollonian oracle with which Psyche's spiritual adventure began:

                    shee must see hell;
And yet by some notorious deede,
Obtaine a Patent from that place
Neuer to die.   (95)

It is Psyche's consignment to hell in search of the box of Beauty which brings Cupid again to her side. Heretofore music and voice have either admonished or caused blindness. But now the inner eye is opening upon a new dimension, which is immediately suggested by Cupid's cry: "It is the sound of hell wakes pitties eye" (142). This is prelude to the almost synesthetic ambient of Psyche's educational ritual of descent. She must ignore the disturbing cries of Oblivion as she crosses Styx; she must ignore the pleading of the idle hags (as she had not ignored the terrestrial sisters); she must keep the box tight shut—"let not thy daring eye / Behold the wealth that in the boxe doth lie" (143). Shutting both senses to these temptations, as to the softer allurements to dine and rest, Psyche obtains her end, and, though Pluto is

                    soule-vext, that any mortall eye
Should see our customes, and returne alive,
To blab them to the wide eare of the world,   (150)

she must be let pass unmolested, for this time she has probed the hidden mysteries in the right way—with ears tuned to the command of the gods whom she had earlier ignored. Bringing life out of death, the now-pregnant Psyche joins the goddess of fertility in returning to the light, to the festivities of Phoebus-Apollo, accompanied by the fading voice of the darkness. "So farewell *Plutoes* joy," cries the subterranean king as they depart: "all hell shall mourne / With hiddious cries, till my faire love returne. (*Exeunt. Hiddeous musicke*)" (151). We are moving not only from darkness into light but from noise into the accompanying music supplied by the Muses for the divine dance.

Psyche has earned both fall and resurrection. Yet man does not live eternally by works alone. There must be one more fall, an epicyclical repetition upon a higher level of humility and awareness, before the ultimate ascension.[37] Leaving hell with Beauty in her hands, disfigured and deformed by the scars of experience, she yearns to open the sacred box and "get heavenly beautie, / Rich beautie, ever fresh, never decaying" (152). Heywood avoids sentimentality by arranging a parody at the same time, in which Midas' debased bastard watches his opportunity to steal the box, "for 'tis my duty, / My Mistris being a blowse, to find her beautie" (152). Lest her new temptation and failure be taken as simply a repetition of the first, Cupid becomes a calm audience to oversee and overhear Psyche's actions and to manipulate them outside the range of tragedy.

The clown is treated farcically. Cupid charms him to sleep and substitutes a *"Boxe full of ugly Painting"* for the original at his side. Awakening, he smears his face with the colors and plays Bottom the Ass for his country compatriots, boasting of his new beauty while they shun him. But the farce has a point, for again the spectator who knows the source novel will be reminded of the episode of Lucius' metamorphosis into an ass: it was accomplished by the stolen witch's salve, which he applied to himself in the hope of attaining the power of celestial flight (*Metamorphoses* III. 21–24). There is also a significance entirely internal to *Love's Mistress*, for the clown smugly dismisses his companions' comments: "This 'tis to be meere mortalls, . . . their dull eyes cannot judge of Celestiall beautie" (155). In this last observation before he goes off to the earthly marriage with Amaryllis which is the parody of Psyche's nuptials, the clown has demonstrated the inevitable truth of Apuleius' earlier caveat: "Celestiall raptures" are "subject unto no weake, and fleshly eye" (120). But as woman, as an Eve, as Man, as the Soul, Psyche has fallen through the sights and sounds of this world only to attain a paradise happier far. And so her marriage masque is performed upon another stage, where Jove and all the powers have done even as Apollo petitions Venus to do: "At length with a commiserating eye, / Looke on distressed *Psiche*" (156). And on this new stage the dance of the deities is performed before celestial eyes to a harmony unheard upon the earth. "View as spectators," Cupid cries, "how our joy appears, / Dancing to the sweete musicke of the spheares" (159).

Although it should now be clear that Heywood's development of the Cupid and Psyche myth is a complex and rich pattern of traditional symbols set into dramatic action which gradually develops and refines their significance, nothing has been done to justify those large claims made at the beginning of this discussion: that Apuleius is the primary protagonist of *Love's Mistress* and that the play is a ritual in a precise sense of that much-abused term. It is time to examine the evidence for these claims, having prepared the ground from which we can advance to a wider view of Heywood's accomplishment.

The debate on poetry begins at once. Apuleius seeks the Muses' hill because he "must to them performe a sacrifice" (92), interrupting his journey only to demonstrate to Midas through the Cupid and Psyche story that "all true Poets raptures are divine" (93). Midas' first reaction, as we saw above, is one of annoyance at the triviality—if not immorality—of the play:

> thou bring'st heere on the stage
> A young greene-sicknesse baggage to run after
> A little ape-fac'd boy thou term'st a god;
> Is not this most absur'd? (106)

This literalism has a point, of course. On the face of it, Apuleius' little play is as precious and trivial as any eighteenth-century Arcadian outpouring. Apuleius cries out in exasperation, "Mis-understanding foole, thus much conceive, / *Psiche* is *Anima, Psiche* is the Soule," and so away, coursing the letter of every detail of what he is presenting as a philosophico-religious *roman à clef* by turning the allegorized tenor upmost to the view. But the exasperation is defensive; one can scarcely blame the bewildered Midas, who, despite his admission to his instructor, "Thou promp'st my understanding pretty well," continues to need the author's translation in order really to understand the play.

When Midas' bastard arrives on the scene, the shoe is upon the other foot. Now it is the swains who admire Homer and the poets who "misse of misunderstanding," according to the clown, and with a magnificent display of euhemerism, he rivals the puppets of *Bartholomew Fair* in reducing poetry to its source:

by this *Troy* ranne a small Brooke, that one might stride over; on the other side dwelt *Menelaus* a Farmer, who had a light wench to his Wife call'd *Hellen*, that kept his sheepe, whom *Paris*, one of *Priams* mad lads, seeing and liking, ticeth over the brooke, and lies with her in despight of her husbands teeth; for which wrong, hee sends for one *Agamemnon* his brother, that was then high Constable of the hundred, and complaynes to him.   (113)

By the time the butcher Ajax has exchanged cudgel blows on a holiday with the baker Hector from the other hundred ("And heere was all the circumstance of the *Trojan* Warres"), the swains' spokesman is disposed to admit that the clown has "taught us more than ever I understood before, concerning Poetrie" (114). This is, of course, only an opinion drawn out of him by the audacious rhetoric with which the clown dazzles his companions. But later in the drama—Apuleius' drama as well as Heywood's, or rather Apuleius' drama within Heywood's—we are shown that, strangely enough, the clown's account has been rather accurate. This is the humble, quotidian way in which poetic myths *do* originate.

The demonstration piece is the scene in Vulcan's forge at the beginning of act IV, occasioned by Cupid's need of help in striking off the manacles his angry mother imposed upon him after the Psyche affair. The scene must have been one of Inigo Jones's delights in preparing the sets for Denmark House: a dark cavern, flames and belching smoke, the great lame figure amidst his scurrying workers—yet all made homely by Vulcan's first words:

> Neptune hath broke his Mace, and *Iunos* Coach
> Must bee new mended, and the hind-most wheeles
> Must have two spokes set in; Phoebus fore-horse
> Must have two new shooes, calk'd, and one remove;
> *Pans* Sheepe-hooke must be mended shortly too,
> Plie it of all hands, wee have much to doe.   (135)

This is the daily life of the gods before the poets magnify them into immortals.

Love's Mistress is not the first occasion upon which Heywood deals with the theme; indeed, euhemerism so completely dominates other interests in *The Golden Age* that the play was subtitled "the Deifying of the Heathen Gods."[38] Homer enters to begin the play by explaining that his right to return and sing once more has been given him by his own creatures:

> The Gods of *Greece,* whose deities I rais'd
> Out of the earth, gaue them diuinity,
> The attributes of Sacrifice and Prayer,
> Haue giuen old *Homer* leaue to view the world
> And make his owne presentment.   (III, 5)

The "presentment," of course, is a re-enactment of his original immortalizing song. The play opens with an expository discussion between two followers of a primitive court which is not much different in culture and attitudes from that of Lear or Leontes. Uranus is dead, and the question of a successor is on everyone's lips, since there are two sons, Titan and Saturn. Saturn's succession is largely a function of his public-spirited technology; a country clown explains, amidst familiar jokes and bawdy, that "he hath taught his people to sow, to plow, to reape corne, and to skorne Akehornes with their heeles, to bake and to brue. . . . Besides, he hath deuised a strange engine, called a Bow and Arrow, that a man may hold in hand, and kill a wild beast a great way off" (11). And it is these achievements which draw from his lords at court the first intimations of immortality. As one says for all, "*Saturnes* inuentions are diuine, not humane, / A god-like spirit hath inspir'd his reigne," and another provides the chorus of confirmation: "*Saturne* is a God" (12).

But deity itself is confused by the process of becoming, and if Saturn sometimes begins to believe his flatterers ("The Gods [if there by any boue our selfe] / Enuy our greatnesse" [13]), at other times he desperately petitions the powers:

> Diuine assistance plunge me from these troubles,
> Mortality here failes me, I am wrapt
> In millions of confusions.[39]   (40)

It is a confusion not lightened for the audience by Homer's ambiguity. When Saturn is certain that through an anachronistic Delphic Oracle Jupiter is doomed because "the Gods say he must dy" (52), Homer comments, "men are borne their owne fates to pursue, / Gods will be Gods, and *Saturne* finds it true" (53). But who are the gods? Or, put another way, what are men? Jupiter himself at the play's end claims godhead and yet roots it in the earth:

> Here end the pride of our mortality.
> Opinion, that makes Gods, must style vs higher.

The next you see vs, we in state must shine,
Eternized with honours more diuine.   (77)

And, as though in obedience to his own invention's voice, Homer provides a spectacular dumbshow of the division of the elements among
Jupiter, Neptune, and Pluto:

     ere we further wade,
The ground of ancient Poems you shall see:
And how these (First borne mortall) Gods were made,
By vertue of diuinest Poesie.   (78)

 Throughout *The Silver Age* and *The Brazen Age*, the supernatural
status of the mythological figures is never brought into serious question
by either presenter or players, and in the midst of the latter play Homer
takes the occasion of Jason's return with the Golden Fleece to advance
these claims to a still higher stage of truth. If poetry turns the narratives
of men's lives into the glorified patterns of mythology, myth itself is
in turn but the image of eternal truths—hidden mysteries:

Let none to whom true Art is not deny'd,
Our monstrous Buls, and magicke Snakes deride.
Some thinke this rich Fleece was a golden Booke,
The leaues of parchment, or the skins of Rammes,
Which did include the Art of making gold
By Chimicke skill, and therefore rightly stild,
The *Golden Fleece*. . . .
. . . .
The sages, and the wise, to keep their Art
From being vulgar: yet to haue them tasted
With appetite and longing, giue those glosses,
And flourishes to shadow what they write,
Which might (at once) breed wonder and delight.
So did th'Aegyptians in the Arts best try'd,
In *Hieroglyphickes* all their Science hide.   (III, 221–22)

When Chapman or the Florentine Platonists make such observations
upon the Mysteries in myths they have more importance[40]—and less:
more, because the Platonists were constantly intent upon recovering and
perpetuating the eternal secrets of the Mysteries; less, because Heywood
is dealing with the essential process of poetry as a truly "divine" art or
—to make a serious pun—an art of divining. In the course of his three
plays Homer has created the mythic apotheosis of the pagan gods, but

he does not seem to be certain of—he certainly did not originally intend —their allegorical relationship to the Mysteries.

And that is just the point, not only of his involuted (if insufficiently clarified) relation to his own creations, but of Apuleius' presentation of *"Cupid and Psyche"* in *Love's Mistress.* Poetry makes every history into myth—so the clown had explained in rural Arcadia's version of the Trojan War, so Heywood and Apulieus imply by the scene at Vulcan's forge. But this is not to falsify history; it is to seek the pattern of its inward meaning through its outward show. True poetry tries to image the invisible reality in shadows. But the poet, too, must learn that patience which restrains the merely human from trying to see the mysteries with Midas' "fleshly eye." To create Beauty which is also "true," he must accept his instrumental role, must accept the autonomy of his creation both in itself—as Homer accepts the divinity of his gods—and in the imagination of his audience—as Homer accepts the glosses of the Egyptian sages. And nowhere is this autonomy better seen than on the stage, for the poet is always, after all, himself both playwright and actor, as Heywood reminded us in the old trope with which he introduced his defense of the drama: "The world's a Theatre, the earth a Stage, / Which God, and nature doth with Actors fill."

 As we have observed of *Love's Mistress,* when she enacts the physical image of her fall and resurrection, when she descends into hell in order to begin the rite by which she will be forgiven for experience, the rite which begins in hell that it may end in "the bright Pallace of Eternitie" (158), Psyche fuses into a parallel movement with the returning Proserpina.[41] The goddess comes at Ceres' behest, bringing a fertility shared by the pregnant Psyche and by the world at large. She comes as the Daughter, as one of Western man's most enduring images of life renewed.

But there is a peculiarity about Proserpina's classical resurrection from hell. Arisen, she is greeted by Apollo in a ring of deities:

> Welcome faire sister, from the vaults below,
> Wee two are Twins, of faire *Latona* borne,
> And were together nurst in *Delos* Ile;
> You guide the night, as I direct the day,
> Darknesse and light betwixt us wee divide. (156)

The mythological genealogy, of course, is hopelessly muddled; what Natale Conti had carefully unwound and sundered in his *Mythologia* (where Heywood might have found all of his elements in their most elaborate Renaissance review), Heywood blithely tangles. Proserpina is Ceres' daughter; but through her participation in *Hecate triplex*—identified as Luna in the heavens, Diana on the earth, and Proserpina in the underworld—she is alternately the daughter of Latona and twin to Apollo. Until the moment of Apollo's greeting, Proserpina has been treated as Ceres' daughter because this relationship is elaborated in Apuleius' *Metamorphoses*, where Psyche serves in Ceres' temple before descending to the underworld (VI, 1–2). But Heywood is not being careless. Reidentifying Proserpina as the Moon was a means of widening the scope of the perpetual renewal even beyond the terrestrial realm, uniting Psyche's divine assumption with the older mythic assumption of Proserpina into the heavens themselves. He had made this intent explicit in *The Silver Age*, where Ceres hands in "Proserpine *attired like the Moone*" and promises a chorus of country folk "plenty and increase," "golden stalkes of wheat to bend / Below their laden riches," as she herself is "Queene of all fertility" and "mother of this beauteous childe the Moone" (III, 133–34). Later in the play Jupiter himself adjudicates the dispute for Proserpina's presence. She cannot be taken from Pluto, she cannot be taken from earth—but on earth she is primarily Luna in Jupiter's mind: "Be she confin'd / Below the earth, where be the ebbes and tides?" Thus he divides the year into twelve parts "cal'd *Moneths of the Moone*":

> When *Ceres* on the earth
> Shall want her brightnesse, *Pluto* shall enjoy it,
> When heauen contains her, she shall light the earth
> From her bright spheare aboue.[42]
> (163)

Then too, there is the encouragement of the *Metamorphoses* itself, in which the re-metamorphosed and humbly obedient Lucius is finally initiated into the hidden mysteries of the temple, where the goddess comes to him in a dream vision, "resembling the light of the Moone," to reveal her identity: "My name, my divinity is adored throughout all the world in divers manners . . . for the Phrygians call me the mother of the Gods . . . the Candians, Diana: the Sicilians, Proserpina: the Eleusians, Ceres: some Juno, other Bellon, other Hecate: and principally the Aetheopians which dwell in the Orient, and the Aegyptians which are excellent in all kinds of ancient doctrine . . . doe call mee Queene Isis."[43]

This actually brings us to the most startling departure of all those

Heywood made from the *Metamorphoses*, rather than leading us back to the source: there is no initiation scene in the temple for Apuleius in *Love's Mistress*, no culmination. After the dance of the deities, Midas grumbles; Apuleius says, as he had begun by saying, that Midas has no sense; and Cupid awards Apuleius a laurel and Midas the ears in a final cavalier exit which is really an epilogue for the audience. To realize this is to turn again to the revelation of Proserpina as the Moon, and to discover here that culmination which seems wanting in the narrative, and yet toward which the entire play has been moving, structurally and thematically.

Apuleius confessed that his fall into folly was occasioned by trying to transcend with human wisdom the "sublunarie"—to pierce "Beyond the Moone." And yet his search continued upward once again, toward the Muses' Hill. In his presentation of that play in which he is also actor, he succeeded in retelling the love story of "a young greene-sicknesse baggage" and "a little ape-fac'd boy" with enough insight to transmogrify it into the most universal of myths, that of man's fall through experience and return through love and patience. He juxtaposed it to the prehistoric fertility rites identified with the pagan Proserpina as well as with Christian history and measured its universal dimensions from past to future and from hell to heaven. As Psyche's myth closes, the dance is overseen by Apollo, deity of poetry, while the music of the spheres plays to the voices of the Muses. But now the dance is joined by Apollo's other aspect, his sister Proserpina, the lunar deity of renewal spanning hell and heaven, who is greeted at the gathering of the gods by Vulcan:

> Cousen Queene,
> I am even moone-sicke, and half merry mad,
> For joy of thy arrival.   (157)

The dance which Apuleius half-invents and half-attends is the union of Sun and Moon,[44] poetry and the promise of life eternally renewed, marriage and mystery, Beauty and Truth, in a single harmony. Returning humbly in the winding ascent of the hidden heights which he had once attempted to assault, satisfied now in the knowledge shared with Heywood's Homer and his pregnant Psyche that man is not a god, but the vessel of the gods' grace, Apuleius has found Apollo's peak where the Muses sing. It has led him out of the "sublunarie," "Beyond the Moon." Having sought the right ends in the wrong spirit of pride, he fell as Psyche falls; having found the right spirit of humility and obedience, he rises as she rises, for as he presents the dance of the deities, he is singing *with* the Muses the song of his own Fortunate Fall.

I said in the opening pages of this chapter that ritual is an efficacious re-enactment of a pre-established pattern—efficacious because it predicts a future contingency which fulfills itself in the very evolution of the ritual. The argument of the succeeding pages has been that the Apuleius of *Love's Mistress* is both playwright of and participant in a mythic pattern of resurrection which is as old as Proserpina and as new as the closing moments of the play. *Love's Mistress* presupposes that the act of poetic creation is the road to union between the human and the transcendent, and the play is about a man engaging in that activity until he finds himself at the point of convergence with and through his own creatures. If my assumptions and those of the play have been demonstrated in the course of our discussion, we must readjust our historic prejudices somewhat and agree that *Love's Mistress* is really a specimen of that creature so often thought a chimera: a drama which is in the strictest sense an enactment of ritual.

BEAUMONT: *THE KNIGHT OF THE BURNING PESTLE*

It is fair to say that *The Knight of the Burning Pestle*, from its suggestive title through its satire upon the societal, fictional, and filial pieties of middle-class London, constitutes one of the few enduring triumphs of Beaumont's short-lived dramatic career. It was not immediately popular. Writing a few years after it was first produced, the publisher of the printed version offered an explanation for its initial failure in the theater: "the wide world . . . for want of judgement, or not understanding the privy marke of *Ironie* about it (which shewed it was no of-spring of any vulgar braine) utterly rejected it."[45]

For those who missed the irony, it must have been a confusing theatrical experience indeed. The Prologue enters to speak his piece and is immediately put out by a grocer, who climbs onto the stage, brings up his wife, sits down among the tobacco-taking gallants familiar from Dekker, and insists on injecting into the play his apprentice-boy Rafe, who is tolerated on the stage by the boy players who are attempting to present the city play titled "*The London Merchant*." In that play two plots interweave: Old Master Merrythought's son Jasper is apprentice to Venturewell, the London merchant. Venturewell tries to wed his daughter Luce to a hapless older man, Master Humphrey, but finds his plans balked by her love for Jasper. He is the more mature and pious son of a

Merrythought whose irresponsible and irrepressible good-humor cause his wife and his other son, Michael, to desert him. All goes on in a fashion which would be ordinary domestic romance and bathos, were it not for Merrythought's extravagant moods, until the runaway lovers are met in Waltham Forest not only by Mistress Merrythought but by Rafe, the grocer's boy. He has taken on himself (at the insistence of his patrons) something of a Quixote character, and here he begins to interfere with the planned plot of the "other" play as the grocer urges him to thrash Jasper as a lesson to proud apprentices. This interference gets worse until ultimately, unable to satisfy the ever more urgent demands of the London couple for action, the boy player turns to the audience, shrugs his shoulders, and gives over direction of activities to them. "It shall be done. It is not our fault, gentlemen" (IV, 49). The actions of "*The London Merchant*" are then brought to a ragged conclusion among chivalrous bouts, May Day pageants, and ludicrous allegorical death scenes presented by Rafe on orders from the grocer and his wife by turns.[46]

This, of course, is a satire upon city chauvinism in general ("Why, present something notably in honour of the commons of the City," cries the London grocer; "I will have a citizen, and he shall be of my owne trade. . . . I will have a grocer, and he shall do admirable things" [Induction, ll. 29–35]) and upon Heywood's plays in particular as popular statements of such sentiments ("what was sir *Dagonet*? was not he prentice to a grocer in *London*? read the play of the *Foure Prentices of London*, where they tosse their pikes so" [46–48]). But the extravagance of Rafe's chivalric encounters with illusory monsters and giants goes beyond any of Thomas Heywood's excesses: Beaumont's satiric sights are set upon yet another—if closely related—dramatic manifestation of public bad taste: the meandering romance transferred to the scenes and machines of the stage, whose continuing popularity had been recently demonstrated in *Sir Clyomon and Sir Clamydes* and *The Wisdom of Doctor Doddypol*. But it was, of course, less the plays in these traditions than the audiences that encouraged them which was the butt of the satire. This point is made in the Induction, when the Prologue is interrupted by the grocer clambering over the rails shouting "Hold your peace, good-man boy." "What do you meane sir?" demands the perplexed young actor. The merchant is clear enough: the theater (probably the Blackfriars) has been presenting too many plays like—well, like *The Knight of the Burning Pestle*: "That you have no good meaning: This seven yeares there hath beene playes at this house, I have observed it, you have still girds at Citizens; And now you call your play *The London Merchant*. Downe with your title, boy" (6–10). This satire upon the cits continues throughout, as the running commentary of the grocer and his wife reveals their aesthetic confusions and their narrow class sentiments. Finally, of course, the thespian urge of the unsophisticated is satirized in Rafe's dramatic reputation ("hee will act you sometimes at our house, that all the neighbours cry out on him: he will fetch you up a couraging part so in the garret, that we are all as feard, I warrant you, that wee quake again" [67–69]) and his strutting on the boards, which is similar to the contemporary parody of citizen dramatics by the boys of St. John's College, Oxford, in their *Narcissus* for the Twelfth Night festivities in 1602 or the company of Sir Oliver Owlet's Men in *Histrio-mastix*.[47]

So much for the elements of satire in *The Knight of the Burning Pestle*, which have long been appreciated even if they seem to have been missed by many in its first audience. But the first publisher's dedicatory letter contains a suggestion that the play cuts deeper: "If it bee slighted or traduced, it hopes his father will beget him a younger brother, who shall revenge his quarrell, and challenge the world either of fond and meerely literall interpretation, or illiterate misprision." The irony which provides for the satiric motifs we have noticed is clear enough for any eye even slightly more sophisticated than that of the grocer himself to see, but if the literal interpretation (on which this play might be thought merely a better version of the St. John's College boys' *Narcissus*, say) misses the point, if the irony is not upon the surfaces we have glanced over, where does it lie? A clue is the dedication, which immediately moves on to deny a debt: "Perhaps it will be thought to bee of the race of *Don Quixote*: we . . . may confidently sweare, it is his elder above a yeare." This remark has generated much speculation as to the date of the first presentation;[48] in any event, it protests too much, and points up rather than denying the indisputable adaptation of some episodes from a version of *Don Quixote*. Indeed, Rafe's chivalrous wanderings begin as a fictional plot which emerges gradually from the reading of romances, precisely in the manner of Quixote's own. After being pressed into the dramatic company by his master, Rafe appears acting his own role as grocer's apprentice, but reading "*Palmerin of England*" in the shop, and exclaiming: "But what brave spirit could be content to sit in his shop with a flappet of wood and a blew apron before him, selling *Methridatum* and *Dragons water* . . . that might pursue feates of Armes" (I, 241–44). Thenceforth, in imitation of both spirit and letter of *Don Quixote*, he frightens the innocent and continually finds himself the victim of illusions, sometimes self-invented, sometimes encouraged by the contrivances of others. So far does this world of illusion impress itself upon his usual milieu that the grocer-spectator eventually comes under its paradoxically anti-realistic spell as a part of his reaction to the verisimilitude of literalism. When Jasper has wrenched the burning pestle from Rafe, the self-dubbed knight, and beaten him in Waltham Wood, the grocer turns to reassure his wife: "I have found out the matter, sweete-heart; *Jasper* is inchanted. . . . he could no more have stood in *Raph's* hands, then I can stand in my Lord Maior's. I'le have a ring to discover all inchantments, and *Raph* shall beat him yet" (II, 314–18).

Don Quixote is more than a sympathetic source for those aspects of *The Knight of the Burning Pestle* which satirize the absurdities of the debased literature of chivalry; Cervantes' masterpiece is also a fellow to Beaumont's more modest achievement in the complex spirit with which it approaches the relationship between art and life, spontaneity and tradition. For if *Don Quixote* satirizes the absurd manner in which the literature of chivalry infects the good villager's imagination (at once so literal as to take all fiction as history and so symbolic as to convert all facts into fictions), it also profoundly questions faith in those "facts": Quixote's dream world gradually transmogrifies them not only for himself but for the audience of his madness, who are at once actors in the adventures and readers of that book which Quixote is continually rewriting. The action is located in some ambiguous realm between the manuscript and printed versions of *Don Quixote*—between the pseudo-*Quixote* which the characters all know and discuss and the plains and villages of a Spain too modern for the knight-errant of the shaving-basin helmet. At almost the very moment when Jonson's Zeal-of-the-Land-Busy was being converted by the sexless puppets of *Bartholomew Fair,* Don Quixote was entering a marionette play to aid the hero by thrashing the pagan puppets of Master Peter, demonstrating that same literalness of mind which leads Beaumont's grocer-spectator to pay the innkeeper of the Bell when Rafe (in an adaptation of Quixote's adventure) refuses to pay for his lodging.[49] As the history comes to a close at Don Quixote's deathbed, however, the good man regains his ability to distinguish reality from his visions, and the world of the sane weeps not only at his but at its own disenchantment. The friends who so long tried to dissuade him from folly would now persuade him to join them in a willed pastoral idyll; as Quixote dies, a world is dying. The final fiction is at the close, when the "author," Cid Hamete Benengeli, puts up his pen and warns off all writers who might try to revive either Quixote or knight-errantry—both are dead: "For my sole object has been to arouse men's contempt for all fabulous and absurd stories of knight errantry." But ironically the Arab historian's characters have, of course, escaped him. The world of knight-errantry he pretends to destroy has been immortalized in Cervantes' book, and its symbol is being mourned by the characters. Toward the close of the first part of *Don Quixote*, the protagonist had argued the values of this chivalrous literature with a well-meaning, intelligent canon who doubted the verisimilitude of books of adventure. At first, Quixote reacts with absurd credulousness: "Books which have been printed by royal licence . . . could they be lies and at the same time appear so much like the truth? For do they not specify the father, the mother, the family, the time, the place, and the actions, detail by detail and day by day, of this or that knight?"[50] Then he outlines a typical plot: his presentation is lyric; its magical and glorious elements are childish. But at the close, his comment on it all is an undeniable reminder of that which Heywood's Homer and Apuleius had learned about the myths which were their own literary vehicles: a young green-sickness baggage and a little ape-faced boy may reveal the essence of Love. It is undeniable that Quixote is accurate in reporting: "I can say of myself that since I became a knight errant I have been valiant, courteous, liberal, well-bred, generous, polite, bold, gentle and patient." Art has triumphed over Don Quixote's life, but in the end, that life has raised art to a level undreamed of in the "author" Cid Hamete's intent.

In similar fashion, if *The Knight of the Burning Pestle* satirizes those who are caught up in the "realistic" aspect of drama, its irony also cuts deeper: it attacks the more "sophisticated" assumption that drama is all artifice, a structure controlled by and obedient to the playwright's intentions and limitations. We have seen how Apuleius learned the humility of creation in *Love's Mistress*, a ritual in which the act of writing became itself only a symbol for the larger action of life. We may be prepared by *Don Quixote* and Apuleius to see *The Knight of the Burning Pestle* as a play whose roots in ritual are so strong that they nourish even this, their most debased offspring, turning back the disruptive efforts of its several would-be authors into the original fertile pattern of comedy.

It seems to me no accident that, as dramatic analogues to *The Knight of the Burning Pestle*, *Narcissus*, a university play about a citizen's play prepared for the traditional Christmas revels, comes to mind, or *A Midsummer Night's Dream*, a species of sophisticated *mariazo* which presents both satiric and mythological weddings as offerings at a real one,[51] both in the mood of the traditional May fertility celebration. If drama as we know it is clearly the development of folk rituals so sturdy that they elaborated rather than shriveling away under ecclesiastical attack upon them as pagan vestiges and impious outpourings, then the drama of the folk will always have some recognizable tendency to look back toward these generative forms—if only because they so often exist almost unchanged for centuries alongside their more developed theatrical offspring in the life of the people. Both *Narcissus* and *A Midsummer Night's Dream* are in large part plays about the plays of a popular audience—the audience which we call the "folk."[52] In this they are not ritual plays, of course, but plays *about* ritual plays. As such, they provide the "generic" framework, if we may so style it, for *The Knight of the Burning Pestle.*

Beaumont, however, has taken the final step: his *is* a ritual play. Everywhere it is permeated by the citizen family's sense of the kinship between ritual entertainment and the theatrical experience in which they are both so much at home and so lost (Rafe has played in *Musidorus,* misquotes Hotspur, and once "should have played *Jeronimo* with a Shooemaker, for a wager" [Induction, ll. 82–83]). The first suggestion comes when Rafe's participation in the play has been accepted by the boy Prologue and the grocer sends for music by "the waits of South-warke . . . as rare fellowes as any are in England" (Induction, ll. 101–3), for the Waits were a familiar relic of late medieval minstrelsy whose duty, aside from piping the watches, was to play at pageants and the annual festivals.[53] But what is the particular pageant-that-is-becoming-a-play?

The grocer, tiring of adventures in town and wood toward the close, demands something "to the eternall honour and glory of all *Grocers*": "Let *Raph* come out on May-day in the morning and speake upon a conduit with all his Scarfes about him, and his fethers and his rings and his knacks" (IV, 8–10). Rafe does so in typical fashion—typical, that is, of the age-old incrustations upon the celebrations of spring—May Day, Midsummer Eve:

London, to thee I do present the merry Month of May,
Let each true Subject be content to heare me what I say:
. . . from the top of Conduit head. . . .
. . . .
And by the Common-councell, of my fellowes in the Strand,
With guilded Staffe, and crossed Skarfe, the May-lord here I stand.
. . . .
Rejoyce, ô Citty, Towne, and Country, rejoyce eke every Shire;
For now the fragrant Flowers do spring and sprout in seemely sort,
. . . .
The Morrice rings while Hobby-horse doth foote it feateously:

The Lords and Ladies now abroad for their disport and play,
Do kisse sometimes upon the Grasse, and sometimes in the Hey.

(IV, 25–40)

The doggerel is absurd, and so is the imagery of country freshness, tarnished not only by Rafe's displacement from Robin's dale and the village green into "Conduit-head" and the Strand but also by the displacement of Rafe, rite, and the audience into the precious artificiality represented by the sophisticated theater of the Boy companies. May Day soon seems forgotten as the tawdry tastes and short span of attention of the citizen's wife determine that Rafe shall give up his May Lord role to lead the city militia in a mock skirmish to the tune of guns and drums. He does so, with full satiric review, in the manner of a little Falstaff. For a moment the Boys' "The London Merchant" interrupts, but the citizen spectators want more of Rafe, and since it is the close, the wife wants it done properly: "*Raph*, come away quickely and die boy," shouts the grocer at her request (V, 272).

In dying (and so closing *The Knight of the Burning Pestle*), Rafe reviews his chivalrous adventures, recalls his role as "Lord of the May" and then as a militiaman, and departs in a grocer-like allegory:

> Then comming home, and sitting in my Shop
> With Apron blew, death came unto my Stall
> To cheapen *Aqua-vitae*; but ere I
> Could take the bottle downe, and fill a taste,
> Death caught a pound of Pepper in his hand,
> And sprinkled all my face and body ore,
> And in an instant vanished away.
> . . . .
> Then tooke I up my Bow and Shaft in hand,
> And walkt into *Moore-fields* to coole my selfe,
> But there grim cruell death met me againe,
> And shot this forked arrow through my head,
> And now I faint, therefore be warn'd by me,
> My fellowes every one of forked heads.　　　　(V, 306–19)

All has been made of debased coin, and the citizens are satisfied. The wife smugly orders Rafe to arise for his *plaudite*: "doe your obeysance to the Gentlemen and go your waies, well said *Raph*" (V, 328–29).

"*The London Merchant*" concludes with the love of Jasper and Luce triumphant after their midsummer wanderings in a Waltham Forest which seems in the psychic and symbolic neighborhood of the Athenian woods of *A Midsummer Night's Dream*. As is decorous for a spring celebration, age bows to youth, and Jasper weds his Luce. This is the happy history over which we might well expect Rafe as May Lord to preside as a comic spirit, versifying the renewal of the lovers' season in which "the little birds do sit and sing," and in which he does exhort: "Up then, I say, both yong and old, both man and maide a Maying" (IV, 57). But as we have seen, he discards his May Lord role for that of the militia captain, whose exhortation is to "shew to the world you can as well brandish a sword as shake an apron. St. *George* and on my hearts" (V, 150). In his role of knight-errant he earlier interrupted the history of the young lovers as he attacked Jasper, to the citizen wife's cacophonous chorus of "Breake's pate *Raph*, breake's pate, *Raph*, soundly" (II, 296), in that very Waltham Wood which should have been the symbol of amorous harmony.

We are brought back by all this to Rafe's debt to the example of Don Quixote, which seems to constitute an obfuscation of purpose, an irreconcilable countercurrent to the narrative. The taste of the modern citizen (nurtured by the shoddy chauvinism of Heywood's or Dekker's more opportunistic trivialities) has contorted the performance into a barbarous parody of drama and ritual pageantry. The "actions" of the several abortive plays do not intertwine in the maze-like weaving we saw at work in *Love's Mistress:* they bump and jostle and cut one another short. But in spite of this all are unified in a larger pattern which makes the ephemeral, topical satire on taste and naïveté a mere instrument to express the eternal validity of ritual action. This ritual action is the Renaissance version of the spring renewal rites, the "May" festival of augury and propitiation which was such anathema to the Puritans, who recognized its provenance intuitively, if not historically. Whether falling on May Day or St. John's Day, whether a post-Lenten or a midsummer celebration, it was fertile with the dangers which Phillip Stubbes gained immortality by describing in his often-quoted *Anatomie of Abuses:* "Against May, Whitsunday, or other time all the young men and maids, old men and wives, run gadding over night to the woods, groves, hills, and mountains, where they spend all the night in pleasant pastimes . . . and no marvel, for there is a great Lord present amongst them, as superintendent and Lord over their pastimes and sports, namely, Satan, prince of hell."[54]

These spring rites, which we met as resonant mythology in *Love's Mistress,* are present as contemporary folk form in *The Knight of the Burning Pestle,* and if it is itself a rite rather than an archeological play about folk rites, it is because the satirized "folk" constantly misunderstand and try to frustrate a pattern which enacts itself.

"A rapid historical review of the spring festivals in Italy from antiquity to our own time will be necessary . . . to bring attention to the manner in which all the rites which may be carried out here can be seen to lead back to two inspiring themes: the nuptial and the agonistic." So Paolo Toschi sets forth upon his definitive investigation into the folk aspects of the varied forms of comic and epic drama in Italy.[55] There is no need to discuss here the nuptial forms, the *bruscelli*, the *mariazi*, the *mogliazzi*, which bespeak their own inevitable association with fertility. But it is worth noting briefly that Professor Toschi devotes about half of his exhaustive study to the agonistic forms which, of course, arise in the twilight zone of folk-loristic Ur history from the saturnalian patterns involving diabolic exorcism, the scapegoat, the *charivari*, etc., but which the Renaissance so fully associated with the historic and legendary matter of chivalry:

We now know that in spring rites the motif of struggle is no less petitionary and fecundative than is the sexual motif, and we see them both present in the May festivals, not contrasted but, we might say, in collaboration. . . . The first of May [in the Middle Ages] was the festival of the army: in a *campo di Marte* there took place a general gathering of the armed forces and the commandant passed them in review. . . .The military encampments became also the centers for great massings of the people; fairs and markets were held; the popular poets gathered about themselves a public which enthused over the warlike deeds exalted in their songs; thus epic poetry flowered . . . around the military tents of the fields of May.[56]

Ritual, says Toschi, moved from song to dance—the agonistic dances of battle, the sword dance, the *moresca*—and from dance to the fully developed *Maggi*, whose battles between Turks and Christians remained at least at choreographic as they were dramatic and whose titles so often remind us of Don Quixote's library—*La rotta di Roncisvalle, Le glorie di Rinaldo, l'Orlando matto, il Rinaldo appassionato.*[57] But these comments on Italian literature offer us only convenient touchstones (and more documentation) for the development of such agonistic rites as the sword dance into the morris dance and of the morris dance into the mummers' plays of St. George. These English phenomena of the same order, if less rich than their Italian counterparts, nonetheless followed a parallel history toward incorporation into May celebrations.[58] This agonistic aspect of the spring rites provides a folklore background for Rafe's Quixote-like questing in the trappings of chivalry or for his Hock-tide drill parade of the militia at Mile-End in the name of St. George (protagonist of the Sword Dance in particular, if also of all English chivalric legend in general), no less than for his May Lord speech or the general city-to-country movement of the love action or the youth-over-age motif of the marriage plot. Nature and nuptial and mock-agon all are elements traditionally associated with the spring festivities.

To say all this only directs our attention to Beaumont's employment of certain elements which coalesce in the folk rituals and which drew from those rituals much of the historic force with which they helped to shape drama in the late Middle Ages and Renaissance. Long before we find them in *The Knight of the Burning Pestle*, they had matured into independent life in developed comedy and romance of the most sophisticated sort; we need only recall that, even if the tone of their treatment differs immeasurably, the elements are all discernible in *Philaster* or a baker's dozen of the Beaumont and Fletcher team's tragicomedies. That the tone *does* differ, and that the folk and the folk celebrations constitute the surface as well as the substructure of *The Knight of the Burning Pestle*, are critical observations which can be of the highest significance as the spring traditions lead us to the organizing principle of the play's structure. In short, what one needs if the apparently dispersed motifs are to fully imitate their ritual origins is just that governing force which the citizens' satirized interruptions of the action prevent either the boy Prologue or Rafe himself from becoming.

This force is found in Master Merrythought, the singing, dancing voice of festival, the play's spirit of chaos. He seems bent upon destruction and unmoved by death until his independent stand for harmony and song brings all to a close with the epigraph for the play: "Me thinkes all we, thus kindly and unexpectedly reconciled should not depart without a song" (V, 330–31). In traditional terms, it is justifiable to say that Merrythought is the Lord of Misrule, chosen to direct toward its proper end the spring celebration which is *The Knight of the Burning Pestle*.

We first meet Merrythought in the belligerent description of his wife as she deserts the household: "he hath spent all his owne, and mine too, and when I tell him of it, he laughes and dances, and sings, and cryes, *A merry heart lives long-a*" (I, 300–302). That the description is accurate is clear at once when he enters, with the first of his anthology of catches: "Nose, nose, jolly red nose, / And who gave thee this jolly red nose?" (I, 334ff.). His wife remonstrates, half in bewilderment and half in vexation, "But how wilt thou do *Charles*, thou art an old man, and thou canst not worke, and thou hast not fortie shillings left, and thou eatest good meat, and drinkest good drinke, and laughest." Merry-thought's response is that of absolute irresponsibility: "If all should faile, it is but a little straining my selfe extraordinary, and laugh my selfe to death" (I, 350–57).

This is the beginning of Merrythought's macabre association with death, so paradoxical because he lives in constant proximity to the smell of mortality and yet scorns it by refusing to abate one jot of his joy. He sees his family break up and desert him and, thus abandoned, closes his familial experience with another reminder that death is itself only another joy in his festive existence: "All I have to doe in this world, is to bee merry: which I shall, if the ground be not taken from me: and if it be, *When earth and seas from me are reft, / The skyes aloft for me are left*" (I, 412–16).

When Venturewell comes to him to protest Jasper's elopement with Luce, Merrythought is alone on stage—singing, as is his wont, and, inevitably, it is a gay, grisly song on death:

> *When it was growne to darke midnight,*
> *And all were fast asleepe,*
> *In came* Margarets *grimely ghost,*
> *And stood at* Williams *feete.* (II, 421–24)

The song finished, Merrythought waxes philosophical—in his usual macabre way: "To what end should any man be sad in this world? give me a man that when hee goes to hanging cries, *troule the blacke bowle to mee*: and a woeman that will sing a catch in her Travell. I have seene a man come by my dore, with a serious face, in a blacke cloake, without a hat-band carrying his head as if hee lookt for pinnes in the streete; I have lookt out of my window halfe a yeare after, and have spide that mans head upon *London-bridge*" (II, 430–37). He greets Venturewell's protests with song and dance skits, appropriate in that each lyric expresses his utter lack of concern or sympathy, until the merchant sputters, "Thou art consenting to my daughters losse," and Merrythought turns prosaic only for the moment demanded to reiterate his disregard for death: "Your daughter, what a stur's here wi' yer daughter? Let her goe, thinke no more on her, but sing lowd. If both my sons were on the gallows, I would sing, Downe, downe, downe: *they fall / Downe, and arise they never shall*" (II, 481–86). Enraged, Venturewell tries to threaten: "For this thy scorne, I will pursue that sonne / Of thine to death," which, naturally, only spurs on Merrythought's frenetic dance: "Do; and when you ha kild him, *Give him flowers i'now, Palmer: give him flowers i'now, Give him red, and white, and blew, greene, and yellow*" (II, 496–500).

Venturewell's frustration is shared by Mistress Merrythought when, having lost all her worldly goods in Waltham Wood, she returns home penitently, only to find herself locked out by a partying, singing Merrythought, who sets what she considers an impossible condition for her re-entry. As she stands scolding outside and the sound of his cronies' drinking and his fiddlers' *lavoltos* drifts from the house, Merrythought leans forth to cry:

> Good woman if you wil sing Il'e give you something, if not
> —'*You are no love for me,* Margret,
> *I am no love for you.*   (III, 557–60)

When we briefly meet the old man in act IV, it is to learn from his servants that his credit is exhausted, that "they will trust you for no more drinke," that "I can get no bread for supper." "Hang bread and supper," Merrythought cries, "let's preserve our mirth, and wee shall never feele hunger" (IV, 329–45).

Now it is time to recall that Rafe's last role in *The Knight of the Burning Pestle* is to die—but that his death is only symbolic: it is a tale of an amorous citizen who receives the shaft in the "forked head." This is a death scene which Rafe's ambitious allegory converts into a cuckolding so that he may didactically admonish the audience at the close, "be warn'd by me, / My fellowes every one of forked heads" (V, 318–19)—and well he might, in the context of a May play, if Stubbes's statistics are anything near correct when he passes on the bad news "that of forty, three-score, or a hundred maids going to the wood over [May] night, there have scarcely the third part of them returned home undefiled."[59] In any event, having died satisfactorily, Rafe is immediately resurrected by the grocer's wife so that he may take his leave of the audience.

This resurrection is a thematic bond between Rafe and Jasper, his antagonist Merrythought's son. The latter has himself placed in a coffin and sends a letter of mock-remorse to Venturewell ("hee is dead, / Griefe of your purchas'd anger broke his heart" [IV, 187–88]) in which he requests that his bier be laid before Luce as a last tribute. This done, the weeping *inamorata* sings a heavy dirge and prepares to enter the coffin with her beloved. Jasper carries out the grotesque gaiety of the play by leaping up to assure her that he is hearty once again. Thickening his plot, Jasper then puts Luce in the coffin and flours his own face into a slapstick ghost mask. He then proceeds to haunt good will into a terrified Venturewell and sends Luce home to his father in the coffin. There the bearers announce that they have brought "a Coffin sir, and your dead son *Jasper* in it." Old Merrythought's reaction is proof enough that his earlier mockery of death was no pose but the essential spirit of defiant mirth:

> Dead? *Why fare-well he:*
> *Thou wast a bonny boy, and I did love thee.*
> [*Enter* Jasper.]
> Jasper. *Then I pray you sir do so still.*
> Merrythought. *Jaspers ghost?*
> *Thou art welcome from Stygian lake so soone,*
> *Declare to mee what wondrous things in* Pluto's *court are done.*
> Jasper. *By my troth sir, I nere came there, tis too hot for me sir.*
> Merrythought. *A merry ghost, a very merry ghost.* (V, 177–85)

Twice resurrected, Jasper now brings forth Luce from the coffin, and the inner play of "*The London Merchant*" rapidly comes to a close under the rubric of spring and renewal. Mistress Merrythought finally agrees to sing for her supper and accepts Merrythought's welcome to the paradoxically anti-festive prodigal: "Come, you'r welcome home againe. . . . *You shall go no more a maying*" (V, 220–23). Immediately Venturewell appears at Merrythought's house, still thoroughly frightened by the "ghost" with a weight of guilt that "will sinke me to my grave"; he is the last of the company to be resurrected when Merrythought surprises him with the revived young lovers and, as we have noticed, binds all in a reconciliation song, a song of resurrection:

> *Sing though before the houre of dying,*
> *He shall rise and then be crying.*
> *Hey ho, 'tis nought but mirth*
> *That keepes the body from the earth.* (V, 340–43)

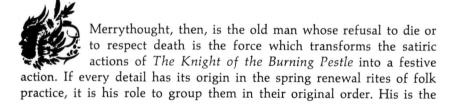 Merrythought, then, is the old man whose refusal to die or to respect death is the force which transforms the satiric actions of *The Knight of the Burning Pestle* into a festive action. If every detail has its origin in the spring renewal rites of folk practice, it is his role to group them in their original order. His is the

spirit of song and dance—and grotesquerie—which the grocer and his wife cannot appreciate, having come too far from the countryside of Robin Hood and the Maypole, and yet it is strong enough to engulf and reinterpret the lath-sword chivalry and mock death of their own dramatic creature, Rafe.

In the spring rites there is always this spirit of Saturnalian satire and sanity. If they are rites of renewal, they must imply death before new life—an underground world in which the corpse winks and pretends until the whiskey and song flows over it and Finnegans Wake again. In the fifteenth- and sixteenth-century *mattacini* which passed into versions of the Death of Samson, the agonistic dance became a gay buffoonery in which the corpse rose to attack its mourners,[60] and in the English mummers' plays the only inevitable figure is the St. George who dies to be gaily resurrected by the Doctor—once so happily named Doctor Ball.[61]

Spring had come to London; the good grocer and his wife had forgotten its meaning but celebrated anyway with a trip to the theater of those titillating little boy-actors. What the actors provided was a play of bourgeois romance; what the cits demanded and invented was a parody of chivalric romance. But what emerged, with the help of Master Merrythought's resurrective powers, was what spring always brought, what Psyche and Proserpina brought with them in another play in which the author allowed his creatures to reinterpret his own efforts. It was a play that refused to be a play and became its own ancestor: as we watch cross-purposes merge into the spiritual unity Merrythought symbolizes, we are attending another enactment of the great ritual of the eternal miracle: life out of death.

The fictional authors of the plays-within-the-plays of *Love's Mistress* and *The Knight of the Burning Pestle,* seeing their artist's autonomy overturned (and thus glorified) by the gravitational pull of ritual forms too powerful for any individual will or intent to resist, might well have declared with their contemporary, "there's a divinity doth shape our ends, / Rough-hew them how we will."

But if Merrythought is the Saturnalian overlord, King Carnival, there is no Lenten season, no mimic sacrifice involved. This raises the question of the play's social function (and ritual is always embedded in a society). There is no Lenten aftermath, no deposition of the mock-king, because the Jacobean society has reversed the order of old holiday: now, as the debased world of George and Nell and their discontinuous relationship to all festivities and civilities indicate, we begin in the world of privation, of Lenten submergence of natural order—witness the Londoners' sympathetic preference for Mrs. Merrythought over her husband, for Humphrey (money) over Jasper (love). It is the world of the audience which John Donne was characterizing at this moment as one in which "all cohaerence" is gone. This incoherence is what the play mirrors in its apparent lack of structure and which it must exorcise if it is to function, as ritual must, to reorder that appearance into a real coherence. The Saturnalian scapegoat, then, is the author who sacrifices his own integrity by abdicating his role as the playwright-god of the dramatic world. Derided by the contemporary audience, reduced by posterity to the status of a social satirist, abused by George and Nell, Beaumont is the magician who has put the world together again for those "understanders" in his audience who can put the dismembered poet together again. He is anonymous because its Lenten social milieu has left the play orphaned—author-less. He is anonymous because the "real" play must be worked out, personally rewritten, as it were, by the auditor who shares his belief that the apparent incoherence of society always masks the eternal order of its renewal. If we have understood, we have watched the world reaffirm the patterns of this renewal which we thought were only old myths. We have *participated* as celebrants against society.

CHAPTER VII Theater of the Dream: Dante's *Commedia,* Jonson's Satirist, and Shakespeare's Sage

Having passed across certain landmarks in two centuries of a dramatic tradition whose self-flaunting theatrical aspect has been sufficiently delineated and, one hopes, explained, it is time to turn to that other aspect of the same tradition, the dream. We have met this dream world often enough in the course of reading plays about the world as theater, for it is the nature of the tradition, as Ortega y Gasset or Artaud sense it, to construct the two metaphors as polar attractions, each shaped by the other's force. But the dream has been an instrument, a shadow guessed by the protagonist in passing, a climactic moment, or, at most—in *Perkin Warbeck* or *The Antipodes*—an ambience. In the plays before us dream becomes an anti-structure which envelops the world wherein man's operations assume the validity of the theatrical metaphor for life. To prepare ourselves for this inversion of emphases, let us turn back to Florence, the historic point of our departure.

From Michelangelo's little drawing of *il sogno* to the vision of Chapman's Count Strozza, we have met a number of echoes of Ficino's own widely disseminated and deeply ambivalent interest in man as a dreamer and his world as a dream.[1] One did not need the *imprimatur* of either an Athenian or Florentine Plato, of course, to dream of the reality beyond or the unreality behind the mask of things, the smoke and evanescence that stirs the nostrils of the senses. Tharsalio was scarcely a Platonist; no more so were erstwhile adventurers in various dimensions of somnambulance such as Trappolin, Perkin, or Peregrine Joyless.

If the world is everywhere spoken of casually as a dream, however, the metaphor was more than metaphor in Ficino's work. It served to express the awareness that the dimensions of quotidian human perspectives are illusions—optical illusions, we might justly say—which are betrayed as such by the moments when visionaries discover in their dreams the divine fourth dimension which surrounds our own; the higher dream awakens man from the lower. The total effect is to re-dimension all structures in the stuff of an anti-structure, the stuff that dreams are made on. If this is a fair reduction of the Christian Platonism at the center of Renaissance Florence's humanistic moment, it is obvious that the nearest approach which could be offered by the Middle Ages to its mode of looking precisely *through* things in a double sense was that Florentine heritage of which Ficino and his more artistic auditors were so continually conscious: *La divina commedia*. Here was the dream vision which dwarfed, by its disciplined systematization of the fluid world beyond conception almost as much as by its poetic quality, all that had gone before. When the sixteenth-century critics turned their attention to art and dream, it was inevitable that the focus should become Dante's poem, and that it should be read through the filter of that great Platonic screen which Ficino had erected between the Renaissance and the Middle Ages. When Boccaccio discussed dreams in his *Genealogia*, it was to classify their species;[2] when Jacopo Mazzoni classifies their species it is only in what he labels "una Digressione della verità e falsità de'sogni."[3] Now the discussion has turned from the dream as psychic phenomenon to the dream as symbolic and aesthetic phenomenon, as a form, in the paradoxical sense we have been coming to understand. This means that the debate about Dante's poem in the late sixteenth century would coordinate one's apparent lack of control over dreams and the equally apparent control exercised by the creative imagination upon the grid of aesthetic structure. And because of the accident that Dante's poem is titled "*commedia*," the form at the heart of the discussion is drama.

It is another of those happy historic coincidences that the issue of dream as form in the sixteenth-century discussion of *La divina commedia* was first suggested by a Florentine who in his youth had whetted his Platonic learning in Ficino's workshop, Girolamo Benivieni.[4] This aging scholar-poet judged that anyone might easily see that Dante had imitated a single action: "I do not say a dream, but rather a waking, and experienced voyage, that he another time passed through."[5] This was to be a point not so casually passed over in the several thousand pages critics devoted to the matter a few years later.

Castelvetro, concerned with Petrarca's sins rather than Dante's (later spokesmen for the defense would reverse the process and justify Dante precisely on the basis of the parallel provided by Petrarca[6]), flatly asserted that the formula Benivieni had so blithely stated was tantamount to making the poem illegitimate: "We must not introduce dreams in which are recounted past things known by the dreamer, as Francesco Petrarca did in his *Trionfi*, telling as if it were historically true how he was conducted into Valchiusa after the death of Laura, [and], after he was actually enamoured of her, writing that he dreamt he was in love with Laura and she died, almost as though he had not known this by seeing it and needed a miraculous dream to realize it."[7] In these two early observations the poles were set up between which the debate on form and creation would be stretched for the next twenty crucial years. The most important statement, as so often in debates of principle, was both early and brief. Someone named Ridolfo or Anselmo Castravilla, who never again appears in literary history (unless he is a more notable figure hidden under a pseudonym which neither his contemporaries nor later commentators were able to penetrate[8]), in 1572 issued an attack on "l'imperfettione della comedia di Dante" which, although never published in his time, was widely circulated in manuscript throughout northern Italy.[9] Tranquillo Venturelli sent a copy from Florence to his learned young fellow Cesenese Jacopo Mazzoni, who immediately put together his *Discorso . . . in difesa della "Commedia" del divino poeta Dante*, first under a pseudonym and soon under his own name.[10]

Belisario Bulgarini, a Sienese scholar, wrote a rebuttal which he privately communicated to Mazzoni, whose respectful admirer and personal acquaintance he remained throughout the ensuing debate. For the next decade Mazzoni's scholarly and pedagogical career took him far from his youthful defense of Dante; then, in 1582, an alleged plagiarism suddenly induced Bulgarini to publish his reply to the *Discorso*. The members of the Accademia Fiorentina were again aroused at desecration worked upon Dante's divine poem, and Lionardo Salviati, a leading academician and close friend of Mazzoni, begged him to reply to Bulgarini. Mazzoni complied, and within a year had completed a mammoth poetics, *Della difesa della commedia di Dante*. Press delays ensued, but the first part appeared in February 1587, dedicated to Ferdinando de' Medici.[11] As a result, Mazzoni was elected to the Accademia Fiorentina and invited to speak before its members, which he did with great success in April, 1587, explicating the first canto of the *Paradiso*.[12] Within a few weeks Francesco Buonamici delivered his *Discorsi poetici* to the same audience, and one must assume that these complementary critics discussed their parallel views of the dramatic process and that Mazzoni may have had some shaping influence upon the *Discorsi poetici*. From Florence, Mazzoni returned to his birthplace Cesena in triumph, and that winter was named to the philosophy chair at the influential University of Macerata. As was observed earlier,[13] in October Ferdinando de' Medici succeeded Francesco as grand duke of Tuscany and immediately recalled Mazzoni to the Florentine sphere of influence by appointing him, as a Platonic authority, to a philosophy chair at Pisa. "Particella terza" of the *Discorso* restated as a militant thesis the question of dream and reality as it had been so briefly formulated by Benivieni: "That in the poem of Dante there is a true imitation of an action and not simply the narration of a dream, as many have believed" (61).[14] Where Benivieni had seen an experience veiled under the dream allegory, Mazzoni—expressing the need of a later century to exalt the artist as creator rather than orator—saw a metaphor which itself was the formal principle on which a vision poetic in every sense was based.

If Castravilla felt that *La divina commedia* could not be called a poem because "it is not the imitation of any action, but only a narration of a dream had by [Dante],"[15] Mazzoni presents over a dozen passages to demonstrate—since each deals with waking from dreams within the dream structure of the poem—"that the poem of Dante is not the narration of a feigned dream, but rather the imitation of actions which he pretended to carry out while awake in his voyage."[16] What seems confusion is really an attempt to explain how dream and waking, the most important symbols of illusion and recognition, interact to make an anti-structural structure for the drama of the Renaissance. Here we have the first instance that I know of a critic's attempting to define that shifting form which refines the life-as-dream trope of the Middle Ages into the Ficinian formula of life as a dream rounded by a sleep, in which we may dream again: in short, seeing becomes a matter of perspectives which melt into vision, and "real" dreams are enveloped in the metaphor of life as a dream.[17] This is a groping toward the aesthetic problem of the epistemological nature of comedy which also led Mazzoni and others to circle back to the theatrical type by examining the illusion-shattering role of the author as actor in a form which is labeled *commedia*. But before that question could be raised directly, Mazzoni felt obliged to examine an intermediate but highly relevant aspect of the complex of creation and vision, theater and dream, namely, the common source of dreams and poems.

Citing Lucretius, Statius, Ariosto, even Dante himself, Mazzoni affirms that Dante called his poem a dream metaphorically, as the others had called their poems "voyages," but with much better reason in that dreams and poetry are founded in the same power of the soul, each arising from the fantasy (on the authority of Aristotle, *De Anima*. 428a–29a). And he concludes with a *"valent'huomo"* 's apposite *sententia*: "Poetry is the dream of man waking, and dreams the poetry of man sleeping."[18]

Once Mazzoni had carried the justification of Dante's *Commedia* to this plane, all of the efforts by Bulgarini, Mazzoni's tenacious if admiring opponent, to argue that the point at issue is not the validity of all dreams, but that of the equation between Dante's poem and true dreams,[19] were automatically relegated to the limbo reserved for windy academic questions. Bulgarini is usually arguing with a straw antagonist of Boccaccio's generation, although Mazzoni himself was academic enough to weary the printers with page upon page of unnecessary rebuttal.

But the crux of the matter was reached here. If Mazzoni defended *La divina commedia* as poem rather than narration of a dream on the purely descriptive basis that its involute form involved dreams wrapped within the basic dream plot (or metaphor, for clearly neither Mazzoni nor his opponents were willing to maintain a distinction between the two in speaking of Dante's *sogno*), he now approached the problem internally, by way of the imagination, to assert that dream is the best metaphor for poetry because it is the most natural—it is a metaphor not invented but discovered hidden in the relationships of things. And yet Mazzoni was too carefully analytic to overlook these distinctions. After rejecting all of Bulgarini's cries that dreams are vain because they are ephemeral, misleading, and so on, he concluded his discussion with a notable warning: the dream is indeed a *vana cosa*, in the sense that it is uncontrolled by the judicial power of the intellect (*giudicio*). And this, of course, fundamentally distinguishes dream from poem (*Difesa*, pp. 207–11). There is no doubt, however, that Mazzoni was fully aware that he only seemed to undermine his defense in admitting so much, since in the preceding chapter he made another important distinction connecting his double defense by way of form and of the formulating imagination. There he was rebutting Bulgarini's objection to the metaphor because, by Mazzoni's own admission, it was founded in the common source of tenor and vehicle within the *"phantasia"*: Bulgarini pointed out (as early as *Alcvne considerazioni* and tirelessly thereafter) that metaphors are legitimate only on the basis of a similitude between diverse things, not their sources. Mazzoni's response was to open his eyes in mock-surprise and to admit it all to be true; he added, however, that "in the metaphor of the dream taken for poetry there is yet another similarity than that of the same source, since the same source always presupposes some similitude in its objects, and as a consequence in its acts."[20]

The *"valent'huomo"* of Mazzoni's first *Discorso* made a handsome but dangerous formula which fused art and life by dissolving them in formlessness; Mazzoni's own analysis of the *Commedia* suggested that it was Dante's intention to perpetrate just such a confusion through simultaneous employment of the dream as shaping plot-metaphor and as episode. But there is an abyss between the man who believes that poems are dreams, dreams poems, and the man who pretends that poems are as divine as (even Bulgarini admitted) some dreams. It is the difference between *la potenza* and *gli atti*, or between the use of *giudicio* and the drift of dreaming. It is also the difference between the poet as creator and the poet as puppet in his own poem. But with this distinction the debate returns to the point of intentional tension between structure and anti-structure.

As early as 1550 Carlo Lenzoni, in a *Difesa* of Dante before the Accademia Fiorentina, had argued that the Florentine's poem was titled *"commedia"* because the author was himself an actor within it, making it representational.[21] It was an opening into which Mazzoni moved in his *Discorso*. Lenzoni was following a tradition as old as Pietro Alighieri in enlisting the aid of pseudo-history to show that Dante simply followed customary medieval terminology; he then went on to discuss the relationships among the varieties of epic and drama.[22] Mazzoni, on the other hand, argued the case from form, and was less ambiguous:

One must primarily recognize that . . . a truly dramatic poem [is that] in which all the personae are necessary to the representation and are in the scene itself; therefore, if it ever should occur that the poet himself were necessary to the scene there is no doubt that he would then not only be a poet, but also an actor in the poem. And then his poem would not be called mixed (as a mixed poem is that in which persons not necessary to the plot speak as well as those who are necessary . . .). . . . Thus I believe that it should clearly appear that in any manner of speaking the poem of Dante cannot be called mixed, but truly dramatic, since the poet is . . . so necessary to it that without him it could not in any way be mimetic.[23]

When Belisario Bulgarini first made known his objections against Dante and Mazzoni in *Alcvne considerazioni*, he easily exposed the disingenuousness of Mazzoni's assertion that *La divina commedia* is an unmixed dramatic poem and made it clear that the fusion of fiction and reality which Mazzoni was trying to describe and defend thoroughly baffled him. Bulgarini could not conceive of such a mode because it would be

some new way of poetizing, neither epically nor dramatically, but [a way in which] in telling of himself the poet would proceed by expounding or imitating one of his own actions (if one can even say that the poet is able to "imitate" himself without at least feigning his name), which might be read as either a true or a false history, but which is clearly not represented as a comedy on the stage nor sung as a rhapsodic epic in the theater. Being aware that it would be necessary, should we wish it to be a comedy, to introduce either the poet in the flesh or others who represent him reciting and narrating at the same time, one cannot see how it might be either in the imagination or set into action upon the stage. And if we should wish to say that it was an epic, the poet would similarly be both narrating and narrated about, both imitating and imitated, a thing impossible in the same part of the same subject simultaneously, from the nature of contraries. . . .[24]

In the *Difesa* of 1587 Mazzoni reprinted Bulgarini's passage verbatim and proceeded to demonstrate that it is not a defect "che la medesima persona sia scritta e scrittore, imitata, e imitante." There is, of course, the example of many historians and orators who have written of their own affairs, but the truly devastating "colpi delle ragioni" aimed at Bulgarini come from Aristotle himself, who

in the second book of the *De Physica* says that the doctor can be the cause of health to himself, but that he will not, however, be considered agent and patient by the same quality. Because if any physician should become ill and should cure himself by means of his own medicine, certainly it could be said that he had caused health in himself, but, however, by one quality he would be agent and by another patient; he would be agent insofar as he is a physician, and patient insofar as he is ill. . . . I say, therefore, that in the same part of him and at the same time, but through diverse qualities, there will be Dante the imitating poet and Dante the feigned persona of an imitated plot."[25]

This is as far as logic could carry one, and Mazzoni's *forte* was logic. He is able here to triumphantly authorize a fusion of art and nature in the name of Aristotle. This distinction, however, was brought into closer proximity to the poetic process proper by an unidentified Florentine, who wrote privately to Bulgarini that the author's "real" character is neither half of the dichotomy, as both Bulgarini and Mazzoni had mistakenly assumed: "It seems to me that Dante imitates not himself . . . but that personage whom it pleased the divine power to attribute to him . . . , which personage is as different from Dante the poet and writer as the truth is different from the feigned."[26] The poet is inspired by the divine science to create two personae while he stands by, paring his nails (to return to the origins of Italian comedy, one might supply the appropriate equation Beolco : Ruzzante : il Reduce).

As far as Bulgarini's attack upon Dante was concerned, the issue was settled, but it had been settled on the level of means, of a method internally clarified and justified. Neither in the discussion of real vs. feigned dreams nor in that of the poet as actor in his own *commedia* did anyone raise the debate to the level of ends, of the final cause. The reason is transparent: to do so would be to relate the poem to an audience, to another imagination which would reopen the structure at one end while it was being so carefully sealed at the other, through which the poet entered in his own persona. And to do so was therefore also tantamount to abandoning formalism for a concept of poetry as transcendence. One critic did make the leap. He was Alessandro Rinuccini, called "*Ardito*" by his fellows in the Florentine Accademia degli Alterati.[27] Rinuccini delivered lectures in defense of Dante on two occasions during the winter and spring of 1587, and the Laurentian Library preserves a full manuscript of notes for these and other planned lectures which Rinuccini either never gave or which have been lost. The manuscript[28] is composed of discontinuous pages marked as if for a commonplace book with headings of "plot," "praise," "blame," etc. These contain defenses of Dante's "science" (a subject also argued by Mazzoni and Bulgarini), quotations from Castelvetro, and questions from Rinuccini to himself. But in a section which was cancelled, with the notation that it was to be employed in "*una lezione*"—hence, a passage which presumably reached the ears of the Florentine Alterati—Rinuccini suddenly sheds a new light upon the whole debate about dreams and imitations, about poets in their poems and out of them, taking as his starting point the paradoxical illusionism of drama as a form involving poet, player, and spectator: "In all, never forget that he as a poet follows not the true, but the verisimilar, the universal, that which is commonly accepted [spoken]; and it should not move you to hear someone say, these things do not stir me because I know that they are not true, since neither his [Dante's] voyage nor anything else of that poem should then move you; even comedies, which one knows certainly represent actions and names which never were, could not then have any effect on us."[29] In comedy pleasure comes through the double awareness of an audience which is always conscious of the unreality of the illusion even while it is "moved" by its verisimilitude. Rinuccini cannot solve the mechanism of this double psyche; it is enough to recognize that it is the source of pleasure in the aesthetic enterprise, to know that it is simply the radical nature of the drama. One may profitably recall at this point the succinct phrases of Ortega y Gasset upon the dual being of Marianinha Rey Colaço and her role of Ophelia: "The stage and the actor are the universal metaphor incarnate, and this is the theater: visible metaphor." But Rinuccini's observation was a prologue, a mere hint which was to be fully developed within the same year in the *Discorsi poetici* which Francesco Buonamici was delivering before the Accademia Fiorentina. But it was a prologue possibly heard, and certainly echoed, by the two great dramatic rivals of the English Renaissance.

 In an earlier chapter we have observed the dramatic vehicle becoming mythic ritual in *The Knight of the Burning Pestle* and *Love's Mistress*, late, sophisticated plays about the nature and limits of artistry in the theater. A decade before the earliest of these and while the principles that emerged from the Mazzoni-Bulgarini debate on Dante's *Commedia* were still being discerned through the settling dust of battle, Shakespeare authored a mythic vehicle for a wedding wherein the masquing carries overtones of efficacy, as well as compliment, which make it his most nearly ritualistic play.

In *A Midsummer Night's Dream* the magic element centers on harmonious generation, while the play itself opens with discord at every level. The central marriage in prospect has itself derived from a literal enactment of the battle of the sexes; Titania and Oberon are at odds over the Indian changeling boy; Hermia's father seeks death as the fruit of her love; the moon is divided, as the patroness of marriage and of a cold chastity;[30] the cosmic weather mirrors this chaotic disorder:

> The spring, the summer,
> The childing autumn, angry winter, change
> Their wonted liveries, and the mazed world,
> By their increase, now knows not which is which.[31]

But moon and changeling are, of course, promises of the close. The former will bring the wedding day of Theseus and Hippolyta, while the latter reminds us that Shakespeare's fairies are benevolent in their final blessing upon the nuptials: the mainstream of folklore saw the fairy changeling as a threatening deformity in human society, while Shakespeare's creatures promise to guard the couples' offspring against just such a deformity.[32] Here the marital "concord of this discord" (IV, ii, 60), emphasized by music and dance throughout the denouement (IV, i, 85ff.; IV, i, 110ff.; V, i, 398ff.), carries onto every level as fairies, man, and nature unite in the fertility rite of May Day-Midsummer. Death is ultimately reduced to theatrical play in the Pyramus and Thisbe interlude, from which Bottom resurrects himself for the final dance much as Beaumont's Rafe had done in his inner play for Midsummer.[33] But myth and ritual, in its archetypal manifestations, as has often been observed, represent the sub-rational (or supra-rational) imagery of human experience displaced into its quintessential forms, as does that related mechanism, the dream.

Thus in *A Midsummer Night's Dream* we have a mythic play which both suggests and blurs its relation to folk ritual by presenting a play-within-a-play which interacts with dreams-within-a-dream. The relations of play and dream are discussed in terms of the aesthetics of the imagination, terms which follow so closely the curve of the Italian critics' discussion of dream, drama, and imagination that the entire play constitutes a dramatic re-enactment of that crucial moment in the history of criticism.[34]

The explicit center is, of course, Duke Theseus' discourse upon the creative imagination, a discourse which turns the action from the waking love dreams of the couples in the forest to the concluding dramatic farce of Pyramus and Thisbe.[35] The position of the Duke is essentially that taken by Bulgarini: the poet creates vain things because he relies upon the inventions of the imagination:

> Lovers and madmen have such seething brains,
> Such shaping fantasies, that apprehend
> More than cool reason ever comprehends.
> The lunatic, the lover and the poet,
> Are of imagination all compact:
> . . . .
> The poet's eye, in a fine frenzy rolling,
> Doth glance from heaven to earth, from earth to heaven;
> And as imagination bodies forth
> The forms of things unknown, the poet's pen
> Turns them to shapes, and gives to airy nothing
> A local habitation and a name.   (V, i, 4–17)

The action would seem in many respects to bear out the Duke's skepticism. At the very opening we are informed by Hippolyta that the events of the play constitute only an evanescent moment imperceptibly punctuating marital desire and fulfillment—"Four nights will quickly dream away the time" (I, i, 8)—and at the close we are invited by Puck to dismiss the poet's inadequate imaginings as the projection of our own fantasy:

> Think but this, and all is mended,
> That you have but slumber'd here
> While these visions did appear.

And this weak and idle theme,
No more yielding but a dream,

a dream enacted by "shadows."

But if, as Lysander observes, love itself is "swift as a shadow, short as any dream" (I, i, 144), Hippolyta responds to Theseus' scornful dismissal of the lovers' tale of waking love dreams with the realization, shared by the audience, that the dream has a substance of truth:

all their minds transfigured so together,
More witnesseth than fancy's images
And grows to something . . .
. . . strange and admirable.[36]   (V, i, 23–27)

We are thus reminded that within the Athenian forest, as in the world of Mazzoni, dreams can be more true than truth. This is first demonstrated when Hermia's nocturnal desertion by Lysander blends into the allegory of the dream from which she awakens calling out to her missing lover:

Help me, Lysander, help me! . . .
Ay me, for pity! what a dream was here!
. . . .
Methought a serpent eat my heart away,
And you sat smiling at his cruel prey.   (II, ii, 145–50)

But Hermia's abandonment and the subsequent lovers' quarrels are truths only in the feeble literal sense which prompts men to believe what they see, and all that is will be made "true" again when Oberon's second application of the juice takes "error" from Lysander's sight and makes "his eyeballs roll with wonted sight" (III, ii, 369–70). In restoring this true nature of things, however, the lovers' vision of the world will have to be inverted so that "when they next wake, all this derision / Shall seem a dream and fruitless vision" (III, ii, 370–71). So, too, with the principal dream action of Bottom's metamorphosis: Bottom is so treated by the fairy lord that waking will merge into his sleep, and he will "think no more of this night's accidents / But as the fierce vexation of a dream" (IV, i, 70–73). The lovers awaken to reject the literal truth of the life they believe they have dreamed in the interest of a greater truth of love and go off to Athens, presumably compliant with the happy suggestion of Demetrius, "And by the way let us recount our dreams" (IV, i, 203). Immediately thereafter Bottom awakens to a more complex view of his experience,[37] but before exploring the relevance of his dream to the imagination and its truth, we must turn to the other pole of Shakespeare's dialectic, the discussion of the nature of drama, and relate drama and dream not only to Theseus' attitude but to Mazzoni's.

At the first appearance of the mechanicals, the assigning of roles in *"Pyramus and Thisbe"* is so dominated by Bottom's player's pride that one is in danger of overlooking the very consistent mimetic theory of dramatic realism which the country troupe shares. Flute cannot play a woman because he has an incipient beard; Quince overcomes the scruple with a mask. At this, Bottom the lover-tyrant-star is prepared to steal the female lead because his "monstrous little voice" is realistically effective. When Snug takes on the lion, Bottom is good for that also because, as he asserts, "I will roar, that I will do any man's heart good to hear me" (I, ii, 72–73). But in the end it is his natural beauty which ultimately dictates the role Bottom must play: "You can play no part but Pyramus; for Pyramus is a sweet-faced man; a proper man, as one shall see in a summer's day" (86–88). All arrangements are predicated upon effective realistic mimesis, and as act III opens with the woodland rehearsal the point is stretched to limits of absurdity rivaled only by Castelvetro's theoretical reductions when the almanac is consulted to determine whether the players can hope "to bring moonlight into a chamber." Fortunately, the moon (new though it should be) will shine clearly on the proposed performance night, and Bottom perceives that "you [may] leave a casement of the great chamber window, where we play, open, and the moon may shine in at the casement" (III, i, 57–59). However, Quince's immediate alternative undermines the realistic conception of presentation and introduces into the preparations for the first time a conception of representational symbolism (a conception analogous to the serpent of love in Hermia's "true" dream which concluded the preceding scene). "Ay," adds Quince, "or else one must come in with a bush of thorns and a lanthorn, and say he comes to disfigure, or to present, the person of Moonshine" (60–62). From this point on, symbolic staging runs rampant in the imagination of the mechanicals: wall will carry plaster and loam, the chink will be represented by parted fingers, etc. Enthusiasm for such outrageous symbolic props among amateur country players, of course, seems to have been a common target of satire. *Narcissus*, the Twelfth Night play presented at St. John's College, Oxford, in 1602, was a sophisticated imitation of some countrymen's version of the Ovidian legend, and it took much joy in explicating such symbolism as that of the "well." *"Enter one with a buckett and boughes and grass,"* reads a stage direction, and in the course of the verses quoted below, other directions are interspersed, such as *"He strawes the grasse about the buckett," "Sprinkles water," "Sets down the bowes"*:

A well there was withouten mudd,
Of siluer hue, with waters cleare,
. . . .
And round about it there was grasse,
As learned lines of poets showe,
Which by next water nourisht was;
Neere to it a wood did growe,
. . . .
And thus least you should have mistooke it,
The truth of all I to you tell:
Suppose you the well had a buckett,
And so the buckett stands for the well;
And 'tis, least you should counte me for a sot O,
A very pretty figure cald *pars pro toto*.[38]

But if *A Midsummer Night's Dream* parodies such mimetic symbolism, as we may call it for want of a better term, we should recall that it is not *Narcissus* and that these rustic aesthetics are embedded in the entire framework of dream and drama theory, including the Duke's speech, which is simultaneously touchstone and target for the whole set of actions. Even such symbols as Quince proposes are a step toward the liberation of the imagination from the search for moonlight at the casements. But in the same rehearsal scene Bottom goes much further into the center of the dramatic transaction as we have come to recognize it and, in so doing, orients us toward the significance of his dream.

I refer to Bottom's objection that there are things in the planned playlet "that will never please," citing the terror the "lion" and the deaths will create among the ladies of the audience. These seem insuperable difficulties to the others, who are ready to censor their piece in the interest of public reaction, but Bottom knows a more familiar solution: "let the prologue seem to say, we will do no harm with our swords, and that Pyramus is not killed, indeed; and, for the more better assurance, tell them that I, Pyramus, am not Pyramus, but Bottom the weaver. . . . you must name his name, and half his face must be seen through the lion's neck; and he himself must speak through, saying . . . 'If you think I come hither as a lion, it were pity of my life: no, I am no such thing; I am a man as other men are'; and there indeed let him name his name, and tell them plainly he is Snug the joiner" (III, i, 17–46).[39]

Here, from the lips of this fatuous country amateur actor, we hear again what Rinuccini told the members of the Accademia degli Alterati, what Ortega y Gasset told us, about the radically double nature of the dramatic experience—at once illusionistic and anti-illusionistic. Bottom is at the center of wonder. To recall Ortega's summary description of the whole transaction, "The stage and the actor are the universal metaphor incarnate, and this is the theater: visible metaphor": thus the relevance of Bottom's dream is that it makes him precisely a "visible metaphor," both himself and a symbol of himself.

The asinine metamorphosis is undergone as the culmination of the rehearsal which we have been examining, and the scene closes with Bottom's ambiguous introduction to Titania's fairy attendants, Peaseblossom, Cobweb, and Mustard-seed. Bottom sees and knows them as functionaries of the fairy queen assigned to assure his bodily comfort and accepts them upon this level (as the noble audience will accept Snug, Bottom, and the others as rural actors performing a ceremonial entertainment for the wedding festivities). But at the same time he is so literal-minded that he reduces each of these creatures to their *nominal* symbolic value ("I shall desire you of more acquaintance, good Master Cobweb: If I cut my finger, I shall make bold with you"), as the noble audience must accept Snout for Wall because

> I, one Snout by name, present a wall;
> . . . .
> This loam, this rough-cast and this stone doth show
> That I am that same wall; the truth is so.   (V, i, 157–63)

This double knowledge of the fairies on Bottom's part echoes the double theory of the actor, but it also focuses the dream.

Whatever the source may have been, and however common the puns upon being made an ass, Shakespeare has put the episode in a context which gives new value to the puns. "I see their knavery," cries the startled compound Bottom when his fellows flee the vision of animality, "this is to make an ass of me" (III, i, 123). But the vision, like all the dreams of *A Midsummer Night's Dream*, is true, both literally and—Bottom having adequately demonstrated his pompous silliness in act I—symbolically. He *is* Bottom and he *is* an ass, as his physically halved person indicates. This is Bottom's unspeakable realization when he "awakens" from the dream that was no dream but a visible metaphor of a truth beyond the literal truth of Bottom's everyday, even holiday, activities: "I have had a most rare vision. I have had a dream, past the wit of man to say what dream it was: man is but an ass, if he go about to expound this dream. Methought I was—there is no man can tell what. Methought I was,—and methought I had,—but man is but a patched fool, if he will offer to say what methought I had" (IV, i, 208–14).

Here is the crucial rebuttal to the Duke's speech on imagination, Shakespeare playing Mazzoni to Theseus' Bulgarini. The drama has borrowed the metaphor which is most appropriate because it is based in that common source of drama and dream, the imagination. If Theseus believes that poetry is "airy nothing," Shakespeare has demonstrated that it, like the life which seems to the lovers a mere dream vision, like the dream which brings to Bottom a truth too essential to look upon with impunity, is a way of knowing "more than cool reason ever comprehends." From the smug security of his rationalism, the Duke is willing to suspend disbelief at a poor play because it is only the spectator's imaginative effort to pretend, to blink the obvious unreality before his eyes, that makes any play viable: "The best in this kind are but shadows; and the worst are no worse, if imagination amend them" (V, i, 213–14). But we have seen the play by this time and know that Oberon, the mythic and dramatic master of ceremonies, the author of events within the play and the surrogate author of the final blessing upon the weddings within and without the play, is—and now the epithet seems inevitable—"king of shadows" (III, ii, 347). The idea that life is a dream has been transformed by Shakespeare, as by Mazzoni, into the idea that drama is a dream; like Mazzoni's argument, Shakespeare's action suggests that the dream-drama opens upon visions of truth that transcend reason. To do so, it develops a double dream world, reminiscent of that articulated by Ficino, in which the dreamer, like the lovers in the Athenian forest, is a somnambulist who awakens into a transcendent dream of truth.

But Shakespeare goes one move farther in validating the metaphor and the imagination which is its justification, adapting but adjusting Theseus' theory that the spectator must participate imaginatively in the dramatic transaction, as Buonamici told the Accademia Fiorentina a few years before *A Midsummer Night's Dream* was performed. The shadow worlds of dreams and drama are symbols, the imagination's visionary epistemology. But their values can only be realized if we are prevented from standing apart from the "visible metaphor" as Theseus stood apart. After all, as Ortega noted, the haunting question which permits us to escape into the *ultramundo* through dream (and drama) is that of whether we are in the dream or the dream is within us, the question which envelops the structure of *A Midsummer Night's Dream* with an anti-structure both encompassed in the same metaphor:

If we shadows have offended,
Think but this, and all is mended,
That you have but slumber'd here
While these visions did appear.
And this weak and idle theme,
No more yielding but a dream.

Jonson's *Every Man Out of His Humour* is not a "dream" play in the literal sense of *A Midsummer Night's Dream*. Yet we may best appreciate the fact that its essence is dramatic rather than satiric if we recognize it as in many ways the clearest paradigm of the Italian argument about the paradox of illusion in its relation to the vision form and the presence of the author as character. Indeed, it is this early play of Jonson's, in conjunction with *A Midsummer Night's Dream*, which can best show us the most traditional—and therefore central—elements in the culmination of Shakespeare's dramatic form, *The Tempest*. The particular interest of Jonson's play lies in a sophisticated effect rising unexpectedly out of an arch obviousness in the mechanisms by which the anti-form is created.

The continual criticism of the *Grex*, who form a bridge to the audience by performing both inside and outside the play, forestalls any which might emanate from that audience. At an early point they give warning about the complexities of structure. Like servant A of *Fulgens and Lucrece*, Cordatus knows the plot and can offer Mitis advance instruction on the play to be performed: "tis strange and of a particular kind by it selfe."[40] The "kind" is one which defies the formal rules of "classical" comedy, rules which, Cordatus points out, have only been built up upon the innovations of many Greek and Roman playwrights. "I see not then, but we should enioy the same license . . . and not bee tyed to those strict and regular formes, which the nicenesse of a few (who are nothing but forme) would thrust vpon vs" (Induction, ll. 266–70). In the midst of this discussion, as if to show the impossibility of delimiting the concept of "form," Mitis simultaneously asserts and denies Jonson's traditionalism. He asserts it by bringing to attention the adherence of *Every Man Out of His Humour* to classical models (in spite of its sprawling appearance and Cordatus' ironic denial) simply by asking a question which the play answers in the affirmative. It may, indeed, with little distortion be said of it that it has "the equall diuision of it into *Acts*, and *Scenes*, according to the *Terentian* manner, his true number of Actors; the furnishing of the *Scene* with GREX, or CHORVS, and that the whole Argument fall within the compasse of a dayes businesse" (ll. 237–41). But embedded in the question is Mitis' ignorance of his double role as simple auditor and as *Grex*; this doubleness causes the structure of the play to overflow the closed stage and envelop the theater, and forces him to surrender his formal part to a permanent sense of contingency. This is a small example of Jonson's experiment: at every level he works to set forth his artifice only to dissolve it. We get another hint of this process in Cordatus' requests that the audience (and Mitis) participate in the playmaking by imagining their own scene changes: "transferre your thoughts to the city, with the *Scene*; where, suppose they speake"; "Let your mind keepe companie with the *Scene* still, which now remoues it selfe from the countrey, to the court"; "let your imagination be swifter then a paire of oares: and by this, suppose PVNTARVOLO, BRISKE, FVNGOSO, and the dogge arriu'd at the court gate"; "I, here he comes: conceiue him but to be enter'd the Mitre, and 'tis enough."[41] This insistence has such an effect upon Mitis that he begins to anticipate the action and criticize not what he sees upon the stage but what takes place only in his imaginative preconstruction of the plot: "your author hath largely outstript my expectation in this *Scene*, I will liberally confesse it." "What?" demands Cordatus, "you suppos'd he should haue hung him selfe, indeed?" "I did, and had fram'd my obiection to it ready" (III, viii, 74–80). This splashing over of London into the Fortunate Isles of the play takes other minor forms, as when two bizarre characters appear in the midst of things, and Mitis is informed that they are *not* in the plot, but "a couple sir, that are meere strangers to the whole scope of our play; only come to walke a turne or two, i' this *Scene* of *Paules*, by chance" (III, i, 17–19).

As usual, the spilling-over works in both directions: the play insists not only upon entering the audience, but upon recalling the dramatic world that impinges from behind its own mimetic screen. This is seen in constant little allusions: Sogliardo inherited his lust for play from his father and dotes on it so strongly that, in the country, "you shall see him turne morris-dancer, he ha's got him bels, a good sute, and a hobby-horse" (II, i, 40–41). In the city, he has come for the puppets: "They say, there's a new Motion of the city of *Niniueh*, with IONAS, and the whale, to be seene at Fleetbridge. . . . I'le see all those deuices, and I come to *London* once" (II, iii, 146–56). Later, waxing ecstatic over his new friendship with Shift, he cries: "I, he is my PYLADES, and I am his ORESTES: how like you the conceit?" and Buffone recognizes its provenance: "it's an old stale enterlude deuice" (IV, v, 57–59). If the city satirists go to the Mitre tavern so that, joining Buffone, they "may bee spectators" of Sogliardo's further discomfiture, (III, iii, 73–74), it is Buffone himself who, once there, puts on a little inner farce reminiscent of the *commedia dell'arte* in the *lazzo* of the drinker who pledges himself until he sets his two glasses to quarreling.[42]

As Jonson never tires of reminding us, all are continuously "spectators" in the worlds of *Every Man Out of His Humour*, from the moment the "author" Asper interrupts his first stage diatribe to watch those watching him:

> I had not obseru'd this thronged round till now.
> Gracious, and kind spectators, you are welcome,
> APOLLO and the MVSES feast your eyes.[43] (Induction, ll. 51–53)

When the play proper begins, Macilente hides to watch Buffone engage in some cony-catching with the countryman Sogliardo, and this "spectator-ship" builds into a pyramid of Chinese boxes through the first three scenes of act II, wherein the audience watches the *Grex* watch Buffone and his companions, who in turn have come to hide and watch Puntarvolo's strange courtship of his own wife. The series rounds back upon itself, though, to fuse playing and reality. It turns out that Puntarvolo's wooing of a wife he acknowledges only as a stranger in courtly grandiosities is a quite unconfused, self-conscious ritual play, which he carries through unabashedly: even when he discovers the spectators, he invites them into that very hall to which he pretends to be a stranger. It is as though Nick Stuff, the tailor of *The New Inn*, were unembarrassed at being discovered courting his wife in the countess' clothes—and the reason is that Puntarvolo has learned that reality in *Every Man Out of His Humour* is play. Indeed, the structure is embodied in that title, for the moment every man *is* out of his humor, all pretensions and pretenses are stripped away, the play is over, the life of the puppets extinguished.

It is, though, in the fragmented figure of the author-satirist that the doubleness of acting and watching is chiefly carried across the several levels of the play. The expanding and controlling center of *Every Man Out* is Macilente, the "envious" spectator who is driven to a mad destructiveness by what he sees, "with which his iudgement is so dazeled, and distasted, that he growes violently impatient of any opposite happiness in another."[44] When Macilente generalizes, it is to cry:

> I looke into the world, and there I meet
> With obiects, that doe strike my bloud-shot eyes
> Into my braine. (I, i, 16–18)

And when he looks at particulars, it is to desire for himself everything. Accepting Deliro's patronage, like a Bussy D'Ambois he laments that "his wealth (but nodding on my wants) / Must make me bow, and crie: (I thanke you, sir.)" (II, iv, 15–16). Seeing Deliro's wife, he jealously and rhetorically asks: "How long shall I liue, ere I be so happy, / To haue a wife of this exceeding forme" (II, iv, 135–36), knowing even as he expresses his wish, that Fallace is a loose and vain woman whom he will delight in exposing. His wild envy goes on and on:

> What mou'd the heauens, that they could not make
> Me such a woman? but a man, a beast,
> That hath no blisse like to others. (II, iv, 159–61)

It is pointless to belabor Macilente's madness, but it is mistaken to explain it away as generic, as is done by Professor Kernan, who utilizes *Every Man Out* as a touchstone for Elizabethan satiric form. Briefly, Kernan finds that in biting satire the persona of the satirist, by the very violence of his outrage, examines the satirized modes of conduct so closely that he appears envious and prurient to a greater degree than his victims— that the exposure is internal at least as much as external.[45] In *Every Man Out of His Humour*, though, Kernan believes that Jonson managed to avoid invalidating his satire dramatically by splitting author and satirist neatly into Asper the actor-author and Macilente the role played by Asper in his own script. Asper "has all of the virtues of the satirist with none of his defects. He is indignant at the time's iniquities; outraged by the impudence of folly; . . . and free from any personal malice, envy, or profit motive. . . . Asper corresponds to the public personality of the satirist and Macilente to the private personality."[46] The difficulty is that a closer look shows that Jonson does less to split than to fuse the pair. Asper, after all, is cast in the role of Macilente in the inner play, a fact emphasized not only at the beginning but at the close, when Macilente in the *plaudite* declines to change back and return "as I was ASPER at the first." Further, if the "character" of Asper prefatory to the dramatic script proper is given out as "an ingenious and free spirit," we must see that his behavior is as wild as Macilente's, and that his stable friend from the *Grex*, Cordatus, apologizes in amazement:

> Why this is right *Furor Poeticus*! Kind gentlemen, we hope your patience
> Will yet conceiue . . .
> This supposition, that a mad-man speakes. (Induction, ll. 147–50)

This is prompted by Asper's uncontrolled impatience to

> strip the ragged follies of the time . . .
> . . . and with a whip of steele,
> Print wounding lashes in their yron ribs. (17–20)

His temper not only forces his friends continuously to warn him ("Be not too bold"; "Forbeare, good ASPER, be not like your name"; "ASPER, I vrge it as your friend, take heed"), but leaves him distracted ("Ha? what? . . . O, I craue pardon, I had lost my thoughts"). Constantly returning to violence, he delays his own play ("But stay, I loose my selfe, and wrong their patience; / If I dwell here, they'le not begin, I see" [209–10]).

There is a further complication of perspective in the person of Carlo Buffone, himself a satirist within the play, who becomes an alter ego of Macilente throughout the middle part,[47] joins with him in exposing the gulls (IV, v), and is drawn imagistically into conjunction with Asper when the latter enters to cry out against the world, "Who can behold such prodigies as these, / And haue his lips seal'd vp?" (Induction, ll. 12–13). (The ultimate punishment inflicted upon Buffone for his satirization of Puntarvolo at the end is exactly this—to have his lips sealed up [V, vi].[48]) This third satirist, furthermore, extends the satiric figure out beyond the Induction to include the "real-life" image of the man Ben Jonson himself, projected by the author Ben Jonson. Entering for a surly drink in the forgetful Prologue's place, Buffone tells the audience:

This is that our *Poet* calls *Castalian* liquor, when hee comes abroad (now and then) once in a fortnight, and makes a good meale among Players, where he has *Caninum appetitum*: mary, at home he keepes a good philosophicall diet, beanes and butter milke: an honest pure Rogue, hee will take you off three, foure, fiue of these, one after another, and looke vilanously when he has done, like a one-headed CERBERVS. . . . He has made a Play here, and he calls it, *Euery Man out of his humor*: Sbloud, and he get me out of the humour hee has put mee in, Ile trust none of his Tribe againe, while I liue.   (334–48)

Here is the familiar, unmistakable portrait of ugly, hard-drinking Ben; Ben of the Mermaid; chief wit and belly of the Tribe of Ben; in short, that same self-portrait which functioned as the dramatic hub for several of the Jonsonian masques. There is yet another complication of identity pointing outward toward the author in society: Jonson is identified with Asper through the agency of Buffone in this miniature, and Buffone says of Macilente that "hee'le blow a man vp with a jest" (I, ii, 216), yet is it Buffone himself who is identified with Jonson by Cordatus: he echoes, in reference to Carlo, the notorious description of Ben as one "given rather to losse a friend, than a Jest."[49]

To these several links which enmesh Buffone, Macilente, Asper, and "Ben" a related phenomenon in Jonson's non-dramatic poetry is added. Few seventeenth-century poets did not provide a little section of "epigrams" sandwiched between the verse epistles and the couplet narratives in their collections. The complicated history of this flourishing of epigram has been recited in relation to early humanism, later Jesuit sacred poetry, and the classical traditions.[50] It is the latter which most influenced Jonson, as the vogue for formal satire in the 1590s brought into prominence Martial's rough but pointed incisions into the anatomy of Roman society. Because "epigram" is essentially a technique rather than a form, subject matter, or attitude, it constantly slips over into other genres, most easily into satire, but also into the epistle, as Martial realized: "Epigrams need no crier, but are content with their own tongue: in whatever page they choose they constitute an epistle."[51] His own collection often uses the epigram to this end; he congratulates friends, eulogizes Domitian, attacks enemies, and gives us glimpses into his own person and history.[52] There is very little of this element in most modern collections,[53] but the Latin poet's precedent permeates Jonson's *Epigrams* ("the ripest of my studies," he called them) in both matter and manner. Chiefly thinking of the tradition stemming from the *Greek Anthology*, no doubt, Puttenham indicated that for the Renaissance "this *Epigramme* is but an inscription or writing made as it were upon a table, or in a windowe, or vpon the walle or mantell of a chimney in some place of common resort . . . where many merry heades meete, and scrible . . . such matters as they would euery man should know & descant vpon."[54] Following this lead, the practice of the age as a whole was to make the epigram the most impersonal and public of genres. If Martial, as his remark indicates, had quite a different view, it probably was not widely recognized because the injection into them of himself, his friends and his work occurs only here and there throughout his collection of over fifteen hundred epigrams, while sixty of Jonson's one hundred and thirty-three epigrams deal with his friends, his children, his person, his critics, and his work.[55] Jonson's more perceptive imitation of Martial has permitted him to forge this most impersonal genre into a tool for self-characterization.[56] We see a world of gullery and nobility, a waste of Elizabethan shame, passing under the outraged eye of an only slightly tamed Asper.

   This digression on the *Epigrams* may seem to have wandered rather far from *Every Man Out of His Humour*, but it is intended to reinforce an important point about the effect and "form" of Jonson's play. In the satiric epigrams, as in the satiric stage play, Jonson has maneuvered in just the opposite direction from that laid down as the norm (and the norm of *Every Man Out*) by Professor Kernan. Far from separating author from satirist, Jonson in both cases saw that the point of satire is engagement and not only provided an angry observer but shaped him into the very image of the author who walks the streets outside the poem. The engagement is not only between the persona and the literary

types of vice and folly, but between these types and their social models:
therefore, the personal authorial image must function as a bridge between model and literary mirror if satire is not to lose its curative value.
But this again leaves us standing simultaneously before and behind the
mirror, so that the idea of form is absorbed into the idea of the author
himself, and he becomes *our* author; he is able to work his corsives and
correctives much more directly than one who merely holds the mirror up
to nature.[57] But such abstract theory has value only when we learn what
it has to tell us about particular practice, and to see what it can reveal
about *Every Man Out of His Humour* we must now turn back to the
play and look at its central metaphor and effect, that of dissolution.

Asper no sooner enters upon the stage in the Induction than he
introduces the image of a world dissolving. He introduces it in company
with the two organs that recur as its instruments at each of its principal
returns, eye and tongue:

> Who is so patient of this impious world,
> That he can checke his spirit, or reine his tongue?
> . . . .
> To see the earth, crackt with the weight of sinne,
> Hell gaping vnder vs, and o're our heads
> Blacke rau'nous ruine, with her saile-stretcht wings,
> Ready to sinke vs downe, and couer vs.   (4–11)

Cordatus reacts by reminding Asper of the tongue's supposed impotence:

> Vnlesse your breath had power
> To melt the world, and mould it new again,
> It is in vaine, to spend it in these moods.   (48–50)

It is only at the close of his raging, when Asper recognizes that he is
delaying his own play, that he implicitly fuses the two organs (and so
implicitly answers Cordatus) by dissolving his own breath into just that
"world" of the play which the spectators will see:

> For these [attentive auditors], Ile . . .
> . . . speake away my spirit into ayre;
> For these, Ile melt my braine into inuention,
> Coine new conceits, and hang my richest words
> As polisht jewels in their bounteous eares.   (204–8)

At the opposite end of the continuum of satirists, Buffone is described in the prefatory "character" as one "*that (more swift then* Circe)

with absurd simile's *will transforme any person into deformity,"* and Cordatus soon confirms this destructive metamorphic talent as the dissolution of sight by tongue: "no honorable or reuerend personage whatsoeuer, can come within the reach of his eye, but is turn'd into all manner of varietie, by his adult'rate *simile's*" (Induction, ll. 361–64).

One could expand upon related phenomena: that Asper's theory of the true "humour" is, if traditional, nonetheless "fluid" in both physiological and psychological senses;[58] that Fastidious Briske's clothes philosophy is an externalized conception of the same ruling principle of change and metamorphosis ("I had three sutes in one yeere, made three great ladies in loue with me: I had other three, vn-did three gentlemen in imitation: and other three, gat three other gentlemen widdowes of three thousand pound a yeere" [II, vi, 32–35]); and that the whole dissolution and metamorphosis at the heart of this heartless world is epitomized in the character whose "maine standing name is CAVALIER SHIFT: the rest are but as cleane shirts to his natures," one who is changeful "as the wind" (II, vi, 190–99). Indeed, as we will see, what is said to Shift could serve as epigraph to the entire world of *Every Man Out of His Humour*: "the fellow were nothing but vapour" (III, vi, 10).

But the real structural significance of the dissolution metaphor, like all else here, is fully clarified only when we turn again to Macilente. He opens the play proper with a set soliloquy on his incapacity for living up to the motto *"Viri est, fortunae caecitatem facile ferre."* The visual tilt of the phrase is taken up immediately because it is just the seeing of the blind goddess' distribution that arouses his gnawing envy:

> I looke into the world, and there I meet
> With objects, that doe strike my bloud-shot eyes
> Into my braine: where, when I view my selfe;
> Hauing before obseru'd, this man is great,
> Mighty, and fear'd: that, lou'd, and highly fauour'd:
> . . . .
> When I see these (I say) and view my selfe,
> I wish the organs of my sight were crackt;
> And that the engine of my griefe could cast
> Mine eye-balls, like two globes of wild-fire, forth,
> To melt this vnproportion'd frame of nature.[59]

Asper having projected a world of folly, Macilente is maddened by it and would, if he could, destroy it. The wish for its dissolution reminds us of Cordatus' warning to author Asper that his rant is vain "Vnlesse your breath had power / To melt the world and moulde it new againe." It also demonstrates that if Asper and Buffone are to be identified primarily with the tongue, Macilente stands identified as a *spectator*, the satiric *eye* of the play. The note is ever-present in Macilente's outrage: "Who can endure to see blinde *Fortune* dote thus?" (I, ii, 157);

> O my senses,
> Why loose you not your powers, and become
> Dull'd, if not deadded with this spectacle? (I, iii, 4–6)

"blind *Fortune* still / Bestowed her gifts on such as cannot vse them" in giving Fallace to Deliro because, in looking at her, Macilente finds that "shee tempts my heart-strings, with her eye, / To knit them to her beauties, or to breake" (II, iv, 133–34, 157–58). This is inevitable in theory because Macilente is the envious man and, as Cordatus explains, this is a spectator's sickness: "the true condition of enuie is, *Dolor alienae foelicitatis*, to haue our eyes continually fixed vpon another mans prosperitie" (I, iii, 164–66).

The author Asper had promised to turn his exasperated vision of the world to creative account when he declared, "Ile . . . speake away my spirit; / Ile melt my braine into inuention," thus reprojecting for the spectators the scene which was the cause of his indignation. But it is into his alter ego, Macilente, that he has passed as he becomes actor, and with Macilente's brain that he has merged his own in order to achieve his aim. Macilente having set up the complex mechanisms of multiple betrayal with which he will put every man out of his humour in act V, Cordatus forewarns us: "Now do's hee . . . store vp a world of malicious thoughts in his braine, till hee is so full with 'hem, that you shall see the very torrent of his enuie breake forth like a land-floud: and, against the course of all their affections oppose it selfe so violently, that you will almost haue wonder to thinke, how 'tis possible the current of their dispositions shall receiue so quick and strong an alteration" (IV, viii, 152–59). As this flood of malice breaks over the characters, destroying the humor—and essence—of one after another, Macilente toward the end gives ironic advice to one victim whose horns have been exposed: "Mee thinkes you should say it were some enchantment, *deceptio visus*, or so, ha? if you could perswade your selfe it were a dreame now, 'twere excellent" (V, xi, 10–13).

This last remark soon deepens into a summary account of the shape of the whole play as Macilente, having crushed all whom he has envied, finds himself self-dishumored: "Why, here's a change! Now is my soule at peace":

> I am so farre from malicing their states,
> That I begin to pitty 'hem. It grieues me

To thinke they haue a being. I could wish
They might turne wise vpon it, and be sau'd now,
So heauen were pleas'd: but let them vanish, vapors.   (V, xi, 61–65)

And so the spectacle of folly has been made a mere *deceptio visus* by its reprojection through the tongue of the author-actor, so it is that his breath *has* "had power / To melt the world" and blow it away as a bubble, mere vapor.

Among the few original passages in the *Discoveries* there are two adjacent and related comments (*de vita humana* and *de piis et probis*) which echo the *topos* of the world theater with a particular pertinency for *Every Man Out of His Humour.* In the first, Jonson says: "I *have* considered, our whole life is like a *Play*: wherein every man, forgetful of himselfe, is in travaile with expression of another. Nay, wee so insist in imitating others, as wee cannot (when it is necessary) returne to our selves."[60] Here is the spectacle of men drawn by their eyes to emulation and envy, the spectacle of Sogliardo's lust for courtly habits, of Briske's lust for Saviolina, Fallace's lust for Briske, Fungoso's lust for Briske's suits, and Macilente's lust for everything he sees. But in the second passage Jonson gives us a glimpse of the conception behind Asper as author: "*Good men* are the Stars, the Planets of the Ages wherein they live, and illustrate the times. . . . These, sensuall men thought mad, because they would not be partakers, or practisers of their madnesse. But they, plac'd high on the top of all vertue, look'd downe on the Stage of the world, and contemned the Play of *Fortune.* For though the most be Players, some must be *Spectators.*"[61]

In *Every Man Out of his Humour* the poet has done what Mazzoni recommended, and become actor in his own play and in his own persona: "In the same subject Dante, . . . but through diverse qualities, there will be Dante the imitating poet and Dante the feigned *persona* of an imitated plot." But this persona, Macilente, refuses to give back an independent identity to the reality level of the author Asper in the end ("I should haue gone in, and return'd to you, as I was ASPER at the first: but . . . wee'le intreat you to imagine it" (V, xi, 75–79). Further, he has done for the play world, which is in so many ways, as we have found, fused with the world of the London audience, just what the original author wished to have the god-like power to do: he has dissolved it and blown it away, leaving himself as the one substantiality for the spectators of his vision. Macilente is that dominant spectator who is also Mazzoni's ideal poet of the ideal poem, he is a *visionary* in the creative sense Mazzoni gave the metaphor: one who both sees and creates the poem. With all the emphasis upon the creative act of the spectator—the spectator in the theater, to whose imagination Cordatus so often appeals and the spectator of the world's folly, who in projecting his vision becomes Jonson's ideal "spectator," Mazzoni's ideal poet—we find ourselves returned again to the creative double sense of vision exfoliated so long before in Cusa's *De visione Dei*.

In our own critical generation, as in those which went before us, *The Tempest* appears as Shakespeare's culmination of traditions almost irrespective of the critics' direction of approach. Now that the worst eccentricities of allegorical severity have been absorbed and corrected, we have become properly accustomed to viewing *The Tempest* as a mythic play in which both natural resurrections and the insinuation of Christian doctrine throughout the imagery combine to create a pattern consonant with what we find in the other late romances and with its seeds in such earlier plays as *Lear*, or even *Much Ado*.[62]

That *The Tempest* is such a play of resurrection and that it is insistent upon specific Christian patterns for a principal sounding board seems clear. Throughout the course of the expository scene in which Prospero introduces Miranda and ourselves to that chapter of disaster in Milanese and human history twelve years ago the emphasis is upon providence, the terminology and the echoes enforcing its Christian lineage.[63] "O, a cherubin / Thou wast that did preserve me"; "How came we ashore?" / "By Providence divine"—such is the dialogue that studs the mage's account of shipwreck, and at its crux he sums up the loss occasioned by his own vain curiosity in magic arts with that explicit paradox which we have come to associate with tragicomic form, the paradox of the Fortunate Fall. "What foul play had we, that we came from thence? / Or blessed was't we did?" demands Miranda, and the magician —who, it should be observed, demonstrates the limits of his power throughout this discourse by laying aside his mantle as he begins— replies:

Both, both, my girl:
By foul play, as thou say'st, were we heav'd thence,
But blessedly holp hither.[64]   (II, ii, 60–63)

Later, speculating upon a benign "rule" should he have "plantation of this isle," the good Gonzalo, who served as providential officer in the earlier salvation of Prospero and Miranda, depicts a "natural" life rooted in total communism of the sort only known to the first parents in the paradisaic state:

> No occupation; all men idle, all;
> And women too, but innocent and pure:
> No sovereignty;
> . . . .
> All things in common Nature should produce
> Without sweat or endeavour . . .
> . . . .
> I would with such perfection govern, sir,
> T'excel the Golden Age.   (II, i, 141–63)

But it has often been noticed that the "natural" state of this utopian idyll is measured by the natural servility of Caliban to the drunken visitors who want—like Caliban himself—no more than the sensual rewards of dominion. Fallen nature is, indeed, "idle" but not necessarily "innocent"; it cries out with Stephano: "the King and all our company else being drown'd, we will inherit here: here; bear my bottle" (II, ii, 42–176).

Gonzalo's merely "natural" community fails (and is justifiably mocked by the depraved Sebastian and Antonio) because it is a vision limited by prelapsarian conceptions, reduced to ridiculous Pollyannism by the necessary implications of isolation.[65] The myth of the Fortunate Fall, of course, informs us that such natural isolation is only "perfect" in the most paradoxical sense—that, indeed, the Golden Age is but a stepping-off point for the responsible enjoyments of experience. Prospero's early recognition that he has abused the highest arts—and duty— by isolating himself in the midst of Milan gives the drama this implication:

> I, thus neglecting worldly ends, all dedicated
> To closeness and the bettering of my mind
> With that which, but by being so retir'd,
> O'er-priz'd all popular rate, in my false brother
> Awak'd an evil nature.[66]   (I, ii, 89–93)

Finally, in every sense, the entire providential resurrection and regeneration tableau with which Prospero arranges to conclude the play before those gathered for the masque of love in his cave is given its ultimate perspective by Gonzalo's marvelling recognition of the Fortunate Fall by which all this evil is turned to greater good. It sounds not unlike the reaction of the astonished happy sinner of Milton's later version of paradisaical loss and gain:

> Was Milan thrust from Milan, that his issue
> Should become Kings of Naples? O, rejoice
> Beyond a common joy! and set it down
> With gold on lasting pillars: in one voyage
> Did Claribel her husband find at Tunis,
> And Ferdinand, her brother, found a wife
> Where he himself was lost, Prospero his dukedom
> In a poor isle, and all of us ourselves
> When no man was his own.[67]　　　　　　(V, i, 205–13)

The Duke of Vienna, whatever the tone may indicate about Shakespeare's intent, tempered justice with mercy much in Prospero's final fashion in *Measure for Measure*, and inset into his tableau is Mariana's apologia for the disillusioning experiment in self-knowledge in which he has involved his subjects:

> They say the best men are moulded out of faults,
> And, for the most, become much more the better
> For being a little bad.　　　　　　(V, i. 437–39)

Here, in little, is the concept of the Fortunate Fall played off against Gonzalo's antelapsarian paradise and Angelo's earlier failure in self-knowledge—also with the qualifier "for the most," a rationale for Sebastian, Antonio, and the beast-man Caliban, who may not recover from the sin of his sire, Satan.[68]

By its very structure, the Fortunate Fall pattern implies the search for self-knowledge, and Shakespeare's happy losers thus naturally converge at the achievement of this deeper view of their own split natures. But it should be observed that one of the important differentiating marks of his middle and late plays, even when they are seen as bringing alive the structural skeleton of the myth, is his employment of varied thematic dangers as obstacles and instruments toward that self-realization. In *Lear* it is the insulation of the ego in the midst of society, in *Measure for Measure* it is confidence in will, in *The Winter's Tale* it is the frightened failure of such confidence, and in *The Tempest* it is isolation. But we may notice a further differentiation of the latter play, a methodological advance in dramaturgy, in that, if isolation is the theme, it is also the setting. The old psychic history is worked out upon an island cut off from participation in the world, and the central heart of that island is a cave where circumstance can breed good and evil in men, but never knowledge.

If we look ahead to the next chapter in this history of dramatic form, we notice the analogy of the isolated dark mountain-tower of Calderón's Prince Segismundo, a protagonist who combines within himself Caliban and Miranda. Anticipating ourselves thus, we realize that in a drama of ethical education resurrection has to be internal, an emergence from the darkness of the ego into the light of participation. We are reminded, by the Platonic tradition which runs through Segismundo's education in and beyond tyranny, of the need for a philosopher-king to grow through *entering* the world of experience even to the point of absolute vision, only that he may *return* to the cave of this world.[69] Segismundo and Prospero alike learn that all knowledge has to be put to use in intercourse within the world, a use called by a later explicator of the Fortunate Fall "Love, by name to come called charity."

This brings us to the really crucial dialectic of *The Tempest*: that between the internal awakening from the dream by raising it to a new power[70] and the recognition of the dreamer as an actor upon this great stage of fools, the theater of the world. The young Shakespeare began his experiments in theatrical dream structures with *The Taming of the Shrew*, a play in which dream fused into drama, and with *A Midsummer Night's Dream*, a dream play about drama, but the conception of life as a dream in conjunction with a motif of miraculous resurrection only begins to emerge seriously with the earliest of his romances, *Pericles*.[71] Therein, as Marina begins to narrate the history which gradually convinces Pericles of her lost and rediscovered genealogy, he cries out, in the midst of his incredible encounter with providence, "This is the rarest dream that e'er dull'd sleep / Did mock sad fools withal,"[72] and, as belief comes, it induces the visionary dream of Diana's instruction, a dream harmonized by the music of the spheres. Waking "dream" here becomes prelude to dream vision. The same double dream level is employed in *Cymbeline*: Imogen awakens to the sight of the decapitated Cloten, whom she imagines to be Posthumus, and cries out: "I hope I dream. . . . The dream's here still: even when I wake it is / without me, as within me."[73] This waking nightmare of deception, however, is itself but a prelude subsumed in Posthumus' own dream vision of Jupiter, from which he awakens saying " 'Tis still a dream. . . . [But] Be what it is, / The action of my life is like it."[74] Always the gods take a hand in turning the course of human destiny through these later dreams, even as the lordly hunter or the fairy king had done in the early versions. But in *The Tempest* all waking is like a dream.[75] Miranda's past seems to her "far off, / And rather like a dream" (I, ii, 44–45); when Ferdinand comes to the first encounter with Prospero and Miranda, his "spirits, as in a dream, are all bound up" (I, ii, 489); when Antonio tempts Sebastian to join him in fratricide and usurpation over the sleeping form of Alonso, the entire episode is couched in dream terms played upon as an extended conceit in duet (II, i, 193–264); when Caliban hears the music of the island, he moves almost indistinguishably between two worlds:

> That, if I then had wak'd after long sleep,
> Will make me sleep again: and then, in dreaming,
> The clouds methought would open . . .
> . . . that, when I wak'd,
> I cried to dream again.   (III, ii, 137–41)

"graves, at my command / Have wak'd their sleepers," claims Prospero (V, i, 48–49) and demonstrates his claim when the Boatswain appears at the cave relating how "even in a dream" he and his fellows have been transported from hellish cacophony to fresh and pregnant harmonies of eye and ear (V, i, 230–44). Encompassing this omnipresent sensation of the dream state, of course, is Prospero's fusion of theater and dream metaphors:

> Our revels now are ended . . .
> And, like the baseless fabric of this vision,
> . . . .
> the great globe itself,
> Yea, all which it inherit, shall dissolve,
> And, like this insubstantial pageant faded,
> Leave not a rack behind. We are such stuff
> As dreams are made on; and our little life
> Is rounded with a sleep.   (IV, i, 148–57)

In this culminative elaboration of our twinned metaphors, as in the dramatic actions and reactions we have reviewed, one hears the clear and universal assertion that life is a dream or, rather, that man is a dreamer and life is a sleep. But this implies that the only awakening must be into the life after death, into the eternal, as is suggested by Segismundo's cry of fideism as he accepts the evanescence of man as dream while at the same time affirming the absolute inheritance of the soul: "Who, if it is a dream, if it is vainglorious, would lose a divine glory for human ephemerality. . . . let us embrace the eternal . . . where deeds do not sleep."

From this perspective, Ariel's song reverberates through the whole drama: body in *The Tempest* has suffered a sea-change that it may become "something rich and strange." That this metamorphic miracle is central is emphasized in the Boatswain's account of the awakening dream of a restored ship, told in the midst of the resurrections which have given not only to Ferdinand, who notes it, but to all "a second life"

(V, i, 195). It had earlier been given scriptural overtones in Ariel's account of the mariners' physical rescue:

Not a hair perish'd;
On their sustaining garments not a blemish,
But fresher than before,   (I, ii, 217–19)

and certainly it is this metamorphic gain which gives point to, and receives added force from, Prospero's boast that "Graves at my command / Have wak'd their sleepers."

Through the dreams of the island, body has been transmuted into a mere symbol of spirit: in this dream as in Segismundo's, all participants come to recognize, through a miracle enacted, the miraculous paradoxes which control experience. The evidence is what we have reviewed, the enhanced quality of the ship, the robes, the bodies "fresher than before." If the sea-change of Alonso, as Ariel describes it ("Of his bones are coral made; / Those are pearls that were his eyes"), is an illusion of Ferdinand's dream, it is an illusion at once symbolic of his changing psychic state and reminiscent of that corporeal glorification promised in scripture: "So also is the resurrection of the dead. It is sown in corruption; it is raised in incorruption . . . it is sown a natural body; it is raised a spiritual body" (I Cor. 15:42–43); "the Lord Jesus Christ . . . shall change our vile body, that it may be fashioned like unto his glorious body" (Philipp. 3:20–21). The Fortunate Fall and the purificatory symbolism of the sea-changes suffered are finally joined by Prospero in that moment of suspended animation before the discovery, when the vanquished all stand within his magic circle before the cave:

The charm dissolves apace;
And as the morning steals upon the night,
Melting the darkness, so their rising senses
Begin to chase the ignorant fumes that mantle
Their clearer reason. . . .
. . . .
. . . Their understanding
Begins to swell; and the approaching tide
Will shortly fill the reasonable shore,
That now lies foul and muddy.   (V, i, 64–82)

Prospero is man who in the midst of life has been a spiritual island of isolation. His punishment is to re-enact his sin symbolically, to be separated and thus educated in the responsibility of man to the otherness, to become the philosopher-prince who knows that life is a dream, that in dreams begin responsibility, and that his own task is to teach these truths to the other sleepwalkers in the dark cave. His method is a masque which teaches that the drama of this *theatrum mundi* is a mere shadow-play, a dream.

We may now note that *The Tempest* weds two of our main Italian heritages with unique skill. Numerous scholars have shown that *commedia dell'arte scenari* lie behind the plot in some fashion. We have seen a bathetic English version in the magic, mistakes, and metamorphoses of *Trappolin Supposed a Prince*, and we can scarcely deny the prevalence of elements from the milieu of the pastoral *scenari*, if we still debate particular sources.[76]

But there is a large difference of tonality established by Shakespeare's crossing of such a plot with the mythological mode of the *intermezzi* and masque.[77] Here we have the island mage, a principal protagonist from the pastoral form in the *commedia improvvisa* tradition, who himself becomes presenter of a betrothal masque, and from there expands his role of theatrical director to present the actual denouement of the outer play as a masque of love in the symbolic chess game.

Both aspects of Shakespeare's debt to tradition have been eloquently and probingly discussed, and this is no place for a renewal or review of those discussions. The question raised here is how Shakespeare organized this crossbreeding in this last, particular vision of the Fortunate Fall as man's quintessential destiny. We should remember that it is precisely at the point of his great speech uniting the tropes of the world theater and life as dream, the point at which he has concluded his own inner revels, in the shape of the hymeneal masque, that Prospero shows his sudden perturbation. The cause is his recollection of the grotesqueries and slapstick threats of Caliban, the seaman, and the fool, whose *lazzi* take them wallowing and grappling through a series of preposterous vaudeville routines well suited for the *zanni* of the *scenari*. The masque world of *The Tempest* is the world of Prospero's magic—spirits and strange music; the *commedia* world of *The Tempest* is the world of violence, drunkenness, gluttony—the world of the body "sown in corruption." As that world cuts short his vision of harmony, it recalls Prospero from the paradoxically beneficent isolation which has been his punishment and yet his initiation into the responsibility of experience. As a mere man he, too, is a shadow of a dream; he must return with his limited powers into the cave of sleepers, even as Plato's philosopher-princes must, once they have had their vision of the reality beyond. He must return to the grotesque theater of the world which is not really the island but Milan. There every third thought shall be the grave, but two must be thoughts for this world. He is now, in short, to put off the garb of playwright and director of these shadows. He has been manipulator only as an actor, knowing that "the best in this kind are but shadows." As in the Epilogue, he says,

> Now my charms are all o'erthrown,
> And what strength I have's mine own,
> Which is most faint,

thus joining all the others whom, as he told Ariel, his charms only introduced to self-knowledge. "My charms I'll break, their senses I'll restore, / And they shall be themselves," but themselves spiritualized with the aura of promise which Gonzalo announced in their recovery:

> O rejoice
> Beyond a common joy, . . .
> . . . all of us [found] ourselves,
> When no man was his own.

From director he has become actor in the dream pageant that takes place on the world stage under the divine playwright's view:

> the world a Theatre present[s],
> As by the roundnesse of it appears most fit,
> Built with star-galleries of high ascent,
> In which *Jehovah* doth as spectator sit,
> And chief determiner to applaud the best
> And their endeavours crown with more then merit,
> But by their evil actions dooms the rest,
> To end disgraced whilst others praise inherit.

This was Thomas Heywood's conception of the world, which was given him, we remember, when "mens bodies tired with the business of the day betaking themselves to their best repose, their never-sleeping souls labored in uncouth dreams and visions, [and] suddenly appeared to me the tragic muse." It is suggestive of a pattern of projection and dissolution which has been with us from the beginning of this chapter, which was basic to the great debate about Dante's *Commedia*, which stunned Bottom with the impossible truth of his dream. It is the pattern we saw when Asper, the playwright of *Every Man Out*, was warned that satiric comedy was useless "Unlesse your breath had power to melt the world, / And mould it new again." And when Asper had written his play and exposed this great stage of fools, he himself became an actor upon it; he, like Prospero, both blessed and dissolved it:

> I could wish
> They might turne wise vpon it, and be sau'd now,
> So heauen were pleas'd: but let them vanish, vapors.

CHAPTER VIII Platonic Perspectives
Dissolved: Calderón's *La vida es sueño*

 This study has been an exploration of some influences and analogues in the history of Italian and English dramatic thought in the early and later Renaissance. As such, it is now ended. But this last chapter is less appendage than coping because no discussion of the dramatic development of the ageless *topoi* of life as play and dream could afford to ignore the greatest of all its exemplars, Calderón de la Barca's *La vida es sueño*. Beyond that, though, viewing Calderón's play from the perspective of the works we have just examined reveals a cohesiveness of its parts different from that offered by the Hispanists' framework. Interpreting any great poem one can claim only that—a different cohesiveness, an unobserved pattern—for great poems, like Cusa's icon, realize themselves only in the eye of an infinity of readers. But that the same historic tradition should be able to cast new light as far from Florence and London as Calderón's Spain suggests its vigor and importance, and may encourage others to complete and make into a true history the intuition of which this book is a first sketch.

In our readings of *La vida es sueño*, critical confusion is engendered in part by historic knowledge. Calderón is the author of the *autos*, and in *La vida es sueño* there are unmistakable resonances of Christian semi-allegory: a man born through original sin into death, the repetition at that man's birth of the sudden solar eclipse which marked Christ's death, faith in the necessity of good works without insistence upon their efficacy for salvation—and all this in a web of language which invokes God's will and help at every turn. But these tease rather than satisfy our sense of the total direction of the *comedia*, leaving much unexplained. What are we to say of the political struggle, of the complicated crossed lovers, of the disguises and mistakes in identity? All of these elements are too easily clarified by literary history. If we look to *Eustorgio y Clorilene* we find, among many other things, much of the matter of *Yerros de naturaleza y aciertos de la fortuna,*[1] and if we conflate the romance with Calderón's earlier drama we can parallel most of the striking particulars of *La vida es sueño*: the names of the protagonists, Segismundo and Rosaura;[2] the threat of tyranny; the tower or cave of dark imprisonment; the pretended-prince plot; the dream sense of reality; even such a detail as the *criado* hurled to his death.[3] Here are indubitable sources which indubitably fail to account for our sense of aesthetic and ideational fulfillment in reading *La vida es sueño*: "the constant sensation that accompanies us is that of crossing through a forest of structures, of geometries, of symbols perfectly hidden."[4]

And more, knowledge draws one near despair of comprehending the particular impact of *La vida es sueño*. If we move from the play's immediate sources back into our larger traditions, we recall that the structural dream metaphor is scarcely more common in Renaissance dramatic literature than that favorite role for self-conscious actors on that great stage, the pretended prince, which is tirelessly replayed from the *scenarii* which fostered Cokayne's Trappolin through *The Taming of the Shrew* to the tragedy of Perkin Warbeck and the triumph of Segismundo. Arturo Farinelli, in his collection of analogues to *La vida es sueño*, documents Calderón's obsession with introducing into play after play what one of his characters calls "aquel proverbio, / . . . que es un sueño la vida."[5] And Farinelli found the dream life and the dream of power drawn together in a rueful moment of human poetry culled from one of those countless guidebooks for the Christian prince which had so little effect upon Renaissance politics: "It is not surprising that we call death a sleep and sleep death, since even life is, as St. Chrysostom says, a brief sleep in which, as in dreams, men are driven by vain imaginings and fantastic furies, having no more substance than does the sleeper, who at times dreams he is rich, at times a king, yet in the morning finds himself poor and miserable as before."[6]

Historicism seeks to recover that it may revivify, but its very success with *La vida es sueño* has reduced the play to shards of tradition—Calderón's immediate background and the background of that background, glued together into a *capa y espada* piece about governing, love intrigues, and the evanescence of "la vanagloria humana" seen in the light a pious author's eye catches from "una divina gloria." Let us, then, explore a by now embarrassingly obvious source which coordinates Calderón's major metaphors, the politics, the ethics, and the epistemology of *La vida es sueño*.[7]

What "source" are we seeking? Clearly, one which shares in some commensurate proportions the elements of Calderón's play: a love plot wherein the protagonist, guided by Beauty, spiritually transcends desire, closely interwoven with a political plot in which the protagonist spiritually transcends the temptation to tyranny. The whole, from the opening instruction that "the action begins at dusk," takes place amidst settings and metaphors of a darkness which seems as much spiritual as physical. And into these plots are injected the two major traditions familiar in theatrical history, the "pretended prince" and the governing metaphor of the dream.

The transcendence of carnality in love and rule, the pursuit of the ideal leading one out of the evanescent shadows of our somnambulist world, is, of course, central to the Platonic tradition we have derived from its Renaissance keeper, Ficino—and it is healthy to remind ourselves that despite the mystique of Spanish cultural isolation Platonism flourished in Renaissance Spain. Menéndez Pelayo[8] has carefully identified the web of Platonic strands, from the later medieval Arabic and Hebraic forces through a widening stream into the dialogues of Leone Hebreo, who carried his own influence into Florence, from whence it returned to Spain in the later sixteenth century in the lost *Tratado de amor en modo platonico* of Francisco de Aldana, the *Apologia en albanza del amor* of Carlos Montesa, the *Tratado de la hermosura y del amor* of Maximilian Calvi, and the discourses of a host of other *tratadistas*.

But Carlos, son of the Mantuan duke in Calderón's *De una causa dos efectos*, is announced in the opening lines to be

> todo el día
> encerrado con Platon
> y Aristotiles, que son
> luz de la filosofía.

This in turn reminds us that the Platonic fashion which ranged over Europe in the Renaissance is based, after all, on Plato, who in the *Phaedo* introduced the cosmological myth of men living in the undersea hollows of a pocked and aqueous globe, "which is just as if a creature who was at the bottom of the sea were to fancy that he was on the surface of the water, and that the sea was the heaven through which he saw the sun and the other stars, . . . having never lifted up his head and seen, nor ever heard from one who had seen, how much purer and fairer the world above is than his own" (*Phaedo* 109). Here is illusion taken as reality in a cosmic context, with man viewing the world from an outsider's perspective which appears to be inside, seeing, from the center, truth and beauty in some dim distance.

This only adumbrates myths and metaphors in *The Republic*, which introduce, of course, all the elements metamorphosed by Calderón into *La vida es sueño*. And even marginal details of the play which may puzzle a reader of Burnet or Jowett emerge in Ficino's pages of commentary. An instance: Basilio's faith in the powers of astrology is the vehicle which draws the entire plot of *La vida es sueño* to the edge of tragedy because of Segismundo's imprisonment as a consequence. Throughout, we would sympathize with him were it not for that first moment of humor when the old king enters to a chorus of mocking praise of his learning which brings all in doubt. Appropriate enough that it should be Estrella first to greet the regal horoscopist—but why as "Sabio Tales"? Perhaps because of the legend that Thales fell into a ditch while star-gazing, passed on as the symbol of philosophy's folly from the *Protagoras* to Diogenes Laertius. But Occam's razor takes us to Ficino's commentary on Book VII of the *Republic*: there it is Thales who holds the dubious primacy of place among those materialists who were said "tam negligentes in rebus divinis fuisse, quam diligentes in naturalibus."[9] This may serve to recall to us Book VII and that allegory of the cave which both orders and reflects the larger myth governing the *Republic*.

Here are the poor prisoners in an underground den watching the flickering shadows that they take for reality. Suppose, says Socrates, that one of these is "dragged up a steep and rugged ascent" into the light. He will squint and doubt and stumble and "will see the sky and the stars by night better than the sun or the light of the sun by day." But ultimately he will be able to contemplate the sun: "The prison-house is the world of sight, the light of the fire is the sun, and you will not misapprehend . . . if you interpret the journey upwards to be the ascent of the soul into the intellectual world. . . . my opinion is that in the world of knowledge the idea of good appears last of all, . . . and when seen is inferred to be the universal author of all things beautiful and right."[10] But we remember, with Prospero, that the allegory concerns the education not of contemplatives but of philosopher-kings, who each, "when his turn comes, must go down to the general underground abode, and get the habit of seeing in the dark." The movement of political preparation is also the curve of knowledge along which one measures the nature of things: from illusions man is educated into reality so that he may carry his vision back to dispel the shadows for others, even as he renounces his own vision of beauty naked. "Our State," Socrates rhapsodizes, "which is also yours, will be a reality, and not a dream" (520b)—paradoxically, it will become a reality when its leaders turn back to participate in the dream world of Plato's cave.

The structure of the entire *Republic* is that of dreams within dreams. The allegory of the cave is set within that "lie" of Book III by which the citizens are to be persuaded to accept a function-based class society: "the audacious fiction, which I propose to communicate gradually, first to the rulers, then to the soldiers, and lastly to the people, [is that] . . . their youth was a dream, and the education and training which they received from us, an appearance only; in reality during all that time they were being formed and fed in the womb of the earth" (414c). The philosopher's dream of the good state leads to the lie of the past as a dream: in this way men may be disciplined for the long ascent out of the dream world of false opinion which is represented by the cave. Of the man who lives by mere opinion we learn, "dreaming and slumbering in this life, before he is well awake here, he arrives at the world below, and his final quietus" (534b); we learn to ask of "he who having a sense of beautiful things has no sense of absolute beauty," "is he awake or in a dream only? . . . is not the dreamer, sleeping or waking, one who . . . puts the copy in place of the real object?" (476a)

But in this world there is another dream, neither the philosopher's dream of absolute beauty creating absolute right nor every man's dream that his shadows are reality. It is nightmare, the distorted dream that can become any man's reality if awakened in the soul. When Socrates comes to his anatomy of tyranny in Book IX he reminds his listeners of the illicit passions in us all: "I mean those which are awake when the reasoning and human and ruling power is asleep; then the wild beast within us, gorged with meat or drink, starts up and having shaken off sleep, goes forth to satisfy his desires (571b). . . . in all of us, even in good men, there is a lawless wild-beast nature, which peers out in sleep" (572a).

The tyrant is the son of that democratic man who earlier came to rest between the extremes of his father's miserliness and his companions' wantonness, accepting "what he deemed moderate indulgence in various pleasures" (572b). The tyrant swings further, drawn by his own wanton tempters and desires. "O heavens!" exclaims Socrates, "can you believe that he would strike . . . his withered old father . . . [that] he will commit the foulest murder . . . or be guilty of any other horrid act. Love is his tyrant, and lives lordly in him and lawlessly, and being himself a king, leads him on, as a tyrant leads a State, to the performance of any reckless deed" (574a–c). With such a sophistication of evil "he becomes always and in waking reality what he was [before] very rarely and in a dream only" (574c—indeed, the dream analogy ultimately ceases to be analogy and is used by Plato as definition for "the character of the worst man": "he is the waking reality of what we dreamed" [576a]). In dreams begin responsibility—and its opposite—for Plato and for Calderón's Segismundo.

This cursory résumé of the *Republic*'s metaphoric pattern may suggest Segismundo's imprisonment in his dark tower, his education through the double fiction of dream as reality, his initial tyranny, and his ultimate emergence as the philosopher-king his father only appears to be. But the *Republic* does not concern itself with romantic love, and *La vida es sueño* emphatically does. Segismundo lusts, loves, and finally betrothes himself. Rosaura is wronged and righted and betrothed. Can we tease out the evidence that this romantic plot strand, too, is created directly by the metamorphosis of the visual symbols of the *Republic* into narrative? It seems improbable. Rosaura arrives in Poland a disguised and dishonored outcast accompanied by a treacherous, self-seeking *graçioso*. She draws her father (himself her mother's betrayer) into moral dilemmas, cuts off the love of Segismundo for herself and prevents the marriage of her errant seducer, Astolfo, to Estrella, and ultimately wins back her honor by accepting Astolfo from the hand of Segismundo. We can feel no more comforted than we do with the repossession of Claudio by Hero, of Angelo by Mariana, of Bertram by Helena. Nor are we delighted that Segismundo renounces Rosaura, for the sake of both their honors, to accept that lesser light Estrella, scarcely a commonplace destiny for romantic protagonists.

The women are boldly allegorical. If Estrella needed any translation, she receives it in the astronomico-amatory observation of Rosaura when she speaks of "Estrella (que lo puede ser de Venus)"[11] and Rosaura would not have to be unscrambled into "aurora" (dawning) were hers not a stock name popular in the less philosophic fiction and drama of the *Siglo de oro*.[12] When she adopts the pseudonym of Astraea in the Polish court, we are reminded that Ficino's subtitle for the *Republic* was "de justo." Segismundo's response to her as the one enduring truth of his shifting existence confirms the unity of truth and beauty; his abandonment of his claim to her joins her pseudonym, Astraea, in confirming the unity of truth, beauty, and justice.

The limitations of Rosaura in the active world of Poland remind us that it is a fallen world: she enters it by precipitous descent (Clarín declares "del monte hemos rodado" ["we have rolled down the mountain"] [30]) through the darkening twilight toward Segismundo's cavernous prison, where "desde su centro / nace la noche" ("from its center night is born") (71–72). Indeed, her descent here at the opening prefigures Segismundo's own, and the prison not only gives birth to night but seems, in her description,

> a las plantas
> de tantas rocas . . .
> que al sol tocan la lumbre,
> peñasco que ha rodado de la cumbre.

> [at the foot of so many rocks . . . that touch the sun a huge stone which has fallen, rolling from the summits.] (61–64)

The prison is both Poland and the Platonic cave in which we all live.[13] Segismundo is like Socrates' prisoner, "reluctantly dragged up a steep and rugged ascent, . . . forced into the presence of the sun himself." He is dazzled, his eyes "pained and irritated" (516a), when he first gazes upon Rosaura:

> viendo que el ver me da muerte,
> estoy muriendo por ver.
> . . . .
> si el verte muerte me da,
> el no verte ¿qué me diera?

> [seeing that sight gives me death, I am dying to see. If seeing you brings me death, what might not seeing you bring?] (231–36)

She descends that he may ascend; having ascended the *scala* of vision he abandons her that he may descend again, in that paradoxical double journey of the philosopher who must also be king.

But the play begins with the descent, and the fatality of vision felt by Segismundo is more than metaphoric. In the realm of the prison valley all are disguised: Segismundo as the man-beast, Rosaura as a man, Clotaldo and the guards with those face coverings which prompt Clarín's impertinent question, "¿Enmascaraditos hay?" (295). This last masking reveals that all who see must die by decree of the King, who will have no one view the prodigy chained among the rocks. Segismundo embraces his imprisonment in darkness because his bestial nature makes him a fatal rebel against the power of light which has come to him disguised as the dazzling Rosaura:

> ¡Ah, cielos,
> qué bien hacéis ne quitarme

la libertad; porque fuera
contra vosotros gigante,
que para quebrar al sol
esos vidrios y cristales,
sobre cimientos de piedra
pusiera montes de jaspe!

[o, heavens, you are right in taking liberty from me because I would be as one of the rebel giants against you, heaping mountains of jasper on foundations of rock to burst the glass and crystal of the sun.]

(329–36)

The prison world, I have said, is also the world of Poland, of Basilio's apparently enlightened court where a king seems a philosopher. But, though less calculated in its deceptions, the palace world is more dangerous, for here, too, there are darkness, failures of vision, mistaken views at every turn—all disguised as knowledge.

The moment we enter the palace, Astolfo is seen to be courting Estrella. But his courtship is ironically misplaced. Rather than praising her in the stellar imagery of courtly love, he addresses her as a solar figure: her eyes are those "de quién el sol fue una sombra / y el cielo un amago breve" ("of which the sun was only a shadow, / and the heavens a mere adumbration") (1742–43):

Donde entra Estrella no tiene
lugar la sombra, ni estrella
donde el sol

[Where Estrella enters, darkness has no place, nor has any star where the sun gleams.] (1771–72)

But the mistaking of one love for another, of a star for a sun, is most explicit when he addresses Estrella with Rosaura's own anagram: "os saludan . . . los pájaros como a Aurora" ("the birds salute you as the dawn") (485–87). Segismundo, risen to rule, repeats the metaphoric mis-identification. Clarín explains to him that she "Es, señor, tu prima Estrella." "Mejor dijeras el sol," replies Segismundo (1390–91).

It is Clotaldo who offers us a preparatory paradigm of such delu-sion as he is on the point of ascending with Rosaura into the court. He should be aware of dangerous appearances, having just remarked that

no sé determinarme
si tales sucesos son
ilusiones o verdades.

[I don't know how to decide whether such happenings are illusions or realities.]   (396–98)

But caution is thrown away when he cries "este es mi hijo" (413) because the eye confirms the heart's intuition:

[el corazón] hace
lo que aquel que está encerrado,
y oyendo ruido en la calle
se asoma por la ventana,
y él así, como no sabe
lo que pasa, y oye el ruido,
va a los ojos a asomarse,
que son ventanas del pecho.

[(the heart) does as one who, being imprisoned, hears a noise in the street—it looks out the window, and so, not knowing what is happening, and yet hearing the noise, it comes and appears in the eyes, which are the windows of the breast.]   (418–25)

The prison analogy is an appropriate reminder of Segismundo's dark world of illusion because, in point of fact, Clotaldo's eyes do not look upon his son, as he supposes, but Rosaura—or, rather, not even Rosaura but the disguise with which she hides her identity.[14]

Clarín, too, adapting the window image to the world-stage metaphor, believes that sight is knowledge:

no hay ventana más cierta
que aquella que, sin rogar
a un ministro de boletas,
un hombre se trae consigo.

[there is no better window than that which, without appealing to a ticket-seller, a man carries about with him.]   (1171–74)

These are but metaphoric and minor preparations for the imminent transformation of knowledge through the windows of the eyes, through vision, into action. When, in Calderón's version of the pretended-prince plot, Segismundo is drugged and reawakens not in his prison chains but upon the regal couch, he first emphasizes his new vision of things: "¡Válgame el cielo, qué veo! / ¡Válgame el cielo, qué miro!" (1224–25). He wonders what strange journey his imagination has taken in sleep "que aqui me he llegado a ver" (1243), but seeing is believing, so "sea lo que fuere, / ¿quién me mete en discurrir?" ("be that as it may, / who will argue it now?") (1244–45). He intends to be served no matter how the servants have been provided. When Clotaldo and Astolfo both are threatened by his barbaric pride, it is a *criado* in the mold of Lear's Kent who tries to intervene. Segismundo's first reaction is to threaten to hurl him from the window ("os eche por la ventana" [1315]) and when he ultimately does so, it is as ocular proof to himself, as to the others, that he possesses the powers he has feared to be only imagined ("¿Qué es esto que lego a ver?" ["What is this that I come to see?"] cries Astolfo, and Segismundo responds, "Cayó del balcón al mar: / ¡vive Dios, que pudo ser!" ["He fell from the balcony into the sea: / God be praised that I am able really to be!"] ([1428–31]). The high hopes for visual knowledge, then, for the eyes as the soul's window, for the emergence into real light fade as the window opens onto death, the ultimate darkness—literal death for the *criado* and metaphoric death for Segismundo, whose action once again brings about his isolation from a world which will be made to appear mere dream. Appropriately, it is an arrangement engineered by Basilio, a would-be philosopher who is really a king only in the shadow world. Basilio knows, without understanding it, that "todos lo que viven sueñan" (1149). As Ficino observed in his commentary to Book VII of the *Republic*, "diuina enim, . . . doceri non possunt, sed purgando potius atque conuertendo" (*Opera*, p. 1411).

From the first encounter between Rosaura and Segismundo at his prison door through this first experience of the prince in the false light of the court, the reader and Segismundo alike have become gradually aware of Rosaura in her true identity, that which her name implies: a dawning, a new light, a vision of reality which will permit Segismundo in his own time to grasp the import of his father's dream-world metaphor. It is prophetic, then, not of the court life but of his deepening involvement with Rosaura that when Segismundo is first prepared by Clotaldo to enter the palace he is compared to the eagle soaring "en las regiones supremas / del fuego" (1041–42), soaring into the sun. And so it is that, returned to his prison, Segismundo awakens to the sense of having dreamed all—except the vision of Rosaura: "pues veo estando dormido, / que sueñe estando despierto" (2106–7); "no diré lo que soñé; / lo que vi" (2110–11); "sólo a una mujer amaba . . . / que fue verdad" (2134–35) ("then I see, having slept, / what I might dream being awake;" "I will not say what I dreamed, / what I saw;" "only that I loved a woman . . . / that was true").

We can begin to see how the dream and the light metaphors make a mutual commentary upon one another: *La vida es sueño*, like the *Republic*, is about knowing and acting; it concentrates our attention on the psyche's awakening into choice. But this leads us to an as yet unmentioned aspect of the plot: its astrological determinism. Here the *Republic* offers an explicit model for Basilio's learned ignorance. But Calderón has worked more subtly to use this Platonic hint better than Plato in explaining the stages of knowing evoked by the *scala* of light.

As Estrella is mistaken for Rosaura, the reflected starlight for the true dawn, so Basilio's folly in following the stars will suggest why even Rosaura is a metaphoric light, bright shadow of beauty, but shadow only because only beauty—and, as Socrates tells us, "in the world of knowledge the idea of good appears last of all . . . universal author of all things beautiful and right, parent of light" (517c). Perhaps, then, it is no dramatic accident that Rosaura's father Clotaldo should be Segismundo's tutor and that it should be he who, hard upon Segismundo's insistence that his love for Rosaura was a reality even in the dream world, first introduces the ethical dimension with a gloss upon the prisoner-prince's recent experience: "aun en sueños / no se pierde el hacer bien" (2146–47).

Immediately following upon the allegory of the cave, Socrates turns to the mathematical education of the philosophers—to their development from arithmetic through geometry to astronomy, the "practical" science of number:

You [Glaucon] . . . have in your mind a truly sublime conception of our knowledge of the things above. And I dare say that if a person were to throw his head back and study the fretted ceiling, you would still think that his mind was the percipient, and not his eyes. . . . but, in my opinion, that knowledge only which is of being and of the unseen can make the soul look upwards, and whether a man gapes at the heavens or blinks on the ground, seeking to learn some particular of sense, I would deny that he can learn, for nothing of that sort is matter of science; his soul is looking downwards, not upwards. . . . The spangled heavens should be used as a pattern and with a view to that higher knowledge [of absolutes]; their beauty is like the beauty of figures or pictures excellently wrought. . . . And will not a true astronomer have the same feeling when he looks at the movements of the stars? Will he not think that heaven and the things in heaven are framed by the Creator of them in the most perfect manner? But he will never imagine that the proportions . . . can also be eternal and subject to no deviation—that would be absurd; and it is equally absurd to take so much pains in investigating their exact truth. (529b–530a)

When Basilio enters the drama it is to a chorus of epithets, "Sabio Tales," "Docto Euclides" (579–80), epithets which immediately draw out the tale of *hubris* by which Segismundo's imprisonment has been destined before birth.

The first *décimas* of Segismundo on his fate ruefully recognize some original sin: "el delito mayor / del hombre es haber nacido" ("the greatest crime of man is being born") (111–12), and Clotaldo affirms a law by which Segismundo died even before being born ("antes de nacer moriste / por ley del cielo" [321–22]). Such a law explains, of course, why Segismundo has less freedom than the streams and their fish, than the beasts, than the birds, and sets responsibility as a theme: choice also carries with it the obligation of reason. But it is only later at court that we learn the crime lay not in Segismundo's will but in Basilio's, that the law of the heavens was written in the stars, but interpreted in the court.[15]

As Basilio details the prodigies attending Segismundo's birth, including the threat of civil war and tyranny in his horoscope, he revives the death-in-birth idea voiced in Segismundo's first soliloquy, but joins it to omens of power without responsibility.[16] His wife's womb was a "sepulcro vivo" (665) in that, giving birth to Segismundo, she died; her fears, half in dreams, were of a monster in human form, that "fiera de los hombres" (212) which Segismundo now feels himself to be. And when Basilio turned to read this son's future in the stars, all was confirmed: sun and moon struggled "a luz," and the sun was bested in

> el màs horrendo
> eclipse que ha padecido
> el sol, después que con sangre
> lloró la muerte de Cristo.
>
> [the most horrible eclipse suffered by the sun since it wept the death of Christ in blood.]   (688–91)

Like the rubber-necked astronomer of Plato's *Republic*, like the Thales of Ficino's commentary upon it, and like Astolfo, Basilio has sought too literally among the stars. We should be warned about misinterpretations because Basilio's entrance has been to the satiric chorus praising his learning, and Astolfo's myopic wooing of Estrella in Rosaura's name has immediately preceded that stellar entrance. Life and death *are* always coupled, but Basilio sees the wrong face of the paradox, as the Christ analogy suggests. He forgets that the man-beast compounded in passion is saved by the sacrifice of the god-man, that the solar eclipse at the crucifixion heralded the coming of a greater son. Segismundo too will, in the event, be the light-bringer. But the philosopher-kings cannot, like mere philosophers, bask in the light of the blessed isles (519c), as the learned Basilio has attempted to do. It will be Segismundo who sees reality in Rosaura's solar strength but accepts his terrestrial destiny as spouse of Estrella.[17]

This process begins when, like Shakespeare's Sly, Segismundo first awakens in the palace and accepts its shadows fully for their own sake—even attempts a violent physical possession of Rosaura. Clotaldo has offered him the "truth" about his imprisonment and heritage, but this hindsight, like the foreknowledge of Basilio, is fatal—for the *criado* hurled from the balcony, and (metaphorically) for Segismundo, who is forced to return to the prison. The first court experience draws Segismundo, however, to confront his identity. In psychic combat with his father he affirms "sé quién soy" ("I know who I am") (1538). And when his violence has returned him to the prison, to the tutelage of Clotaldo and to the memory of Rosaura, Segismundo finally masters the lesson which will have its political consequences at the close of the action, when he renounces tyranny after defeating his father. That existence may be a dream is not important—Segismundo has found the phantasmagoric equally present in cave or court. In awakening to a renewed realization of the prison, Segismundo half-remembers himself risen to "la anchurosa plaza / del gran teatro del mundo" (2072–73). Once again we hear the playwright crossbreeding those two favorite metaphors for the illusory nature of life: man's world as theater and as dream. The experience of his double existence teaches Segismundo "que el hombre que vive, sueña / lo que es" (2156–57). The dream, as critics have pointed out, is not existence but essence: "lo que es," not *that* one is, but *what* one is.[18] In brief, we dream the role we are to act on this great stage, for Segismundo a role of rule in borrowed robes:

> Sueña el rey que es rey, y vive
> con este engaño mandando,
> disponiendo y gobernando;
> y este aplauso, que recibe
> prestado.

> [The king dreams he is a king, and lives with this delusion, giving commands, disposing, and governing; and the praise that he receives is only lent him.] (2158–62)

In his early *auto, El gran teatro del mundo,* the same ephemeral view of power speaks from Calderón's stage when Mundo informs Rey as he exits from the stage into the *sepulcro* that all of his robes were but theatrical garments, not his own: "porque dado non fueron, no; prestados / sí para el tiempo que el papel hiciste."[19] In this *auto* the advice of the chorus to mankind is a constant refrain: "obrar bien," because the role we play is an ethical role. So, as Segismundo awakens at the close of act II to the realization that "toda la vida es sueño, / y los sueños, sueños son" (2186–87), it is appropriate that Clotaldo should gloss his discovery with an ethical conclusion: "aun en sueños, / no se pierde el hacer bien" (2146–47). In the final act Segismundo is returned to the world to act out the role of king he reluctantly reassumes and to demonstrate that he has learned "hacer bien."

"The lawless wild-beast nature, which," Plato reminds us, "peers out in sleep" slew the *criado*, threatened Clotaldo, insulted Astolfo, and almost assaulted Rosaura when Segismundo first awoke to the court world as tyrant. But even in this worst moment, as in his first view of her at the prison door, Segismundo instinctively is awed by the brilliant beauty of Rosaura. "No juntes el ocaso y el oriente, / huyendo al primer paso" ("Do not join the sunset to the dawn, / fleeing even upon your arrival") (1573–74), he pleads with her at court, depriving us of

> el sol, a cuya llama
> aquella estrella vive,
> pues de tus rayos resplandor recibe.
>
> [the sun, in whose fire that star lives, and from your rays receives her light.]   (1593–95)

Rosaura alone had remained a reality in the dream world of both his lives, and in act III she falls into Segismundo's power on the battlefield. His internal struggle with the beast of passion is difficult. Lust invokes as *carpe diem* the lesson which Segismundo has just learned under the rubric of a *memento mori*:

> Esto es sueño; y pues lo es,
> soñemos dichas ahora,
> que después serán pesares.
>
> [This is a dream; and since it is, let us dream of pleasures now, since later sorrows will come uninvited.]   (2964–66)

But the vision of life as a dream taught him better than this, in the end. If the light of Rosaura remains a constant reality throughout his dreams, the vision of her has educated him to another constant, the union of the dark illusory dream world and the transcendent light of the real world through that mandate "hacer bien":

> Si es sueño, si es vanagloria,
> ¿quién por vanagloria humana
> pierde una divina gloria?
> . . . .

acudamos a lo eterno;
que es la fama vividora
donde ni duermen las dichas,
ni las grandezas reposan.

[If it is a dream, if it is a mere vanity, who for human vainglory would lose divine glory? Let us turn to the eternal, which is an ever-living fame wherein neither pleasures nor grandeur sleep.] (2969–85)

He renounces possession of Rosaura, then, but in doing so he must avert his eyes from the vision he has followed:

ni ti miro, porque es fuerza,
en pena tan rigurosa,
que no mire tu hermosura
quien ha de mirar tu honra.

[nor do I look at you, because it is necessary in such strong pain, that he who must look to your honor must not look upon your beauty.]
(3012–15)

The renunciation is the act of humility which tells us that the beast-man has become the philosopher-king. As the action unfolds, Segismundo defeats Basilio in battle, only to humble himself and belie the mistaken inference drawn from his ominous birth. And in his final act, now formally recognized by Basilio's happy cry "principe eres" (3250), he returns Rosaura to Astolfo and her honor, taking Estrella for his consort and comfort as he enters upon the new dream of just rule.[20] His last words are as measured and rueful as Prospero's when that other Renaissance philosopher-king had to return to rule in Milan, his every third thought the grave:

pues así llegué a saber
que toda la dicha humana,
en fin, pasa como sueño,
y quiero hoy aprovecharla
el tiempo que me durare,
pidiendo de nuestras faltas
perdón.

[this I have learned: that all human pleasure, in the end, passes like a dream, and I wish now to profit from the time left to me by asking pardon for all our failures.] (3312–18)

In commenting upon the allegory of Plato's cave, Ficino noted that "in tribus gradibus mentionem hic facit de lumine, scilicet in cauerna, in nocte, in die," which correspond to the three absolute degrees of light, "uisibile scilicet, & intellectuale super uisum, & diuinum super intellectum" (*Opera*, p. 1410). Having gazed, with the true philosopher, upon the image of the divine light which radiated from Rosaura's beauty, Segismundo now, as a true prince, returns to the cave with that mortal reflection Estrella, for men in the darkness, as Plato said, "will see the . . . stars by night better than the . . . sun by day." But this reflected light of the intellect will dispel the flickering shadows passing for reality on the dreamers' prison wall when they, too, learn, with their philosopher-king, "hacer bien." Then, Socrates said, "our State, which is also yours, will be a reality, and not a dream."

APPENDIX Guarini, Chapman, and the Form of Tragicomedy as the Fortunate Fall

 The crucial incident upon which *The Gentleman Usher* turns is Strozza's wounding and its consequences. When one seeks the background for that incident, it is discovered to be a plot *topos* from the epic which was variously adapted to other genres in the Renaissance. I suggest that its natural milieu was tragicomedy, the genre in which this recurrent incident could assume a central place, becoming a microcosm of the rationale by which this form purged the mingling complexions of man, as Guarini argued that it must.

We have seen the importance of Hercules transformed from *furens* to *patiens* in the Italian mythographers and in Chapman's play, and I have insisted upon the importance of Ficino as a stimulus for the ideas of both. M. Jacquot also looked to the world of Ficino in search of the source which inspired Strozza's wounding and found in Pomponazzi's work the account of a man from whose body an arrowhead was removed only after a thaumaturge's incantations and a similar case in a medical treatise by Antonio Benivieni.[1] But reading Ficino was a not uncommon Renaissance sport; that Chapman did so does not guarantee that he read lesser Italian treatises on miracle practices in medicine. While Jacquot's emphasis upon Platonic influences affecting Chapman's Herculean plot is justified, it is unnecessary to seek quite such recondite sources for the crucial incident of *The Gentleman Usher.*

Let me make an initial generalization: tragicomedy moves to one of two poles, triviality or transcendence. When successful, it is a genre in which character chooses a symbolic providence that reverses the direction of inner pressures, in which man is, in all but the most literal sense, reborn. It is, in short, essentially constructed upon some version of the Fortunate Fall. This is why, I believe, mixed drama learned to adapt to its peculiar needs an event originating in Homer, becoming ambiguous in the romance epics, christianized in Tasso, and dramatized as both symbol and plot center in Guarini's *Il pastor fido.*

The surprising thing is that the early commentators should have made so little of the incident. Chapman himself, for instance, did not bother to gloss the episode in the *Iliad* (Bk. IV. 126–219) wherein Menelaus, pierced by an arrow, is cured by Machaon, the physician who removes a recalcitrant arrowhead and cures his thigh wound. More important than this prototype is Virgil's imitation, in which Aeneas rushes to kill Turnus in the final book of the *Aenead* (XII. 318–440), only to be struck down by an arrow. His suffering allows Turnus to bloody the field while Aeneas tears futilely at the shaft, and Iapas the physician applies herbs and pincers in vain. It is only when Venus, taught by the medical mythology of Aristotle and Theophrastus, which passed into wide currency through Cicero's *De natura deorum* and Pliny's *Natural History*, treats Aeneas with dittany from Crete that the arrow falls from the wound and the protagonist of history is enabled to resume the sword and salvation of Rome.[2] Even the indefatigable Virgilian commentaries made little of this. Giovanni Fabrini da Fighine was typical in concentrating upon the botanical tradition, indicating that while the plant grew everywhere it was most potent on Crete, "where, they say, the deer and goats when wounded by some dart or arrow, the iron remaining lodged within, pasturing on this herb immediately cast out the steel."[3]

Boiardo adapted the incident freely but tangentially in the *Orlando inamorato* (XXI, 39–42), where the daughter of the King of the Distant Isles instantaneously and miraculously restores Brandimarte, wounded "per colpo di Marfusto furioso." It was readapted, with much closer attention to Virgil's model, by Ariosto (*Orlando furioso* XIX, 13–26) in Angelica's use of dittany to cure Medoro's sword gash. It is at this point in its history that the incident begins to be moralized, but the moral drawn is generally negative. Lodovico Dolce says it illustrates the nature of ungrateful females,[4] chorused with variations by such eminent sixteenth-century scholiasts as Giuseppe Bononome, Tommaso Porcacchi, Orazio Toscanella, and Clemente Valvassori,[5] but never more bitterly than by Aluigi Gonzaga in his "allegory," where he notes that Angelica's action "expresses gracefully . . . the nature of woman, in truth, ungrateful and lacking caution; so that . . . it is always naturally inclined to the worst things."[6]

It is an interesting side reflection upon Guarini's acumen that there were a number of French stage adaptations of the love between Angelica and Medoro—usually bearing "tragicomedie" on the title page—which, missing the opportunity afforded by the incident, consistently omit the miraculous cure, either in the interest of stressing Orlando's Ajax-like love madness (as in Jean de Mairet's *Roland furieux* of 1640 and Philippe Quinalt's *Roland* of 1685) or of turning Medoro into a précieux love-debater who conquers Angelica and France's knights while disguised, as in Gabriel Gilbert's *Les amours d'Angélique et de Medor* of 1664.

Returning to the mainstream, however, one finds that Tasso (*Gerusalemme liberata* XI, 53–54, 68–75) incorporates the medical commentary into his text and reverses the allegorical tradition: he describes how Goffredo, wounded by a pagan arrow, is cured by his guardian angel with dittany, elaborating how the Cretan plant held power to heal the mountain goats and the arrow fell out immediately and Goffredo's vigor was renewed. Since Strozza's vision and cure in *The Gentleman Usher* are brought about by "that good angel / That by diuine relation spake" to him, Chapman may have been remembering Tasso, who christianized the episode in keeping with his epic theory, not only naming "l'Angiol custode" as Goffredo's deliverer, but allowing the physician Eròtimo to emphasize the new element by observing "un angiol":

> I believe an angel
> Made into a doctor for you, has descended upon the earth;
> Because I see the signs of a celestial hand.   (XI, 75)

But now let us take a fresh start in tracing the *topos* of the wound and its miraculous cure. Leonard Grant has assured us that the *venatoria* form was among the less common in Renaissance Neo-Latin pastoral,[7] and the most celebrated of these centered upon an incident which transferred the *topos* from war to the hunt in 1494—that is, even before Ariosto's development of its epic status. In the familial 1513 collection *Strozzi poetae pater et filius* Lucrezia Borgia is presented with a lengthy hexameter "venatio" by her crippled, elegant, and ill-starred confidant Ercole Strozzi or Strozza. This hunting poem is an anachronistic *chasse a cléf* in which Pico, Bembo, Ariosto, and others go hunting in a wood where Cesare Borgia, under the pseudonym Alcimous, stumbles upon the baths and sacristry of Diana, carries off the sacred boar, and returns triumphantly. At Diana's plea, Jove strikes him down under a falling oak tree. Thus blasted, he recovers only when, Jove's anger spent, Apollo reanimates him miraculously with a touch from his wand.[8]

It is within this hunt milieu that Guarini adopts the *topos* of the wound miraculously cured into *Il pastor fido*. In this first full-blown dramatic tragicomedy, a play noted by Chapman in the preface to *The Widow's Tears*, one in which he could find oracles, a hunt both allegorical and literal, Hercules, and the crucial wounding, there are three turns which draw the action from potentially tragic to finally comic form. The three are the wounding of Dorinda by Silvio in the hunt, the discovery that Mirtillo is Montano's son, and the final realization that his union with Amarilli can fulfill the demands of Diana's justice happily, averting an imminent sacrifice of son by father. The latter two work out a straight causal line of events, recognitions without reversals, but the wounding and cure of Dorinda by the scornful hunter Silvio not only opens the way to later developments but completely alters Silvio's character, making Guarini's employment of the *topos* a natural metaphor for his conception of tragicomedy as a mixed genre which functions as a medicine to purge the human temperament of excesses and so bring men, like Silvio, to a happier balance. We may remember many remarks in Guarini's *Compendio* such as "from this there results a poem of most excellent and tempered form . . . corresponding to the human complexion, which exists entirely in the proper tempering of the four humors."[9]

The problem of character correction in *Il pastor fido* is stated in the opening scene, where Silvio is chided for his lack of love interest by the wise tutor Linco. If, like Adonis, he prefers to hunt the boar, Linco warns him, his own breast is the wood and his cruelty the enforested boar he should hunt (a conceit suggestive of Strozza's allegorical explications of the masque that opens *The Gentleman Usher*). Silvio counters that his ancestor Hercules was a hunter. Again suggesting echoes in the masque within Chapman's play, Silvio sees the possibilities for symbolic metamorphosis inherent in the boar hunt when he contrasts Diana's own followers with those of Venus.

> Your followers kill wild boars
> But hers are miserably
> Slain by wild boars. (IV, viii)

Linco reminds him that Hercules was also a lover, a breeder of life, and the subdued promise of this fertile ancestry is realized in the actual boar hunt of act IV. Silvio, "true child of Hercules," kills the boar which has made barren the soil of Arcadia:

> O glorious youth! by whom these plains depriv'd
> Of tillage . . . retriv'd
> Their fruitfull honours have.[10]

But this is made the type and promise of a greater conquest:

> Such peradventure was that famous Boar
> *Alcides* slew. . . . But with wilde Beasts thy infant valour playes,
> To kill worse monsters in thy riper days. (3767–72)

The inner conquest of "cruelty" is foreshadowed here, and when Silvio wounds Dorinda, the boar hunt and the love hunt fuse and Silvio is converted from adamant Adonis to *inamorato*. Transformed, he kneels and bares to Dorinda's dart that breast in which he has lodged the boar of abnormal passion: "I strike thee? strike thee Love," she replies (4113). With this, Silvio takes her home, and our *topos* for the first time is enacted in a context of harmonious and legitimate love. Silvio, attempting to remove the arrow, leaves the head embedded in Dorinda's thigh:

> It was not possible by hand of man,
> Or iron instrument, or ought beside
> To get it out. Perchance t'ave open'd wide
> The wound . . . had
> Effected the great cure. But *Silvio's* hand,

Too pitifull, too much with love unmann'd
The Surgeon was, so cruelly to heal.   (5258–65)

But love knows the ways of traditional magic medicine; Silvio assures her that

By hunting I have learn'd to cure
. . . A plant there is much us'd by the wild Goat
When there's a shaft into her body shot.

This obtained, the narrator cries,

O wonderfull! As soon as that was laid
Upon the wound . . . The iron coming without pain away,
Did the first summons of the hand obey.   (5273–88)

In a play of oracles and providential discoveries this incident which opens the way to harmony must itself be interwoven with a sense of guiding forces at work, punishing and yet restoring the distempered humors of Silvio, the new Hercules, so that he, like the tragicomic genre for which his experience is symbol, should not show us only "the atrocity of chance, blood and deaths, which are," Guarini said, "horrible and inhuman visions."[11] Linco, from first to last Silvio's voice of conscience, bitterly declares when he discovers the accident:

If thou think (fond childe)
This *chance* by chance befell thee, th'art beguild.
These monstrous things without Divine decree
Hap not to men.   (4045–48)

But, indeed, Dorinda could justifiably join Amarilli in the chorus of praise for the *felix culpa* with which *Il pastor fido* concludes:

Basta à me, ch'l destino
T'usò per felicissimo stormento
D'ogni mia gioia, avventurosi inganni,
Tradimenti felici.

[Yet my fate us'd thee as her instrument to work my blisse, and that's enough: for me, 'twas a good Treason, a blest Fallacy.]   (5536–38)

This brings us back to the opening generalization: tragicomedy achieves substance through inner reversal, the metamorphosis of character, and transcendent rebirth through that metamorphosis. Since the generic movement is from tragic event to comic harmony, this reversal would seem inevitably to constitute always some version of the Fortunate Fall, the "tradimenti felici" of Guarini's protagonists.

The plot *topos* of the wound magically healed gradually developed more miraculous overtones as it was Christianized in Tasso's epic and moved toward the center of interaction between character and event in *Il pastor fido*. It was Chapman's distinction to seize upon the central issue of the tragicomic genre when he read its first great exemplar and, at least insofar as structure would take him, to transcend the Italian master from whom he borrowed. It is in *The Gentleman Usher* that the miraculous cure, crossed with Guarini's Herculean hunter's metamorphosis, becomes the central metaphor which organizes a truly Platonic poem about transcending the self.

NOTES

ABBREVIATIONS

The following abbreviations are used for journal titles throughout the notes:

AJP	*American Journal of Philology*
BH	*Bulletin Hispanique*
BHR	*Bibliothèque d'Humanisme et Renaissance*
CL	*Comparative Literature*
EC	*Essays in Criticism*
ELH	*English Literary History*
ELN	*English Language Notes*
Ét. Angl.	*Études Anglaises*
GSLI	*Giornale Storico della Letteratura Italiana*
HLQ	*Huntington Library Quarterly*
HR	*Hispanic Review*
JEGP	*Journal of English and Germanic Philology*
JHI	*Journal of the History of Ideas*
JWCI	*Journal of the Warburg and Courtauld Institutes*
KFLQ	*Kentucky Foreign Language Quarterly*
KR	*Kenyon Review*
MLN	*Modern Language Notes*
MLQ	*Modern Language Quarterly*
MLR	*Modern Language Review*
MP	*Modern Philology*
NLH	*New Literary History*
N&Q	*Notes & Queries*
PMLA	*Publications of the Modern Language Association of America*
PQ	*Philological Quarterly*
RN	*Renaissance News*
RR	*Romanic Review*
SEL	*Studies in English Literature*
SP	*Studies in Philology*
SQ	*Shakespeare Quarterly*

PROLOGUE

1. In Greek διαβασις: an action of crossing over; a transition. I employ the term for its double sense of a bridging and an act of passage between interchanging elements, and because the Renaissance adapted it in just this sense in Henry More's *Brief Reply*, 1672, cited in *OED*.

2. *Metatheatre: A New View of Dramatic Form* (New York, 1963). My quotations are from pp. 76–79 passim. Cf. pp. 83, 105, 112–13. An adumbration of some of the historic connections treated by Abel was made by Oscar Büdel, "Contemporary Theater and Aesthetic Distance," *PMLA*, 76 (1961), 277–91, but from a negative standpoint.

3. *La Littérature de l'âge baroque en France: Circé et le paon* (Paris, 1954), p. 226. All translations from non-English texts are my own unless otherwise indicated.

4. On the symbolic origins and flourishing of the amphitheater-within-the-theater see Richard Bernheimer, "Theatrum Mundi," *Art Bulletin*, 38 (1956), 225–47; Frances A. Yates, *The Art of Memory* (London, 1966) and *Theatre of the World* (Chicago, 1969), with the critique and criticism of I. A. Shapiro, "Robert Fludd's Stage-Illustration," in *Shakespeare Studies*, II, ed. J. Leeds Barroll (Cincinnati, O., 1967), pp. 192–209; Herbert Weisinger, "*Theatrum Mundi*: Illusion as Reality," in *The Agony and the Triumph: Papers on the Use and Abuse of Myth* (East Lansing, Mich., 1964), pp. 58–71; Thomas B. Stroup, *Microcosmos: The Shape of the Elizabethan Play* (Lexington, Ky., 1965); Frank J. Warnke, *Versions of Baroque: European Literature in the Seventeenth Century* (New Haven, Conn., 1972), pp. 66–89. Bernini's *Comédie des deux théâtres* is commented upon by Rousset, p. 73, and by Bernheimer, pp. 242–43. Confirmatory evidence for the Renaissance respect for theatricality is offered in a survey of Italian *Cinquecento* non-dramatic texts made by Mario Costanzo, *Il "Gran Theatro del Mondo": schede per lo studio dell'iconografia letteraria nell'età del Manierismo* (Milan, 1964), pp. 7–46; in Peter Rusterholz' reading of Gryphius, Hoffman von Hoffmanswaldau, and Von Lohenstein as "Barock" playwrights in *Theatrum vitae humanae: Funktion und Bedeutungswandel eines poetischen Bildes*, Philologische Studien und Quellen, No. 51 (Berlin, 1970)—a book heavily influenced by Rousset—and in W. Tatarkiewicz, "Theatrica, the Science of Entertainment," *JHI*, 26 (1965), 263–72. Tatarkiewicz notes that the listing of "theatrica" as a science of spectator games and shows among the "mechanical" arts was initiated in the twelfth-century *Didascalicon* of Hugh of St. Victor, that this "science" essentially disappeared in the later Middle Ages, and that it was reinstated in the popular *Margarita philosophia* of Georg Reisch (1496, with numerous editions through 1583) and systematically expanded in Johann Alsted's seventeenth-century *Encyclopedia*.

5. Rousset's work influenced Imbrie Buffum, *Studies in the Baroque from Montaigne to Rotrou* (New Haven, Conn., 1957), who elaborates many points and examines at length Rotrou's *St. Genest*. Robert J. Nelson, *Play within a Play: The Dramatist's Conception of His Art, Shakespeare to Anouilh* (New Haven, Conn., 1958), gathered a set of readings within a casual and frequently misleading "historic" framework. Leslie Fiedler, "The Defense of the Illusion and the Creation of Myth: Device and Symbol in the Plays of Shakespeare," in *English Institute Essays, 1948*, ed. D. A. Robertson, Jr. (New York, 1949), pp. 74–94, made a brief but ambitious investigation into Shakespeare's use of the inner play. Anne Righter, in *Shakespeare and the Idea of the Play* (London, 1962), found a native tradition of theatrical self-consciousness, raising many issues which impinge upon our conceptions of medieval and Renaissance attitudes (some of which are touched on below). The essential observations in regard to Shakespeare were originally sketched in S. L. Bethell's analysis of what he labeled the "multi-consciousness" which "is the essence of this popular dramatic tradition—of the perennial psychology of the popular audience" (*Shakespeare and the Popular Dramatic Tradition* [London, 1944],

pp. 25–29; cf. pp. 13–40 passim). Righter, like Rousset, finds self-reflexive devices passing into triviality just when, in fact, they are being turned to the most creative philosophic uses: see pp. 204–7.

6. *El espectador*, 2nd ed. (Madrid, 1921), I, 13.

7. I, 17–18. Cf. VI. Steph. 500.

8. The lecture, delivered in Lisbon on April 13, 1946, and again in Madrid on May 4, was published in greatly abbreviated form in the *Revista nacional de educación*, 62 (1946), but first appeared in full in the "Revista de occidente" edition of the *Obras ineditas* along with the important unfinished appendix, or companion piece, titled "Máscaras," from which these quotations are drawn. See *Idea del teatro* (Madrid, 1958), p. 17.

9. The name is that of the daughter of the most illustrious actress of the Teatro de Dona Maria in Madrid, a girl who made her theatrical debut in *Hamlet* shortly after Ortega's lecture (*Idea del teatro*, pp. 39, 41).

10. All quotations are from *The Theater and Its Double*, trans. Mary Caroline Richards (New York, 1958).

11. Artaud not only directed but designed costumes and sets and played Basilio: see Eric Sellin, *The Dramatic Concepts of Antonin Artaud* (Chicago, 1968), p. 3; for details of Artaud's interest in Elizabethan drama see pp. 37–42. For a hyperbolic but interesting statement of Artaud's influence upon the return to radical theater see Jacques Derrida, "Le théâtre de la cruauté et la cloture de la representation," *Critique*, 22 (1966), 595–618.

12. Righter, *Shakespeare and the Idea of the Play*, is a useful ancillary work insofar as it carefully collects evidence that in the later medieval English drama, which was un-self-conscious about its Christian premises as well as subjects, "the player was urged to associate illusion with his own life and reality itself with the dramas enacted before him" (15). These plays had an audience which identified itself as player of the part of Mankind so obviously, Righter feels, that the actors could engage in direct audience address without raising any "self-conscious" theses concerning reality (19). "Not until the Renaissance does the King become a beggar in the epilogue, and from the ruins of the play world appeal for grace to the reality represented by the audience" (15). This is to conclude that the late medieval drama was still essentially pure rite, "dramatic" without a sense of contingency. And the assumption carries into her analysis of theatrical imagery in the Shakespearean canon, an analysis which finds Shakespeare passing from casual use of the world-as-stage metaphor through a bitter denigration of man as an actor, until in the romances he reverts to a ritualistic conception of dramatic function: "In the theatrical images of the last plays there is a curious sense that Shakespeare was now out of contact with his own theatre, that the drama had come to mean for him not the Globe or Blackfriars but the festivals of the country, the traditional celebrations . . . holidays, puppets, hobby-horses, horn-pipes, Whitsun queens. . . . Out of these and certain other elements he created a world in which illusion and reality are indistinguishable" (192). C. L. Barber's *Shakespeare's Festive Comedy* (Princeton, N.J., 1959) should have made this concept seem much less peculiar to Shakespeare. Righter, though, offers us another richly documented confirmation of a renewed Renaissance awareness of the theatricality of the theater even though, like Rousset, she seems to interpret her evidence in sociological categories rather than grasping its epistemological significance.

13. *A Natural Perspective: The Development of Shakespearean Comedy and Romance* (Princeton, N.J., 1965).

14. Having elaborated my understanding of Frye's *modus operandi* elsewhere (*The Metaphoric Structure of Paradise Lost* [Baltimore, 1962], pp. 15–18), I shall risk this flat assertion here.

CHAPTER I

1. *European Literature and the Latin Middle Ages* (New York, 1953), pp. 138–44.

2. "Le théâtre du monde de Shakespeare à Calderón," *Revue de littérature comparée*, 31 (1957), 341–72.

3. Menander, *The Principal Fragments*, ed. and trans. Francis G. Allison (London, 1921), pp. 442–43.

4. "Le théâtre du monde," p. 371.

5. Ernst Cassirer, *The Individual and the Cosmos in Renaissance Philosophy*, trans. Mario Domandi (1927; rpt. New York, 1963), emphasized Cusa's putative influence upon Ficino in spite of the latter's relative silence concerning his predecessor. Cassirer later admitted the absence of evidence in his review-essay of Paul Oskar Kristeller's *Philosophy of Marsilio Ficino*, "Ficino's Place in Intellectual History," *JHI*, 6 (1945), 492. Giuseppe Saitta, *Marsilio Ficino e la filosofia dell'umanesimo*, 3rd ed. (1923; rpt. Bologna, 1954), p. 62, was no more cautious in fact, if careful in his provisos. However, Saitta has emphasized (perhaps overemphasized) Cusa's reciprocal debt to the Italian humanists in *Nicolò Cusano e l'umanesimo italiano con altri saggi sul rinascimento italiano* (Bologna, 1957). Eugenio Garin, *Giovanni Pico della Mirandola: vita e dottrina* (Florence, 1937), pp. 120–21 et passim, carefully weighed Cassirer's attempt to derive the mainstream of Italian Platonism from Cusa and found his influence on Pico important but not crucial. However, Michael Seidlmayer, "Nikolaus von Cues und der Humanismus," in *Humanismus, Mystik und Kunst in der Welt des Mittelalters*, ed. Josef Koch, 2nd ed. (1952; rpt. Leiden-Cologne, 1959), pp. 1–38, took the extreme position that there is no direct historic link between Cusa and the Ficinian circle but that Cusa's reputation was in eclipse before the Brunonian revival. Seidlmayer's position was elaborated by Garin in "Cusano ed i platonici italiani del Quattrocento," in *Nicolò da Cusa: relazioni tenute al convegno interuniversitario di Bressanone nel 1960*, Pubblicazioni della Facoltà di Magistero dell'Università di Padova, No. 4 (Florence, 1962), pp. 75–100. These essays dismiss as unimportant Pico's express desire to visit Cusa's library during his prudent self-exile to the north in 1488. Cf. the careful evaluation of the evidence in the second edition of Edgar Wind, *Pagan Mysteries in the Renaissance*, 2nd ed. (1958; rpt. London, 1967), pp. 239–40. However, Garin in his later essay emphasizes Cusa's relations with the Florentine *scienziati*, and, although he is reserved about Cusa's influence among the Ficinians, André Chastel, *Marsile Ficin et l'art* (Geneva, 1954), pp. 107ff., 113, n. 14, argues Alberti's influence at Careggi and points out his early interest in the geometric problems dealt with by Cusa. Giovanni Santinello elaborates the points of coincidence between Cusa and Alberti in "Nicolò Cusano e Leon Battista Alberti: pensieri sul bello e sull'arte," in *Nicolò da Cusa . . . convegno . . . di Bressanone*, pp. 147–78. Cf. Joan Gadol, *Leon Battista Alberti* (Chicago, 1969), pp. 196–97, 206.

6. Nicolas Cusanus, *Of Learned Ignorance*, trans. Fr. Germain Hawkins (London, 1954), p. 35. All translations are from this edition. Latin page references and, where individual images are at stake, citations (with abbreviations expanded) are from *Opera* (Basel, 1565).

7. P. 7; "Omnes autem inuestigantes, in comparatione praesuppositi certi, proportionabiliter incertum iudicant. Comparatiua igitur est omnis inquisitio, medio proportionis utens" (*Opera*, p. 1).

8. Cf. Saitta, *Nicolò Cusano e l'umanesimo*, pp. 145–74.

9. Pp. 47–48: "The lesson we here learn in our ignorance is that the Maximum, which is at once the minimum, is incomprehensible; and in it the centre is the circumference"; "Ex quo docetur ignorantia nostra, incompraehensibile maximum esse, cui minimum non opponitur, sed centrum est in ipso circumferentia" (*Opera*,

p. 16). For the history of the figure from the twelfth-century *Liber XXIV philoso-phorum*, see Georges Poulet, *Les métamorphoses du cercle* (Paris, 1961), pp. iii–xxxi, esp. xii. Alexandre Koyré, *From the Closed World to the Infinite Universe* (Baltimore, 1957), pp. 5–28, examines Cusa's adaptation of the infinite circle for its cosmological impact because he finds Cusa the first to make a "transference to the universe of the pseudo-Hermetic characterization of God" (p. 18).

10. P. 108; "aequedistantia praecisa ad diuersa extrà Deum, reperibilis non est, quia ipse solus est infinita aequalitas. Qui igitur est centrum mundi, scilicet Deus benedictus, ille est centrum terrae, & omnium sphaerarum, atque omnium quae in mundo sunt" (*Opera*, p. 38).

11. Giovanni Santinello, *Il pensiero di Nicolò Cusano nella sua prospettiva estetica* (Padua, 1958), pp. 152–57 and nn., indicates Cusa's relations with earlier Renaissance art both in the north and in Italy. This important study finds an aesthetic conception (formulated in terms of form, harmony, and splendor) dictating Cusa's ontology and metaphysics (see pp. 37, 151, 154–57, 221, 224–26). Santinello skillfully clarifies Cassirer's view that Cusa held a dynamic conception of the world in all which that phrase implies concerning the relations of God : world : artist : work (pp. 15–16, 85, 124–25, 181–82, 247–48).

12. P. 79; "sicut ueritas in imagine, ac si facies esset in imagine propria, quae ab ipsa multiplicatur distanter & propinque, quo ad imaginis multiplicationem : non dico secundum distantiam localem, sed gradualem a ueritate faciei, cum aliter multiplicari non possit, in ipsis multiplicatis ab una facie, diuersis imaginibus, diuersimode & multipliciter una facies appareret" (*Opera*, p. 27). Cf. the more self-conscious passing statement of the "Idiota" in *De mente* 9.89.

13. London, 1646. There was a translation of *Idiotae de sapientiae* in 1650: see Paolo Rotta, *Nicolò Cusano* (Milan, 1942), p. 330. I have not seen this text.

14. Nicholas of Cusa, *The Vision of God*, trans. E. M. Salter (New York, 1928), Preface, p. 3. All translations are from this edition. "Sed inter humana opera, non repperi imaginem, imagine omnia uidentis, proposito nostro conuenientiorem. Ita quod facies, subtili arte pictoria, ita se habeat, quasi cuncta circumspiciat. Harum etsi multae reperiantur optime pictae . . . figuram cuncta uidentis tenentem : quam iconam Dei appello" (*Opera*, p. 181). Cassirer, *Individual and Cosmos*, pp. 31–34, examines this passage, believing it central to Cusa's speculation, but he develops a thesis which contrasts Cusa's mathematical conception of form with the aesthetic conceptions of the Florentine Platonists; contrast Santinello's views (*Il pensiero nella prospettiva estetica*, pp. 238ff.), which subsume Cusa's concern with "value" in an aesthetic of form which engages spectator and author in a mutual transaction.

15. Cf. Santinello, *Il pensiero nella prospettiva estetica*, pp. 213–31.

16. Pp. 43–44; "animasti me Domine . . . ut uim mihi ipsi faciam: quia impossibilitas, coincidit cum necessitate, & repperi locum, in quo reuelate reperieris, cinctum contradictoriorum coincidentia, & iste est murus Paradisi, in quo habitas, cuius portam, custodit spiritus altissimus rationis, qui nisi uincatur, non patebit ingressus" (*Opera*, p. 189).

17. See Saitta, *Nicolò Cusano e l'umanesimo*, pp. 82, 100, and Santinello, *Il pensiero nella prospettiva estetica*, pp. 27, 140–41, 172, 174–75, on the importance of the incarnation of the word as treated in the book of the world by Cusa.

18. It may be worth recalling here, to underline the difference rather than the similarity, Ficino's elaborate system of musical and visual proportions and their interactions: see Paul Oskar Kristeller, *The Philosophy of Marsilio Ficino* (New York, 1943), pp. 307–9; D. P. Walker, *Spiritual and Demonic Magic from Ficino to Campanella* (London, 1958), pp. 99–104; Chastel, *Marsile Ficin et l'art*, pp. 99–104.

19. Cf. n. 22 below.

20. Cf. pp. 17–18 above.

21. P. 24; "Sic igitur compraehendo, uultum tuum Domine, antecedere omnem faciem formabilem, & esse exemplar ac ueritatem, omnium facierum, & omnes facies, esse imagines faciei tuae. . . . Omnis igitur facies, quae in tuam potest intueri faciem, nihil uidet aliud, aut diuersum à se, quia uidet ueritatem suam" (*Opera*, p. 185).

22. Pp. 127–28; *Opera*, pp. 207–8; this is the conclusion of *De visione Dei*. Cf. *Dialogus de Genesi* (written in 1447); *Opera*, p. 134, where "Nicholaus" demonstrates how God in a manner "paints" the world into being; and Santinello, *Il pensiero nella prospettiva estetica*, pp. 179–81, 184–89.

23. Santinello, *Il pensiero nella prospettiva estetica*, pp. 184–85, 268.

24. *Opera* (Basel, 1563), pp. 893–94. The influence of Alberti upon this description is discussed by André Chastel, *Art et humanisme à Florence au temps de Laurent le Magnifique* (Paris, 1961), pp. 148–51.

25. The stylistic history of pictorial space which prepares for this Renaissance moment was written by Erwin Panofsky in *Die Perspektive als "symbolische Form": Vorträge der Bibliothek Warburg: 1924–1925* (Leipzig, 1927). This monograph has been translated and incorporated into a survey of earlier and subsequent studies of graphic perspective in Panofsky, *La prospettiva come "forma simbolica" e altri scritti*, ed. Guido D. Neri (Milan, 1961). "Perspective was a double-edged tool," explains Panofsky, in reference to the post-Alberti mastery of the "visual pyramid" formula: "it creates a distance between man and things . . . but then it eliminates this distance, in a way absorbing the world of things that exist autonomously before him into the eye of man; it reduces artistic phenomena to well-defined rules, even mathematically precise rules, but on the other hand, makes them depend on man, moreover, on the individual. . . . Thus the history of perspective can be conceived simultaneously as a triumph of the sense of reality which distances and objectifies and as the triumph of the will to power of man which tends to annul every distance" (*La prospettiva*, p. 72). This fusion appears with the artistic movement which refuses to make coincident the beginning of the visual space and the graphic "frame" of the picture, so that "the picture has become a 'fragment of reality' in the measure and in the sense that the imagined space now proceeds in all directions *beyond* that which is figured" (p. 65; cf. also p. 80, which elaborates on the "ideal of creating an interior image in the most pregnant sense of the word, of an interior, that is to say, which seems to include even the spectator in the figured space"). Interesting in connection with the Ficino-Pico experience with the villa is Panofsky's concluding remark on the emphatically graphic vision which the Renaissance inherited as a potential form from its mastery of mathematical perspective: "Through this peculiar transposition of artistic objectivity into the field of phenomenalism, the perspective conception . . . disclosed a region completely new, the region of the visionary, in the ambiance of which the miracle becomes an immediately lived experience of the spectator, since the supernatural events erupt into the apparently natural visual space, which is to say, they erupt to *him* and so permit him to properly penetrate their supernatural essence." On the fusion of proscenium framing and Italian perspective staging, with the consequent fusing of symbolic and illusionistic stage conventions, see George R. Kernodle, *From Art to Theatre: Form and Convention in the Renaissance* (Chicago, 1944), esp. pp. 176–215.

26. The Neroni letter should be read with that immediately following, titled "Res uerae sunt in mundo inuisibili, in mundo uerō uisibili sunt umbrae rerum" (*Opera*, pp. 837–40). In a letter to Guido Cavalcanti titled "Theologi uigilant, caeteri somniant," while defending his close imitation of Plato, Ficino identifies himself with the philosopher who alone is awake in the dream world (*Opera*, p. 628).

27. See Chapter VIII, pp. 248–50, below.

28. Kristeller, *Philosophy of Ficino*, p. 361, has pointed out the great significance of such interpretations: "In this way Ficino eliminates all material punishment and by an allegorical interpretation attempts to reduce the mythical concepts of Plato and of the other ancient philosophers to the same, spiritual meaning." While this is true, it makes it only more interesting to observe the markedly physical quality of the language controlling this "spiritualization." In the passage cited above there is the mythic sense of place itself, the gates of Tartarus, and a continuous downward movement: "prolapsae sunt . . . profunde . . . profundiore gravari." For general commentary upon life as a sleep in Ficino's work see Chastel, *Marsile Ficin et l'art*, pp. 42–45, 141–56; Robert Klein, "L'Imagination comme vêtement de l'âme chez Marsile Ficin et Giordano Bruno," *Revue de métaphysique et de morale*, 61 (1956), 18–39, esp. 28–29.

29. In the following chapter Ficino's personal as well as theoretical attitude toward the magic aspect of dreams and visions will be discussed in relation to George Chapman's adaptation of it: cf. pp. 44–45.

30. See Nesca A. Robb's account of Palmieri's *La città di vita* and others in *Neoplatonism of the Italian Renaissance* (London, 1935), pp. 135–63.

31. Eugenio Garin, "Una fonte ermetica poco nota: contributi alla storia del pensiero umanistico," *La Rinascita*, 3 (1940), 202–32.

32. Chastel, *Marsile Ficin et l'art*, pp. 107–8, 112. Cf. Arnaldo della Torre, *Storia dell'Accademia Platonica di Firenze* (Florence, 1902), pp. 577–79, on Alberti's relations with Ficino's group. An interesting oblique reflection of the Florentine vogue is Francesco Colonna's *Poliphili Hypnerotomachia*, which, although northern in origin, yet seems to owe a great deal to Florentine humanism, in the opinion of Chastel (pp. 148–49). He cites the insistence upon dreams more true than life, the architectural lectures taken from Alberti's *De re aedificatoria*, and the sacerdotal rituals in association with "mysteries." Giovanni Pozzi has questioned the latter, claiming that Colonna was merely secularizing the liturgy he knew as sacristan of SS. Giovanni and Paolo in Venice, but he does detail the debt to Alberti: see Maria T. Casella and Giovanni Pozzi, *Francesco Colonna: Biografia e opere* (Padua, 1959), II, 11–27, 32–49. The title itself carries the Ficinian paradox that life is a mere dream, but that only in dreams is there true knowledge: *Poliphili Hypnerotomachia. Ubi humana omnia non nisi somnium esse ostendit, atque obiter plurima scitu sane quam digna commemorat*. Here in Polia's history of Poliphilo's account of his own love swoon we recede even into a dream within a dream (II, chaps. 1–12). Yet the interior spaces of the dream are physical and perspective, illustrated with disquisitions upon the architecture of temples and palaces. Indeed, the physical detail is so elaborate as to have made the presumptive allegory inaccessible even to persistent scholars: see the literature cited in Casella and Pozzi, *Francesco Colonna*, I, xviii–xxvii.

33. See A. M. Nagler, *Theater Festivals of the Medici* (New Haven, Conn., 1964), pp. 13–15, 21–24, 102–3.

34. See the illustration on p. xi above. Panofsky attributes this drawing to Ficino's direct influence in *Studies in Iconology* (1939; rpt. New York, 1962), p. 224. Cf. Ludwig Goldscheider, *Michelangelo: Drawings* (London, 1951), pp. 49–50, and Robert J. Clements, *Michelangelo's Theory of Art* (New York, 1961), p. 180: "The inability of the baroque mind to view life as a positive or a reality with well-defined values led him to the Calderonian premise that life is a dream. . . . No work shows this so clearly as his curious drawing." Clements rejects Panofsky's Platonic reading of "Il sogno" (p. 232), but the view has remained standard among most interpreters: see the review of scholarship in the reissue of *Studies in Iconology*, p. xiii. Elsewhere Clements acknowledges Ficino's influence upon the artist: see pp. 29–35, 405–6.

35. "Nel quel tempo" was about 1463, according to the anonymous "Vita Secunda"

from which this quotation is taken. See Raymond Marcel, *Marsile Ficin* (Paris, 1958), p. 705, for the text, pp. 180–81 for comment. Eugenio Garin, "La vita di Marsilio Ficino," *Rinascimento*, 1 (1951), pp. 96ff., attributes the MS to Piero Caponsacchi, but Marcel (pp. 690–93) raises dating difficulties for the attribution.

36. "Sommario della vita di Marsilio Ficino raccolta da Ms Piero Caponsacchi filosofo Aretino," from the text in Marcel, *Marsile Ficin*, p. 731. Cf. Chastel, *Marsile Ficin et l'art*, pp. 39–40.

37. *The Crisis of the Early Italian Renaissance: Civic Humanism and Republican Liberty in an Age of Classicism and Tyranny* (Princeton, N.J., 1955), pp. 169–71; cf. pp. 160–77 and the texts, pp. 517–20.

38. Gadol, *Leon Battista Alberti*, has as a principal thesis the ubiquity of "perspectivist" theories in the many varied aspects of Alberti's work. Chastel has related the obsession with perspective in Florence from Alberti to Leonardo to Ficino's commentary on the *Timaeus* (*Art et humanisme*, pp. 302–8). Straws sometimes signify the strength of the wind. Around 1450 there arises a generic tendency to subordinate figures to elaborate perspective frames in the highly popular *trompe-l'oeil* wooden mosaics. Their origins are generally traced to northern Italy, but Chastel argues that the initiation of the practice was Florentine: see "Marqueterie et perspective au XVe siècle," *La revue des arts*, 3 (1953), 141–54.

39. "Vt est centrum quidem, est in omnibus, ut circumferentia uero, est extra omnia. In omnibus, inquam, non inclusus, quia est & circumferentia. Extra omnia quoque non exclusus, quia est & centrum. Quid ergo Deus est? Vt ita dixerim, circulus spiritalis, cuius centrum est ubique, circumferentia nusquam. At enim si centrum id diuinum in aliqua mundi parte imaginariam aliquam aut perspicuam operationis sedem habeat, potissimùm in rerum medio dominant, tanquam rex in medio corporis, Sol in medio planetarum. In Sole igitur, id est, in tertia mediàque rerum essentia Deus posuit tabernaculum suum" (*Opera*, p. 403). Kepler's heliocentric cosmology was greatly influenced by such premises, Arthur O. Lovejoy argued, leading him to find the sun to be "that which alone we should judge to be worthy of the Most High God if he should be pleased with a material domicile and choose a place in which to dwell with the blessed angels" (quoted in *The Great Chain of Being* [Cambridge, Mass., 1936], p. 105). Cf. E. A. Burtt, *The Metaphysical Foundations of Modern Physical Science*, rev. ed. (London, 1932), pp. 47–49. Frances Yates, *Giordano Bruno and the Hermetic Tradition* (Chicago, 1964), p. 153 et passim, supplies the Dionysian hermetic background for Ficino's sun emulation, and that it was emulation is suggested in Ficino's response to a letter in which John Colet addressed Ficino himself as the sun: Sears Jayne, *John Colet and Marsilio Ficino* (Oxford, 1963), pp. 19ff.

40. See p. 17 above. Chastel, *Marsile Ficin et l'art*, pp. 58–59, 62, exaggerates his claims for the "physical" quality of Ficino's image only to the extent that he does not recall Cusa's earlier treatment of the infinite circle.

41. Kristeller, *Philosophy of Ficino*, pp. 218–55; cf. Ernst Cassirer, "Ficino's Place in Intellectual History," *JHI*, 6 (1945), 483–501.

42. *Opera*, p. 410. Cf. pp. 418–24 passim and the statement on our daily soul motion: "non est etiam contra naturam aliquod ē sublimibus spiritibus huc quasi descendere quotidie atque ascendere" (p. 375). See Kristeller, *Philosophy of Ficino*, pp. 392–401.

43. "Ac licet animus per naturam essentiae tertiae, Iani bifrontis instar utrumque respiciat, corporeum scilicet et incorporeum" (*Opera*, p. 375).

44. In a letter addressed "to all men," Ficino declares that he has an image to depict man's state in this life: "Praecipuam mihi quaerenti hodie rationem qua homines tam laboriosam in terris uitam continuē ducent, uenit in mentem ludus quidem eiusmodi, in quo nonnulli cruribus extensis in altum interim palmis & capitis

uertice gradiantur. Praeterea conentur altero quidem oculo terrena undique omnia, altero autem coelestia circumspicere. Deinde quicquid humi occurrerit, naribus, labijs, digitis, prensare nitantur. Rursus si quid ab alto his imminet, pedibus attrectare conentur & carpere, & quaecumque attigerint, portanda suscipiant. O turpissimum spectaculum" (*Opera*, p. 755).

45. The ultimate source is Plato's *Republic* VI (Steph. 507–11), where the primacy of sight is discussed in conjunction with the sun as an analogue to the Good. For Ficino, *De amore* 5.3 (*Opera*, pp. 1335–36) seems to be the *locus classicus*. Cf. Kristeller, *Philosophy of Ficino*, pp. 226–28, 394; Chastel, *Marsile Ficin et l'art*, pp. 109–10; Panofsky, *Studies in Iconology*, p. 133; Eugene F. Rice, Jr., *The Renaissance Idea of Wisdom* (Cambridge, Mass., 1958), pp. 65–66. On Alberti's medallion of the winged eye see also Renée Watkins, "L. B. Alberti's Emblem, the Winged Eye, and His Name, Leo," *Mitteilungen des Kunsthistorischen Institutes in Florenz*, 9 (1960), 256–58, and Gadol, *Leon Battista Alberti*, pp. 69ff. The early sources are discussed in R. C. Kissling, "The OXNMA-TNEYMA of the Neo-Platonists and the *De Insomniis* of Synesius of Cyrene," *AJP*, 43 (1922), 318–30. A later direct development from Ficino's metaphor to Campanella's total involvement of the senses in contemplation is traced in Eugenio Garin, *Italian Humanism: Philosophy and Civic Life in the Renaissance* (1947; rpt. New York, 1965), pp. 197, 217–20.

46. *Liber de sole* 3 (*Opera*, pp. 968–69) presents the theme of God-sun as eye ("coeli oculum"). Cf. the letter on "Mens quia est diuina uultus imago, Deum semper suspicere debet" (*Opera*, p. 706). Colet, annotating Ficino's sun metaphor, noted "Angeli oculi"; see Jayne, *Colet and Ficino*, pp. 105–6. Cf. C. R. Ligota, "L'Influence de Macrobe pendant la Renaissance," in *Le soleil à la Renaissance: sciences et mythes*, Travaux de l'Institut pour l'Etude de la Renaissance et de l'Humanisme, Université Libre de Bruxelles, No. 2 (Brussels, 1965), pp. 475–78.

47. *Opera*, p. 296. I am indebted to Chastel, *Marsile Ficin et l'art*, esp. pp. 59–60, 82–83, for these points of emphasis; cf. also Klein, "L'Imagination chez Ficino," esp. pp. 25–26, 32–33.

48. "Quapropter diuina mens cum sit infinita, meritō nominatur ab Orphicis απείρομμα, id est, oculus infinitus" (*Opera*, p. 105).

49. "Et sicut plura uidet tanquam finitam, id est, tanquam rem quandam essentiae omnino simplicem, sed quoadammodo ratione multiplicem, quia formam suam re uera unam, uigore & respectu quodam considerat omniformem, perinde ac si Solis lux, colorum fons omnium, quae (ut ita loquar) unicolor est, se tanquam omnicolorem percipiat" (*Opera*, p. 105).

50. Translated by Nancy Lenkeith in *The Renaissance Philosophy of Man*, ed. Ernst Cassirer et al. (Chicago, 1948), pp. 387–93. In relation to these later epicycles in the Platonic field of force stimulated by Ficino, it is useful to recall Cassirer's emphasis upon dynamism and becoming in *The Individual and the Cosmos* as Ficino's contribution; cf. Rice, *Idea of Wisdom*, pp. 93–123.

CHAPTER II

1. *Poems of George Chapman*, ed. Phyllis Brooks Bartlett (New York, 1941), p. 49. All citations from the poems are taken from this edition.

2. The evidence, both textual and contextual, was first gathered by Frank L. Schoell, *Études sur l'humanisme continental en Angleterre à la fin de la Renaissance*, Bibliothèque de la revue de littérature comparée, No. 29 (Paris, 1926), and "George Chapman and the Italian Neo-Latinists," *MP*, 13 (1915), 24–38. Schoell's work was incorporated and developed in Bartlett's edition of the *Poems*; cf. her Introduction, pp. 1, 7–9, 11–12, and Notes, pp. 422–28, 430–31, 446–47, 453–54, 462–63, 474–75,

486, for detailed accounts of Chapman's borrowings. Neoplatonic interpretation of myth is briefly annotated for the tragedies as well in Roy W. Battenhouse, "Chapman and the Nature of Man," *ELH*, 12 (1945), 87–107. Jean Jacquot, *George Chapman: sa vie, sa poésie, son théâtre, sa pensée* (Paris, 1951), pp. 199–231, treats Chapman's debt to Ficino, relying largely on the earlier findings. In spite of this preparation, only three full-scale readings have demonstrated a structural coherence in individual works based on platonically oriented mythological interpretation. See Raymond B. Waddington, "Chapman's *Andromeda Liberata*: Mythology and Meaning," *PMLA*, 81 (1966), 34–44, and "Prometheus and Hercules: The Dialectic of *Bussy D'Ambois*," *ELH*, 34 (1967), 21–48; the latter thickly develops points partially anticipated in Eugene M. Waith, *The Herculean Hero in Marlowe, Chapman, Shakespeare and Dryden* (New York, 1962), pp. 88–111. These ideas themselves were partially adumbrated in Jean Jacquot, "*Bussy D'Ambois* and Chapman's Conception of Tragedy," *English Studies Today*, 2nd ser., ed. G. A. Bonnard (Bern, 1961), pp. 129–41.

3. See the Preface to the translation of Dante's *De monarchia* in Paul O. Kristeller, *Supplementum Ficinianum* (Florence, 1937), II, 184ff. See Raymond Marcel, *Marsile Ficin* (Paris, 1958), pp. 325–34, for a thoroughly political analysis of the Dante translation which minimizes the sincerity of Ficino's statement of platonically oriented syncretism. But on this point and others I follow the discussions of mythic patterns in Florentine culture by André Chastel, *Marsile Ficin et l'art* (Geneva, 1954), pp. 141–56, and *Art et humanisme à Florence au temps de Laurent le Magnifique* (Paris, 1959), pp. 195–206, 517–18.

4. See Chapter I, p. 24, above.

5. The climax of Chastel's studies is a detailed review of the manner in which Saturn, Eros, and Hermes were first revivified as symbols and then fused in Orpheus by Ficino, only to be dispersed again in the attitudes and attitudinizing of Raphael, Leonardo, and Michelangelo (*Marsile Ficin et l'art*, pp. 118–79, *Art et humanisme*, pp. 487–513). This point is emphasized also in the survey by Robert Klein, "La crise de la Renaissance italienne," *Critique*, 16 (1960), 322–40.

6. D. P. Walker, *Spiritual and Demonic Magic from Ficino to Campanella* (London, 1958), pp. 15, 21–22. Cf. E. H. Gombrich, "*Icones Symbolicae*: The Visual Image in Neo-Platonic Thought," *JWCI*, 11 (1948), 175–78.

7. Pico della Mirandola, *De hominis dignitate*, ed. Eugenio Garin (Florence, 1942), p. 156. The history of "mysteries" and their interpreters has been written by Don Cameron Allen, *Mysteriously Meant: The Rediscovery of Pagan Symbolism and Allegorical Interpretation in the Renaissance* (Baltimore, 1970). Important interpretations focusing upon the Florentine circle have been made by Edgar Wind, *Pagan Mysteries in the Renaissance* (Princeton, N.J., 1958), and Erwin Panofsky, *Studies in Iconology* (1939; rpt. New York, 1962).

8. Sears Jayne, *John Colet and Marsilio Ficino* (Oxford, 1963), pp. 92–93.

9. "A Sleight Man," ll. 59–64.

10. "To the Most Worthily Honored, my Singular Good Lord, Robert, Earle of Somerset, Lord Chamberlaine, &c." prefatory to the *Odysseys* (*Poems*, p. 407), ll. 40–56 of the prose interpolation. But one wonders what Chapman intended in the piece he never wrote, "my Poeme of the mysteries / Reueal'd in Homer" ("To the Reader," *Iliads*, ll. 61–62 [*Poems*, p. 393]).

11. See Jackson I. Cope, "*Bartholomew Fair* as Blasphemy," *Renaissance Drama*, VIII (Evanston, Ill., 1965), pp. 127–52.

12. *Poems*, p. 327.

13. *Poems*, p. 86; published as part of *Ovids Banquet of Sense*.

14. *The Revenge of Bussy D'Ambois*, I, i, 319–74. Citations of the tragedies are

from *The Plays and Poems of George Chapman*, ed. Thomas Marc Parrott (London, 1910–14).

15. This is the principal burden of Gombrich, *"Icones Symbolicae,"* esp. pp. 169–73, where he documents the Renaissance exaltation of visual symbols over discourse because they mirror the "immediate" knowledge of higher things available in "visions." Cf. also Panofsky's observations on the role of graphic perspective in making "vision" directly available to the Renaissance spectator (see Chapter I, n. 25, above).

16. In Chapter VII, pp. 212–16, below, the Renaissance discussions of the point which center on Dante's *Commedia* are reviewed.

17. *Herculean Hero*, pp. 88–111; I quote p. 93. Cf. T. W. Baldwin's earlier insistence upon the influence of the sophisticated Blackfriars audience on the tone of *The Gentleman Usher*, "the first full-fledged tragicomedy" (*The Organization and Personnel of the Shakespearean Company* [Princeton, N.J., 1927], pp. 315–17).

18. *Herculean Hero*, p. 111. Waddington, by his discernment of the interacting Prometheus myth, refines upon the analysis and makes a *concordia discors* of Bussy's antithetical split journeys ("Prometheus and Hercules").

19. Henry M. Weidner, "The Dramatic Uses of Homeric Idealism: The Significance of Theme and Design in George Chapman's *The Gentleman Usher*," *ELH*, 28 (1961), 121–36, treats the play from the perspective of true and false ceremony, reading the whole as an exercise in sophisticated ritualism. It will become clear that I believe Weidner pursued some proper elements in improper directions.

20. I, i, 15–16. All citations from the comedies are to the still incomplete *Plays of George Chapman: The Comedies*, ed. Allan Holaday (Urbana, Ill., 1970).

21. Cynanche's entire commentary places her as a Venus-type in a long tradition:

> My Lord I fancie not these hunting sports,
> When the bold game you follow turnes againe,
> And stares you in the face: let me behold
> A cast of Faulcons on their merry wings,
> Daring the stooped prey, that shifting flies:
> Or let me view the fearefull Hare or Hinde,
> Tosst like a musicke point with harmonie
> Of well mouthed hounds. This is a sport for Princes,
> The other rude; Boares yeeld fit game for Boores.   (I, i, 50–57)

Don Cameron Allen, "On *Venus and Adonis*," in *Elizabethan and Jacobean Studies Presented to Frank Percy Wilson in Honour of His Seventieth Birthday* (Oxford, 1959), pp. 100–11, has shown how the boar was traditionally associated with the "hard hunt" of the virtuous life and death, the hind and the hare with the soft hunt of love. But Cynanche emerges as the chaste Venus-Diana who presses the ideal of virtue, merging Venus, Grissel, Diana. The courtesan Cortezza fuses the two hunts as she leads Alphonso to "hunt at view" the young lovers who play at "loue-sports" while the Duke is thought to be "still a hunting" (IV, iv, 48–53).

22. An analogue to the cannibalism of the regal horses at Duncan's unnatural murder (*Macbeth*, II, iv).

23. The role of prophet of doom clings to Poggio throughout the play: cf. IV, i, 1–10; IV, ii, 202–18; V, ii, 64–79.

24. Vestiges of a similar metamorphic hunt in which Queen Aegiale and *"Isis Nymphes"* hunt a boar which "may fall, / Slayne with our beauties more than swordes or dartes" appear in *The Blind Beggar of Alexandria* (iii, 13–26), but the mutilated text does not pursue the suggested hunt. The masque of boarhunting with which Richard II captures the "tyrant" Gloucester in *Woodstock* may be a relevant

antecedent: see *Woodstock: A Moral History*, ed. A. P. Rossiter (London, 1946), IV, ii, 80–218.

25. Cf. the similar view, in another context, expressed by Weidner, "Homeric Idealism," pp. 125–26. Alphonso later ironically gives high significance to the misunderstood masque by begging Margaret that she will

> thinke it was not a mere festiuall shew,
> But an essentiall type of that you are
> in full consent of all my faculties.   (III, ii, 278–80).

Alphonso is just at the point of recovering his rational faculties, of course, when he conforms to Strozza's real reading of the boar hunt masque.

26. Wind, *Pagan Mysteries*, pp. 71–77, 158–75. Wind (163) attributes this habitual representation to a neoplatonic law of "self-contrariety" within the conception of the gods: "With every shift of argument a new harmony or discord may be discovered between the gods." Notice that if we shift from the male to the female viewpoint, Wind's equation is almost a translation of the "Enchanters'" explication of Strozza's vision.

27. In a more "impervial" mood, Chapman had also treated Hercules as a purifier:

> Fall Hercules from heauen in tempestes hurld,
> And cleanse this beastly stable of the world:
> Or bend thy brasen bow against the Sunne,
> ....
> Now make him leaue the world to Night and dreames.
>   ("Hymnus in Noctem," *Poems*, ll. 255–61)

The union of purification and the dominance of dreams is, of course, suggestive of the pattern emergent in *The Gentleman Usher*. The protagonist applies the same image of Hercules' solar shaft to his own efforts to purify French justice in the *Tragedy of Chabot* (II, ii, 81–85).

28. Waith, *Herculean Hero*, pp. 16–59, traces the development into union of initially incompatible versions of Hercules, summing up: "The meaning of Hercules in the Renaissance approaches a paradox when it includes both justifiable pride and reason subduing passion" (p. 41).

29. For a general discussion of relevant aspects of Herculean mythology see Erwin Panofsky, *Hercules am Scheidewege* (Leipzig, 1930); Angelo Castelluccio, *Il dio Eracle come espressione di religiosità primitiva* (Salerno, 1951), esp. pp. 33–36, on the fifth-century union of self-cremation and stellar apotheosis forming a new image of purifying sacrifice; Marcel Simon, *Hercule et la Christianisme* (Paris, 1955). Waith has, of course, surveyed much of the most relevant material.

30. *Imagini delli Dei de gl'Antichi* (Venice, 1674), pp. 172–73. For demonstration of Chapman's employment of Cartari see D. J. Gordon, "Chapman's Use of Cartari in the Fifth Sestiad of 'Hero and Leander,'" *MLR*, 39 (1944), 280–85. Cesare Ripa, *Iconologia* (Rome, 1603), p. 508, repeats an added element at least as old as Fulgentius, also found in Boccaccio's influential compendium; in explicating a medal of Trajan he writes: "it represents Hercules, nude, who with the right hand holds the club on his shoulder in a graceful attitude, and with the left hand drives a lion and a wild boar harnessed together. By Hercules nude with the club one should understand the idea of all virtues; by the lion magnanimity and strength of soul; by the boar, corporal virtue."

31. *Iconologia*, p. 507. However, Ripa also reminds us that Hercules was only a demigod, and that in his human aspect he found it necessary to struggle for tran-

scendence of passion, even as do Chapman's protagonists Bussy and Strozza: see "Vertù heroica nella Medaglia di Geta," p. 507.

32. Anguillara's *Metamorfosi* was published in 1561 (with numerous editions through the nineteenth century) under the influence of Ariosto and his imitators. It was "something like a poetic romance" (Giuseppe Toffanin, *Il Cinquecento* [Milan, 1954], p. 523), which makes it all the more revealing of the tenacity of tradition that, in 1563, Horologgi should have appended his brief but familiar interpretations, with their medieval roots.

33. *Le Metamorfosi di Ovidio, ridotte da Gio. Andrea dall'Anguillara . . . con l'annotationi di M. Gioseppe Horologgi* (Venice, 1588), pp. 172–73. The scriptural reference is a reminder of the typological interaction between pagan and biblical figures. The definitive history of their general movement into the Renaissance is Allen's *Mysteriously Meant*. On Hercules, in particular, in addition to Panofsky, Simon, and Castelluccio, see Michael Krouse, *Milton's Samson and the Christian Tradition* (Princeton, N.J., 1947), and Compton Rees, "Hercules as Symbol in the Sixteenth Century" (Diss. Rice University 1962). Panofsky cites Berchorius' early use of Hercules "nicht nur als fleischgewordne virtus, sondern u. a. als präfigurierten Erlöser" (*Hercules am Scheidewege*, p. 146). Some reflections of this tradition inevitably enter the mythographic handbooks, as when Ripa cites Hercules as one who approaches the angels, or when Cartari unites Jove and Hercules in recounting out of Plutarch the hunting of the flies from the temple (pp. 373–74). But the backbone of late Christianizations must be sought, as noted, in the Ovidian commentators, and if we turn to the Raphael Regius-Jacobus Micyllus paraphernalia which accompanied most Renaissance texts of the *Metamorphoses*, we find the emphasis clearly shifted from classical *virtus* to Christian virtue. Hercules is the soul struggling with bodily passions, and Nessus the devil who burns man with the poison of vice. Hercules' voluntary self-immolation represents man's ability to burn away the poisonous passions through terrestrial suffering, thus not only substituting a figurative flame for the fire of hell, but also gaining beatification at the side of God the Father through the strength of spiritual endurance (*Metamorphoseon Pub. Ouidii . . .* [Venice, 1553], p. 102).

34. Chapman has redeveloped in a dramatic context the narrative of his early "Hymnus in Cynthiam" from *The Shadow of Night* (1594). In that poem on the state of souls, Diana (Euthimya) changes herself into a panther "now turnd a Bore" (378) who leads the passion-driven hunters to destruction; the account of her action is presented as "An Argument to rauish and refine / An earthly soule, and make it meere diuine" (154–55).

35. Quoted in *Plays and Poems of George Chapman: Comedies*, ed. Thomas Marc Parrott (London, 1910–14), p. 760.

36. See Appendix, n. 1, below.

37. Cf. Clarence in *Sir Giles Goosecap* on his beloved Eugenia, who represents the "soul exempt from flesh in flesh inflam'd," etc. (Parrott, *Comedies*, III, ii, 7–10). I cannot, however, accept the long-orthodox view that *Goosecap* is Chapman's work, a view rejuvenated by G. A. Wilkes' conjecture that the play constitutes Chapman's palimpsest for the *Children of the Chapel* written over an earlier manuscript for the *Admiral's Men* ("Chapman's 'Lost' Play, *The Fount of New Fashions*," *JEGP*, 62 [1963], 77–81). This is no place to argue the case; I shall only point out that while Clarence embodies many of Chapman's themes, he overstates, distorts, and even makes them appear contradictory. As a simple test not involving "tone," one might sample I, iv, 121–46, where it is proved by Momford that reason and anti-reason are both exclusive tools to work women to one's will. But III, ii as a whole seems the firmest evidence that we are dealing with a parody of Chapman's Platonism, when Clarence demonstrates (1) that women have the power of the distillation of souls, (2) that they have no souls, and (3) that on both counts he must get to wooing on

a "philosophic" principle infused into his aquatic mentality by Momford. The editors of the University of Illinois edition of Chapman tacitly reject Chapman's authorship by omitting *Goosecap* from the canon.

38. George Sandys, *Ovid's Metamorphosis Englished, Mythologiz'd* (Oxford, 1632), p. 321.

39. See Hardin Craig, "The Shackling of Accidents: A Study of Elizabethan Tragedy," *PQ*, 19 (1940), 1–19; Rolf Soellner, "The Madness of Hercules and the Elizabethans," *CL*, 10 (1958), 309–24; Waith, *Herculean Hero*, passim.

40. *Opera*, p. 294; cf. pp. 292, 764; Soellner, "The Madness of Hercules," p. 314; Chastel, *Marsile Ficin et l'art*, pp. 174–75.

41. Cf. Chapter I, pp. 23–24, above.

42. *Bussy D'Ambois*, I, i, 18–19. The *topos* is Pindaric, but cf. Ficino on the body as shadow (*Opera*, p. 628).

43. Cf. the text with Italian translation and notes in *Prosatori Latini del Quattrocento*, ed. Eugenio Garin (Milan, 1952), pp. 932–69; Paul Oskar Kristeller, *Philosophy of Marsilio Ficino* (New York, 1943), pp. 215ff., and *Studies in Renaissance Thought and Letters* (Rome, 1956), pp. 272ff.; Giuseppe Saitta, *Marsilio Ficino e la filosofia dell'umanesimo*, 3rd ed. (Bologna, 1954), pp. 136ff.

44. Kristeller, *Philosophy of Ficino*, pp. 292–97.

45. Kristeller's best summary of the part of contemplation in Ficino's systems is "The Platonic Academy of Florence" in his *Renaissance Thought II* (New York, 1965), pp. 94–98. But the clearest brief explanation of the role of "patience" is the following (*Philosophy of Ficino*, pp. 299–300):

The moral situation expressed by man's inward overcoming of fate is discussed at length by Ficino in his consideration of patience. . . . [His] moral theories . . . are based essentially on the experience of contemplation. We may now understand why he connects philosophical knowledge so closely with the moral life. For him philosophy is no mere theoretical doctrine whose truth can be learned and understood solely by reason. Instead he follows the true Platonic tradition, according to which knowledge can be acquired only by a profound moral and spiritual regeneration of the entire person. Ficino therefore ranks the philosopher first among those who arrive at a higher insight through a temporary separation of the soul from the body.

In Chapman's *The Revenge of Bussy D'Ambois*, Clermont D'Ambois offers a long discussion of "patience" as the virtue which puts man in harmony with the will of the "All" (IV, i, 128–57), and again the context is suffering occasioned by a tyrant.

46. *Opera*, p. 788: "patientia vero sola in bene patiendo consistit."

47. *Opera*, pp. 802–3; cf. *Supplementum Ficinianum*, ed. Paul Oskar Kristeller (Florence, 1937), II, 172. The above and immediately following translations are from Kristeller, *Philosophy of Ficino*, to which I am obviously indebted for comprehension of the importance of "patience" to Ficino's thought (see pp. 299–300). Ernst Cassirer, *The Individual and the Cosmos in Renaissance Philosophy*, trans. Mario Domandi (1927; rpt. New York, 1963), pp. 110–15, and Eugene F. Rice, Jr., *The Renaissance Idea of Wisdom* (Cambridge, Mass., 1958), pp. 58–92, examine the results of the paradox by which patience produces power.

48. *Opera*, p. 758. This passage could constitute a source for the Ferrarese court masque of 1501 honoring Lucrezia Borgia and Duke Ercole d'Este, the latter an associate of Lorenzo il Magnifico: *Lotta fra la fortuna ed Ercole*. In the masque Hercules subdues fortune. Chapman would not have known the masque, but very possibly would have known Giordano Bruno's adaptation of it in *Spaccio della bestia trion-*

fante, wherein fortune fails in her petition for Hercules' place among the stars even as Hercules is being identified as *fortezza.* Cf. Cassirer, *Individual and Cosmos,* pp. 73–74, 121–22, and the elaborate development of Hercules' conquest of vice and symbolic apotheosis by Cristoforo Landino, Ficino's companion at Careggi, in *Testi inediti di Cristoforo Landino e Francesco Filelfo,* ed. Eugenio Garin (Florence, 1949).

49. Chapman's earliest published poem, the *Hymnus in Noctem (Shadow of Night),* had framed the achievement of celestial vision in the endurance of suffering. The persona in his "torture" (17), through "skill of my griefs" (21) "For euer murmur[ing] forth my miseries" (287), is rewarded

> with grauer dreames inspir'd with prophesies,
> Which oft presage . . .
> We proouing that awake, they shew in trances. (353–55)

Twenty years later Chapman repeated the conception in *Eugenia: or, True Nobilities Trance, for death of . . . William Lord Russell* ("Vigilia Tertia"), where he developed the superiority of weakness overcome to mere untried strength in the image of a wounded, dying man who accepts the offerings of providence and rejects pretended strength which might "beare . . . with so false a patience" (896–908; cf. the whole passage, 882–941). Obversely, *Biron's Conspiracy* shows the folly of transcendence sought impatiently, as Biron cries: "Tis immortality to die aspiring / As if a man were taken quick to heaven" (I, ii, 31–32). Cf. III, iii, where defiance of fate and prophecy both underline Biron's fatal impatience. Again, in *Biron's Tragedy* (V, i, 109–27) Biron's lack of "patience" during imprisonment is contrasted with the behavior of D'Auvergne. Cf. V, ii, 2–3, on his "impatience"; V, iii, 109–11, for Biron's ironic account of "patience" "ask'd on bended knee."

50. *Opera,* p. 633.

51. "The Madness of Hercules," p. 314.

52. See D. P. Walker, *Spiritual and Demonic Magic from Ficino to Campanella* (London, 1958), for a fully developed account of Ficino's system and its sources.

53. *Opera,* pp. 644–45. For detailed accounts of this prophetic-visionary strain in Ficino, his parents, and his system, see Kristeller, *Philosophy of Ficino,* pp. 309–15, and, especially for biographical detail, Marcel, *Marsile Ficin,* pp. 121–31. John Colet's marginalia to Ficino's *Epistolae* include the remark that "the good [daemons] strive to purify us even by dreams; but we do not know how to read their writing" (Jayne, *Colet and Ficino,* p. 124). Thomas Nashe's satire in "Terrors of the Night" suggests the early notoriety of Chapman's own "visions," however: Chapman publicly laid claim to a visit from Homer's spirit in authorization of his translations (*Euthymiae Raptus,* 75–89), and in *The Revenge of Bussy* (V, i, 36–56) there is a distinction drawn between the imagination's "waking dreams" and genuine visions which "presage something."

54. *Opera,* p. 1365, discussed by Walker, *Spiritual and Demonic Magic,* pp. 20–22, and by Chastel, *Marsile Ficin et l'art,* pp. 129–35.

55. While any conjectures about numerological symbolism are dangerous, and never more so than when dealing with traditions surrounding "seven," it is worth noting that the repeated association of that number with the several cures in *The Gentleman Usher* possibly is derived from the complex of Ficino's ideas I have been detailing. Ficino found seven things capable of drawing celestial influences, the seventh and highest being the divine insight which comes with contemplation and which is astrologically entered under his own sign of the Saturnine philosopher: *"Septimum secretiores simplicioresque intelligentiae, quasi iam a motu seiunctae, con iunctae diuinis, destinate Saturno"* (*Opera,* p. 561). See Walker, *Spiritual and*

Demonic Magic, pp. 14ff., 126–27, 140–44. In *Eugenia: Or True Nobilities Trance, for death of . . . William Lord Russell*, Chapman depicted death as an angel drawing man into eternity, who would "croune him with the Asterisme of seauen: / To show he is the death of deadly sinnes" (555–56).

56. Cf. Baxter Hathaway, *The Age of Criticism: The Late Renaissance in Italy* (Ithaca, N.Y., 1962), pp. 210ff., 285ff., and the interesting suggestions in T. S. K. Scott-Craig, "Concerning Milton's Samson," *RN*, 5 (1952), 45–53.

57. Cf. *Bussy D'Ambois*, II, ii, 198–204; *Revenge of Bussy*, II, i, 117–22; *Caesar and Pompey*, V, ii, 1–18.

58. A few lines earlier Alphonso had accepted his messenger's warning that "your subjects breathe / Gainst your vnnatural fury" (V, iv, 35–36). It should be noted that Strozza himself when wounded first defied "slauish Nature," which subjects man to such torment (IV, i, 34–37).

59. Sandys, *Ovid*, p. 329. Cf. Margaret's outcry against Alphonso, which begins with the epithet "Tyrant" (V, iv, 12–26) and Strozza's entering demand, "Where is the tyrant?" (V, iv, 40) when Vincentio is carried in.

60. Cf. Chapman's continuation of *Hero and Leander* in which "the Goddesse Ceremonie" descends to chide Leander for his premature lovemaking,

> his vnceremonious part,
> In which with plaine neglect of Nuptiall rites,
> He . . . fell to his delites.   (Sestyad III, 105–60)

61. Within the scene itself, though, there is a parodic but promising little play upon providential salvation as Cortezza in dead-pan earnest reports the girl in "Saint Marks streete" who, when she tried suicide by a leap for love, found that

> her clothes
> Flew vp about her so, as she had no harme:
> And grace of God your clothes may flie vp too.   (10–13)

62. Strozza addresses him as "reuerend Doctor" (V, ii, 56) and recognizes him as one who bears "choice *Antidote*[s]" for poison, but also "good spirits and prayers" for exorcism of diabolical effects (60–64). Later Strozza identifies Benevenius as a divine agent brought by the angel who spoke to him (V, iv, 197–204).

63. *Herculean Hero*, pp. 44–45.

64. *The Gentleman Usher* reappeared strangely metamorphosed but still recognizable in Richard Brome's late romantic comedy *The Queen and Concubine* (1635–39). Brome's surface source for this long and not very characteristic play was *Penelope's Web*, one of Greene's lesser novellas setting the "patient Grissel" theme in an Egyptian court (E. Koeppel, "Brome's *Queen and Concubine*," *Quellen und Forschungen*, 82 [1897], 209–18). But Brome shifted the scene to Sicily, giving the characters Italian names—including Strozza and Poggio. Moreover, he centered the entire action around the providential power of "patience," a quality which takes on all the divine magic it bears in Chapman's Platonic play.

    Briefly, the lecherous King Gonzago deposes his longtime queen, Eulalia, under trumped up charges of adultery in order to replace her with the ambitious young courtesan Alinda, a woman whose ambition is consistently emphasized in images of flight, climbing, and ascent. Exiled, Eulalia behaves so patiently that a "Genius" appears to her in sleep

> to make sweet thy Dreams;
> Thy Dreams which truly shall relate
> The Passages of thy Estate.
>   (*Dramatic Works of Richard Brome* [London, 1873], II, 45ff.).

In this dream the Genius reveals the whole intricate plotting at court, then announces:

> I thy Brain inspire
> With a Divine Prophetick Fire;
> Thou shalt be able to Fore-doom
> The ends of many things to come.
> Into thy Breast I next infuse
> The Skill of Med'cine how to use.

Awakening from her trance, Eulalia feels as immediately empowered as Strozza had in Chapman's play:

> sure I have
> The Spirit of Prophecie, the Gift of Healing,
> And Art of teaching hidden Mysteries.
> Thanks Heaven, that first didst send me Patience. (II, 47)

"Patience" has been to Eulalia "a sweeter servant than Gentilitie" (II, 44), and with these new gifts (soon used to cure the sick population of the countryside) it leads her to Strozza-like transcendence. "O happy woman," cries a courtier,

>   now no more a Queen,
> But Holy Saint: I see how Providence
> Means to advance thy injur'd innocence. (II, 55)

Hers has been, of course, a Fortunate Fall, a *felix culpa*, and Brome interweaves both versions of the *topos* when Eulalia realizes her own transcendence:

> Who says our State is low, or that I fell
> When I was put from Court? I did not rise
> Till then, nor was advanc'd till now. I see
> Heaven plants me 'bove the reach of Treachery.

And a loyal follower speaks her epigraph: "O happie, happie Saint" (II, 90). As Eulalia rises above earthly things, Alinda begins to fall under the sheer weight of her passions, pride and ambition. The King feels himself "awak'd" from the "Lethargie" of his lust (II, 75, 98; cf. Chapman's penitent Alphonso) and sets off seeking Eulalia in what Alinda believes is a murder hunt. Finding her, the King dethrones his concubine, announcing to Eulalia: "Thy povertie and patience have restor'd thee / By the just Providence" (II, 114). But it is Eulalia with her magical powers who must do the true restoring—the healing of Alinda, whose surging passions have been quelled in a "trance." Her noble father threatens the girl, but he too is calmed by Eulalia's magic word: "Patience good *Sforza*" (II, 127–128). All passion spent, all wounds healed by the visionary purgations made possible by patience, the King writes finis in explaining how Eulalia's Fortunate Fall has included the entire country in its beneficence, making it a blessed garden wherein "the Air disperseth pleasure and the Earth / Of fresh delight to every step gives birth":

> *Eulalia*, thou art happy, and didst rise,
> Not fall from Court into this Paradise.
> Nor can it move my admiration much,
> Thy vertue wrought the change, and made it such. (II, 123)

It will be clear from this brief résumé that Greene's novella plot has been overlaid with a thematic treatment of patience, vision, prophecy, and magical cures—

elements making up *The Gentleman Usher* as well. This points toward Chapman's play as the "philosophic" source for restructuring Greene's plot, as do the names Strozza and Poggio and a wise fool much like the latter, who is Brome's innovation without a counterpart in *Penelope's Web*.

As we will see in Chapter V below, Brome was interested in the interaction of life and dream, and even more in theatrical manipulations within his plays, and thus would no doubt have found Chapman's earlier play interesting. But he was scarcely a Platonist, and the aura of natural magic is alien to his other works. His attention may have been drawn to *The Gentleman Usher* by Chapman himself, however, since the collector Abraham Hill late in the century saw a manuscript he listed as "Christianetta or Marriage & hanging goe by destiny Chapman & Brome," and an S. R. entry of 4 August 1640 lists "Christianetta" among six plays by Brome (G. E. Bentley, *The Jacobean and Caroline Stage* [Oxford, 1941–68], III, 58–59).

65. See the Appendix on Guarini's formula and *The Gentleman Usher*.

66. Dating problems for Chapman's plays, particularly the earlier comedies, are insoluble. In the account which follows I have treated stages of development for a theme to which the playwright persistently returns in plays which probably span fifteen years of his mature career, but his interest cannot be construed as a steady chronological growth. The earliest "testing" play was probably *All Fools*, which may well be *The World runs on Wheels* mentioned in Henslowe as early as 1599 (Parrott accepts this identification; E. K. Chambers, *The Elizabethan Stage*, 4 vols. [Oxford, 1923], suggests as late as 1604 tentatively; Q1 is 1605). *The Gentleman Usher* is very tentatively placed by Parrott and Chambers in 1602, although the latter thinks 1604 an equally good possibility: Q1 is 1606 (S. R. entry 26 November 1605). *The Widow's Tears* is placed by Parrott in late 1605 or early 1606, while Chambers leaves it undetermined, somewhere between 1603 and 1609. The S. R. entry of 17 April 1612 is for "twoo play bookes, th'one called, the revenge of Bussy D'Amboys, beinge a tragedy, thother called, The wydowes teares, beinge a Comedy, both written by George Chapman." *The Revenge of Bussy* is placed by Parrott in late 1610 or early 1611, by Chambers probably in 1610, possibly anywhere between 1608 and 1612. Q1 of the comedy is 1612, of the tragedy 1613. *Chabot* is very tentatively placed by both Parrott and Chambers in 1613 (licensing, 1635; S. R. entry, 1638; Q1, 1639), a date later rejected by Parrott in his review (*JEGP*, 29 [1930], 300–304) of Norma Dobie Solve's *Stuart Politics in Chapman's Tragedy of Chabot* (Ann Arbor, Mich., 1928), where he accepts her hypothesis that the play alludes to events of 1621–1624. John W. Wieler, however, carefully analyzes the improbability of Solve's argument and returns to a date ca. 1612–1613 (*George Chapman: The Effect of Stoicism upon His Tragedies* [New York, 1949], pp. 112–15). The problems and a theory of initial composition between 1612 and 1614 with a revision by Chapman in the 1620s and a further revision by Shirley in 1634 are discussed by Thelma Herring, "Chapman and an Aspect of Modern Criticism," *Renaissance Drama*, VIII, pp. 167–70.

67. There is no novelty in the notion, of course. To take an early instance, the English adapter of Grazzini's *La spiritata* had added to the original source in his *Bugbears* (1563) a consolation by the servant Squatacantino: "a poore horne inviseble / Tutte, no man shall see it, nor you your self shall fele it" (IV, v, 24–25).

68. See Parrott, *Comedies*, pp. 800–801 and nn.; Jacquot, *George Chapman*, pp. 102–3. The latter has several illuminating remarks upon the play.

69. More mechanical is the repetition of another element from the earlier canon. The double self-cuckolding of the disguised Irus in *The Blind Beggar of Alexandria* (scene v) has echoes in the abortive adultery attempted by Lysander upon his own wife. The origins of the self-cuckolding trial are probably to be found in Italian developments of the Cephalus myth in both pastoral (Niccolò da Correggio's *Il Cefalo*) and black farce (Ruzzante's *La moschetta*), but Charles R. Baskervill attributes them to the very popular jig of "Rowland" (*The Elizabethan Jig* [Chicago, 1929], pp. 229–30).

70. Chapman, the translator of Homer, would have found the positive sense in the *Iliad*, 21.589 and 19.169, the negative in the *Odyssey*, 17.419 and 19.91.

71. The question has been addressed. Samuel Schoenbaum, "*The Widow's Tears* and the Other Chapman," *HLQ*, 23 (1960), 321–38, finds the author to be revealing a seldom recognized cynical side in expressing his own gynephobia through the realist Tharsalio; his position seems to be roughly supported by Herring, "Chapman and an Aspect of Modern Criticism," pp. 157–67, who is, however, principally interested in attacking Henry M. Weidner, "Homer and the Fallen World: Focus of Satire in George Chapman's *The Widow's Tears*," *JEGP*, 62 (1963), 518–32. Weidner sees Tharsalio as a dupe whose absolutism is disappointed when he seeks Golden Age perfection in the Iron Age of decline, something of an inverted Ulysses. The latter parallels my broadest generalizations about the play.

72. The 1612 quarto has only act divisions, usual for Chapman, but the stage is cleared and place changed after 162 lines of the first act. The economy with which the problem is set forth and important leitmotivs introduced is Chapman the dramatist's, not the accident of modern editing.

73. It is tempting to conjecture that the mirrors in which both brothers project their own images may be cracked versions of Ficino's mirror image for the mind's expression of itself in its works (*Opera*, p. 229).

74. It would seem natural to associate the peacock with the courtier, but Eudora, not he, has used Tharsalio's "erection, with such lowe respect," as he complains (I, iii, 9–12).

75. There is nothing arbitrary in singling out this particular aspect of the peacock's symbolic history for application to what might seem a casual comment. Quite aside from the nucleus of Juno allusions which appear at important junctures of the plot, one must recall that the bird received its glories when Juno transplanted the eyes of Argus to its tail, Argus having failed as guardian of the Ionian cow when Hermes lulled him to sleep. The gentleman usher to Eudora is "*Argus* that bold Asse that neuer weighs what he does or saies; but walkes and talkes like one in a sleepe" (II, ii, 5–7). It is, naturally, Argus who is bribed to betray Eudora into Tharsalio's hands.

76. Parrott, *Comedies*, pp. 815–16.

77. See pp. 35–36 above.

78. It is with this conception that Argus has been won to aid Tharsalio's cause: "Are you squint ey'd? can you not see afore you? A little foresight I can tell you might sted you much" (II, iv, 88–89), and when the gentleman usher is convinced, he is characterized by Tharsalio as a man of "forwarder insight then yee all" (98).

79. *The Revenge of Bussy* introduces the problem in Montsurry's assertion that one must feign chastity in lust (I, ii, 33–48). But Montsurry also recognizes the deeper sense of essential metamorphosis, of a real *concordia discors* between Venus and Diana, when he calls attention to a "strange cross in nature; purest virgin shame / Lies in the blood, as lust lies." The Petronian story must have bulked large in Chapman's mind at the time of the composition of this play as well as that of *The Widow's Tears*, since Maillard alludes in passing to widows who are whores until they capture a husband, then honest women again (IV, i, 60–62). Finally, Clermont himself describes how Democritus

> Saw he a youthful widow
> Never so weeping, wringing of her hands,
> For her lost lord, still the philosopher laugh'd.
> Now whether he suppos'd all these presentments
> Were only maskeries, and wore false faces,
> Or else were simply vain, I take no care.   (I, i, 364–74)

80. Cynthia and Lysander alone among major characters never place an overt meta-

phoric foot in Venus' camp: Tharsalio implies his allegiance (I, i, 60, 73–75; II, iv, 124–26) and ultimately states it outright (III, i, 76–77). Eudora swears by the Cyprian goddess (I, ii, 39, 149), as do Arsace the panderess (II, ii, 51) and Ianthe and Sthenia the ladies-in-waiting (II, 15–16, 71). It is a favorite epithet and greeting with Argus (III, ii, 18–19). Eudora's daughter Laodice petitions Venus for success in love (III, ii, 87); Lysander's son Hylus masques as Hymen, but is called a Cupid in disguise (III, ii, 16–19); and even Lycus swears by Venus (IV, i, 105). These are but samplings of ubiquitous allusions.

81. Lysander is explicit on the limits of subterranean love: "in the height of her mourning in a Tomb . . . to change her faith, exchange kisses, embraces, with a stranger; and but my shame with-stood, to giue the vtmost earnest of her loue" (V, ii, 34–39).

82. Professor Raymond Waddington has pointed out to me that in *The Widow's Tears* there are several allusions to Hercules in his distaff role and to Virgil the lover in a basket as well as to the Actaeon myth, all symbols of lust which were also grouped in *The Merry Wives of Windsor*: see John M. Steadman, "Falstaff as Actaeon: A Dramatic Emblem," *SQ*, 14 (1963), 231–44.

83. Schoenbaum, "*The Widow's Tears* and the Other Chapman," pertinently observes that the Governor is a Lord of Misrule in a Saturnalian structure (pp. 330–31).

84. S. L. Bethell, "The Diabolic Images in *Othello*," *Shakespeare Survey*, 5 (1952), 62–80.

85. Cf. IV, ii, 84; V, ii, 40; V, iii, 13, 60.

86. Weidner, "Homer and the Fallen World," pp. 521–24 et passim, comments in complementary fashion upon a shattered "idealism" which tempers the viciousness of Tharsalio's motives.

87. The closest parallel to this male version of the patient Grissel legend is Heywood's *The Royal King and the Loyal Subject* (ca. 1620), wherein sycophants of a carefully anonymous "King of England" induce him to test the loyalty of "the Lord Martial" with fairy-tale intensity. But here the serious psychological potential is dissipated in a tragicomic harmony at the close. There is, of course, a novella tradition of jealous probing which passes from the *Decamerone* into the "Curious Impertinent" tale set into *Don Quijote*. But Chapman was unusually persistent in returning to the problem, and his trials are more varied than the jealousy theme (which becomes epistemological only in Cervantes, never in Shakespeare). Something of a context, and possibly the importance of his own explorations, can be suggested by glancing at a few more casual plays which suggest the popularity of the thematic structure of *The Widow's Tears*. John Ford's *The Lady's Trial* (1638) irradiates its entire action from a calibrated series of trials provided for Spinella, young wife to a poor Genovese gentleman, Auria. Auria first submits her to testing indirectly and blamelessly (although with warning from some acquaintances) by going to the wars to win back lost fortunes. Adurni, an otherwise noble young man, tries her faithfulness wantonly by attempting seduction at a private banquet. Aurelio, Auria's friend, sees and interrupts, judging all on Othello's "ocular proof." Auria himself concludes all with an actual staged "trial" scene in which all characters are brought to judgment, Spinella being justified, Adurni and Aurelio chided, but the one let off as a mere Platonic gentleman (!) and the other warned of "over-busy curiosity." The end is harmony, and Auria is left untouched by the author's potential vision of self-righteous confidence, as if Lysander had emerged unschooled in disaster by his folly.

Speaking even more tellingly for a tradition, perhaps, is the creaking "trial" mechanism in Thomas Randolph's *The Jealous Lovers* (1632), since this play involves two sets of trials, motivated respectively by the jealously of a male and a female lover, and since it carries the trial theme into the tomb, as does *The Widow's*

Tears. But finally the jealous tempters are allowed to realize that their lovers are, in fact, their brother and sister, respectively, and so are allowed to marry each other happily, without a word of reproof for their distrust and dangerous masquerading in a false death adapted from *Romeo and Juliet;* indeed, the last note is a naturalization of such temptations:

> I see our jealous thoughts were not in vain.
> Nature, abhorring from so foul a sin,
> Infus'd those doubts into us.
> (V, vii, *Poetical and Dramatic Works of Thomas Randolph,*
> ed. W. C. Hazlitt [London, 1875], I, 168)

Finally, I suggest the probability that Edward Sharpham's sadistic farce *Cupid's Whirligig* (1607), which centers on the cure of old Troublesome's jealousy of his chaste wife by the extreme measures of divorce and self-castration, is the King's Revels group's answer at Whitefriars to the Blackfriars success with the jealous trial theme in *The Widow's Tears.* If this is true, it would support Parrott's dating of the latter as 1605–1606 (for Sharpham see Chambers, *Elizabethan Stage,* III, 490–91). Further, it was about this date that Marston made his essay at the theme in the "trial" of Beatrice by Freevill in *The Dutch Courtesan* (*Plays of John Marston,* ed. H. Harvey Wood [London, 1934–39], II, 116, 120, 128, 130). Entered and published in 1605 (dated by Chambers in 1603–1604), this derivative play, which borrowed from Bandello, Montaigne, Painter, Shakespeare's *Much Ado,* and—for the dizzy machinations of Cockledemoy—perhaps from Chapman's own demon plotter Irus of *The Blind Beggar,* may be evidence to support the earliest dating of *The Widow's Tears.* Not only does it contain the trial theme but also an aborted approach to the temptation of the widow in Mistress Mulligrub's response to Cockledemoy's approaches in the very van of her husband's execution parade (*Plays,* II, 134–36). Cf. n. 66 above. With different foci Thomas Stroup has written upon "the testing pattern" in Chapman and other dramatists in *Microcosmos: The Shape of the Elizabethan Play* (Lexington, Ky., 1965), pp. 179–206.

88. In I, i, 203–20 by implication; explicitly in II, ii, 86–87 and III, i, 209–11.

89. Cato's suicide is the only means by which he can remain free and just at the same time, and he behaves much like a less effective Chabot throughout act V of *Caesar and Pompey:* see esp. V, ii, 1–18, 177 (which provides the subtitle quotation for the 1631 and 1653 quartos: "Only a just man is a freeman" [Parrott, *Plays,* p. 677]).

CHAPTER III

1. O. B. Hardison, "The Place of Averroes' Commentary on the *Poetics* in the History of Medieval Criticism," in *Medieval and Renaissance Studies: Proceedings of the Southern Institute of Medieval and Renaissance Studies, Summer, 1968* (Durham, N.C., 1970), pp. 57–81.

2. Bernard Weinberg, "Castelvetro's Theory of Poetry," in *Critics and Criticism,* ed. R. S. Crane et al. (Chicago, 1952), p. 349.

3. See Baxter Hathaway, *Marvels and Commonplaces: Renaissance Literary Criticism* (New York, 1968), pp. 60–64. An illustration of the difficulty imposed by the undigested size of Castelvetro's commentary is the contrast between Weinberg's view that his chief departure from the spirit of the *Poetics* is "the removal of the principal emphasis from the poem to the audience" (p. 351) and the citations by Galvano della Volpe supporting his view of Aristotle as one whose emphasis was upon the poem-as-object (*Poetica del Cinquecento* [Bari, 1954], esp. pp. 45–51, 164–66).

4. Robert C. Melzi, "*Gl'ingannati* and Its French Renaissance Translation," *KFLQ*, 12 (1965), 180–90, has convincingly drawn up the evidence for Castelvetro's authorship.

5. *Commedie del Cinquecento*, ed. Aldo Borlenghi (Milan, 1959), I, 161–66.

6. Cf. Bernard Weinberg, *A History of Literary Criticism in the Italian Renaissance* (Chicago, 1961), Index, under "Prologue"; Emilio Goggio, "Dramatic Theories in the Prologues to the *Commedie Erudite*," *PMLA*, 58 (1943), 322–36, and "The Prologue in the *Commedie Erudite* of the Sixteenth Century," *Italica*, 18 (1941), 124–32; Borlenghi, *Commedie del Cinquecento*, I, 17–18, 949–1094; Franco Fido, "Reflections on Comedy by Some Italian Renaissance Playwrights," in *Medieval Epic to the "Epic Theater" of Brecht*, ed. Rosario P. Armato and John M. Spalek, University of Southern California Studies in Comparative Literature, 1 (Los Angeles, 1968), pp. 85–95.

7. "Non picciola differenza si veda essere tra le cose che egli scrisse nella giovinezza e quelle che andò scrivendo di tempo in tempo diventando vecchio," as Castelvetro's nephew said ("no small difference is to be seen between the things that he wrote in his youth and those which he continued to write from time to time as he grew old"); see Melzi, *Gl'ingannati*, p. 182.

8. See pp. 90–97, 212–17 below.

9. Ludovico Castelvetro, *Poetica d'Aristotele vulgarizzata, et Sposta*, Poetiken des Cinquecento, 1 (Vienna, 1570; rpt. Munich, 1968), pp. 12–13. This limits the sense of comedy as well as of drama in general, as H. B. Charlton remarked: "Castelvetro has no idea of the comedy which is not ludicrous; he is thus mainly concerned with farce" (*Castelvetro's Theory of Poetry* [Manchester, 1913], pp. 134–37). In this, Castelvetro is reversing the position of his principal predecessor, Francesco Robortello, who insists upon making rules for a wise audience rather than for the "vulgar, rude men," the "imbecile populace" (*In librum Aristotelis de arte Poetica explicationes* [Florence, 1548], pp. 142–46).

10. Castelvetro returns to the twelve-hour limit on pp. 212^r, 219^v, and 296^v. One should take into account, however, actual practices which make his position less absurd. In 1598 Angelo Ingegneri (*Discorso sulla poesia rappresentativa*), in writing prescriptions for *sacre rappresentazioni*, said they should not go beyond three and one-half to four hours: "quella che arriverà alle cinque per dilettevole ch'ella sia, non ischiferà il tedio di molti degli uditori" (cited in Alessandro D'Ancona, *Origini del teatro Italiano*, 2nd rev. ed. [Turin, 1891], I, 421).

11. In the same place Castelvetro says that neither the audience ("in which there are children and shy women") nor the actors should be exposed to the embarrassment of love scenes ("carnal embraces and amorous kisses").

12. Giuseppe Spezi, "Parere di Ludovico Castelvetro sopra ciascuna comedia di Plauto tratto di un codice Vaticano," *Il propugnatore*, I (1868), 61–74. The MS is Vatican No. 5337. Like criticisms appear in Muratori's edition of Castelvetro's posthumous papers, *La vita ed opere varie critiche* (Bern, 1727), pp. 165, 168, 171.

13. "Parere," p. 66. This view of Plautus' Mercury closely echoes that in Giraldi Cinthio's *Intorno al comporre delle commedie e delle tragedie* (1544; rpt. Milan, 1864), II, 73–74. And Castelvetro's own stand against prologues and staged horror was still being echoed at the end of the century in Tommaso Campanella's *Poetica*, ed. Luigi Firpo (Rome, 1944), pp. 186–87. Conservatism dies hard.

14. Alessandro D'Ancona, *Sacre rappresentazioni dei secoli XIV, XV, e XVI* (Florence, 1872), I, 1–39.

15. D'Ancona, *Origini*, pp. 411–12. Virginia Galante Garrone, *L'Apparato scenico del dramma sacro in Italia* (Turin, 1935), argues persuasively for a simplicity of setting in these plays by youngsters and novice nuns which originates in Feo Belcari's

Abramo ed Isac (1449) and continues throughout the fifteenth century, singling out *Abraam cacciò Agar* as particularly inspired by Belcari's sparse, almost symbolic, mountings (pp. 72–75). But for the ducal nuptials of 1589 this same group's successors presented Cecchi's *Esaltazione della croce*, with most elaborate machinery and perspective scenery, in an open-air playing area protected by an allegorically ornamented awning extending about three hundred feet on each side (*Descrizione dell'apparato e de gl'intermedii fatti per la storia dell'esaltazione della croce rappresentata in Firenze . . . nell'anno 1589*, in D'Ancona, *Sacre rappresentazioni*, III, 121–38). If these preparations were special to the occasion, there are lines in the *frottola* to *Abraam cacciò Agar* which suggest a semi-enclosed staging area ("Oh be', noi ci appressiamo, / Et è la porta aperta") and ornamented or perspective hangings ("E questo è un bel parato. / Si bene, in simil lato"). Cf. Vincenzo de Bartholomaeis, *Origini della poesia dramatica italiana*, 2nd ed. rev. (Turin, 1952), pp. 396–97, on l'Aquilini.

16. D'Ancona, *Sacre rappresentazioni*, I, 1–2.

17. On the *frottola* (the term is generic) and the less elaborate but related *annunziazioni dell'angelo* see D'Ancona, *Origini*, I, 379–91. He examines and rejects the hypothesis that the *annunziazioni* derived from the prologues of Latin comedy (I, 380). Paolo Toschi, *Le origini del teatro italiano* (Turin, 1955), pp. 692–93, traces the fusing of the complicated interaction of comic and sacred structures in the Florentine *sacre* to the fact that the same companies of players frequently presented bawdy farces for *carnevale* and *sacre* for *quaresima*; cf. Toschi, *Teatro italiano*, pp. 695–701. As this applies to L'Aquilini, D'Ancona (*Origini*, I, 412) shows their survival as a vehicle for Metastasio's *melodrammi* as late as the eighteenth century.

18. D'Ancona, *Sacre rappresentazioni*, I, 2.

19. *Sacre rappresentazioni* were traditionally presented during the hours between vespers and dark; cf. the statement by Ingegneri, n. 10 above.

20. Luca Landucci, *Diario fiorentino dal 1450 al 1516*, ed. Iodoco del Badia (Florence, 1883), p. 204 (November 1, 1499).

21. *Origini*, I, 395–97.

22. Cited in Francesco Palermo, *I manoscritti palatini di Firenze ordinati ed esposti* (Florence, 1853–68), II, 485–86.

23. D'Ancona, *Origini*, I, 404–11; II, 157–62.

24. *Ibid.*, II, 159, n. 1.

25. Emphasis upon this audience is the principal focus of Garrone's *L'Apparato scenico del dramma sacro in Italia*.

26. Aldo Borlenghi centers upon this social criticism and the thick local color in drawing *Abraam cacciò Agar* into his thesis that the Boccaccian *novelle* crossbred with regular New Comedy to produce a freer drama of satiric and farcical content: "Regolarità e originalità della commedia del Cinquecento," *Studi di lètteratura italiana dal '300 al '500* (Milan, 1959), pp. 142–48.

27. A frequent synonym for the *sacre rappresentazioni*: see D'Ancona, *Origini*, I, 372–73.

28. The director, whose position of authority over his little singing troupe corresponds closely to that of the Elizabethan masters of the boy singing companies, "era insieme impresario, capocomico, trovarobe, macchinista e suggeritore, un po' d'ogni cosa, si prendeva anche la cura dell'ammaestrare i recitanti nelle parti loro assegnate" (D'Ancona, *Origini*, I, 422).

29. Toschi, *Teatro italiano*, pp. 212–18. The emergence of this symbolic *carnevale* figure is another reminder of the close ties between sacred and profane celebrations and drama. See, for instance, the comic *sacra*, *La guerra di carnevale e quaresima*

(1552), which recounts a war of personifications fought out with sausages, sauce-pans, and such, but nonetheless presided over by the familiar annunciatory angel (in *Laude drammatiche e rappresentazioni sacre*, ed. Vincenzo de Bartholomaeis [Florence, 1943], III, 165–85). Evidence of another order is brought to bear in Orville K. Larson, "Spectacle in the Florentine *Intermezzi*," *Drama Survey*, 2 (1963), 344–52, where he demonstrates that machines for later sixteenth-century *intermedii* were inspired by and sometimes borrowed from the earlier machines made for the *sacre*.

30. See Robert J. Rodini, *Antonfrancesco Grazzini: Poet, Dramatist, and Novelliere, 1503–1584* (Madison, Wis., 1970), pp. 20–25, and Grazzini's letter, reproduced there on p. 206.

31. In *Termini di mezzo rilievo e d'intera dottrina tra gl'archi di casa Valori in Firenze col sommario della vita d'alcuni* (Florence, 1604), pp. 15–16. Giovan Maria Cecchi was designated the modern Plautus.

32. On the anticlassical bent in Grazzini and what he considers its partial failure in practice, see Ireneo Sanesi, *La commedia*, 2nd ed. rev. (Milan, 1954), I, 360–62, 366–67. On dating see Antonfrancesco Grazzini [Il Lasca], *Teatro*, ed. Giovanni Grazzini (Bari, 1953), pp. 181, 573–78. All citations are from this edition.

33. Grazzini, *Teatro*, p. 187; cf. *La gelosia*, pp. 9–10, and *La spiritata*, p. 125.

34. The distinction between Fiesolan and Roman stocks in Florence in Dante's *Inferno*, 15, 73–78, appears to be the origin. Cf. Nicola Zingarelli, *Il canto XV dell' Inferno: Lectura Dantis* (Florence, 1900), pp. 35–36.

35. Grazzini enthusiastically describes the zestful acting of the *commedia dell'arte* troupes in a *canto carnascialescho* "di Zanni e di Magnifichi," in *Le rime burlesche edite ed inedite di Antonfrancesco Grazzini*, ed. Carlo Verzone (Florence, 1882), pp. 207–8.

36. "In Firenze . . . non ci si usano figliuoli adottivi, non ci vengono i ruffiani a vender le fanciulle, né i soldati dal dí d'oggi nei sacchi delle città o de' castelli pigliano più le bambine in fascia, e allevandole per lor figliuole, fanno loro la dote" ("in Florence . . . adopted sons are not customary, bawds don't come to sell little girls, nor do today's soldiers still, in sacking of cities and castles, take away babies in swaddling clothes and, raising them as their daughters, give them a dowry") (187).

37. The *fiorentinismo* of Grazzini in this archaeological sense is a major concern of Rodini, *Antonfrancesco Grazzini*, esp. pp. 38–77.

38. Rodini notes some *comedia dell'arte* debts by Grazzini (*ibid.*, pp. 116, 124) but views Taddeo as a *miles gloriosus* type.

39. *Teatro*, p. 149. For the origin of the plot see p. 138.

40. Of the large literature the most thorough studies are Allardyce Nicoll, *Masks, Mimes and Miracles* (London, 1931), and Toschi, *Teatro italiano*, pp. 166–227.

41. "E Farfanicchio suo ragazzo bisogna che abbia una mascheraccia col ceffo con-traffatto e brutto, la quale con uno uncinazzo si attacchi dietro, e, . . . se la metta al viso e se la levi, ma destramente, e di maniera che Taddeo non se ne avvegga; e questo faccia la prima e la seconda volta che egli viene seco in scena" (182).

42. Michele Maylender, *Storia delle accademie d'Italia* (Bologna, 1929), V, 363–67; Rodini, *Antonfrancesco Grazzini*, pp. 5–14.

43. *Discorsi poetici nella accademia fiorentina in difesa d'Aristotile* (Florence, 1597), sig. a2ᵛ.

44. His indebtedness to the Medici is acknowledged by Buonamici himself in the *Discorsi poetici*, p. 155. On Buonamici's career, writings, and reputation as one of the great polymaths of the century, see Valori, *Termini di mezzo rilievo*, pp. 7–8

(the *Discorsi* were dedicated to the scholar-senator Baccio Valori); Jacopo Rilli, *Notizie letterarie, ed istoriche intorno agli uomini illustri dell'accademia fiorentina* (Florence, 1700), pp. 213–16; Giulio Negri, *Istoria degli scrittori fiorentini* (Ferrara, 1722), pp. 187–88; Giammaria Mazzuchelli, *Gli scrittori d'Italia cioè notizie storiche, e critiche* (Brescia, 1763), II, iv, 2317–19.

45. On the question of love and the *trattatisti d'amore* see Nesca Robb, *Neoplatonism of the Italian Renaissance* (London, 1935), and, particularly, the comments of Baxter Hathaway, *The Age of Criticism: The Late Renaissance in Italy* (Ithaca, N.Y., 1962), pp. 341–48, which illuminate the relationship of this tradition of Petrarchan commentary to Ficino's influence and the main body of critical doctrine of a more theoretical sort.

46. Hathaway, *Age of Criticism*, p. 143.

47. Torquato Tasso, *Prose*, ed. Ettore Mazzali (Milan, 1959), p. 793.

48. "La [Accademia] fiorentina divenne quasi una corporazione dello Stato," says Maylender, *Storia delle accademie*, III, 4.

49. See pp. 213–14 below and Pierantonio Serassi, *La vita di Jacopo Mazzoni* (Rome, 1790), pp. 85–106.

50. *Ibid.*, pp. 85–99. The early theses were published as *De triplici hominum vita* in 1576. After his Pisan professorship, Mazzoni published *In universam Platonis et Aristotelis philosophiam praeludia, sive de comparatione Platonis et Aristotelis* (1597). See Serassi, *Vita di Mazzoni*, pp. 8–20, 103–6, 145–46.

51. Cf. Felix Gilbert, "Bernardo Rucellai and the Orti Oricellari," *JWCI*, 12 (1949), 101–31, and Amando L. De Gaetano, "The Florentine Academy and the Advancement of Learning through the Vernacular: The Orti Oricellari and the Sacra Accademia," *BHR*, 30 (1968), 19–52. On p. 43 we are reminded of the importance of productions of comedies in the Accademia Fiorentina. For information on Diacceto I am principally indebted to Paul Oskar Kristeller, "Francesco da Diacceto and Florentine Platonism in the Sixteenth Century," *Studies in Renaissance Thought and Letters* (Rome, 1956), pp. 287–336. Cf. also André Chastel, *Marsile Ficin et l'art* (Geneva, 1954), p. 24, and Eugenio Garin, *Italian Humanism: Philosophy and Civic Life in the Renaissance* (1947; rpt. New York, 1965), pp. 114–17, who cites Diacceto's comment: "noi, tutto quello che siamo, se siamo cosa alcuna, siamo da Marsilio Ficino."

52. Kristeller, "Un uomo di stato e umanista fiorentino Giovanni Corsi," *Studies in Renaissance Thought and Letters*, pp. 175–90.

53. On Vettori see Kristeller, "Diacceto," pp. 322–23; Negri, *Istoria*, pp. 471 and 95 (on Varchi's discipleship); on Grazzini and Varchi see Rodini, *Antonfrancesco Grazzini*, pp. 10, 80, 100, and Grazzini's homage in *Le rime*, p. 482; for Varchi's tribute to *Stradino* see *La suocera*, Biblioteca classica italiana, secolo XVI (Trieste, 1858), IV, vi, p. 33.

54. Salvino Salvini, *Fasti consolari dell'accademia fiorentina* (Florence, 1717), cited by Maylender, *Storia delle accademie*, III, 5.

55. Girolamo Sommai, cited from manuscript annotations in Mazzuchelli, *Scrittori d'Italia*, II, iv, 2318.

56. This aspect of Buonamici's theory and recognition of his importance as an interpreter of contemporary stage practice has been touched on by Cesare Molinari in an interesting essay which focuses upon stage decors as indicators of the manner of audience involvement. However, Molinari denies the importance of imagination for Buonamici, seeing his audience separated from the stage world as mere decipherers of signs. This, of course, is a misinterpretation. See "Les rapports entre la scène et les spectateurs dans le théâtre italien du XVIᵉ siècle," in *Le lieu théâtral à la renaissance*, ed. Jean Jacquot (Paris, 1964), pp. 61–71.

57. "Il tirare dietro à quello, che è stato, diminuirebbe del diuino ingegno del poeta, il quale deue essere faccitore, & ritrouatore, non recitatore" (83). The allusion to divine genius in the poet is a mark of Buonamici's Platonic bent. In treating the vexing passage in the *Poetics* (1455a) Castelvetro initiated an anti-Platonic rejection of poetic fury (see O. B. Hardison, in O. B. Hardison and Leon Golden, *Aristotle's Poetics: A Translation and Commentary for Students of Literature* [Englewood Cliffs, N.J., 1968], pp. 218–19) by amending the text to read "la poetica è da persona fornita di buona natura, & non da furiosa" (*Poetica*, 203^r). He explained that Aristotle's phrase had been corrupted by those who had already "beuuta quella opinione del furore poetico" (207^v), an absurd opinion because "la poesia sia trouamento . . . non della furiosa come diceuano alcuni, non essendo il furioso atto a trasformarsi in varie passioni, ne solicito inuestigatore di quello che si facciano & dicano i passionati" (207^v). Buonamici takes Castelvetro extensively to task on the point, invoking Plato on Apollo and the Muses, but ultimately pays tribute to the direct influence of Ficino as he attributes the poetic fury to the Florentine philosopher's inspiring humor of genius, melancholy: "i poeti sono mossi, & in che modo mossi? dal furore, & dall'affetto, il quale è efficacissimo nel malencolico" ("poets are moved, and in what way moved? By fury, and by love, which is very efficacious in the melancholy") (153).

58. "L'historia è come di cosa rappresentata, & come idea, la poesia è come di cosa rappresentante, & participante" (10).

59. Hathaway, *Marvels and Commonplaces*, pp. 80–87, uses the term in treating this aspect of Buonamici's thought; cf. also his *Age of Criticism*, pp. 141–43, 183–84.

60. "Egli suppone vn particolare, ma che in lui considera l'idea, che è vniuersale, perchioche egli non descriue a punto come egli è, & quello che egli fece, ma innalza le attioni e' costumi a quel grado di che può esser' capace la natura humana . . . di maniera che imitando in questo suggetto questo, & quel fatto particolare, come vn fatto pietoso d'Enea, tratta, & imita il particolare, ma inalzando il fatto a maggior grado, che non fu in effetto . . . lo viene a considerare secondo l'idea sua astratta dalla materia, & vniuersalmente; cosi considera il particolar' vniuersalmente" (48–49).

61. "Douendo la poesia muouere li affetti, inducendone de'nuoui . . . è di necessità, che c'interuenga l'assenso, cioè che l'animo nostro creda, che la cosa poss'essere passata così" (38).

62. "Composto di verso, suono, & ballo: nel quale s'ingeriuano li histrioni soli, ne il poeta se n'impacciaua" (58).

63. "Si commouueno li histrioni ci commouiamo anchor' noi, & con esso loro piangiamo, & ridiamo, . . . tal che si richiede nella purgatione questo moto fatto dal rappresentante poeta solo con la fauella, & histrione, co' gesti, & con la fauella" (122).

64. "Diceret Plato in libro de furore Poetico, poetas non arte vlla instrui, sed afflatu Apollinis, & musarum impelli, neq. poetas tantum, sed etiam recitatores, & interpretes poetarum, non secus ac magnete cathenati anuli trahi solent" (*In librum Aristotelis de arte poetica explicationes*, p. 3).

65. At this important juncture, the *Discorsi poetici* is mispaginated. The sequence under discussion is as follows: pp. 105, 110, 111, 108, 109.

66. "Hora questa disuguaglianza di grandezza si riconosce ne' segni i quali sono i rappresentanti, perche se egli si fingerà vn Re, il quale veste d'ostro, & di perle di grandissima valuta, si rappresenterà con vna veste di dommasco."

67. "Nel poeta è il costume la sentenza, li habiti, i gesti sono nell'histrione, & esterni al poeta."

68. "Nelle cose rappresentate stà la verisimilitudine, che le parti dell'attione sieno connesse, che l'inclinino l'animo dello spettatore à credere che sia stato così; ne giamai può tanto l'opera del verisimile nello spettatore, se egli non è vn balordo,

che e' pigli la cosa rappresentante per la rappresentata, come fanno le donnucce qualche volta il venerdì Santo. Et sappiamo noi benissimo, che noi siamo alla commedia, & che quello è il prologo, il quale ha imparata la commedia, & come da vna breue informatione, & quell' è Roscio, quell'altro Calliopio, non il Re Agamennone, ò lo Stradino; & riconosciamo la prospettiua il palco, le tende, il coro, & vedendo quel giouane vestito di bianco con vn torchio acceso in mano, sappiamo che egli è quel Panfilo inamorato."

69. Sanesi, La commedia, I, 245, attributes it to Ottonaio's circle. A bit of theatrical history confirms Buonamici's attendance at the theater. He complains that when a brief space of time is supposed to elapse between scenes, in order to give a sense of temporal verisimilitude, "fanno hoggidì i nostri di riempiere quello spatio della rappresentazione per farlo vguale al tempo rappresentato di ragionamenti scurrili, & di inetti soliloquij" ("our [actors] today fill that space of the presentation, in order to make the time equal to that represented in the plot, with scurrilous discussions and inept soliloquies") (109). Certainly such practice must represent the influence of the commedia dell'arte improvisations upon the commedia erudita.

70. On the tradition of gathering anecdotes around a mythologized contemporary as it moved from novelle into drama, see Borlenghi, "Regolarità e originalità," pp. 206–20.

CHAPTER IV

1. K. M. Lea, Italian Popular Comedy: A Study in the Commedia dell'arte, 1560–1620 with Special Reference to the English Stage (London, 1934), I, 231–54; Vito Pandolfi, La commedia dell'arte: Storia e testo (Florence, 1958), I, 9–14.

2. The Mediaeval Stage (Oxford, 1903), II, 180–81; cf. 180–87.

3. M. C. Bradbrook has discerned the implications of Chambers' synthesis in The Growth and Structure of Elizabethan Comedy (London, 1955), pp. 14–15, and has developed it thoroughly and carefully from the point of view of the effect of "hall" playing upon the ultimate structure and techniques of professional playing companies; see The Rise of the Common Player (London, 1962), esp. pp. 24–38, 96–100, 257–58, 280–81. My own analysis of Renaissance dramatic structure is antipodal to Miss Bradbrook's thesis that Marlovian and Shakespearean tragedy represent a triumph of "a new kind of attention to the object, free from the cauls of 'dream' and 'shadow' in the older storyteller's art, which established his imaginative relation with his audience. The dramatist leaves the establishing of direct relationship with the audience to the actors; his art involves a kind of abdication" (pp. 127–28). Nonetheless, I am deeply indebted to this careful and imaginative study for illuminating the background of the current chapter. T. W. Craik, The Tudor Interlude (Leicester, 1962), pp. 19–20, 24–25, et passim, also emphasizes the dramatic effects of "hall" upon drama.

4. Rise of the Common Player, pp. 29–30.

5. Bradbrook qualifies her account with a proper proviso, however: "gorgeous garments were the players' chief resource, and a change of garment was often the climax to a play, the simple forerunner of the transformation scene" (30).

6. See Orville K. Larson, "Spectacle in the Florentine Intermezzi," Drama Survey, 2 (1963), 344–52. The opera was the Dafne of Jacopo Peri and Ottavio Rinuccini, presented at Florence in continually altered and more "melodramatic" versions for the carnevali celebrations from 1595 through 1599: cf. Mario Apollonio, Storia del teatro italiano (Florence, 1954), I, 648–57, esp. 655. On the intermedii and masques see pp. 111–13 below.

7. See Inga-Stina Ewbank, "These Pretty Devices, A Study of Masques in Plays," in A Book of Masques in Honour of Allardyce Nicoll (Cambridge, 1967), pp. 407–48.

8. "Reflective showmakers and spectators might have shared the perception that the passing show concretely and compactly exemplifies the evanescence of the seemingly lasting beauties of this world. . . . one of the best manifestations of this transitory glory was the pageant—a symbol of short-lived beauty celebrating worldly achievement. . . . these persons almost daily observed preparations for some pageant or water display or parade. . . . After the day of the spectacle had passed, those same citizens saw the razing of the structures" (Alice S. Venezky, *Pageantry on the Shakespearean Stage* [New York, 1951], p. 202). There is incidental interest for our present discussion in the fact observed by Venezky that as early as the fifteenth century Skelton's elegy on Edward IV uses "pageant" in the sense of a dramatic role: "Now I sleep in dust / I have played my pageant" (p. 216, n. 72).

9. *I Henry IV*, III, ii, 55–59. Cf. Anne Righter, *Shakespeare and the Idea of the Play* (London, 1962), passim, esp. pp. 113–38.

10. Roper, *Life* (1577), cited in Chambers, *Mediaeval Stage*, II, 193: see also Chambers' notes on More and the preservation of this improvisational tradition in the late play *Sir Thomas More* and elsewhere.

11. The play was almost certainly provided for the 1497 Christmas festivities at Morton's palace in honor of the Flemish and Spanish ambassadors: see the introduction to the edition by F. S. Boas and A. W. Reed, *Fulgens and Lucres. A Fifteenth-Century Secular Play* (Oxford, 1926). On the *débat* as a formal source see C. R. Baskervill, "Conventional Features of Medwall's *Fulgens and Lucrece*," *MP*, 24 (1927), 419–42. The under-plot beating of *A* and *B* by Joan during their "joust at fart prick in cule" is a *fabliau* trick, and the patter of the *parade* must lie somewhere behind *A* and *B*'s self-exaltations as artists: see Chambers, *Mediaeval Stage*, II, 85. Glynne Wickham, "Dramatic Qualities of the English Morality Play and Moral Interlude," in *Shakespeare's Dramatic Heritage* (London, 1969), p. 28, suggests the impact of Lydgate's "Mumming at Hertford." I will not press a historic point which must always remain moot, but in the light of our earlier chapters it is worth recalling that More was very directly aware of Ficino's circle as Pico's translator and otherwise, and knew not only its attitudes but the images which might well induce a man to see with more than ordinary profundity into the implications of theatricality as a philosophic tool. Medwall's own play was based on the *Disputatio de nobilitate* of Buonaccorso de Montemagno, one of the early documents of fifteenth-century Florentine humanism which had been translated into French, German, and English just when Ficino and More were emerging as Christian Platonists: see Hans Baron, *The Crisis of the Early Italian Renaissance: Civic Humanism and Republican Liberty in an Age of Classicism and Tyranny* (Princeton, N.J., 1955), pp. 364–73, 623–28.

12. Madeleine Doran, *Endeavors of Art* (Madison, Wis., 1954), p. 313, shoehorns the choice into the argument of her study, i.e., that romance forms and attitudes dominated the structure of Elizabethan drama. But R. J. Mitchell, *John Tiptoft, 1427–1470* (London, 1938), pp. 182–85, and Baron, *Crisis of the Early Italian Renaissance*, pp. 625–28, make it clear that both Medwall and Tiptoft, the English translator of the Caxton edition, reduced rather than stressed the original emphasis upon an unambiguously bourgeois choice on the part of Lucrece. The obvious conclusion is that Medwall was adapting a popular debate which had been important in the ambient of early fifteenth-century Florentine politics but which now served as a device to flatter his learned patron, yet carefully tempering it so as not to insult the patrician guests.

13. Cf. Craik, *The Tudor Interlude*, pp. 1–26 (with special reference to *Fulgens and Lucrece* on pp. 2–4, 26). The most detailed study of theatricality in this play is Robert C. Jones's "The Stage World and the 'Real' World in Medwall's *Fulgens and Lucrece*," *MLQ*, 32 (1971), 131–42.

14. I, 715–16. All quotations are from Boas and Reed, *Fulgens and Lucres*.

15. Entered in the Stationers' Register in 1562, but clearly written for the reign of Mary and usually dated 1553–58, although H. N. Hillebrand has argued for 1552. Attribution of authorship to Nicholas Udall has been made by W. H. Williams and Hillebrand and is tentatively accepted by Smart and Greg. See Chambers, *Mediaeval Stage*, II, 457–58; *Early English Dramatists: Anonymous Plays*, 3rd series, ed. John S. Farmer (London, 1906), pp. 278–79; *Jack Jugeler*, ed. W. H. Williams (Cambridge, 1914), pp. x–xvii; *Jack Juggler*, ed. E. L. Smart and W. W. Greg, Malone Society Reprints (Oxford, 1933), pp. v–vi (all citations are from this edition). H. N. Hillebrand, review of the Williams edition, *JEGP*, 15 (1916), 317–21; H. N. Hillebrand, *The Child Actors* (Urbana, Ill., 1926), pp. 72–73. The play has received negligible critical attention, the most illuminating account of structure and intention being that by R. Marienstras, "*Jack Juggler*: Aspects de la conscience individuelle dans une farce du 16ᵉ siècle," *Ét. Angl.*, 16 (1963), 321–30. Marienstras views the "farce" as a new genre, combining medieval and classical elements to create a sharp satire not only on transubstantiation but on the corruption of the individual by power: "l'aliénation qui résulte du viol de la conscience" (327). Jaegus Voisine (with comments by Marienstras) cites earlier redactions of *Amphytrion* which might have influenced *Jack Juggler*: "À-propos de *Jack Juggler*," *Ét. Angl.*, 18 (1965), 166–68.

16. It is the failure to understand the place of this address to the audience in the total economy of *Jack Juggler* which led Righter to cite the play as falling between medieval and Renaissance modes—but it is difficult to follow the logic which lumps it with *Fulgens and Lucrece* because "*Jack Juggler* was still trying, like Medwall and [John] Heywood, to accommodate the spectators within the play, to transform their traditional symbolic role into something purely realistic" (*Shakespeare and the Idea of the Play*, p. 51).

17. Cf. the background provided by Bradbrook, *Growth and Structure of Elizabethan Comedy*, pp. 27–32, esp. p. 30.

18. The source was *Amphitryon*, but cf. Charles Mills Gayley, ed., *Representative English Comedies* (London, 1903–36), I, lxxviii–lxxix, and F. J. Child's introduction to *Four Old Plays* (Cambridge, Mass., 1848), cited by Farmer, *Early English Dramatists*, pp. 278–80, and Righter, *Shakespeare and the Idea of the Play*, pp. 50–51. All these commentators indicate, from various approaches, the divergence from the Plautine source in *Jack Juggler* which is tantamount to independence.

19. On the doctrinal aspects of the play, which will not concern us here, see Gayley, *Representative English Comedies*, and Marienstras, "Aspects de la conscience."

20. He says:

> I durst a good mede and a wager laye,
> That though laiest doune and slepest by the waye
> And dreamist all this.   (959–61)

21. John Summerson, *Inigo Jones* (Harmondsworth, 1966), p. 17.

22. Allardyce Nicoll, *Stuart Masques and the Renaissance Stage* (London, 1938); Glynne Wickham, *Early English Stages: 1576–1660* (New York, 1962), II, ii, 267–68; Summerson, *Inigo Jones*, pp. 21–22. George R. Kernodle, *From Art to Theatre: Form and Convention in the Renaissance* (Chicago, 1944), pp. 212–14, offers a caveat on overemphasizing the immediate effect of Jones's Italian studies.

23. *Ben Jonson*, ed. C. H. Herford and P. and E. Simpson, 11 vols. (Oxford, 1925–52), VII, 301.

24. For the entire celebration see A. M. Nagler, *Theater Festivals of the Medici* (New Haven, Conn., 1964), pp. 93–100.

25. *The Court Masque: A Study in the Relationship between Poetry and the Revels* (London, 1927), pp. 174–80, 196–202, 217–43 passim.

26. The Platonic iconography with which Jonson implemented his humanistic aims in the masques is examined in John C. Meagher, *Method and Meaning in Jonson's Masques* (Notre Dame, Ind., 1966).

27. *The Jonsonian Masque* (Cambridge, Mass., 1965). Cf. Angus Fletcher, *The Transcendental Masque: An Essay on Milton's 'Comus'* (Ithaca N.Y., 1971), pp. 11–12, 78, 87–115, esp. 104–6 on the Platonic "style of imagination."

28. "To Make Boards To Speak: Inigo Jones's Stage and the Jonsonian Masque," *Renaissance Drama*, N.S. I (Evanston, Ill., 1968), pp. 121–52; cf. Glynne Wickham, "Emblème et image: Quelques remarques sur la manière de figurer et de représenter le lieu sur la scène anglaise au XVIe siècle," in *Le Lieu théâtral à la Renaissance*, ed. Jean Jacquot (Paris, 1964), pp. 317–22; and Glynne Wickham, "The Stuart Mask," in *Shakespeare's Dramatic Heritage*, pp. 103–17.

29. Allan H. Gilbert, *The Symbolic Persons in the Masques of Ben Jonson* (Durham, N.C., 1948).

30. Orgel, "To Make Boards To Speak," p. 127.

31. *Ibid.*, pp. 135, 140.

32. *Ibid.*, pp. 146ff.; and Orgel, "The Poetics of Spectacle," *NLH*, 2 (1971), 367–89, esp. 369–71, 386–89.

33. The detailed history of the performance is given in *Jonson*, X, 573–86; cf. Orgel, "To Make Boards To Speak, "pp. 144–46.

34. Gian Lorenzo Bernini, *Fontana di Trevi*, ed. and introd. Cesare D'Onofrio (Rome, 1963), p. 22. Cf. Filippo Baldinucci, *Vita di Bernini*, ed. Sergio Samek Ludovici (Milan, 1948), pp. 77, 104–5.

35. *The Diary of John Evelyn*, ed. E. S. DeBeer (Oxford, 1955), II, 261 (19 November 1644).

36. Baldinucci, *Vita*, pp. 149–50.

37. Cf. the remarks of John H. McDowell in *The Renaissance Stage: Documents of Serlio, Sabbatini and Furttenbach*, ed. Barnard Hewitt (Coral Gables, Fla., 1958), p. 37; and Irving Lavin, *Art Bulletin*, 46 (1964), 570–71 (in the course of a review of D'Onofrio's edition of *Fontana di Trevi*). One might add that the conceptions even antedate the machines in some cases. The Prologo to Donato Giannotti's *Il vecchio amoroso* (1533–36) warns his Florentine audience: "La strada che m'è in fronte, è il Lungarno. E voi spettatori vi trovate a vedere questa festa in Arno. Ma state sicuri che si andranno le cose, che non vi bagnerete."

38. My understanding of Bernini's drama opposes Cesare Molinari's description of a hypothetical dichotomy between the scenarist and the scenic technician, as well as his suggestion that there is an essential difference between the multiple star system of the *commedia dell'arte* troupes and Bernini's dictatorial insistence upon directorial dominance: see Molinari, "Note in margine all'attività teatrale di G. L. Bernini," *Critica d'arte*, 9, no. 52 (1962), 57–61, and *Le nozze degli Dèi: Un saggio sul grande spettacolo italiano nel seicento* (Rome, 1968), pp. 105–20.

39. The background through the celestial amphitheater, a courtly audience, and a mythological stage, especially in the Florentine *intermezzi*, has been traced in Richard Bernheimer, "Theatrum Mundi," *Art Bulletin*, 38 (1956), 225–47, esp. 242–43, on Bernini.

40. *Vita*, p. 151.

41. Domenico Bernini, *Vita del G. L. Bernini* (1773), quoted in D'Onofrio, *Fontana di Trevi*, pp. 109–10.

42. Baldinucci, *Vita*, p. 151. I cannot agree with Lavin (*Art Bulletin*, pp. 569–70, 572) that the *Fontana di Trevi* manuscript is to be identified with this "bella idea."

43. See n. 34 above. The playlet, untitled, is in MS italienne 2084 of the Bibliothèque Nationale, Paris.

44. Cf. an analogous adaptation of the epigrammatic genre by Jonson discussed in Chapter VII, pp. 230–31, below.

CHAPTER V

1. *Works*, ed. William Gifford and Alexander Dyce (London, 1869), I, 13–15 (all references to Ford's works are to volume and page number in this edition unless otherwise designated). Cf. *Pericles*, IV, Prologue, 25–27, for an analogue not previously noted.

2. The case is not altered fundamentally if we accept the hypothesis of a Ford-Dekker collaboration: see Alfred Harbage, "The Mystery of Perkin Warbeck," in *Studies in the English Renaissance Drama in Memory of Karl Julius Holzknecht*, ed. Josephine W. Bennett et al. (New York, 1959), pp. 125–41; and Sidney R. Homan, Jr., "Dekker as Collaborator in Ford's *Perkin Warbeck*," *ELN*, 3 (1965), 104–6. Peter Ure, in the introduction to his Revels Plays edition of *Peter Warbeck*, p. lii, comments on the comparative isolation of our play from the rest of the Fordian canon. This in itself he views as only another aspect of a larger condition: the comparative isolation of *Perkin* from the rest of Caroline drama. The latter generalization should be adequately refined by the analyses in this chapter.

3. All citations are from *The Chronicle History of Perkin Warbeck*, ed. Peter Ure (London, 1968).

4. On the dating of *Perkin Warbeck*, entered and printed in 1634, see G. E. Bentley, *Jacobean and Caroline Stage* (Oxford, 1941–68), III, 454–56, and Ure's introduction to the play, pp. xxviii–xxx. Homan, "Dekker as Collaborator," suggests a date as early as 1621–24, but only in passing. Sir Aston Cokayne's *Trappolin*, although not printed until 1658, has been shown to derive from his attendance at a 1632 performance of the *Affezionati* in Venice and to have been written during his return trip to England in 1633: see K. M. Lea, "Sir Aston Cokayne and the 'Commedia dell' Arte,'" *MLR*, 33 (1928), 47–51. On the "pretended-prince" theme in *commedia scenari* see Lea, *Italian Popular Comedy* (Oxford, 1934), I, 193–94 (*Trappolin* was revived in an adaptation which is close to plagiarism in Nahum Tate's *A Duke and No Duke* [1685]). In relation to these dates we may notice also Richard Brome's *The Novella*, a comedy acted in 1632. The details of its Venetian setting may be the result of Brome's reading of Coryat's *Crudities* (R. R. Sharpe, "The Sources of Richard Brome's *The Novella*," *SP*, 30 [1933], 69–85) and Jonson's guidance in such matters. But the action and characters of *The Novella* seem much more directly related to the *commedia dell'arte* than those in the earlier plays examined by Lea (*Italian Popular Comedy*, II, 412–30). The allied fathers who are trying to force their children into money marriages are called Pantaloni and Guadagni. The former is a lecher who is shamed by the substitution of a disguised Moor when he sneaks to the bordello (this incident possibly echoing an episode in Fletcher's *Monsieur Thomas*, which Brome edited in 1639). The *zanni*-type Nicolo turns the tables upon his master in collaboration with the son. The Spaniard is introduced quite outside the plot economy to act the traditional cowardly bravo. There is an elaborate slapstick *lazzo* between the *zanni* and a "zaffo" concerning a chest. There is a recurrent cry of "magic" and "inchantment." Finally, there is an extremely complex interaction of disguises which, as so often in the *commedia* scripts, effects a series of intentionally slapstick confrontations and yet attempts to become serious at the hasty denouement, in which the whore is revealed as the lost virgin, the pimp is revealed as a friar, and the fathers are ready to bow to their childrens' amorous wills. Of later English plays aside from Cokayne's *Trappolin*, I would judge *The Novella* the

one most likely one day to prove the exception to Miss Lea's proper reminder that "it is hardly to be expected that we should find the precise original of any English play among the miscellanies of the Commedia dell'arte" (*ibid.*, p. 411). Some external support for the conjecture is provided by the discovery masque in Brome's *The City Wit* (ca. 1629–1631), which the pedant Sarpego says "should be done after the fashion of *Italy* by our selves, only the plot premeditated to what our aim must tend: Marry the Speeches must be extempore" (*The Dramatic Works of Richard Brome Containing Fifteen Comedies Now First Collected in Three Volumes* [Pearson rpt.; London, 1873], I, 364). Unless otherwise noted, all citations are to volume and page number of this edition, lineation not being provided. On the dating of *The City Wit*, cf. Bentley, *Jacobean and Caroline Stage*, III, 59–61, and R. J. Kaufmann, *Richard Brome, Caroline Playwright* (New York, 1961), pp. 47–57, 179. The reference to "de *Comedien* dat act de shangling" in *The Damoiselle* (1638; *Works*, I, 454) also seems a probable allusion to the popular gallicized Italian troupes. Less conclusive, because of the obvious Jonsonian echo, is Brome's allusion in *Covent-Garden Weeded* (1632–1633) to the "Mountebank" who in London "drew such flocks of idle people to him, that the Players, they say, curst him abominably" (*Works*, II, 10–11). Kaufmann (*Richard Brome*, pp. 67–87) has conclusively demonstrated that this play was stuffed with topical allusions, and one notices especially numerous references to licensed mountebanks in England in the early 1630s— although the only specific notice for 1632 (three men with a troupe exhibiting "Italian motion with divers and sundry storyes in it") is at Coventry (Lea, *Italian Popular Comedy*, II, 361–62). At any rate, Brome's numerous references to the *commedia* and the very surge of the mountebanks themselves at this time, taken together with *Trappolin*, suggest that *Perkin Warbeck* was written at a time of revived English interest in the Italian theatrical troupers and their methods. See also n. 28 below.

5. *Trappolin Creduto Principe*, in *The Dramatic Works of Sir Aston Cockain*, ed. James Maidment and W. H. Logan (Edinburgh and London, 1874), p. 202; all references to Cokayne's works are to this edition.

6. As well as the general play of *dédoublement* in *Trappolin*, there is continuous breaking through illusion in two directions: by dramatic reference to the audience itself (as when Trappolin alludes to his *zanni* role and to the *commedia dell'arte* cast explicitly, in angrily demanding: "You take me for a doctor,—Gracian of Franckolin, I warrant you,—or a fool in a play" [190]) or inwardly, with a mythological masque (141–45). That the *commedia* tradition impressed its mark permanetly upon Cokayne is evidenced by the large role played by Captain Hannibal in *The Tragedy of Ovid* (ca. 1658), a Capitano Spaventoso type of *miles gloriosus* who is clearly developed from the Captain Mattemores of *Trappolin*.

7. It must be noted, even in claiming the uniqueness of *Perkin Warbeck* in the Ford canon, that *The Lover's Melancholy* is an abortive attempt which nevertheless moves very much in the direction of *Perkin*. It is a play involving madness and feigned madness; Palador, Prince of Cyprus, is sick with lost love and neglectful of his realm; yet he at one point seems to be playing a double Hamlet with the courtier Rhetias—both putting on the antic disposition to cover their true feelings (I, 37–38). The cause of what is genuine in Palador's melancholy is Eroclea, the girl lost through his own late father's lusting attempts upon her, attempts which, when thwarted by her father, Lord Meleander, led to Meleander's imprisonment by the old king and the consequent shock which has made him an older Segismundo-cum-Lear, as he raves and wonders in a castle prison. Palador is cured of his psychic malaise through the instrumentality of a masque of melancholies presented by his physician and friends (I, 24, 51, 63–69, 82), and the old Meleander is brought back to himself by a similar dramatic mirroring of his own state (I, 74–78), a return which he makes in a confusion of reality and dream:

O, I have slept belike; 'tis but the foolery
Of some beguiling dream. So, so! I will not
Trouble the play of my delighted fancy,
But dream my dream out.   (I, 95–96; cf. 88)

The arranged dramatics, however, are only part of the double cure: they are complemented by the miraculous reappearance of the lost Eroclea. If the nightingale legend noticed at the opening of the chapter shows art triumphing destructively over nature, the theatrical masque of melancholy and the "dreams-awakening" plot arranged around Meleander demonstrate art triumphing over nature to resurrect and restore life. The ambiguity will be made explicit in the simultaneous triumph and death of Perkin Warbeck in the later play.

Ford seldom missed an opportunity to incorporate a masque within his plays, but always it is a masque of murder, in *The Spanish Tragedy* tradition ('*Tis Pity She's a Whore*, I, 172; *The Broken Heart*, I, 270, 274, 308; *Love's Sacrifice*, II, 70–71). Only in *The Lover's Melancholy* do the internal theatricals serve in the elaborately medical sense which will become the plot predication for Brome's *The Antipodes*.

8. Irving Ribner, *The English History Play in the Age of Shakespeare*, rev. ed. (New York, 1965), pp. 313–20.

9. *The Mirror of Monsters* (London, 1587), sig. E5^r.

10. St. Augustine, *Soliloquies* II.10 (*PL*, XXXII, 895). I owe the quotation to Charles S. Singleton, ed., *Dante Studies 1* (Cambridge, Mass., 1954), pp. 63–64.

11. Anne Righter, *Shakespeare and the Idea of the Play* (London, 1962), pp. 121–38, esp. 137–38, has glanced at *Perkin Warbeck* in the context of Shakespeare's "player-kings." Especially pertinent are her comments on the Lord of Misrule role developed in *Richard II* (p. 122) and in *I Henry IV* (p. 128), although she does not perceive the relevance for *Perkin Warbeck*.

12. Ure edition, p. 5. Citations from Bacon's *History* are from the James Spedding, Robert Ellis, and Douglas Heath edition of the *Works* (London, 1861). The *History* appeared in 1622: cf. *Works*, VI, 5–6.

13. Cf. John Speed, *The History of Great Britain* (1609; rpt. London, 1650), p. 750: "Yet the Lady *Margarets* course to vent her Creature at the first was exquisite; for shee (as in a Magicke practice) having kept him secret . . . he sayles into *Ireland* . . . where . . . he so strongly enchanted that rude people with the charmes of false hopes, and mists of seemings." See the "preface" to *The History of Henry VII* in *Works*, VI, 16–18, on Speed's use of a yet earlier sketch of Henry VII drawn up by Bacon. But it is clear from the purely imagistic echoes that Bacon's much more circumstantial account drew heavily enough on Speed's chronicle to repay the debt.

14. Bacon had taken the phrase from Speed, who had extracted passages from the original of Harl. MS. 283ff., 123ff., "Perkyn Warbecks his Proclamation." The entire proclamation is reprinted as Appendix II to *The History* in *Works*, VI, 252–55.

15. I am, of course, disinclined to accept the judgment of recent years, perpetuated in Ure's edition, that Thomas Gainsford's *The True and Wonderful History of Perkin Warbeck* (1618) was the principal source for Ford's play. However, it is probable that Ford did consult it, and in doing so he would have found a less coherently developed undertow of theatrical metaphor: "here is our stage of variety" (536); "she set up another puppet . . . to act the part of wonder on the stage" (539); "nor seemed this mischief simply to be acted on the stage of fiction, like an historical tragedy" (552); "Perkin, who played the counterfeit so exactly, that his words resembled forcible incantations" (558); "Perkin like some strange meteor or monster; or . . . like a triumphant spectacle" (589); "the last act of his tragedy and catastrophe was now in hand" (590). Of the imagery of evanescence discussed

below, Gainsford has only one demi-exemplar: "in this our story . . . the best excuse ariseth from shadows, smoke, vapours" (537) (pagination from the reprint in *The Harleian Miscellany*, ed. William Oldys and Thomas Park [London, 1818], VI, 534–94).

16. "To a Vain, Young Courtier; occasion'd by his speaking contemptibly of the Players," in *Complete Works of William Wycherley*, ed. Montague Summers (London, 1924), IV, 241.

17. Speed had affirmed, in beginning his account of Perkin's history, that "there is in humane nature . . . a kinde of light matter, which will easily kindle, being toucht with the blazing hopes of ambitious propositions" (*History*, p. 750); that "the whole Stratageme, was smoakt out of France" (*ibid.*). And Bacon had taken up the metaphor in reporting that Margaret, having tutored Perkin in his role, "began to cast with herself from what coast this blazing star should first appear, and at what time. It must be upon the horizon of Ireland; for there had the like strong meteor influence before" (135–36). Perkin was "smoked away" out of France as a political sacrifice (138), and at the desperate climax of his career, "as it fareth with smoke that never leeseth itself till it be at the highest, he did now before his end raise his stile, intitling himself . . . Richard the Fourth, King of England" (190).

18. Cf. the ironic reversal of the terms when Perkin scorns hopeless desperation, as a "poverty our greatness dares not dream of" (III, ii, 184).

19. Speed reports that in Scotland "there wanted not some, who with many arguments advised the King *to repute all but for a meere dreame, and illusion*" (*History*, p. 753). But the world as dream was one of Ford's few persistent semi-structural metaphors. We have already noticed Meleander's "awakening" in *The Lover's Melancholy* (*Works*, I, 95–97), and it threads throughout *'Tis Pity She's a Whore*, especially in the willful illusionism of Giovanni, although never becoming an ordering principle: cf. *Works*, I, 126, 162, 179, 192–93, 198. In *The Broken Heart* Penthea has a set piece on the world as dream and theater at once (I, 275–76) which is casually echoed later (281, 290).

20. There has been an early preparation for just this startling speech when the Countess of Crawford comments shortly after Perkin's arrival in Scotland that "'twere pity now if ha' should prove a counterfeit" (II, i, 4), and Katherine, enamored, agrees that "I should pity him / If ha' should prove another than he seems" (II, i, 119–20).

21. It is pertinent at this point to recall that the ambiguity (which I would prefer to call ambivalence) of Perkin's identity within the dream is heightened by the absence of soliloquies; from this point onward we can never determine what Perkin Warbeck believes his own identity to be. It was a point first made in an admirable note appended to his edition by William Gifford: "Whatever might be his own opinion of this person's pretensions, [Ford] has never suffered him to betray his identity with the Duke of York in a single thought or expression. Perkin has no soliloquies, no side-speeches, to compromise his public assertions; and it is pleasing to see with what ingenuity Ford has preserved him from the contamination of real history, and contrived to sustain his dignity to the last with all imaginable decorum, and thus rendered him a fit subject for the tragic Muse" (*Works*, II, 217). The fullest endorsement and critical development of Gifford's observation is in Jonas Barish, "Perkin Warbeck as Anti-History," *EC*, 20 (1970), 151–71, where it is demonstrated that no moment within the play offers a hint that Perkin is a pretender. My own reading, which assumes an audience with a "set" toward historic backgrounds in viewing a history play, perhaps stands between Barish's and Ure's sense of the experience of *Perkin Warbeck*: cf. Ure's introduction to his edition, pp. xli–xliii, lxxviii–lxxix.

22. *History*, p. 750.

23. *Works*, VI, 139.

24. Speed, *History*, p. 757; Bacon, *History*, VI, 195–96, 201–3. Cf. Barish, *"Perkin Warbeck,"* p. 154.

25. The evidence and speculation are gathered in Kaufmann, *Richard Brome*, pp. 19–23, 176–77.

26. The sixteen extant plays span the years 1629–1641; a lost *Fault in Friendship* was licensed October 2, 1623: see Bentley, *Jacobean and Caroline Stage*, III, 69.

27. See *ibid.*, pp. 86–87, and Kaufmann, *Richard Brome*, p. 179.

28. That Brome apparently utilized this plot trope at the historic moment when the Venetian *"Trappolin"* *scenario* was being Englished by Cokayne and the *commedia dell'arte* troupes and traditions generally seem to have been undergoing something of a revival in England (see n. 4 above) is further evidence of his direct consciousness of the Italian players and *scenari*. Since *The Queen's Exchange* bears certain marked resemblances to the Calderónian version of the "pretended prince," it is perhaps not inappropriate to notice a further historic coincidence: *La vida es sueño* appeared in 1635.

29. *Works*, III, 476–77.

30. Cf. Kaufmann, *Richard Brome*, p. 65: "It is true that as early as *King Lear* state doctors prescribed some therapy for mental illness, but Ford's play [*The Lover's Melancholy*] and Brome's [*The Antipodes*] after it are the first to build a whole layer of a play on the bases of diagnosis (in systematic terms) and treatment of an illness." Cf. n. 7 above.

31. In order to point up the continuity of Brome's concerns, it is appropriate to notice that the cure of melancholy is a major interest in plays other than those examined here. In the early (1629) romance *The Northern Lass*, Constance (the lass) is thrown into the hands of a benevolent conspirator-pretending-psychiatrist-pretending-physician, a position she is willing to accept because she agrees with her family that love for Sir Philip has crippled her: "I know I am not weell too" (*Dramatic Works*, III, 60; cf. 50–53). But Constance also knows more than the doctors: "I'le have no Doctor but Sir *Philip*," she insists, and the mock doctor Pate agrees to dissipate all the psychiatric potential in the pleasing mist of a romantic denouement. If Constance's governess "doubt[s] not of your speedie address to the cure," Pate can prescribe at once: " 'Tis done in three words. The partie that she loves, must be the Doctor, the Medicine, and the cure" (84). In the later *Covent Garden Weeded* (1632) one strand is the cure of an elder brother, Gabriel Crosswill, of his Puritan extremism by means of a drink-induced sleep, from which he awakens in martial gear to believe his Puritan phase a mere

> thousand vain imaginations
> . . . dust
> Contracted by a whirlwinde,
> . . . lodg'd in the rich Seat of Contemplation,
> Usurping there the room of vertuous thoughts.   (II, 90; cf. 86–91)

In such a military recovery one must see not only the dream cure but the seeds of Peregrine's Quixotic resurrection among the puppets and plumes behind the stage in *The Antipodes*.

32. On the contract, dating, and composition of the two plays see Bentley, *Jacobean and Caroline Stage*, III, 52–55, 56–57, 67–69; Kaufmann, *Richard Brome*, pp. 28–33. On the plague and the surreptitious reopening of the Cockpit by the elder Beeston during the prohibition, see Ann Haaker, "The Plague, the Theater, and the Poet," *Renaissance Drama*, N.S., I (Evanston, Ill., 1968), pp. 283–306, where the documents of the litigation between Brome and Heton are reproduced and analyzed. The points

of central convergence between these two plays which were the fruits of the mortality bills would seem sufficient to lay forever to rest the scholarly myth that *The Antipodes* was Brome's imitation of Thomas Randolph's negligible *Muses' Looking-Glass*, a verse satire on stage which has no more in common with Brome's play than with Jonson's *Every Man Out of His Humour*, which Bishop Hurd thought formed *its* source. Cf. C. E. Andrews, *Richard Brome: A Study of His Life and Works* (New Haven, Conn., 1913), p. 122 ("In structure Randolph's *Muses' Looking-Glass* . . . is so much like *The Antipodes* that we may say that together they form a special type of which, as far as I know, there are no other examples in the period"; cf. 124ff.); Joseph Lee Davis, "Richard Brome's Neglected Contribution to Comic Theory," *SP*, 40 (1943), 520–28, and *The Sons of Ben* (Detroit, Mich., 1967), pp. 59–66, 70–80; Kaufmann, *Richard Brome*, p. 64n. The *Muses' Looking-Glass* (1630) treats the theater as purgation, but makes it into a Gascoignean true glass in which deformities are seen by, and convert to reality, two purveyors of clothes, the symbolic stuff of unreal surfaces. Brome's *Antipodes* works toward an opposite thesis: that theater can convert the imagination to a truce with reality because its pretense is more potent than "life." It should be said in all fairness, though, that Davis' thesis seems confused because of his dependence upon Andrews, and that it comes close to the point in asserting that Brome surpasses Randolph's conception of comedy as the traditional "mirror" and shows in *The Antipodes* that catharsis is possible where "inversions . . . of a purely fantastic or topsy-turvy world, present a version of life in which incongruity is carried to the unpredictable extremes of its quaint logic" (528). Kaufmann's treatment of *The English Moor* as a "usury" play smacks of L. C. Knights' sociology and is among the most mistaken of his often perceptive readings in Brome (*Richard Brome*, pp. 131–50).

33. When Millicent is ordered into blackface by Quicksands, he remarks:

> Illustrious persons, nay, even Queens themselves
> Have, for the glory of a nights presentment,
> To grace the work, sufferd as much as this. (*Works*, II, 38)

Jonson's *Masque*, presented in January, 1605, was described by Sir Ralph Winwood, an eyewitness: there was "a Skallop, wherein were four Seats; on the lowest sat the Queen with my lady *Bedford*. . . . Their Apparell was rich, but too light and Curtizan-like for such great ones. Instead of Vizzards, their Faces, and Arms up to the Elbows, were painted black" (*Ben Jonson*, ed. C. H. Herford and P. and E. Simpson, 11 vols. [Oxford, 1925–52], X, 448).

34. When Meanwell and Rashly—supposed dead—expatiate on their almost motiveless disappearance in the final act, I prefer to believe that their "awkward" pointers indicate an unnoticed aside in the exchange of testiness between Jonson and Brome rather than ineptness or hurry on Brome's part—especially in a manuscript which the author was at leisure to rewrite. Certainly *The Staple of News* and *The New Inn* are the target of Rashly's explanation:

> Nor was it onely to make tryal of
> What husbands they would be; how spend, or save;
> How manage, or destroy; how one or both
> Might play the Tyrants over their poor Tenants,
> Yet fall by Prodigality into th' Compters:
> And then the dead by pulling off a Beard,
> After a little chiding and some whyning,
> To set the living on their legs again,
> And take 'em into favour; pish, old play-plots. (73)

35. See the effective argument of Harriett Hawkins, "The Idea of a Theater in Jonson's *The New Inn*," in *Renaissance Drama*, IX (Evanston, Ill., 1966), pp. 205–26.

36. Alfred Harbage, "Elizabethan-Restoration Palimpsest," *MLR*, 35 (1940), 304, describes the "guilty heroine" formula which dominates the surface action of a number of Brome's plays and adds that "in his best comedies *The Antipodes* and *The Jovial Crew*, Brome departs from his own formula." Kaufmann, *Richard Brome*, p. 61, echoes this in concluding that *The Antipodes* is "Brome's most unusual play." Both judgments are correct if one adds that the quality and character of these plays lies in their fealty to the "main tradition" of philosophic drama of which Brome was more conscious than any of his contemporaries. Ian Donaldson has observed the familiarity of the "Antipodes" as a *topos* before Brome employs it (*The World Upside-Down: Comedy from Jonson to Fielding* [Oxford, 1970], pp. 78–98).

37. *The New Inn*, I, vi, 95–97. All quotations are from Herford and Simpson, *Ben Jonson*, VI, 395–498.

38. The Courts of Love concluded and the denouement imminent, Jonson ostentatiously returned to making the controlling trope explicit. "The Court's dissolu'd, remou'd, and the play ended," asserts the player-queen Prudence (IV, iv, 247), and Lovel, unaware that his love conquest is approaching, choruses in lament

> How like
> A Court remoouing, or an ended Play
> Shews my abrupt precipitate estate   (IV, iv, 251–53)

because he has been, he believes, "baffuld by a Chambermaid, / And the good Actor, her Lady" (IV, iv, 277–78). The chambermaid, chafing under her lady's reprimands meanwhile, is casting off her regal role with more than a player's dignity:

> Why, take your spangled properties, your gown
> . . . I will not buy this play-boyes brauery,
> At such a price.   (IV, iv, 319–22)

And at the beginning of the last act, the Host-Frampul articulates his disappointment only to sharpen the contrast with the harmonious discoveries of the close: "I had thought . . . like a noble Poet, to haue had / My last act best: but all failes i' the plot" (V, i, 2–7). With this comment, of course, the theatrics of the Court of Love within the theater of the Light Heart Inn reach out to embrace the yet larger milieu of the "noble Poet" Jonson, writing his last act for the unappreciative Blackfriars audience—a last faint emanation from the Jonsonian persona which had bridged audience and artifact, the strutting of Asper upon the Globe thirty years before (see Chapter VII below).

39. *Dramatic Works of Thomas Heywood* (Pearson rpt.; London, 1874), IV, 231–32. On the authorship and date (1634) see Bentley, *Jacobean and Caroline Stage*, III, 73–76. If Harbage's elaborate argument is correct in tracing Dryden's *Mistaken Husband* (1675) to a lost Brome manuscript, we have probable evidence for another instance of impotence, insofar as Dryden's Mrs. Manley has suffered seven years of unconsummated marriage ("Elizabethan-Restoration Palimpsest," pp. 304–7).

40. *Dramatic Works*, III, 240.

41. It is useful here to notice that the play has large and small versions of sexual confusion at center and periphery: Blaze's fantasy life prevents him from accepting his wife because she is his wife; the Doctor jokes upon the "Antipodes" where

> the maids do woe
> The Batchelors, and tis most probable,
> The Wives lie uppermost;   (252)

Peregrine's imaginative crippling makes Martha a married virgin, and focuses the plot. This last central case literally frustrates nature in its generative aspect. It is an observation to be remembered when reading *The Jovial Crew*, where the question of "nature"'s power is presented (with a coherence and force more integral than in any English drama during the thirty years since *The Winter's Tale*) in terms both of procreation and what might almost—but not quite—be called man's "mythic" sympathy with physical nature and its fertility. That sexual order will be restored within *The Antipodes*, incidentally, is foreshadowed at the outset when Blaze tells Joyless of Hughball's cure upon a woman who sought seven years to love her husband

> Untill this Doctor tooke her into cure,
> And now she lies as lovingly on a flockebed
> With her owne Knight, as she had done on downe,
> With many others. (235)

42. On Brome's earlier use of the dream device, see *The Queen and Concubine* (II, 44–47, and the discussion in Chapter II, n. 64, above) as well as *The Queen's Exchange*, III, 526–29, discussed on pp. 134–40 above.

43. The familial inversions of *The Antipodes* constituted a long strand in the plot of the Heywood-Brome *Late Lancashire Witches* (1634), where one effect of witchcraft is to make the elderly Seely couple obey their children, while the children themselves are in thrall to the family servants: "This is quite upside downe," marvels one observer of the familial farce: "the sonne controlls the father, and the man overcrowes his masters coxcombe, sure they are all bewitch'd" (*Dramatic Works of Thomas Heywood*, IV, 183; cf. 179, 208, 217, 252–55).

44. "Probably quite directly" because Beeston's Boys at the Cockpit, for whom *The Antipodes* was intended by Brome, were given full title to *The Knight of the Burning Pestle* by the Lord Chamberlain's edict of 10 August 1639, and the old Beaumont comedy had been presented at St. James on 28 February 1635–1636 by Queen Henrietta's Company, which, under Christopher Beeston, was the nucleus and predecessor of the mixed group which became The King and Queen's Young Company, or "Beeston's Boys" (Bentley, *Jacobean and Caroline Stage*, I, 236, 250, 330–31). In short, the earlier play was being revived by Brome's friends just prior to the composition of *The Antipodes*. M. C. Bradbrook, *Shakespeare the Craftsman* (London and New York, 1969), pp. 44–48, has some astute comments on this scene of havoc and Shakespeare's company as an allegory of theatrical history.

45. See n. 4 above.

46. Her fantasy life, like Peregrine's, is rapidly finding itself projected into the dramatic proceedings, as evidenced by her response: "I love this playne Lord better than / All the brave gallant ones, that ere I dream't on" (262).

47. We find ourselves again at the motive so powerfully treated by Chapman in *The Widow's Tears*. The difference in the effect of arbitrary trial here, as in those other versions from the 1630s Randolph's *The Jealous Lovers* and Ford's *The Lady's Trial* (see Chapter II, n. 87, above), is, in my view, historic. Imagination does not make people over, does not metamorphose Diana into Venus (the coincidence of names in Chapman's and Brome's "testing" plots is a touchstone to sharpen the difference); artifice, life as a theatrical plot, makes over the imagination among the Carolines.

48. With the discovery of Letoy's life-long manipulation of his world, one in retrospect understands that the explicit relation he bears to his servants is but a symbol of his dramatic control of that world itself

> My owne men are
> My Musique, and my Actors, I keepe not
> A man or boy but is of quality:
> The worst can . . .

. . . act his part too in a comedy.
. . . .
I love the quality of Playing I, I love a Play with all
My heart . . . and a Player that is
A good one too, with all my heart: As for the Poets,
No men love them, I thinke, and therefore
I write all my playes my selfe.   (246)

49. Bentley, *Jacobean and Caroline Stage*, III, 71–73. The comments which follow will make clear my thorough rejection of Kaufmann's "escapist" reading of the drama, which seems to go out of the way to depict Brome as a desperate and frustrated reactionary (*Richard Brome*, pp. 169–73). Ann Haaker's introduction to *A Jovial Crew* (Lincoln, Neb., 1968), pp. xiii–xxi, is the best placing of the play in its social context. The mechanical impact of Jonson's *The Gypsies Metamorphosed* upon *A Jovial Crew* is manifest.

50. The motif is carried on at another remove in Oldrents' "cure" of a minor character, the young booby gentleman Talboy who has lost his betrothed Amy through the elopement described below. Oldrents drowns him in sack, hunting, and pleasures, until he is challenger for the title of merriest man alive (419–20, 441–42). Of course, the "play" at the close is the final play to purge melancholy at its root rather than symptomatically.

51. Too habitually to suit loyal but somewhat skeptical old Randall, who sighs: "The old wonted news, Sir, from your Guest-house, the old Barn. We have unloaden the Bread-basket, the Beef-Kettle, and the Beer-*Bumbards* there, amongst your Guests the Beggars. And they have all prayed for you and our Master, as their manner is, from the teeth outward, marry from the teeth inwards 'tis enough to swallow your Alms; from which I think their Prayers seldom come" (362).

52. A red herring which badly misled Kaufmann into making it the pivot for his analysis of *A Jovial Crew* (*Richard Brome*, pp. 172–73).

53. Master Talboy, Amy's amiable booby suitor, who must owe something of his childlike charm to Bartholomew Cokes, joins Peregrine and Diana of *The Antipodes* as one who "never saw any *Players*" (441), a spice of expected naïve illusionism which is another red herring, since the play is not calculated to betray anyone's reactions in the direction followed by "*The Antipodes*" of Letoy and Hughball.

54. The strange destiny of blood is woven tightly when the "Patrico" within the inner play explains how Oldrents' grandfather had beguiled an earlier Wrought-on (great-grandfather to Springlove) of "half the Lands / That are descended to your hands" (444).

CHAPTER VI

1. The printer Walter Burre emphasized the point in his dedicatory letter for the 1613 quarto of *The Knight of the Burning Pestle*: "this unfortunate child . . . was by his parents (perhaps because hee was so unlike his brethren) exposed to the wide world."

2. *Shakespeare's Festive Comedy* (Princeton, N.J., 1959), pp. 220–21; cf. pp. 193–94, 205–7. The most elaborate construction of ritual-art relations in general, of course, is that of Northrop Frye (*Anatomy of Criticism* [Princeton, N.J., 1957]), incorporating his earlier essay on the "Argument of Comedy." But, since Francis M. Cornford's 1914 studies in Aristophanes, probably the most widely read development of theoretical relations between ritual and drama proper has been Francis Fergusson's *The Idea of a Theatre* (Princeton, N.J., 1949). It is instructive for a realization of the contemporary mood—so clearly expressed by Barber—to read the introductory essay and cumulative bibliography of caveats against the excesses of the original in

Theodore H. Gaster's annotated reissue of Cornford's *The Origin of Attic Comedy* (Garden City, N.Y., 1961) fifty years later. Fergusson's study has been questioned, as I will indicate in my brief review of the objections raised by Robert J. Nelson, *Play within a Play* (New Haven, Conn., 1958), pp. 3–6. On the other hand, it is proper to point out that Nelson, in discussing Rotrou's *Saint Genest* (pp. 35–46, esp. p. 45), himself points to one instance in which drama does return to a ritual function.

3. *Shakespeare's Festive Comedy*, pp. 61, 72–73, 83. It is true that *Summer's Last Will and Testament* lacks the essential dramatic quality of complex viewpoint, but even with such a marginal effort one can never underestimate the controls exercised by the Elizabethans, and Barber's comments on the simple "norm" adapted by Nashe's satiric speakers seem less sophisticated than the rhetorical tradition warrants. They should be reconsidered in the light of Alvin Kernan's discussions of satiric personae in *The Cankered Muse* (New Haven, Conn., 1959). *The Sun's Darling* (ca. 1624), a Ford-Dekker-Rowley collaboration, seems much closer to uncomplicated pageantry while utilizing the same seasonal structure which dominates *Summer's Last Will*. Into this "moral masque" the authors have introduced a spring morris dance (121–22), a country dance and hymning of the "Summer Queen" in holiday before Summer himself (140–41), and other festival interludes (127, 165–77) whose folkloristic origins are only slightly veiled by mythological paraphernalia. Still there is the running satire of Humour's servant Folly, which removes *The Sun's Darling* to a semi-dramatic dimension not enjoyed by pageantry (page references are to vol. III of John Ford, *Works*, ed. William Gifford and Alexander Dyce [London, 1869]).

4. All quotations that follow are from *Play within a Play*, pp. 3–6. Essentially concerned with French dramatists, Nelson also briefly discusses Shakespeare, Schnitzler, and Pirandello. The following analysis should be compared with Fergusson's own brief comments on comedy and audience in *The Idea of a Theatre*, pp. 178–79.

5. As has been demonstrated by Norman Rabkin, "Dramatic Deception in Heywood's *The English Traveller*," *SEL*, 1 (1961), 1–16.

6. *An Apology for Actors* (London, 1612), sigs. G^v–G2^v. Cf. M. C. Bradbrook, *The Rise of the Common Player: A Study of Actor and Society in Shakespeare's England* (London, 1962), pp. 89–92, on the *Apology* and the *topos*; she finds that Heywood "pushed comparison between microcosm and macrocosm to its utmost limits."

7. Sigs. B^v–B2^v. The "dream" trope as an account of life is not frequent as either image or instrument in Heywood's plays, but it does recur in *A Challenge for Beauty* (*The Dramatic Works of Thomas Heywood* [Pearson rpt.; London, 1874], V, 50, 56, 71; all references to Heywood's plays are to volume and page number in this edition). The Spanish Lord Bonavida even suggests that the world is a dream of the theater (V, 66, 71), as had the earlier *Apology for Actors*, but the point is not developed.

8. Sigs. B3^v–B4.

9. As at the close of act IV in *I The Fair Maid of the West*, where a chorus enters to lament:

Our Stage so lamely can expresse a Sea,
That we are forst by *Chorus* to discourse
What should have beene in action. Now imagine
Her passion ore, and *Goodlacke* well recovered   (II, 319–20)

or even more elaborately at the close of act III of the much later *II The Fair Maid of the West*, where the chorus appears abruptly to demand of the audience, "Imagine Besse and Spencer under sail" and goes on for thirty-four lines, interrupted by a dumbshow, to recount a sailing, a pirate encounter, a battle, two shipwrecks, and a joust, before allowing the actors to continue their presentation (II, 386–87).

10. Homer fulfills this role in *The Golden Age*, *The Silver Age*, and *The Brazen Age* (ca. 1611–1613) but, surprisingly enough, does not appear as a framing figure in the two-part *Iron Age*, which dramatizes the Trojan War and its aftermath.

11. *The Silver Age*, III, 97; cf. *The Golden Age*, III, 20: "Thinke kinde spectators seventeene sommers past."

12. W. W. Greg, *A Bibliography of the English Printed Drama to the Restoration* (London, 1939), I, 44. Cf. G. E. Bentley, *The Jacobean and Caroline Stage* (Oxford, 1941–68), I, 232.

13. The complications among work, audience, and author are slightly expanded if one accepts the biographical conjectures of A. M. Clark, *Thomas Heywood, Playwright and Miscellanist* (Oxford, 1931), pp. 129–43, 223–26.

14. In Midas' continual need for an allegorical key, one hears an ironic echo of Ben Jonson's comment in the 1609 *Masque of Queens*: "to haue told, vpon they^r entrance, *what they were* . . . had bene a most piteous hearing, and vtterly vnworthy any quality of a *Poeme*: wherein a *Writer* should always trust somewhat to the capacity of the *Spectator* . . . Men, beside inquiring eyes, are vnderstood to bring quick eares and not those sluggish ones of Porters and Mechanicks, that must be bor'd through, at every act, with Narrations" (*Ben Jonson*, ed. C. H. Herford and P. and E. Simpson, 11 vols. [Oxford, 1925–52], VII, 287).

15. William Adlington in his "Epistle Dedicatory" to *The Golden Ass* (1566), ed. Charles Whibley (London, 1893), mentions "Mydas" whose legend of the golden touch signified "the foul sin of Avarice" (p. 5), but only in an extensive catalogue of "feined fables" moralized.

16. The only other occasion upon which Heywood utilized the Midas legend emphasized the greed for gold and associated it with the ass's ears, while insisting that it was a concomitant of spiritual blindness: see *The Royal King and the Loyal Subject* (VI, 18–20).

17. "To the Reader" (V, 86). In this passage, as in others where no imagistic or staging crux is involved, I have silently corrected printing and pointing inadvertencies in the Pearson edition, a notorious example of nineteenth-century editing but indispensable until we receive Professor Arthur Brown's long-announced edition. The Jones sets were prepared for the second royal performance at Denmark House.

18. Thus setting before a Christian background the authentically Apuleian lie by which the jealous sisters induce Psyche to gaze upon Cupid: they tell her how they saw in her paradisiacal meads "a serpent gliding," "writhing his head / Proudly into the ayre, first hist at heaven" (117). Cf. *Les métamorphoses*, ed. D. S. Robertson, trans. P. Vallette (Paris, 1940–46), V.17–18, and Adlington, *The Golden Ass*, pp. 111–12, in neither of which does one receive the visual image or the Christian implication, nor does the original abandonment of Cupid by Psyche contain any parallel to Cupid's orders to blast and wither the place of the sin (V.25; Adlington, *The Golden Ass*, p. 112). The skeleton of the Christian commentary is, of course, the character Apuleius' "allegory," and this is drawn almost verbatim from Fulgentius, *Mythologicon*, the section "De Psyche & Cupidine" being frequently published as a preface to the *Metamorphoses* in the Renaissance. See n. 36 below.

19. In "Fortunate Falls as Form in Milton's 'Fair Infant,'" *JEGP*, 63 (1964), 660–74, I have illustrated Milton's use of very similar techniques to fuse Christian and classical myths of the Fall in a poem almost contemporary with *Love's Mistress*.

20. Two remarks in his first dialogue with Midas make it clear that Apuleius does not wear the ears, as would be expected for the sake of an almost inevitable piece of slapstick humor, but inconveniently carries them. The first is Apuleius' aside

upon meeting Midas, spoken although he has already confirmed that he still "bears" the ears—"I hope my Asses shape is quite shooke off" (92); in the second, Midas grumbles, "take heede Poet that your rimes be sound, / Else with thine owne Asse eares thou shalt be crown'd" (93).

21. The classical study of Renaissance views of proper and vain knowledge is Howard Schultz, *Milton and Forbidden Knowledge* (New York, 1955). His conclusion, after tracing attitudes from patristic literature through a massive body of religious, philosophic, and literary comment in the Renaissance, is that no science was generally considered forbidden but that all were evaluated according to the spirit of humility or self-exaltation in which they were pursued. The relevance of Schultz's conclusions for *Love's Mistress* will become apparent in the course of the discussion.

22. The frequent citations of this sort by Jonson and others offer testimony to Apuleius' popularity, which was stimulated by his reputation as Platonist and magician: see, for example, the citations, especially of the *Apologia*, in Ficino, *Opera* (Basel, 1563), pp. 294, 724, 740, 759, 769ff., 899, 997, 1132, 1358, 1715, 1836 (a catalogue borrowed from Paul Oskar Kristeller, *Il pensiero filosofico di Marsilio Ficino* [Florence, 1953], p. 452), and Frances Yates, *Giordano Bruno and the Hermetic Tradition* (Chicago, 1964), pp. 9–11, 169, 172–74. Surely, too, the attractive prose of Adlington's 1566 translation of *The Golden Ass* had not become so antiquated as to have lost all popularity among the court ladies who crowded Denmark House on the king's birthday to watch the spectacle of Psyche's struggle with the gods amidst the engineering triumphs of Inigo Jones.

23. This Apollonian music is another substructure of *Love's Mistress*. Here it introduces the oracle whose words presage the theme of the Fortunate Fall paradox as applied to Psyche. Later it establishes the value of poetry in the contest between Pan and Apollo, and ultimately it is the Muses' singing which provides the harmony for the dance of the deities welcoming Psyche to immortality—a dance which is part of the rites performed under the auspices of Apollo.

24. Heywood has entirely reworked the original prophecy in two ways, both of which are important to this argument. First, he concludes with a direct immortality paradox—eternal life can be gained from death (hell); second, he focuses the whole upon visual images for which there is no hint in the original (*Metamorphoses* IV.33; Adlington, *The Golden Ass*, p. 101, follows Apuleius more closely than usual in translating the oracle, as one might expect).

25. Heywood portrays a similarly angry Venus persuading Cupid to pierce Daphne with misplaced disdain in "*Apollo and Daphne*" (*Pleasant Dialogues and Dramas*, VI, 288). One may note that Venus' visual image is not in the original *Metamorphoses*; cf. IV.31.

26. Pp. 115, 143–46. Turning versifier upon his mistress, Amaryllis, he shocks his friend, who says "the veriest dowdy in all *Arcadia*, even Mopsa compar'd with her, showes like a Madam," and goes on to illustrate the point (144).

27. When Psyche has betrayed him, Cupid cries:

> did I not give thee charge,
> To taste the pleasures of Immortal love,
> But not to wade too deepe in mistery? (129)

and Apuleius must explain once more after her fall to Midas:

> because poore soule,
> She aym'd to search forbidden mysteries,
> Her eyes are blasted. (134)

28. *Metamorphoses* IV.7, 27.

29. A conclusion further illustrated in the play, I infer, by the simultaneous conversion of the clown to love and poetry (115). It is perhaps worth recalling that this is the same destructive urge for possession and certainty which is the theme of Chapman's *Widow's Tears*, although Heywood, of course, raises his protagonists from the infernal metamorphosis with which Chapman concludes.

30. Psyche's father, failing to recognize her, refuses to soothe her ear ("Nor my tongue grace thee with a daughter's name"), and she reacts by again shunning sight: "Oh whether shall a wretch convert her eyes, / When her owne father shall her teares despise?" (130).

31. Cf. Fulgentius' gloss upon Apuleius' *"Psyche et Cupidine"* cited in n. 36 below, where Adam's recognition of nakedness is directly invoked as an allegorical gloss to the *Metamorphoses*.

32. See Chapter I above, esp. pp. 27–28.

33. An echo of Cupid's epithet for the sisters in *Metamorphoses* V.12 (retained by Adlington, *The Golden Ass*, p. 108).

34. Perhaps Heywood's union of the two myths—Cupid's and Midas'—was inspired by a very brief and indirect hint in the *Metamorphoses*. Immediately after her fall, Psyche is desperately contemplating suicide by drowning but is dissuaded by Pan, who pipes and encourages her hope of regaining Cupid's love (V.25; Adlington, *The Golden Ass*, p. 114).

35. Cf. n. 21 above.

36. For the Renaissance developments of Plato's *Aphrodite Urania* and *Aphrodite Pandemos*, see the brief history in Erwin Panofsky, *Studies in Iconology* (1939; rpt. New York, 1962), pp. 139–46. The Heywood passage, so rich in its dramatic context, is in fact an almost verbatim rendering of Fulgentius' allegory *"De Psyche & Cupidine,"* a passage from which I quote at length (Heywood has divided it between two parts of Apuleius' gloss) to indicate the simpler introduction of the Christian parallels: "Huic invidet Venus, quasi libido; ad quam perdendam cupidinem mittit. sed quia cupiditas est boni & mali, cupiditas animam diligit, & ei velut in conjunctionem miscetur: quam persuadet ne suam faciem videat, id est, cupiditatis delectamenta discat: unde & Adam, quam vis videat nudum se, non videt, donec de concupiscentiae arbore comedat" (*Apuleivs madavirensis platonicus Opera* [Amsterdam, 1624], sig. *5ᵛ–*6ʳ).

37. To the obvious objection that Heywood is simply following his source (*Metamorphoses* VI.21–22) one must oppose the evidence of thematic intention present in the otherwise unmotivated reintroduction and elaboration of the clown at this juncture.

38. E. K. Chambers, *The Elizabethan Stage*, 4 vols. (Oxford, 1923), III, 344, notes "deifying" as a correction from the "defining" found in some copies. On the entire series of "Ages" plays see pp. 174–75 above. It is worth noticing, in the light of the opening remarks in this chapter, that although *Love's Mistress* originated as a Caroline court play (the first production at the Phoenix Theatre was attended by the royal family and presumably served as a dress rehearsal for the Denmark House spectacle [see Bentley, *Jacobean and Caroline Stage*, I, 232–33]), *The Golden Age* was written for the Red Bull soon after that house had been satirized for catering to city tastes in *The Knight of the Burning Pestle* (IV, i, 45–50): see Chambers, *Elizabethan Stage*, II, 445–48. As late as 1638 and 1639 Heywood was still—this time in a tone of pedantic instruction—euhemeristically accounting for the myths of Proteus (*Porta Pietatis*, V, 265) and of Janus (*Londini Status Pacatus*, V, 363–64) in the public context of the lord mayoralty pageants.

39. The confusion is general. Saturn is not sure whether the Titans are "Gods aboue" or "infernall" (43); when Saturn is temporarily defeated, the Titans sneer

at the "Godhead / With which the people Auee'd thee to heaven" and yet imply that they suspect he is allied with anonymous divine powers (47), and Saturn himself decides that "the Gods freely gaue me" life in order that he might be a scourge and minister to Titan's blasphemies against these anonymous forces (49). Even while he is admitting that he obeys the gods, in victory he cries "Neuer was *Saturn* deifi'd till now, / Nor found that perfectnesse the Gods enioy" (51). Cf. Jupiter, who thinks himself only aided by deities and yet greater than kings (65).

40. Cf. Chapter II, pp. 29–32, above.

41. Prosperpina does not rise with Psyche in Apuleius' *Metamorphoses*; after she has presented the box to Psyche we see no more of her until the closing pages, where we find her in the person of the omniform Isis, as noted below.

42. Cf. *Pleasant Dialogues and Dramas*, VI, 288, and *The Wise Woman of Hogsdon*, where the witchcraft aspect of the triple deity is alluded to, a note carefully subdued in *Love's Mistress*: "You inchantress, you Sorceresse, Shee-devill; you Madam Hecate, Lady Proserpine" (V, 295).

43. Adlington, *The Golden Ass*, p. 233 (*Metamorphoses* XI.5). Cf. Willi Wittmann, *Das Isisbuch des Apuleius* (Stuttgart, 1938), and the notes to Robertson's *Les métamorphoses*, III, 140–44, on Apuleius' Hellenizing assumption that Isis was primarily a lunar deity.

44. As another possible seed for the imagistic union of which Heywood has made so coherent a structure, cf. the opening argument of Apuleius' *Liber de deo Socratis*, in *Apuleivs Opera*, pp. 327–30.

45. All citations are from the text by Cyrus Hoy in *The Dramatic Works of the Beaumont and Fletcher Canon*, ed. Fredson Bowers (Cambridge, 1966); cf. I, 7. Dramatic references are to act and line numbers.

46. This Blackfriars play upon the attitudes of Globe audiences reflects whatever social fact lies behind the doubtless exaggerated account of the popular theater preserved by Edmund Gayton, *Pleasant Notes upon Don Quixot* (London, 1654), p. 271 (although it should be recalled that Gayton was born in 1608):

men come not to study at a Play-house, but love such expressions and passages, which with ease insinuate themselves into their capacities. . . . if it be on Holy dayes, when Saylers, Water-men, Shoomakers, Butchers and Apprentices are at leisure, then it is good policy to amaze those violent spirits, with some tearing Tragedy full of fights and skirmishes: As the *Guelphs and Guiblins, Greeks and Trojans*, or the three *London Apprentises*, which commonly ends in six acts, the spectators frequently mounting the stage, and making a more bloody Catastrophe amongst themselves, then the Players did. I have known upon one of these *Festivals*, . . . where the Players have been appointed, notwithstanding their bils to the contrary, to act what the major part of the company had a mind to; sometimes *Tamerlane*, sometimes *Jugurth*, sometimes the Jew of *Malta*, and sometimes parts of all these, and at last, none of the three taking, they were forc'd to undresse and put off their Tragick habits, and conclude the day with the merry milkmaides.

47. See *Narcissus: A Twelfe Night Meriment*, ed. Margaret L. Lee (London, 1893), 1–18, 78–133, 740–55, Introduction, pp. xi–xiii, xix–xxi. Cf. pp. 222–23 below.

48. It seems reasonable to conclude that it was probably a Blackfriars play of 1607: cf. *The Knight of the Burning Pestle* and *Philaster*, ed. Raymond M. Alden, Belles Lettres Series (London, 1910), pp. 166–69; Chambers, *Elizabethan Stage*, III, 220–21; Alfred Harbage, *Shakespeare and the Rival Traditions* (New York, 1952), pp. 102, 106, 348.

49. Ortega y Gasset has very interesting observations on the scene's symbolic value for dramatic illusion in *Idea del teatro* (Madrid, 1958), pp. 45–47.

50. *Don Quixote*, trans. J. M. Cohen (Middlesex, 1950), pp. 440–42.

51. On the highly developed *mariazi* and *mogliazzi* of the Italian Renaissance, see Paolo Toschi, *Le origini del teatro italiano* (Turin, 1955), pp. 413–35; on the wedding as a part of May game rituals see *ibid.*, pp. 344–58; E. K. Chambers, *Mediaeval Stage*, 2 vols. (Oxford, 1903), I, 143–44, 165, 169–74. On the not unusual displacement of May Day rituals to Midsummer's Eve see *ibid.*, p. 114, and Barber's discussion of *A Midsummer Night's Dream* in *Shakespeare's Festive Comedy*, esp. pp. 119–25.

52. If Muriel Bradbrook is correct in her reading of Laneham's letter describing the Kenilworth Entertainments of 1575 as a fictionalized account, probably by Robert Wilson the player-playwright of Leicester's Men ("Robert Laneham . . . never existed; he is a 'ghost' "), we have another document in which a theater man gives an ambiguous judgment, half-satiric, half-indulgent, upon the Hock-Tuesday "storial show" and other folk dramatics of the occasion (see *The Rise of the Common Player*, pp. 141–61).

53. Chambers, *Mediaeval Stage*, I, 51–52. Of course, there is present also the more quotidian satiric tradition scornful of the Waits' talents represented in the tavern scene of Henry Glapthorne's *Wit in a Constable*, act V. Master Humphrey, the citizen-suitor of "*The London Merchant*" inner play, is equally festival-conscious. In comic metaphor he can think of no intenser description of his passion than that it could "put to flight / Even that great watch of Mid-summer Day at night" (I, 136–37).

54. *The Anatomie of Abuses* (1583), ed. F. V. Furnival (London, 1877–82), p. 149.

55. *Le origini del teatro italiano*, p. 17. A very detailed scheme of genres and masks organized in view of their ritual origins can be found useful by students of English dramatic forms as well: see pp. 71–73.

56. *Ibid.*, p. 452.

57. *Ibid.*, pp. 501–53, esp. 521, on the morris dance and the *Maggi*; I draw the titles from p. 524. Much detail is available in Bianca Maria Galanti, *La danza della spada in Italia*, Studi e Testi di Tradizioni Popolari, No. 2 (Rome, 1942).

58. Chambers, *Mediaeval Stage*, I, 182–227, esp. pp. 190–91, 207; and the recent and authoritative Alan Brody, *The English Mummers and Their Play: Traces of Ancient Mystery* (Philadelphia, 1969). In passing, it may be pointed out that Chambers (see pp. 192, 199n) was unaware of the diabolic buffoon whose legacy was the inevitable grotesque (often the "Bessy") of the sword dance as well as Arlecchino (cf. Toschi, *Le origini del teatro italiano*, pp. 166–277, 514–18). The point will become significant in respect to *The Knight of the Burning Pestle* in the course of our discussion.

59. *The Anatomie of Abuses*, p. 149.

60. Toschi, *Le origini del teatro italiano*, pp. 498–99.

61. Chambers, *Mediaeval Stage*, I, 206–14.

CHAPTER SEVEN

1. See Chapter I, pp. 23–24, above.

2. *Genealogia de gli Dei* (Venice, 1627), pp. 21–22.

3. *Della difesa della Comedia di Dante* (Cesena, 1587), pp. 176–96 (hereafter cited as *Difesa*); facing the last page there is a chart of medical and what Mazzoni calls "scholastic" classifications not far different from Boccaccio's ordering. The documents in the "quarrel over Dante" have themselves been exhaustively classified in Bernard Weinberg, *A History of Literary Criticism in the Italian Renaissance*

(Chicago, 1961), II, 819–911, and in Aldo Vallone, *L'Interpretazione di Dante nel Cinquecento: studi e ricerche*, 2nd ed., Biblioteca dell' "Archivum Romanicum," Ser. 1, Vol. 97 (Florence, 1969), and are more synthetically organized around rival conceptions of the imagination in Baxter Hathaway, *The Age of Criticism: The Late Renaissance in Italy* (Ithaca, N.Y., 1962), pp. 349–89. Michele Barbi, *Della fortuna di Dante nel secolo XVI* (Pisa, 1890), pp. 36–37, gives the most detailed chronological history of the stages consequent upon Castravilla's attack and Mazzoni's first defense. He also prints Belisario Bulgarini's correspondence over almost twenty years concerning his replies to Mazzoni (pp. 327–53). An annotated bibliography of items constituting the entire debate is in Colomb de Batines, *Bibliografia Dantesca* (Prato, 1845), I, 419–37.

4. One would be more insistent about the historic effect of Ficino thus indirectly coming to bear upon the analyses of the dream in art were it not that Benivieni's comment appears in a manuscript (Marucelliana A. 137) written in his advanced years (1525–1542), long after he had moved from under the shadow of Ficino to that of Pico and ultimately Savonarola: see Arnoldo Della Torre, *Storia dell'Accademia Platonica di Firenze* (Florence, 1902), pp. 691, 759–66 (but also see Benivieni's moving letter defending the Careggi meetings against accusations of magic and occultism, written in 1515 in Raymond Marcel, *Marsile Ficin* [Paris, 1958], pp. 540–42).

5. Quoted by Weinberg, *Literary Criticism in the Italian Renaissance*, II, 821; cf. 820–21 and the note on provenance, p. 1117.

6. Cf. Jacopo Mazzoni, *Discorso . . . in difesa della "Commedia" del divino poeta Dante* (1572), ed. Mario Rossi, Collezione di opuscoli Danteschi inediti o rari, Vols. 51–52 (Florence, 1898), pp. 66–67. All text references are from this edition, hereafter cited as *Discorso*.

7. *Poetica d'Aristotele Vulgarizzata, et Sposta*, Poetiken des Cinquecento, 1 (Vienna, 1570; rpt. Munich, 1968), p. 261.

8. Speculations on identification are summarized and evaluated in Barbi, *Fortuna di Dante*, pp. 38–52.

9. Cf. Weinberg, *Literary Criticism in the Italian Renaissance*, pp. 831–34, on Castravilla's attack upon both the epic and the satiric aspects of Dante's poem, and pp. 1121–22, for the extant MSS. The earliest printed publication came after the debate had finished, under the auspices of Bellisario Bulgarini, in *Annotazioni, ovvero Chiose Marginali* (Siena, 1608).

10. Weinberg, *Literary Criticism in the Italian Renaissance*, pp. 834–35. The treatise was enthusiastically received by members of the Accademia Fiorentina; Castravilla, on the other hand, was savaged in brutal satire by Antonfrancesco Grazzini: see Pierantonio Serassi, *Vita di Jacopo Mazzoni* (Rome, 1790), pp. 19–23, and Grazzini's "A Ridolfo Castrovilla" in *Le rime burlesche, edite ed inedite di Antonfrancesco Grazzini*, ed. Carlo Verzone (Florence, 1882), pp. 98–99.

11. Serassi, *Vita di Mazzoni*, pp. 55–56, 66–68.

12. *Ibid.*, pp. 76–78; Marcello Vannucci, *Dante nella Firenze del' 500: studi danteschi dell'Accademia Fiorentina* (Florence, 1965), p. 61.

13. See pp. 90–92 above.

14. Torquato Tasso accepted Mazzoni's view that *La commedia* was the imitation of an "azione de l'intelletto, la contemplazione," since it would be unworthy of a poet to imitate a dream on Platonic grounds: "because the Idea stands in the first level of truth, in the second stand the natural form and the thing itself, in the third its imitation or image. But the imitator who imitates not a true action but a dream, the image [dream] being further from the truth than the action, would as a consequence be more imperfect; nor can one conclude otherwise according to the doctrine of Plato, although Synesius may have written that fictions had their beginning in

dreams and that it is not unsuitable that the dream should be the end of fiction, as it is the origin" (*Discorsi del Poema Eroico*, in *Prose*, ed. Ettore Mazzali [Milan, 1959], pp. 494–95). The *Discorsi*, published only in 1594, were largely the reconstruction of his *Discorsi dell'arte poetica*, a reconstruction which Tasso began and nearly completed immediately following publication of the earlier version in 1587. Therefore, the interpolation of the defense of Dante's dream form is an immediate reaction to Mazzoni's own 1587 *Difesa*. The two were admiring friends who in 1574 carried on a famous debate on the heroic poem and drama for the pleasure of the court of Urbino during carnival season in Pesato: see Serassi, *Vita di Mazzoni*, pp. 23–26. Tasso alludes to the influence of Mazzoni's book upon the revised *Discorsi* on pp. 524–25.

15. "Poscia che non è imitatione di fauola alcuna, ma solamente vna narratione d'vn sogno fatto da lui" (*Discorso*, p. 61). Castravilla's actual argument that Dante's is no poem by Aristotelian standards because it is not an imitation runs thus: "la 'Comedia' di Dante non sia imitazione d'azione . . . poi che né quella che Dante referisce in quell'opera è una azione, ma uno insogno; né quel tale insogno è da lui imitato, ma raccontato. Che quel di Dante sia uno insogno, o una visione, o una fantasia si deduce dalle parole medesime di quell' opera . . . propii de' somnianti, come *'parea'* et simili. Che tal sogno non sia da Dante espresso per imitazione è manifesto, poi che egli non induce una persona . . . ma parla sempre l'autore, e sempre in persona propria" (*I Discorsi di Ridolfo Castravilla contro Dante*, ed. Mario Rossi, Collezione di opusculi Danteschi inediti o rari, Vols. 40–41 [Florence, 1897], pp. 21–22).

16. "Da tutti questi luoghi assai manifestamente, s'io non m'inganno, può apparire che 'l poema di Dante non è narratione d'vn sogno finto; ma sí bene vna imitatione dell'attioni, ch'egli finse di fare, desto, in questo suo viaggio" (*Discorso*, p. 64).

17. The conception of the life-as-dream metaphor serving as formal (as well as philosophic) envelope for Dante's *Commedia* is raised by Mazzoni when he discusses "nel mezzo del camin di nostra vita" as the sleep with which life is half-occupied, upon the authority of the *Ethics*: see *Discorso*, pp. 61–62; *Difesa*, pp. 196–97.

18. "Però che metaforicamente chiamò il suo poema sogno. . . . E se, come appare, questa [nautica] metafora è lecita, é molto più lecita quella del sogno, poscia che 'l sogno e la poesia sono fondati in vna medesima potentia dell'anima, perciò chè e l'vno e l'altro ha per suggetto la fantasia. Onde quel valent'huomo in questo proposito fece vna di quelle metafore ch'Aristotile chiamò nella *Poetica* metafore per proportione, cioè che la poesia era vn sogno d'huomini desti, e 'l sonno [sic] era la poesia d'huomini dormentati" (*Discorso*, pp. 67–68). Bulgarini in passing seems to question this psycho-physiology in *Alcvne considerazioni . . . Sopra 'l Discorso di M. Giacopo Mazzoni, Fatto in difesa della Comedia di Dante* (Siena, 1583), pp. 35–36, a passage in which he also skeptically wonders who this *valent'huomo* might be. In the extended *Difesa* of 1587 (pp. 197–99) Mazzoni exhaustively cites the authority of Aristotle, Synesius (who, on the powers of reveries and dreams, is close to Mazzoni on poetry when he says, "all this is in the waking state of the dreamer, or the dream of the awakened, for in each the underlying thing concurs, i.e., the fantasy" [Migne, *PG*, LXVI, 1305c]), Pausanius, Plutarch, and others on the fantasy and attributes his quotation to Plutarch. Now, however, he adds a remark which may have gotten to the ear of Shakespeare's Duke Theseus, if we are correct in assuming that the poet was a late addition to the speech on the creative imagination of the lunatic, the lover, and the poet (*Midsummer Night's Dream*, V, i, 1–22): "E non come dicono alcuni le Phantasie de Poeti per l'efficacia loro sono sogni: ma egli è piùtosto vero delle Phantasie de gli amanti" ("And it is not [true], as some say, that the fantasies of poets are as inefficacious as dreams; this is rather true of lover's fantasies") (*Difesa*, p. 198).

19. Cf. Bulgarini, *Alcvne considerazioni*, pp. 28–40; and *Repliche . . . alle risposte del Orazio Capponi sopra . . . Sue Considerazioni, intorno al Discorso di M. Giacopo Mazzoni* (Siena, 1585), pp. 84–93, esp. 90–91, where he insists that only the *Commedia* true dream metaphor is in question, and p. 93, where he agrees that other poets may modestly call their poems trifles or caprices, etc., but never *farnetichi* ("frenzies"), as Mazzoni believes; see also his *Difese di . . . Bulgarini in risposta all'apologia, e palinodia di Monsig. Alessandro Cariero* (Siena, 1588), pp. 35–43. Cariero was not a Mazzonian but an "ally," whom Bulgarini accused of plagiarizing his own manuscript attacks on Dante written soon after Mazzoni's original *Discorso*: see Serassi, *Vita di Mazzoni*, pp. 67–68, and Weinberg, *Literary Criticism in the Italian Renaissance*, II, 861–65. The views on dream metaphor in his *Breue et ingenioso discorso contra l'opera di Dante* (Padua, 1582) are almost identical with those so frequently expressed by Bulgarini. Not only Mazzoni in the *Discorso* but others in manuscript replies to Castravilla had affirmed the legitimacy of the dream metaphor (Weinberg cites Antonio degli Albizzi's lecture before the Accademia degli Alterati in Florence in 1573 and Filippo Sassetti's lecture to the same group at about this time [*Literary Criticism in the Italian Renaissance*, II, 840–41, 844]), but it remained for Mazzoni to exhaust the matter with the arsenal of authorities and aspects which he introduced when he arrived at the dream form in his *Difesa*, pp. 159–211.

20. *Difesa*, pp. 206–7.

21. *In Difesa Della Lingva Fiorentina, Et Di Dante* (Florence, 1556), p. 52, cited by Weinberg, *Literary Criticism in the Italian Renaissance*, II, 824; cf. 823–25. Cf. Vallone, *L'Interpretazione di Dante*, pp. 188–91. Vallone also draws attention to the Platonizing "Il Lenzone," a dialogue in the anonymous *I Ragionamenti Accademici sopra alcuni luoghi difficili di Dante* (Florence, 1567), in which Lenzoni is the major speaker and Ficino and Alberti are cited as revered authorities by the Accademici Fiorentini.

22. Giovan Batista Gelli was later to give the Academy a more circumstantial account of Dante's dramatic heritage through Plautus and Terence: see his *Lettere edite ed inedite sopra la commedia di Dante*, ed. C. Negroni (Florence, 1887), I, 39–42. Cf. Vannucci, *Dante nella Firenze del '500*, pp. 43–45.

23. *Discorso*, pp. 89–90. Antonio degli Albizzi's rebuttal of Castravilla before the Accademia degli Alterati in 1573 made a similar distinction, although he was less certain about genres: "non fà di mestiero sapere chi fosse Dante ueramente, et di che conditione, ma quale, et di che costumi ei sia nel poema introdotto" (cited by Weinberg, *Literary Criticism in the Italian Renaissance*, II, 840–41). Mazzoni probably is tacitly responding to Castelvetro's flat assumption, in his recently published commentary on the *Poetics*, that the poet of tragedy cannot enter into the tragedy itself on the same principle of realistic mimesis for the maintenance of illusion which ruled against prologues. He denies that "vogliamo che la persona narrante che è il poeta conseruando la sua persona di narrante trapassi dal modo narratiuo al rappresentatiuo percioche con parole senza fare veramente vedere nuoua persona induce altrui in atto a parlare" (*Poetica d'Aristotele Vulgarizzata*, p. 60ʳ). On prologues cf. pp. 79–80 above. Tommaso Campanella was still quite specific at the close of the century: "mai parla il poeta" in tragedy (*Poetica*, ed. Luigi Firpo [Rome, 1944], pp. 186, 130), and the *Commedia* was written to be read, not represented (pp. 193, 138).

24. *Alcvne considerazioni*, pp. 62–63; cf. pp. 57–63. Cf. also Bulgarini's return to the same argument in *Repliche . . . alle risposte del Capponi*, pp. 74–80; *Risposte . . . a' ragionamenti del Sig. Ieronimo Zoppio* (Siena, 1586), pp. 31–35, 158–66; *Difese . . . in risposta all'apologia, e palinodia di Cariero* (Siena, 1588), pp. 35–43.

25. P. 278.

26. Biblioteca Nazionale di Firenze MS. VI, 164, fol. 17, cited in Weinberg,

Literary Criticism in the Italian Renaissance, II, 892–94. The exchange of letters occurred in March, 1589.

27. For a diary of literary discussions held by this academy, including two defenses of Dante by Rinuccini, reproduced from Ashburniano MS. 558 of the Biblioteca Laurenziana in Florence, see Bernard Weinberg, "Argomenti di Discussione Letteraria nell'Accademia degli Alterati (1570–1600)," *GSLI,* 131 (1954), 157–94. Cf. Weinberg, *Literary Criticism in the Italian Renaissance,* II, 837–41, on the Alterati, and pp. 884–87 on Rinuccini.

28. Ashburniano MS. 562 of the Biblioteca Laurenziana in Florence contains Rinuccini's notes bound with several other MSS. On a separate sheet and also at the top of p. 1 it is titled, with almost Dantesque pride in its subject, *"Maggiorente,"* i.e., "the great one."

29. "In somma non ti scordar mai che' segue come Poeta non il uero, ma il uerisimile, l'universale, quel che si dice, e non ti muoua il dire, queste cose non mi muouono perch'io so che non son uere, che ne ancor la sua gita, ne nulla di quel poema ti mouerebbe, anzi le Commedie che si sa certo che rappresenton cosa e nomi che non furno mai non opererebbone in noi cosa ueruna" (fol. 6). Unhappily, I can neither here nor elsewhere in the manuscript locate a passage to support entirely Weinberg's exciting assertion that Rinuccini "goes so far as to say that such fictions are moving because they are not true" (*Literary Criticism in the Italian Renaissance,* II, 887). However, he may have been thinking of such passages as this on verisimilitude and "knowledge": "Puossi ancora dire che i piu non sanno se è fu ò non fu, e che [per] questi è scritta la poesia, ma che ne possono sapere gli scienzati? non si sa egli che Orlando fu? che Giove fu? e se bene si tien per fermo che è non facessero quelle gran cosa, non è percio che e non ne fusse qualche cosa che cosa poteua dir di piu forza piu intelligibile e piu persuadibile" (fol. 10).

30. See Ernest Schanzer, "The Moon and the Fairies in *A Midsummer Night's Dream, UTQ,* 24 (1955), 234–46.

31. II, i, 111–14. All references are to the text in *Complete Works,* ed. Hardin Craig (Chicago, 1951).

32. In regarding Oberon's petition that

> Never mole, hare-lip, nor scar,
> Nor mark prodigious, such as are
> Despised in nativity,
> Shall upon their children be (V, i, 418–21)

Minor White Latham observes that Shakespeare inverts "the fairies' passion for stealing human children from their cradles and their known practice of disfiguring them with withered arms and elvish marks is changed into an excessive solicitude about the welfare of babies. Even the changeling in *A Midsummer Night's Dream* has not been obtained by violence and human woe. He has been adopted by Titania out of friendship for his mother" (*The Elizabethan Fairies* [New York, 1930], p. 183; cf. pp. 148–62, 176–97). The emphasis here upon Shakespeare's originality in this respect, however, should be corrected by the more informed folklore background provided by K. M. Briggs, *The Anatomy of Puck* (London, 1959), pp. 44–55.

33. C. L. Barber, *Shakespeare's Festive Comedy* (Princeton, N.J., 1959), pp. 119–62, provides the standard study of the play's derivation and elements; see pp. 119–21 on May Day and Midsummer. Of particular interest because it draws together some implications of the relationship between folk fairy beliefs and the conception of the creative imagination in both *Midsummer Night's Dream* and *The Tempest* is Robert Weimann's essay on these plays in *Phantasie und Nachahmung: Drei Studien zum Verhältnis von Dichtung, Utopie und Mythos* (Halle, 1970), pp. 68–90. Cf. also James E. Robinson, "The Ritual and Rhetoric of *A Midsummer Night's Dream,"*

PMLA, 83 (1968), 380–91. Certainly May Day is most conspicuous, but we have been shown how Midsummer associations "extend the natural so as to accommodate madness, mystery, and the super-natural in the form of the spirits" (David P. Young, *Something of Great Constancy: The Art of A Midsummer Night's Dream* [New Haven, Conn. 1966], pp. 20–24). Also, it would seem that Lanthorn-Moon and the moonlight washing of the eyes with flowers represent direct Midsummer elements (see Joseph Strutt, *The Sports and Pastimes of the People of England*, ed. William Hone [London, 1876], pp. 462–64), while Midsummer celebrations, too, were dominated by make-believe animals, such as Shakespeare's emphatic ass and lion (*ibid.*, pp. 30–32). Bottom's metamorphosis, of course, has also been traced quite rightly to Apuleius (and is enveloped in a theory of the creative imagination which will remind the reader of the internal discussions of Heywood's Midas and Apuleius in *Love's Mistress*): see Sister M. Generosa, "Apuleius and *A Midsummer Night's Dream*: Analogue or Source, Which?," *SP*, 42 (1945), 198–204; a broader analysis of the utilization of the *Metamorphoses* is in D. T. Starnes, "Shakespeare and Apuleius," *PMLA*, 60 (1945), 1021–50, esp. 1030–32; and the remarks by Frank Kermode, "The Mature Comedies," in *The Early Shakespeare*, Shakespeare Institute Studies, 3, ed. John Russell Brown and Bernard Harris (New York, 1966), pp. 214–20. Cf. also, however, Robert R. Reed, Jr., "Nick Bottom, Dr. Faustus, and the Ass's Head," *N&Q*, 204 (1959), 252–54. Interesting is Sears Jayne, "The Dreaming of *The Shrew*," *SQ*, 17 (1966), 41–56, which, in controversially treating the entire inner play as Sly's dream, draws parallels with *Midsummer Night's Dream* and includes a bibliography of Renaissance dream treatises. Robert Presson examines some of Shakespeare's developments of typical dreams from simpler sources in "Two Types of Dreams in the Elizabethan Drama, and Their Heritage: *Somnium Animale* and the Prick of Conscience," *SEL*, 7 (1967), 239–56.

34. Richard Cody, *The Landscape of the Mind: Pastoralism and Platonic Theory in Tasso's Aminta and Shakespeare's Early Comedies* (Oxford, 1969), argues Shakespeare's adoption of "the attitudes and vocabulary of Florentine Platonism" in the early comedies (p. 87) and a Platonized *"serio ludere"* interpretation of dreams in *Midsummer Night's Dream* in particular (pp. 142–46). John Vyvyan, *Shakespeare and Platonic Beauty* (London, 1961), argues Florentine influence less seriously. The thesis is attractive historically in the light of the debt of Chapman to Ficino. Professor Cody's development, however, rests more upon interpolation of earlier paradoxes of mythological unions than upon interpretation of those found within the text. Further, his basic thesis concerning the union of pastoral and Platonic in Renaissance drama is based on a misunderstanding of Guarini's revolutionary restructuring of the genre; see the Appendix for further discussion of this point and cf. *Landscape of the Mind*, pp. 81–82.

35. The set speech is historically all the more tantalizing as a possible direct reflection of the Dante debate when we recall that the discussion of the poet was somehow inserted late, as a catalyzing afterthought. See n. 18 above and E. K. Chambers, *William Shakespeare: A Study of Facts and Problems* (Oxford, 1930), I, 360–61. The mislineation is in all early editions, but differs slightly in Q1 from Q2 and F1, which agree.

36. Howard Nemerov, "The Marriage of Theseus and Hippolyta," *KR*, 18 (1956), 633–41, has some remarks on the relevance of the exchange to poetic theory, remarks much extended by J. A. Bryant, Jr., *Hippolyta's View: Some Christian Aspects of Shakespeare's Plays* (Lexington, Ky., 1961), 1–18; cf. Young, *Something of Great Constancy*, pp. 115–26, 137–40; Elizabeth Sewell, *The Orphic Voice* (New Haven, Conn., 1960), pp. 110–16.

37. At the level of narrative confusion implemented by dreams, one notes the sanction of Castelvetro, who bases comic laughter in varied types of *inganni*, a list of sources for error which sounds suspiciously under the influence of Ariosto's

suppositi, but which includes "inganni che procedono . . . o per sogno o per farnetico" (*Poetica d'Aristotele Vulgarizzata*, p. 51ᵛ).

38. *Narcissus: A Twelfe Night Merriment played by youths of the parish at the College of St. John the Baptist in Oxford, A.D. 1602*, ed. Margaret L. Lee (London, 1893), 494–511. For the play's provenance as a university production and a detailed comparison with *A Midsummer Night's Dream*, see Frederick S. Boas, *University Drama in the Tudor Age* (Oxford, 1914), pp. 278–85.

39. This is, of course, the solution accepted, and when the playlet is presented in act V, not only do Snug and "Wall" continually remind the audience of their roles, but Bottom carries theory past the limits of drama to step in and out of the play and keep the audience informed of what is to come in an *ex tempore* running interchange. "Moon" reduces the theory of mimetic symbolism to equal absurdity when he finally becomes so literal as to annihilate imagination: "All that I have to say is, to tell you that the lanthorn is the moon; I, the man in the moon; this thorn-bush, my thorn-bush; and this dog, my dog" (V, i, 261–63).

40. "Induction," ll. 230–33. All quotations are from the text of *Ben Jonson*, ed. C. H. Herford and P. and E. Simpson, 11 vols. (Oxford, 1925–52). Thelma N. Greenfield, *The Induction in Elizabethan Drama* (Eugene, Ore., 1969), pp. 72–83, examines Jonson's influence upon "critical" prologues.

41. Cf. II, iii, 314–15; III, viii, 98–102; III, ix, 153–54; IV, viii, 175–82; V, iii, 92–93; V, ix, 4. A late Jonsonian play has been analyzed as an exploration of illusion in life through the techniques of dramatic illusion-breaking in Harriet Hawkins, "The Idea of a Theater in Jonson's *The New Inn*," *Renaissance Drama IX* (Evanston, Ill., 1966), pp. 205–26.

42. Herford and Simpson (*Ben Jonson*, IX, 475) trace the scene to Fynes Moryson's account of Dutch drinking (*Itinerary*, III, ii, 4, 99). I have found no identical *lazzi*, but cf. the chaotic exchange drinking in "Il Lazzo della Caracolla," preserved in the eighteenth-century manuscript collection of *concetti comici* of P. D. Placido Adriani (Vito Pandolfi, *La commedia dell'arte: storia e testo* [Florence, 1957–61], IV, 274).

43. The term "spectator" is itself recurrent: Induction, ll. 52, 136; II, i, 141; II, iii, 300–301; III, iii, 73–74.

44. "Maciliente his Character," prefatory to the dramatic text proper (*Ben Jonson*, III, 423).

45. Alvin Kernan, *The Cankered Muse: Satire of the English Renaissance* (New Haven, Conn., 1959), pp. 14–30.

46. *Ibid.*, pp. 161–62. Cf. 137–38, 158–63.

47. Oscar J. Campbell, *Comicall Satyre and Shakespeare's* Troilus and Cressida (San Marino, Calif., 1938), pp. 79–80, emphasized the Buffone-Macilente split as being characteristic of the satiric norm set up in drama after verse satire was banned, while missing the significance of the Asper-Macilente relationship. Robert C. Jones, "The Satirist's Retirement in Jonson's 'Apologetical Dialogue,'" *ELH*, 34 (1967), 447–67, errs interestingly in the other direction while discussing Jonson's own ambivalence toward the satirist's audience, and ignores Buffone while separating a (Jonson?-)Asper poet from a Macilente "satirist."

48. Buffone, in closing the Induction, advises the audience: "if any here be thirsty for it [his bottle], their best way . . . is, sit still, seale vp their lips, and drinke so much of the play, in at their eares" (351–53).

49. *Conversations with Drummond*, l. 681, in *Ben Jonson*, I, 151. Jonson, of course, openly boasted of the myth in having his alter ego Horace described in *Poetaster* as one who "will sooner lose his best friend, then his least iest" (IV, iii, 110–11).

50. Leicester Bradner, *Musae Anglicanae: A History of Anglo-Latin Poetry, 1500–1925* (New York, 1940); Hoyt Hudson, *The Epigram in the English Renaissance*

(Princeton, N.J., 1947); Austin Warren, *Richard Crashaw* (Baton Rouge, La., 1939), pp. 77–90.

51. *Epigrams,* ed. and trans. Walter C. A. Ker (London, 1919), Epistle Introductory to Book II.

52. See esp. I. 117; II. 90; III. 95; IX. 18, 97; X. 65, 103. I am aware that much of our "knowledge" of Martial is based upon subjective evaluations of this or that passage as ringing autobiographically true, evaluations which sometimes can lead into contradictory positions: see Ker's introduction to *Epigrams,* I, xii.

53. For instance, in Sir Thomas More's *Epigrammata* (expanded edition of 1520) the only "personal" pieces are the Brixius group and a few scattered dedications and epitaphs, the whole constituting only fifteen items in a collection of more than two hundred and fifty.

54. George Puttenham, *The Arte of Englishe Poesie* (1589), in *Elizabethan Critical Essays,* ed. G. Gregory Smith (Oxford, 1904), II, 56.

55. See esp. 1–3, 14, 17–18, 22, 28, 36, 43, 45, 49, 52.

56. Wesley Trimpi, *Ben Jonson's Poems: A Study of the Plain Style* (Stanford, Calif., 1962), 167–90, comments on Jonson's "personal" style in the epigram and attributes the quality to the plain style, an English *genus humile.* But Trimpi's argument has been severely questioned by Arnold Stein, "Plain Style, Plain Criticism, Plain Dealing, and Ben Jonson," *ELH,* 30 (1963), 306–16.

57. Douglas Duncan, "A Guide to *The New Inn,*" *EC,* 20 (1970), 311–26, argues persuasively for the divided presentation of an image of Jonson the comic poet as the idealist Lovel and as the ironist Host of *The New Inn.* Cf. the discussion of Jonson's dramatization of himself in the masques in Chapter IV, pp. 113–16, above.

58. Induction, ll. 96–108:

> what soe're hath fluxure, and humiditie,
> As wanting power to containe it selfe,
> Is Humour. So in euery humane body,
> The choller, melancholy, flegme, and bloud,
> By reason that they flow continually
> In some one part . . . Receiue the name of Humours. Now thus farre
> It may, by *Metaphore,* apply it selfe
> Vnto the generall disposition:
> As when some one peculiar quality
> . . . doth draw
> All his affects, his spirits, and his powers,
> In their confluctions, all to runne one way.

59. Chrisoganus, in *Histriomastix,* identified on more general grounds with Jonson (in addition to the earlier studies by Penniman and Small, the point is made again in Henryk Zbierski, *Shakespeare and the "War of the Theatres": A Reinterpretation* [Poznan, 1957], p. 41), parodies precisely the dissolution imagery which binds Asper and Macilente (*Plays of John Marston* [London, 1934–39], ed. M. Harvey Wood, III, 281):

> The poor Chrisoganus, who'le envy thee,
> Whose dusky fortune hath no shining glosse
> That *Envies* breath can blast? . . .
> . . . .
> O! I could wish my selfe consum'd in aire.

60. *Discoveries,* ll. 1093–99, in *Ben Jonson,* VIII, 597.

61. *Ibid.,* ll. 1100–1109.

62. Cf., among other studies, the overlapping chorus of confirmations which rises even out of the debates in E. M. W. Tillyard, *Shakespeare's Last Plays* (London, 1938); S. L. Bethell, *The Winter's Tale* (London, 1947), esp. pp. 71–76; Arthur Sewell, *Character and Society in Shakespeare* (Oxford, 1951), pp. 122–45; Derek Traversi, *Shakespeare: The Last Phase* (Stanford, Calif., 1954); H. M. V. Matthews, *Character and Symbol in Shakespeare's Plays* (Cambridge, 1962), pp. 179–208; Frank Kermode, *Shakespeare: The Final Plays* (London, 1963); Northrop Frye, *A Natural Perspective* (New York, 1965). The original impetus, of course, arose from G. Wilson Knight's 1929 essay *Myth and Miracle*, incorporated and expanded in *The Crown of Life* (Oxford, 1947).

63. Allusions include Paul's shipwreck upon Malta; Acts 27:34 is called up twice at I, ii, 30–31, 217–19. See the annotations in *The Tempest*, ed. Frank Kermode (New Arden ed.; London, 1954). All citations are from this edition.

64. On the Fortunate Fall, see the comments by Kermode in his introduction to *The Tempest*, pp. xxix–xxx, and *Final Plays*, pp. 39–42. Cf. *Cymbeline* (ed. J. M. Nosworthy [New Arden ed.; London, 1955], IV, ii, 403), where Lucius reassures the grieving Imogen: "Some falls are means the happier to rise." Jupiter in Posthumus' dream vision echoes the trope:

> Whom best I love, I cross; to make my gift,
> The more delay'd, delighted. Be content,
> Your low-laid son our godhead will uplift. (V, iv, 101–3)

65. A few supporting observations may merit mention. First, Gonzalo's failure in "authority" over "nature" has earlier been challenged by the Boatswain in the tempest scene (I, i, 19–27). Second, the plot balances several versions of isolated naïveté against each other. Thinking the island their inheritance *because* it is isolated, the fool and drunkard, depraved and unnatural, cry hopefully to Caliban (sired by the devil): "O brave monster! lead the way" (II, ii, 188). From the ignorance of her isolation Miranda looks out over the fallen humanity of the Neapolitan group with equally blithe expectations in her "O brave new world" ejaculation, which is placed in the perspective of experience by Prospero's "'Tis new to thee" (V, i, 182–84). Finally, we may measure the limitations of such idyllic isolation against the explicit debate between Belarius and his wards in *Cymbeline*, III, iii, 10–103.

66. On vain curiosity as self-isolation in one's studies, see Paul H. Kocher, *Science and Religion in Elizabethan England* (San Marino, Calif., 1953), pp. 72–76; Howard Schultz, *Milton and Forbidden Knowledge* (New York, 1955); there is also considerable discussion of Shakespeare and the tradition in Gordon Worth O'Brien, *Renaissance Poetics and the Problem of Power* (Chicago, 1956), pp. 1–56.

67. Prospero's manipulation has looked to this end from the beginning: "My charms I'll break, their senses I'll restore, / And they shall be themselves" (V, i, 31–32).

68. There are valuable observations upon the unregenerate in *The Tempest* and upon the "indestructibility of evil" in Robert Grams Hunter, *Shakespeare and the Comedy of Forgiveness* (New York, 1965), pp. 239–41.

69. Notice the image with which we learn that Plato's philosophers will naturally attempt to ignore their duty to rule, as Prospero does: "they will not act at all except upon compulsion, fancying that they are already dwelling apart in the islands of the blest" (*Republic.* VII [519]).

70. Cf. Traversi, *Shakespeare, the Last Phase*, pp. 206–16, 240, 244–48, on the awakening, especially in relation to Miranda and Alonso.

71. Cf. Anne Righter, *Shakespeare and the Idea of the Play* (London, 1962), pp. 192–94.

72. *Pericles*, ed. F. D. Hoeniger (New Arden ed.; London, 1963), V, i, 161–62; cf. IV, vi, 103, and V, i, 228–63, which recount the dream of Diana mentioned below.

73. IV, ii, 291–332.

74. V, iv, 146–50; cf. IV, ii, 345–53.

75. Cf. Don Cameron Allen, *Image and Meaning: Metaphoric Traditions in Renaissance Poetry* (Baltimore, 1960), p. 61 of his essay on *topoi* of ephemerality in *The Tempest*; D. G. James, *The Dream of Prospero* (Oxford, 1967), pp. 134–53; and Alan Hobson, *Full Circle: Shakespeare and Moral Development* (London, 1972), pp. 78–98.

76. Ferdinand Neri, *Scenari delle maschere in Arcadia* (Città di Castello, 1913); Henry David Gray, "The Sources of *The Tempest*," *MLN*, 35 (1920), 321–30; K. M. Lea, *Italian Popular Comedy: A Study in the Commedia dell'arte, 1560–1620 with Special Reference to the English Stage* (London, 1934), II, 443–53; Valentina Capocci, *Genio e mestiere: Shakespeare e la commedia dell'arte* (Bari, 1950); Allardyce Nicoll, *The World of Harlequin* (Cambridge, 1963), pp. 118–20; Sharon L. Smith, "The Commedia dell'arte and Problems Related to Source in *The Tempest*," *Emporia State Research Studies*, 13 (1964), 11–23.

77. Enid Welsford, *The Court Masque* (Cambridge, 1927), pp. 324–49, climaxes her discussion of the form with an examination of *The Tempest*, in which "we experience not only what the masque was, but what it might have been." Cf. Kermode's introduction to *The Tempest*, pp. lxxi–lxxvi; *Final Plays*, pp. 43–49; Righter, *Shakespeare and the Idea of the Play*, pp. 201–5; Robert J. Nelson, *Play within a Play* (New Haven, Conn., 1958), pp. 30–35.

CHAPTER VIII

1. Cf. George T. Northrup, "*Los yerros de naturaleza y aciertos de la fortuna*, by Don Antonio Coello and Don Pedro Calderón la Barca," *RR*, 1 (1910), 411–25, and the fuller analysis in Albert E. Sloman, *The Dramatic Craftsmanship of Calderón* (Oxford, 1958), pp. 250–77; J. A. Van Praag, "*Eustorgio y Clorilene*: Historia Moscovica," *BH*, 41 (1939), 236–65, esp. 240–41, and J. A. Van Praag, "Un Fuente de *La vida es sueño*," *Neophilologus*, 25 (1940), 250–51. Cesáreo Bandera, "El itinerario de Segismundo en *La vida es sueño*," *HR*, 35 (1967), 69–84, reads some of the same matter with medieval spectacles.

2. Northrup, *Los yerros de naturaleza*, p. 422, gathers evidence for these being stock names.

3. *Ibid.*, p. 423.

4. Vittorio Bodini, *Segni e simboli nella "Vida es sueño"* (Bari, 1968), p. 7.

5. Coriolano, in *Las armas de la hermosura*, cited in Farinelli, *La vita è un sogno* (Turin, 1916), I, 237; cf. II, 165–66.

6. Juan de Torres, *Philosophía moral de príncipes para su buena criança y gouierno* (1602), cited in *ibid.*, II, 364.

7. Suggested in the essays of Michele F. Sciacca, "Verdad y sueño de 'La vida es sueño' de Calderón de la Barca," *Clavileño*, 1, no. 5 (1950), 1–9, and "Verità e sogno, un' interpretazione della 'Vida es sueño,'" *Humanitas*, 6 (1951), 472–85. Sciacca's sketches of Platonic parallels drew little reaction. Anton L. Constandse, *Le Baroque et Calderón de la Barca* (Amsterdam, 1951), pp. 76–88, made a negative critique, and Otis H. Green, *Spain and the Western Tradition* (Madison, Wis., 1963), I, 258–63, preferred to see Calderón's tradition as that of *dolce stil nuovo* lovers, Platonic but in contradistinction to Plato.

8. *De las vicisitudes de la filosofía platónica en España* (1889), in *Edición nacional de las obras completas* (Madrid, 1948), XLIII, pp. 9–115.

9. *Opera* (Basel, 1576), p. 1411.

10. All translations are from Jowett, with Stephanus numbers.

11. Ll. 1901–2. Quotations are from the text of Everett W. Hesse (New York, 1961).

12. Cf. n. 2 above and William W. Whitby, "Rosaura's Role in the Structure of *La vida es sueño*" in Bruce W. Wardropper, ed., *Critical Essays on the Theatre of Calderon* (New York, 1965), pp. 101–13, esp. 107, n. 13 (reprinted from *HR*).

13. Calderón explicitly confirms this interpretation when, with Segismundo's final revolt, Estrella sees Poland as a place in which "cada edificio es un sepulcro altivo, / cada soldado un esqueleto vivo" (2474–75) ("each building is a proud sepulcher, / each soldier a living skeleton").

14. Yet, of course, Clotaldo's instinct is right: he does sense Rosaura's kinship.

15. Alexander A. Parker, "The Father-Son Conflict in the Drama of Calderón," *Forum for Modern Language Studies*, 2 (1966), 99–113, makes the following important observations on the limits of the oracle's determinism: "The horoscope, as Basilio casts it, is fulfilled to the letter, and it is essential . . . that this be realized. What the horoscope predicted is that Segismundo would start a civil war and that Basilio would find himself defeated and prostrate at his mercy. This is exactly what happens. It was natural for Basilio to expect his own death, but his death does not happen precisely because he does not foresee it. What he does not foresee is what depends on Segismundo's free choice; and this makes us realize that what Basilio foresees is only the result of *his own* free act—the result, that is to say, of the imprisonment he chooses to inflict on his son" (108–9).

16. A. E. Sloman, Introduction to *La vida es sueño* (Manchester, 1961), pp. xx–xxi, points out that Clarin, Astolfo (toward Rosaura), and Basilio all suffer and fail through trying to avoid responsibility.

17. Rosaura mistakes the implications of another rebirth paradox, that of the phoenix, when she uses it to characterize her troubles, one born from another (1828–37). The folly of misreading the phoenix emblem is even more explicit in Don Lope's mistakes in *A secreto agravio secreta venganza* (III, vi, xvi).

18. Edward M. Wilson, "*La vida es sueño*," *Revista de la Universidad de Buenos Aires*, 3rd Ser., 8 (1946), 69; Sloman, Introduction to *La vida es sueño*, p. xiv.

19. *Obras completas*, ed. Angel Valbuena Prat (Madrid, 1952), III, 218.

20. Cf. the observations in Margaret S. Maurin, "The Monster, the Sepulchre and the Dark: Related Patterns of Imagery in *La vida es sueño*," *HR*, 35 (1967), 161–78, esp. 173–76.

APPENDIX

1. Jean Jacquot, *George Chapman: sa vie, sa poésie, son théâtre, sa pensée* (Paris, 1951), pp. 94–95, cites Pomponazzi's *De naturalium effectum admirandorum causis seu de incantationibus liber* (1556) as a source for the wounding because in it "a man, having been seriously wounded by an arrow, the iron immediately dropped from the wound after a thaumaturge had spoken some incantations," but he believes that the name of Strozza's physician suggests an even more likely source in a similar incident reported in Antonio Benevieni's *De abditis nonnullis ac mirandis morborum et sanationum causis* (1529). John Hazel Smith, "The Genesis of the Strozza Subplot in George Chapman's *The Gentleman Usher*," *PMLA*, 83 (1968), 1448–53, follows Jacquot's lead by analyzing Benevieni's work more closely and adding some etymological conjectures concerning the names Strozza and Cynanche.

2. Pomponius Sabinus annotates the incident in Virgil's *Opera* (Paris, 1547), col. 1777a, by referring the reader to the accounts of dittany in Theophrastus *Peri*

Photon Hist. IX. xvi. 1–3; Pliny *Nat. hist.* XXV. 92; Cicero *De nat. deo.* II. 127. Aristotle records the powers of the plant in *Hist. animal.* IX. 6.

3. *Opere di Virgilio* (Venice, 1726), p. 519.

4. *Orlando furioso* (Venice, 1554), p. 200.

5. For the respective remarks of these critics see the variorum Ariosto *Opere* (Venice, 1730), I, sigs. C4^{r-v}, 215, C2^r.

6. *Orlando furioso* (Venice, 1547), p. 83^v.

7. Leonard W. Grant, *Neo-Latin Literature and the Pastoral* (Chapel Hill, N.C., 1965), p. 228.

8. "La 'venatio' di Ercole Strozzi nell'autografo Ferrarese," *Instituto Lombardo di scienze e lettere: classe di lettere . . . memorie,* 23 (Milan, 1914–17), 87–124.

9. [Giovanni] Battista Guarini, *Compendio della poesia tragicomica, tratto da i duo Verati* (Venice, 1602), p. 14 (separately titled, but printed as an appendix to *Il pastor fido*).

10. *A Critical Edition of Sir Richard Fanshawe's 1647 Translation of Giovanni Battista Guarini's* Il Pastor Fido, ed. Walter F. Staton, Jr., and William E. Simeone (Oxford, 1964), ll. 3754–56. All English translations are from this source.

11. *Compendio,* p. 14.

INDEX

The note number is given when a note contains a substantive discussion of the topic.

THE JOHNS HOPKINS UNIVERSITY PRESS

This book was composed in Palatino text and Trajanus display
type by Monotype Composition Company from a design
by Victoria Dudley. It was printed by Universal Lithographers, Inc.,
on S. D. Warren's 60-lb. Sebago paper, in a text shade, regular finish.
The book was bound by L. H. Jenkins, Inc., in Joanna Arrestox and Kivar cloth.

Library of Congress Cataloging in Publication Data

Cope, Jackson I.
   The theater and the dream.

   Includes bibliographical references.
   1. Drama—15th and 16th centuries—History and
criticism. I. Title.
PN1791.C6   809.2   72-12782
ISBN 0-8018-1417-0